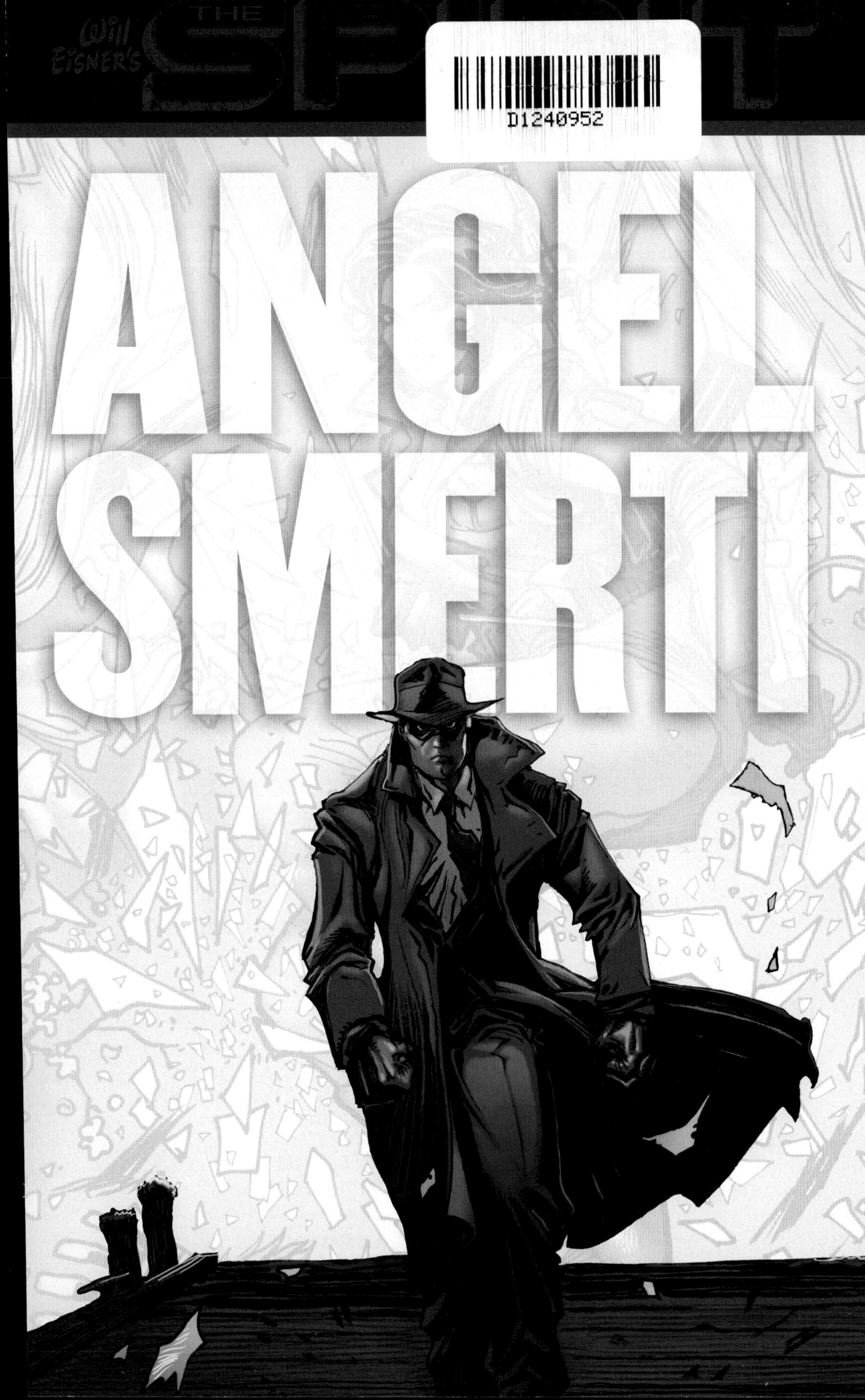
Will Eisner's
THE SPIRIT
ANGEL SMERTI

Will Eisner's THE SPIRIT

ANGEL SMERTI

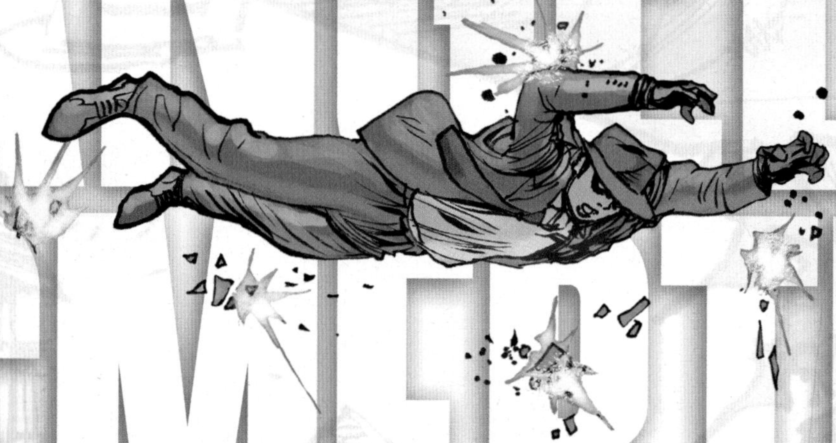

MARK SCHULTZ
WRITER **ANGEL SMERTI**

DAVID HINE
WRITER **FROST BITE**

MORITAT
ARTIST

GABRIEL BAUTISTA
ANDRE SZYMANOWICZ
COLORISTS

ROB LEIGH
LETTERER

LADRÖNN
COVER ARTIST

THE SPIRIT CREATED BY **WILL EISNER**

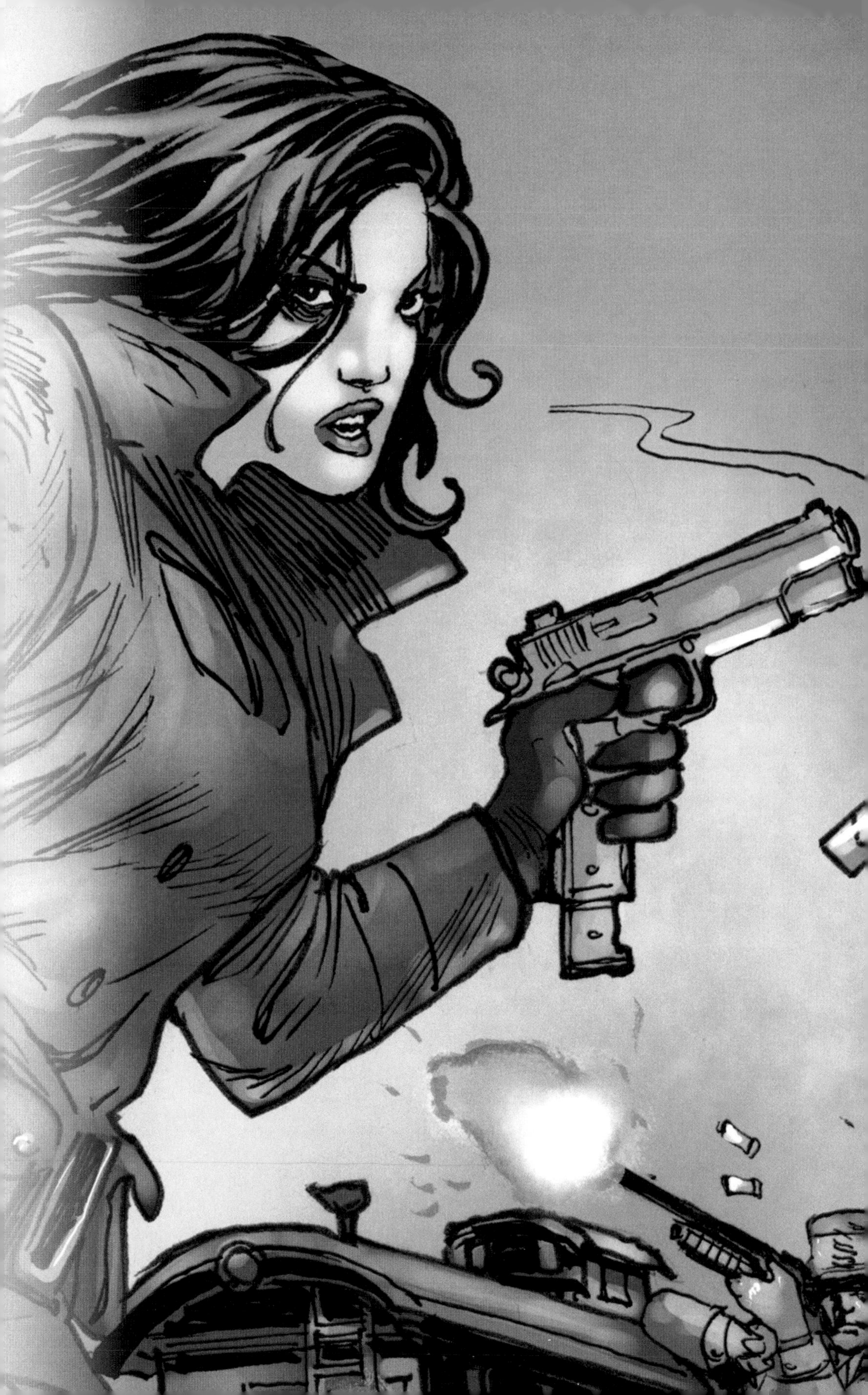

JOEY CAVALIERI
Editor-Original Series

CHRIS CONROY
Assistant Editor-Original Series

BOB HARRAS
Group Editor-Collected Editions

ROBBIN BROSTERMAN
Design Director-Books

CURTIS KING JR.
Senior Art Director

DC COMICS

DIANE NELSON
President

DAN DIDIO and **JIM LEE**
Co-Publishers

GEOFF JOHNS
Chief Creative Officer

PATRICK CALDON
EVP-Finance & Administration

JOHN ROOD
EVP-Sales, Marketing & Business Development

AMY GENKINS
SVP-Business & Legal Affairs

STEVE ROTTERDAM
SVP-Sales & Marketing

JOHN CUNNINGHAM
VP-Marketing

TERRI CUNNINGHAM
VP-Managing Editor

ALISON GILL
VP-Manufacturing

DAVID HYDE
VP-Publicity

SUE POHJA
VP-Book Trade Sales

ALYSSA SOLL
VP-Advertising and Custom Publishing

BOB WAYNE
VP-Sales

MARK CHIARELLO
Art Director

THE SPIRIT: ANGEL SMERTI

Published by DC Comics. Cover and compilation
Copyright © 2011 Will Eisner Studios, Inc.
All Rights Reserved.

Originally published in single magazine form in
THE SPIRIT 1-7. Copyright © 2010 Will Eisner Studios,
Inc. THE SPIRIT, Denny Colt, Commissioner Dolan and
Ebony are registered trademarks owned by Will Eisner
Studios, Inc. The stories, characters and incidents
featured in this publication are entirely fictional.
DC Comics does not read or accept unsolicited
submissions of ideas, stories or artwork.

DC Comics, 1700 Broadway, New York, NY 10019.
A Warner Bros. Entertainment Company

Printed by Quad/Graphics,
Dubuque, IA, USA. 3/11/11. First Printing.
ISBN: 978-1-4012-3026-5

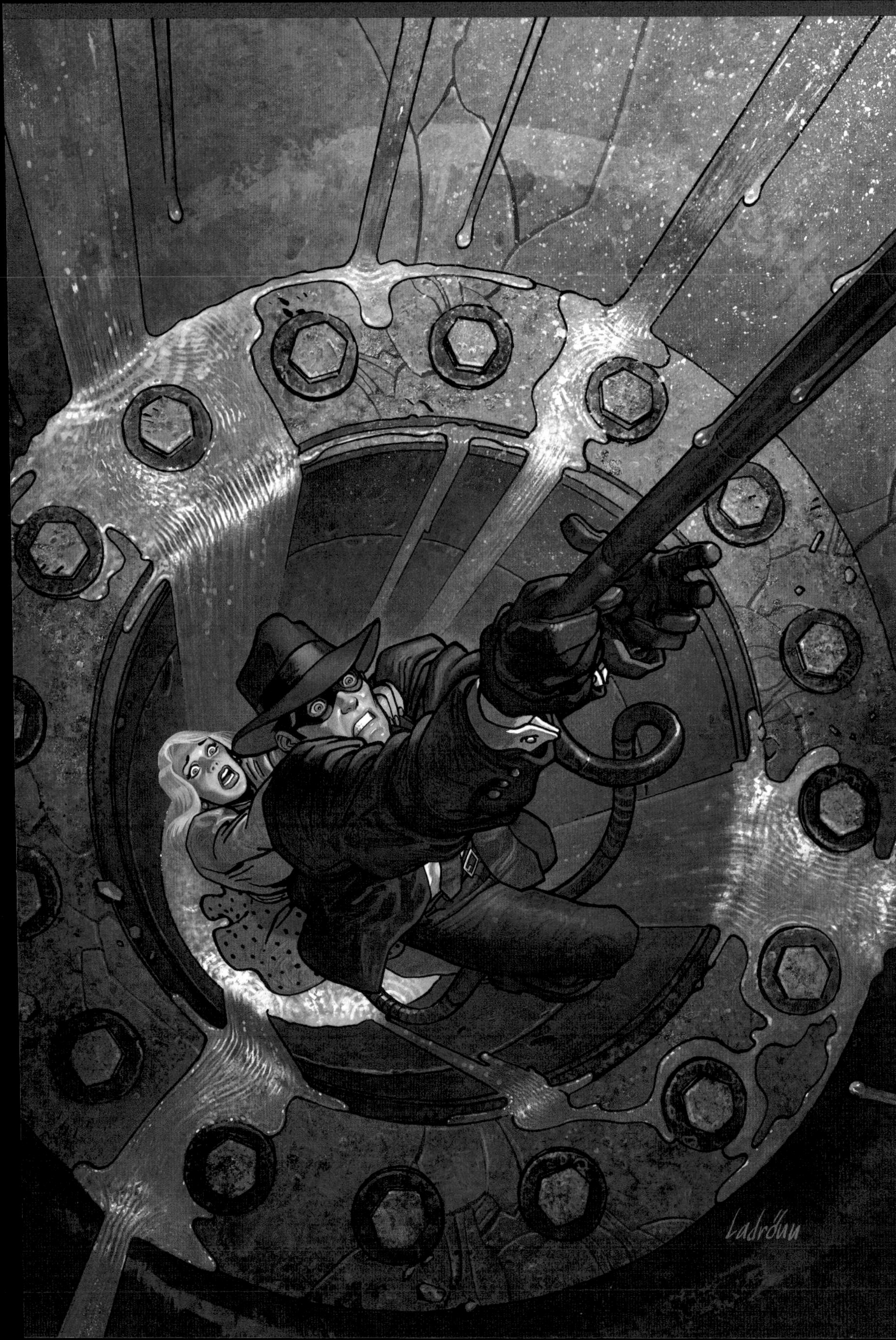
Ladrönn

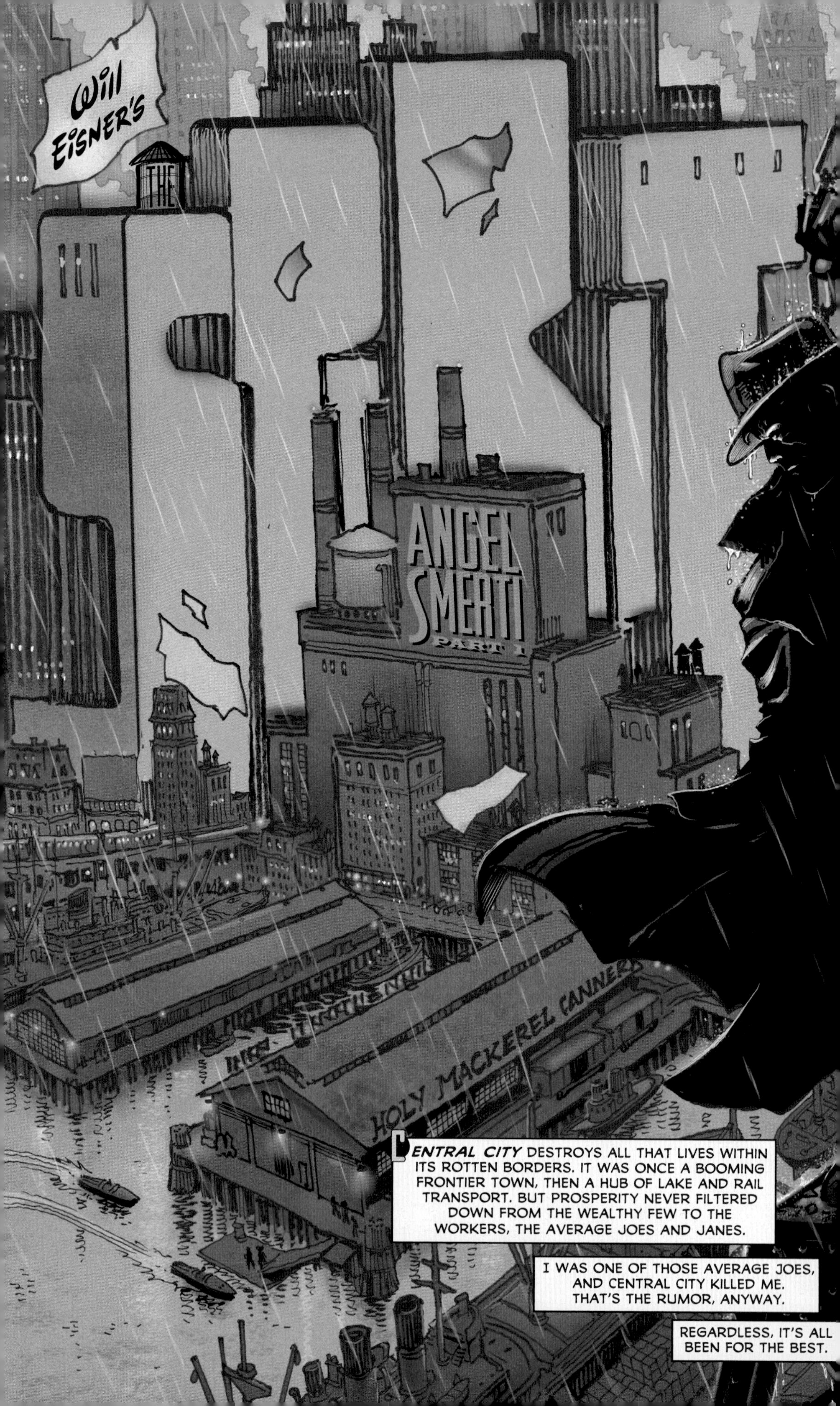
Will Eisner's
THE
ANGEL SMERTI
PART 1
HOLY MACKEREL CANNERY
CENTRAL CITY DESTROYS ALL THAT LIVES WITHIN ITS ROTTEN BORDERS. IT WAS ONCE A BOOMING FRONTIER TOWN, THEN A HUB OF LAKE AND RAIL TRANSPORT. BUT PROSPERITY NEVER FILTERED DOWN FROM THE WEALTHY FEW TO THE WORKERS, THE AVERAGE JOES AND JANES.
I WAS ONE OF THOSE AVERAGE JOES, AND CENTRAL CITY KILLED ME. THAT'S THE RUMOR, ANYWAY.
REGARDLESS, IT'S ALL BEEN FOR THE BEST.

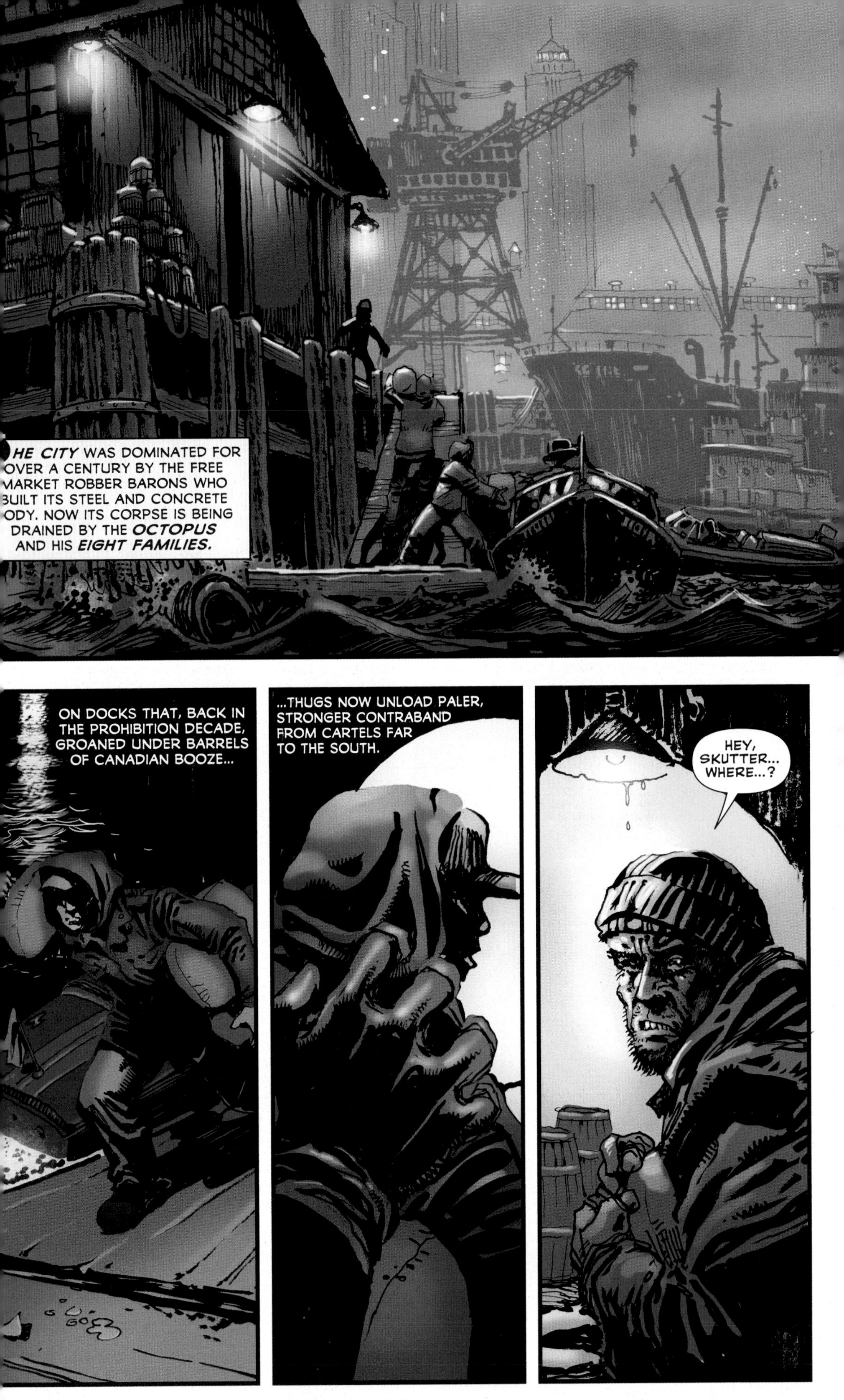
HE CITY WAS DOMINATED FOR OVER A CENTURY BY THE FREE MARKET ROBBER BARONS WHO BUILT ITS STEEL AND CONCRETE ODY. NOW ITS CORPSE IS BEING DRAINED BY THE OCTOPUS AND HIS EIGHT FAMILIES.
ON DOCKS THAT, BACK IN THE PROHIBITION DECADE, GROANED UNDER BARRELS OF CANADIAN BOOZE...
...THUGS NOW UNLOAD PALER, STRONGER CONTRABAND FROM CARTELS FAR TO THE SOUTH.
HEY, SKUTTER... WHERE...?

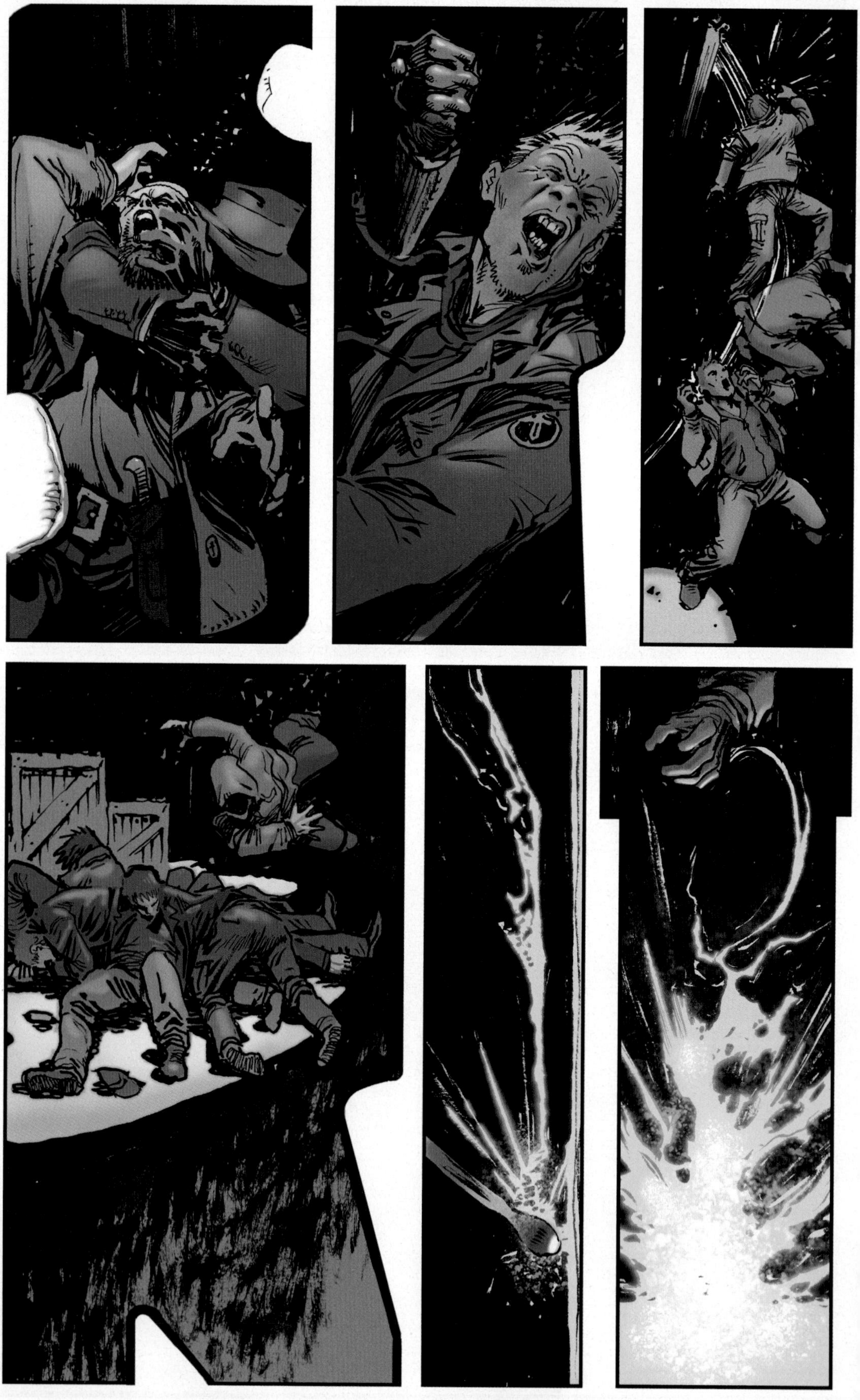

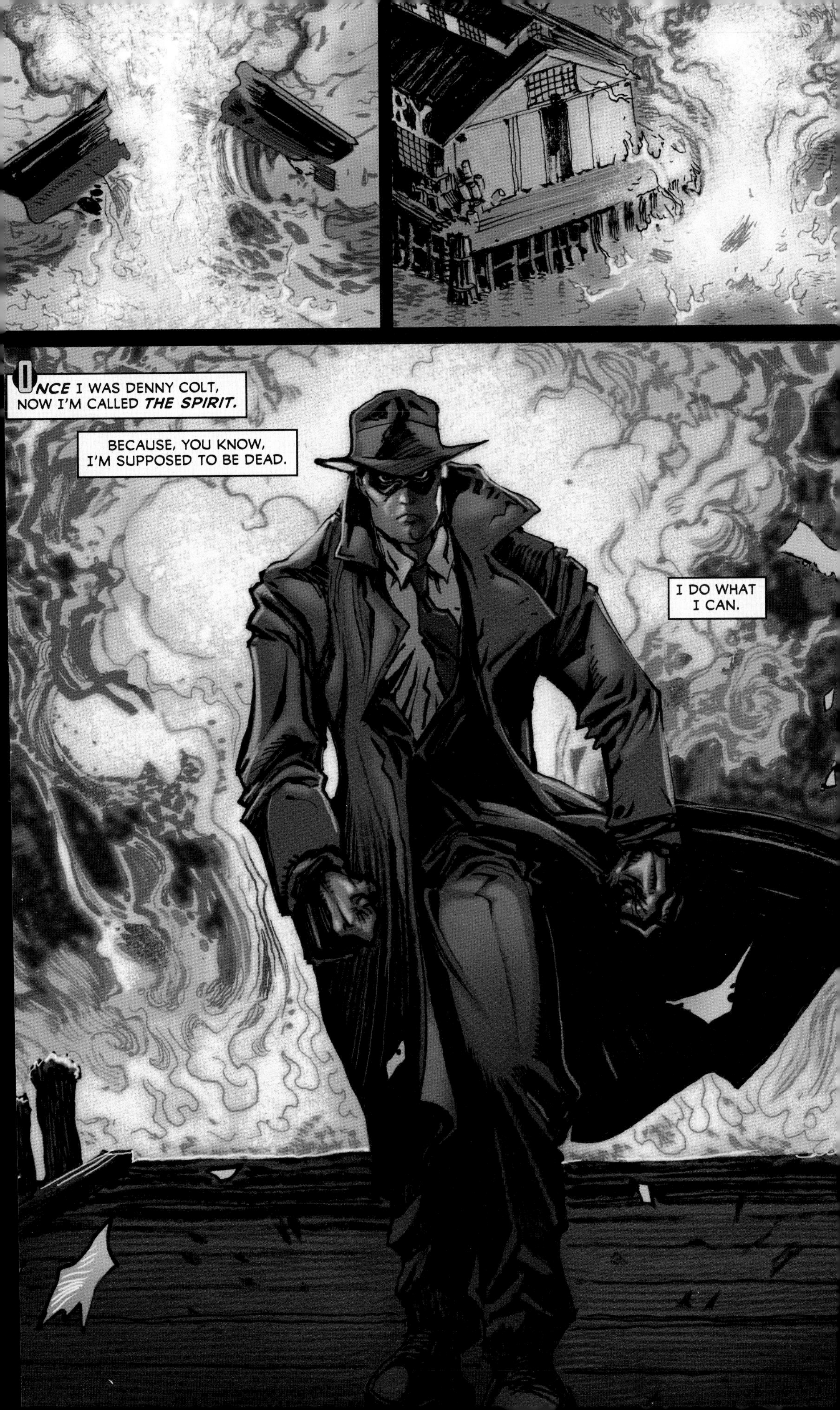
ONCE I WAS DENNY COLT, NOW I'M CALLED THE SPIRIT.
BECAUSE, YOU KNOW, I'M SUPPOSED TO BE DEAD.
I DO WHAT I CAN.

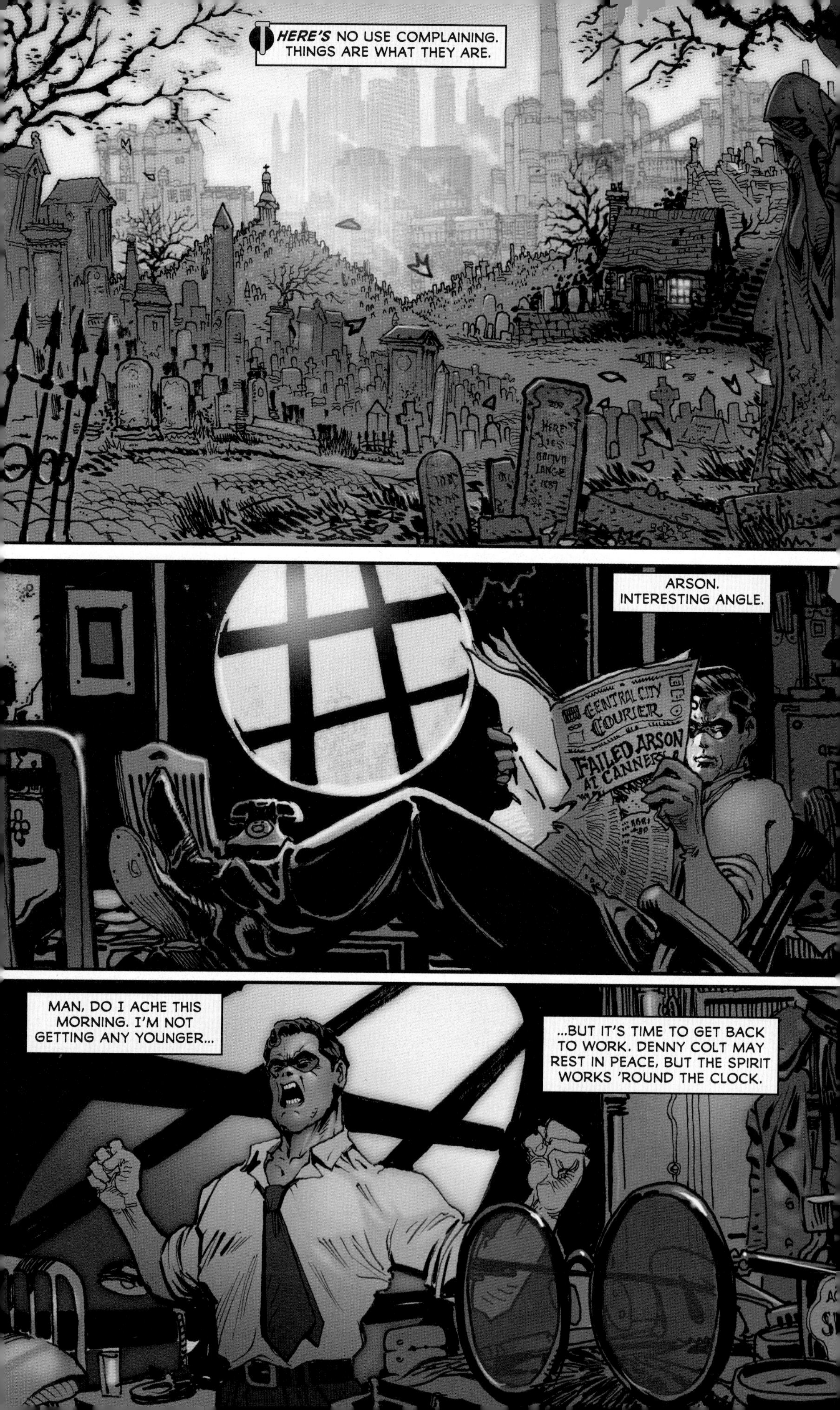
THERE'S NO USE COMPLAINING. THINGS ARE WHAT THEY ARE.
ARSON. INTERESTING ANGLE.
CENTRAL CITY COURIER
FAILED ARSON
MAN, DO I ACHE THIS MORNING. I'M NOT GETTING ANY YOUNGER...
...BUT IT'S TIME TO GET BACK TO WORK. DENNY COLT MAY REST IN PEACE, BUT THE SPIRIT WORKS 'ROUND THE CLOCK.

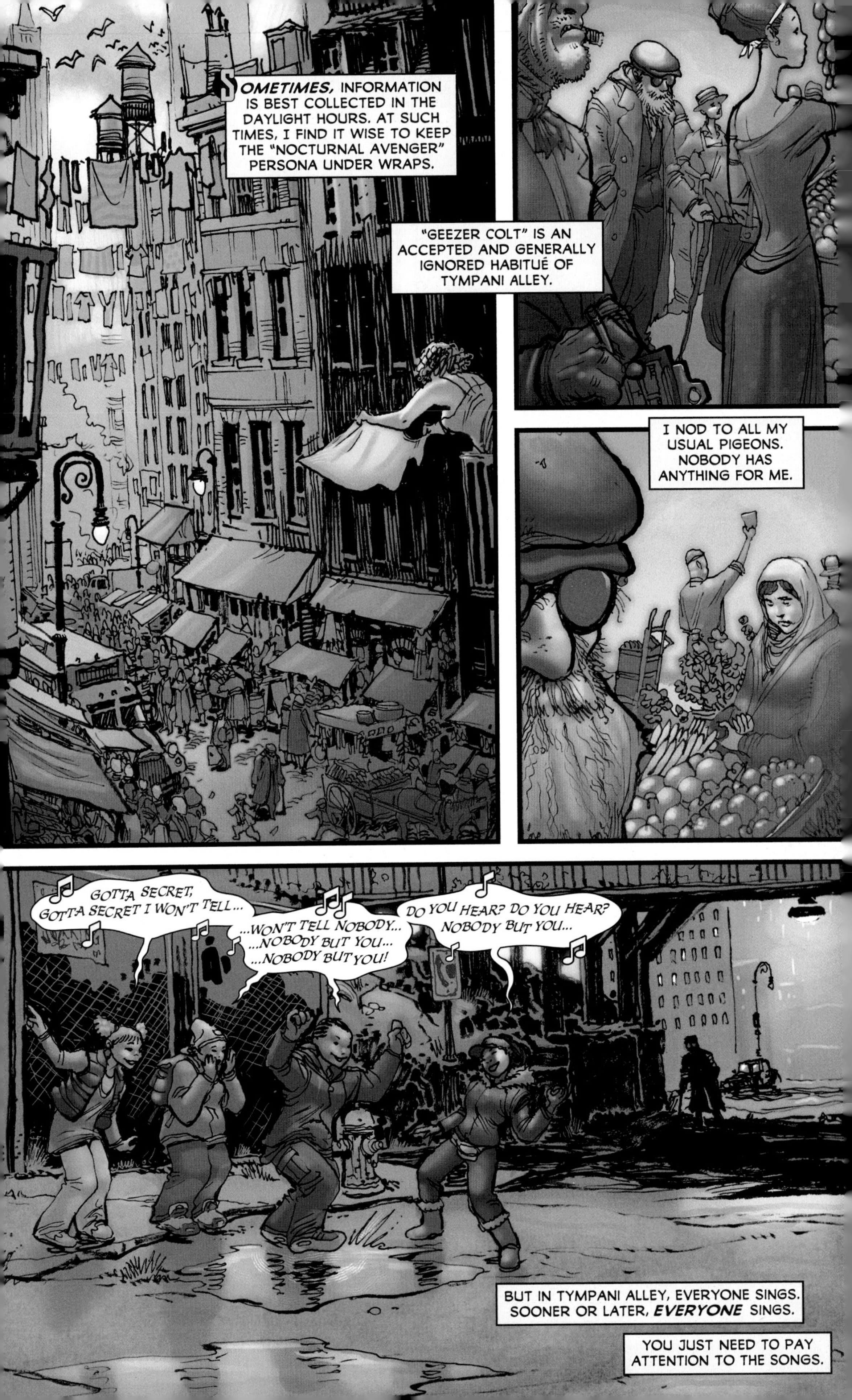
SOMETIMES, INFORMATION IS BEST COLLECTED IN THE DAYLIGHT HOURS. AT SUCH TIMES, I FIND IT WISE TO KEEP THE "NOCTURNAL AVENGER" PERSONA UNDER WRAPS.
"GEEZER COLT" IS AN ACCEPTED AND GENERALLY IGNORED HABITUÉ OF TYMPANI ALLEY.
I NOD TO ALL MY USUAL PIGEONS. NOBODY HAS ANYTHING FOR ME.
GOTTA SECRET, GOTTA SECRET I WON'T TELL...
...WON'T TELL NOBODY... ...NOBODY BUT YOU... ...NOBODY BUT YOU!
DO YOU HEAR? DO YOU HEAR? NOBODY BUT YOU...
BUT IN TYMPANI ALLEY, EVERYONE SINGS. SOONER OR LATER, EVERYONE SINGS.
YOU JUST NEED TO PAY ATTENTION TO THE SONGS.

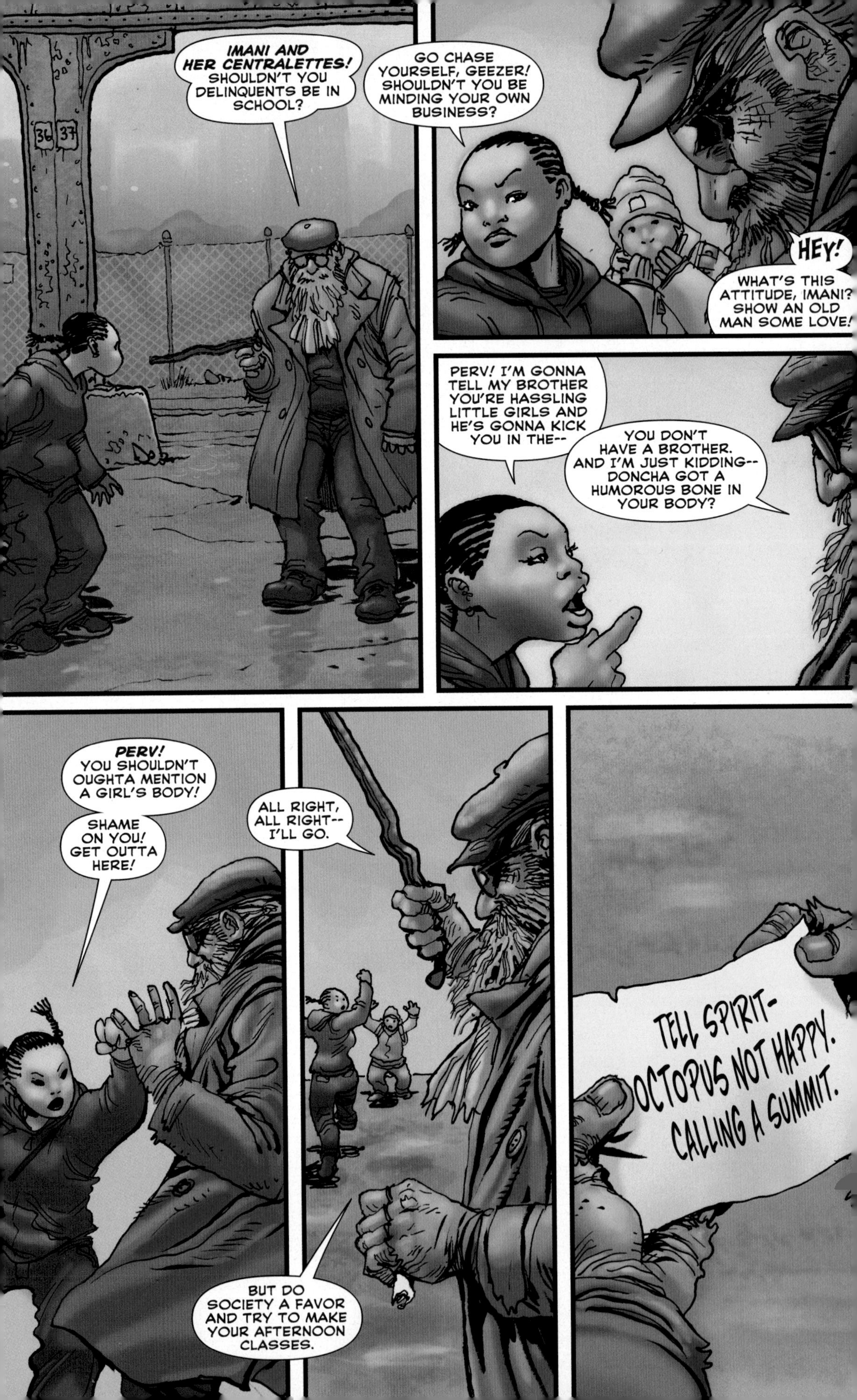

IMANI AND HER CENTRALETTES! SHOULDN'T YOU DELINQUENTS BE IN SCHOOL?
GO CHASE YOURSELF, GEEZER! SHOULDN'T YOU BE MINDING YOUR OWN BUSINESS?
HEY!
WHAT'S THIS ATTITUDE, IMANI? SHOW AN OLD MAN SOME LOVE!
PERV! I'M GONNA TELL MY BROTHER YOU'RE HASSLING LITTLE GIRLS AND HE'S GONNA KICK YOU IN THE--
YOU DON'T HAVE A BROTHER. AND I'M JUST KIDDING-- DONCHA GOT A HUMOROUS BONE IN YOUR BODY?
PERV! YOU SHOULDN'T OUGHTA MENTION A GIRL'S BODY!
SHAME ON YOU! GET OUTTA HERE!
ALL RIGHT, ALL RIGHT-- I'LL GO.
BUT DO SOCIETY A FAVOR AND TRY TO MAKE YOUR AFTERNOON CLASSES.
TELL SPIRIT- OCTOPUS NOT HAPPY. CALLING A SUMMIT.

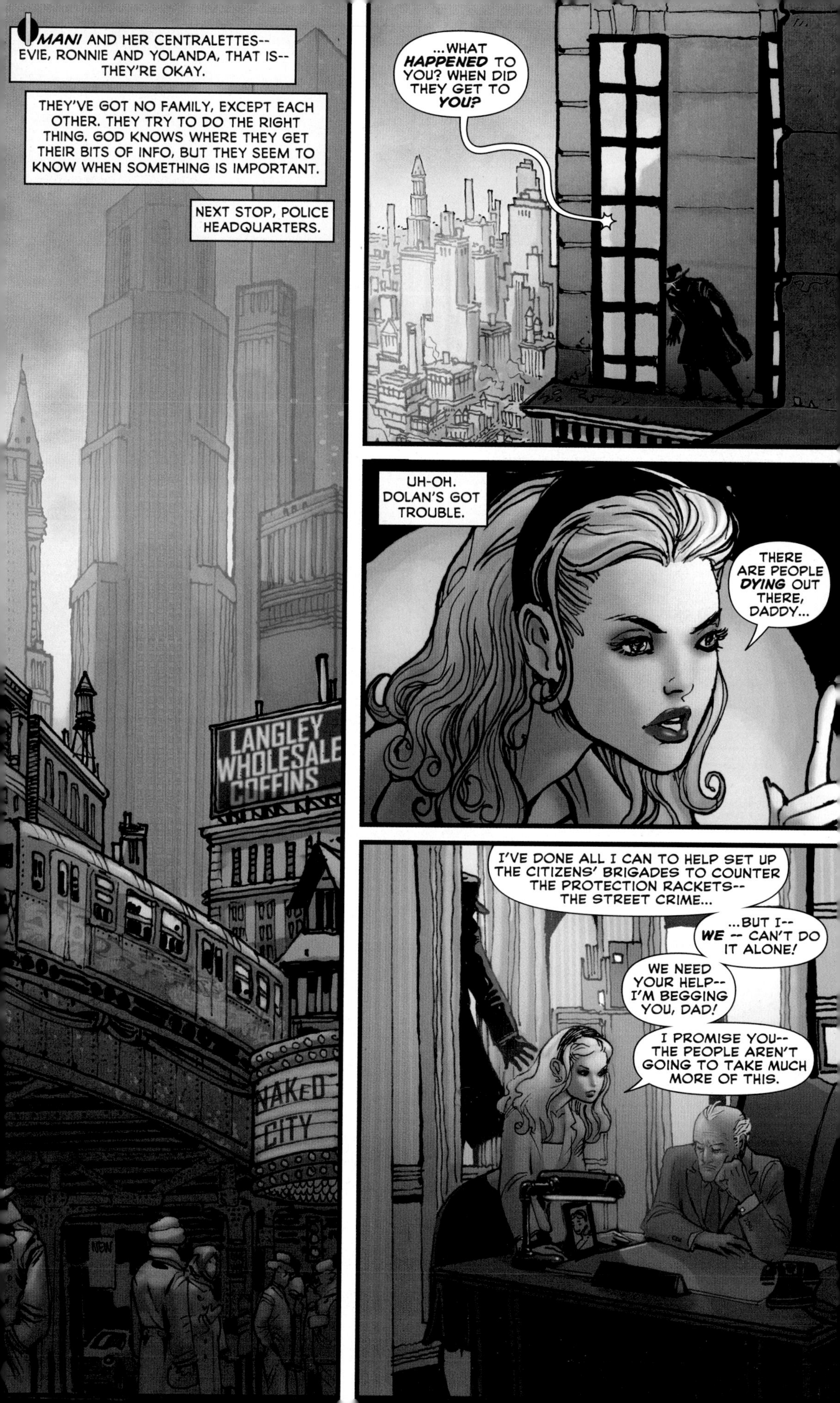
OMANI AND HER CENTRALETTES--
EVIE, RONNIE AND YOLANDA, THAT IS--
THEY'RE OKAY.
THEY'VE GOT NO FAMILY, EXCEPT EACH OTHER. THEY TRY TO DO THE RIGHT THING. GOD KNOWS WHERE THEY GET THEIR BITS OF INFO, BUT THEY SEEM TO KNOW WHEN SOMETHING IS IMPORTANT.
NEXT STOP, POLICE HEADQUARTERS.
LANGLEY WHOLESALE COFFINS
NAKED CITY
...WHAT HAPPENED TO YOU? WHEN DID THEY GET TO YOU?
UH-OH. DOLAN'S GOT TROUBLE.
THERE ARE PEOPLE DYING OUT THERE, DADDY...
I'VE DONE ALL I CAN TO HELP SET UP THE CITIZENS' BRIGADES TO COUNTER THE PROTECTION RACKETS-- THE STREET CRIME...
...BUT I-- WE -- CAN'T DO IT ALONE!
WE NEED YOUR HELP-- I'M BEGGING YOU, DAD!
I PROMISE YOU-- THE PEOPLE AREN'T GOING TO TAKE MUCH MORE OF THIS.

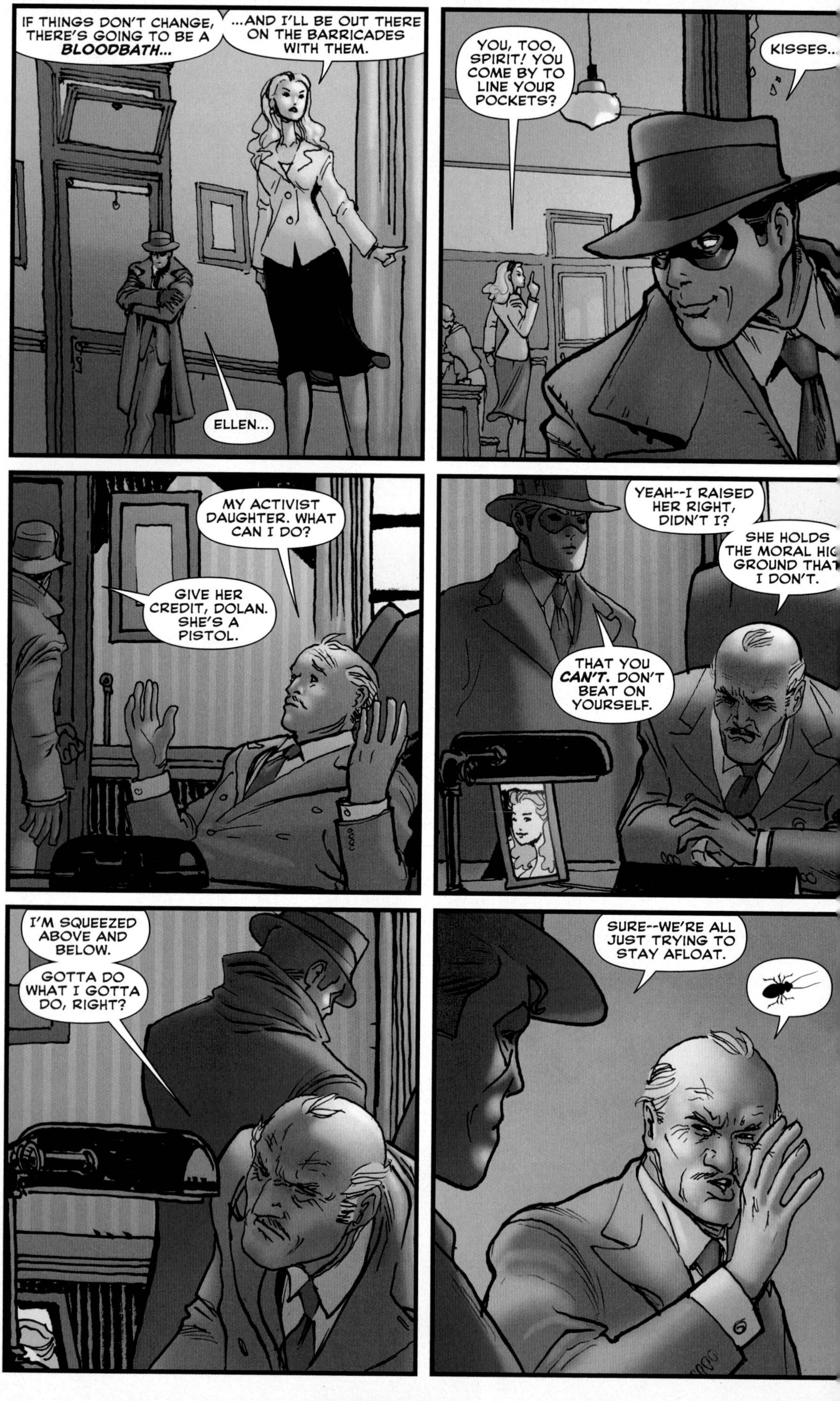
IF THINGS DON'T CHANGE, THERE'S GOING TO BE A ***BLOODBATH...***
...AND I'LL BE OUT THERE ON THE BARRICADES WITH THEM.
ELLEN...
YOU, TOO, SPIRIT! YOU COME BY TO LINE YOUR POCKETS?
KISSES...
MY ACTIVIST DAUGHTER. WHAT CAN I DO?
GIVE HER CREDIT, DOLAN. SHE'S A PISTOL.
YEAH--I RAISED HER RIGHT, DIDN'T I?
SHE HOLDS THE MORAL HIG GROUND THAT I DON'T.
THAT YOU ***CAN'T.*** DON'T BEAT ON YOURSELF.
I'M SQUEEZED ABOVE AND BELOW.
GOTTA DO WHAT I GOTTA DO, RIGHT?
SURE--WE'RE ALL JUST TRYING TO STAY AFLOAT.

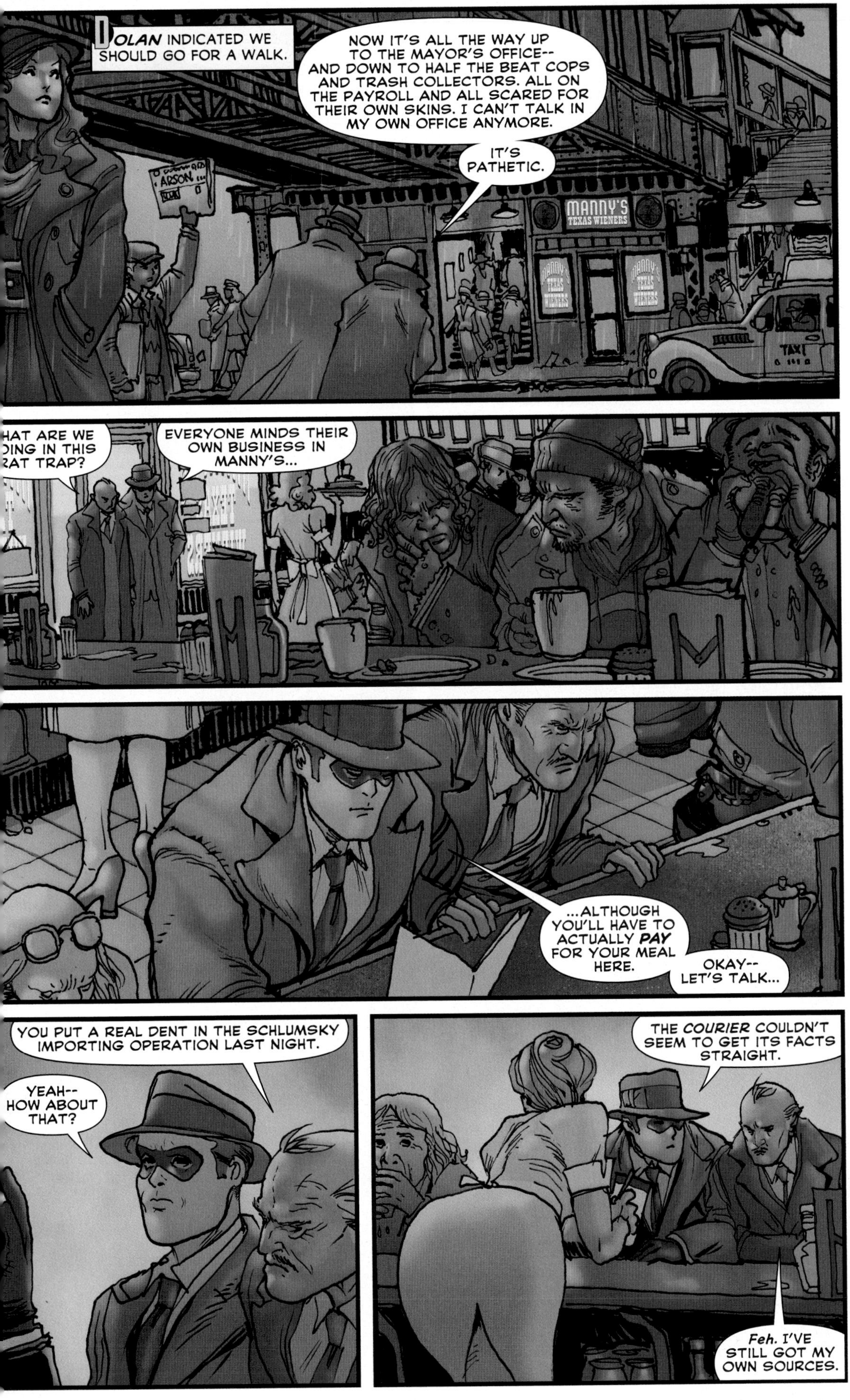
DOLAN INDICATED WE SHOULD GO FOR A WALK.
NOW IT'S ALL THE WAY UP TO THE MAYOR'S OFFICE--AND DOWN TO HALF THE BEAT COPS AND TRASH COLLECTORS. ALL ON THE PAYROLL AND ALL SCARED FOR THEIR OWN SKINS. I CAN'T TALK IN MY OWN OFFICE ANYMORE.
IT'S PATHETIC.
ARSON
MANNY'S TEXAS WIENERS
TAXI
HAT ARE WE OING IN THIS AT TRAP?
EVERYONE MINDS THEIR OWN BUSINESS IN MANNY'S...
...ALTHOUGH YOU'LL HAVE TO ACTUALLY PAY FOR YOUR MEAL HERE.
OKAY--LET'S TALK...
YOU PUT A REAL DENT IN THE SCHLUMSKY IMPORTING OPERATION LAST NIGHT.
YEAH--HOW ABOUT THAT?
THE COURIER COULDN'T SEEM TO GET ITS FACTS STRAIGHT.
Feh. I'VE STILL GOT MY OWN SOURCES.

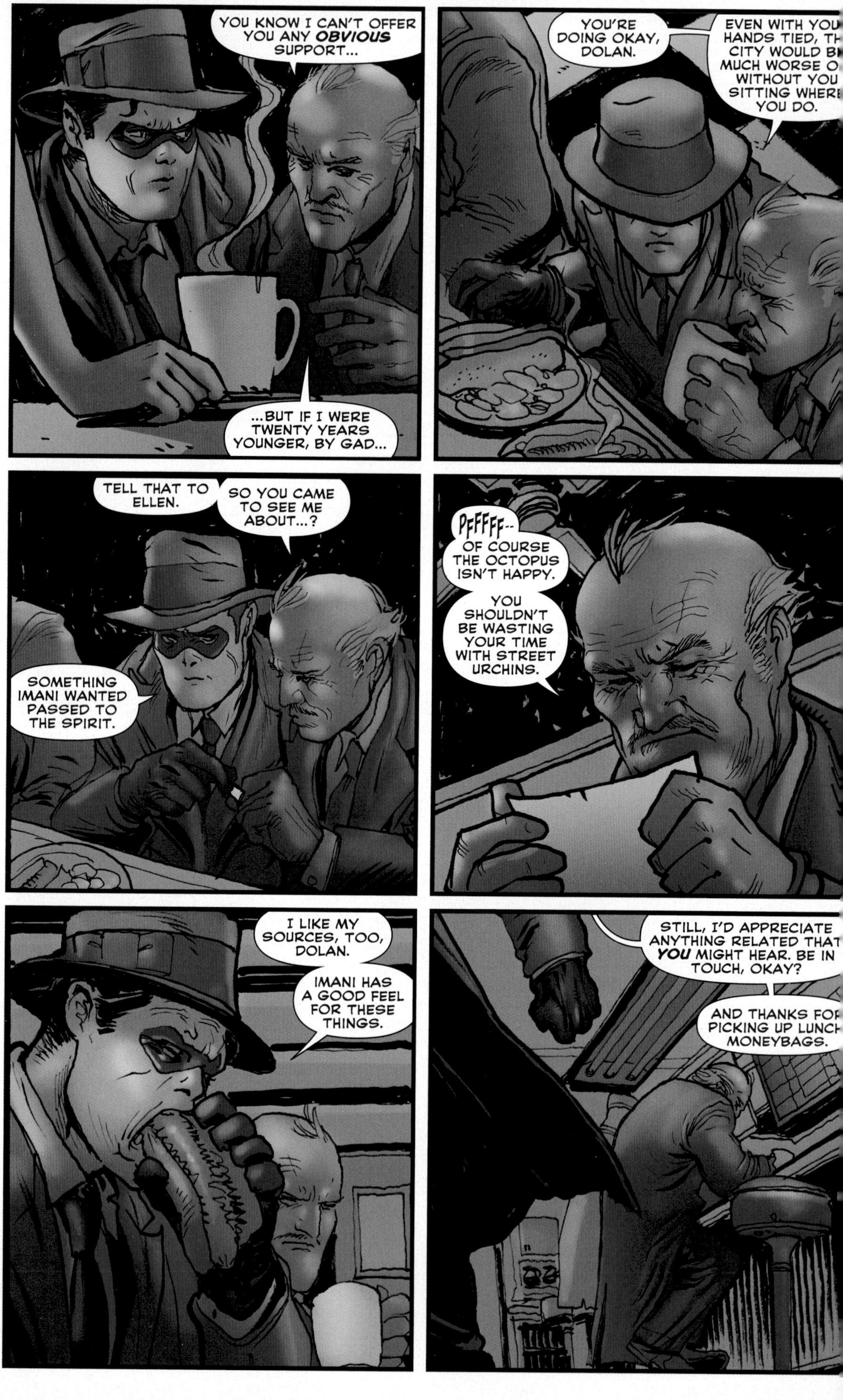

YOU KNOW I CAN'T OFFER YOU ANY OBVIOUS SUPPORT...
...BUT IF I WERE TWENTY YEARS YOUNGER, BY GAD...
YOU'RE DOING OKAY, DOLAN.
EVEN WITH YOU HANDS TIED, TH CITY WOULD B MUCH WORSE O WITHOUT YOU SITTING WHERE YOU DO.
TELL THAT TO ELLEN.
SO YOU CAME TO SEE ME ABOUT...?
SOMETHING IMANI WANTED PASSED TO THE SPIRIT.
PFFFFF--
OF COURSE THE OCTOPUS ISN'T HAPPY.
YOU SHOULDN'T BE WASTING YOUR TIME WITH STREET URCHINS.
I LIKE MY SOURCES, TOO, DOLAN.
IMANI HAS A GOOD FEEL FOR THESE THINGS.
STILL, I'D APPRECIATE ANYTHING RELATED THAT YOU MIGHT HEAR. BE IN TOUCH, OKAY?
AND THANKS FOR PICKING UP LUNCH MONEYBAGS.

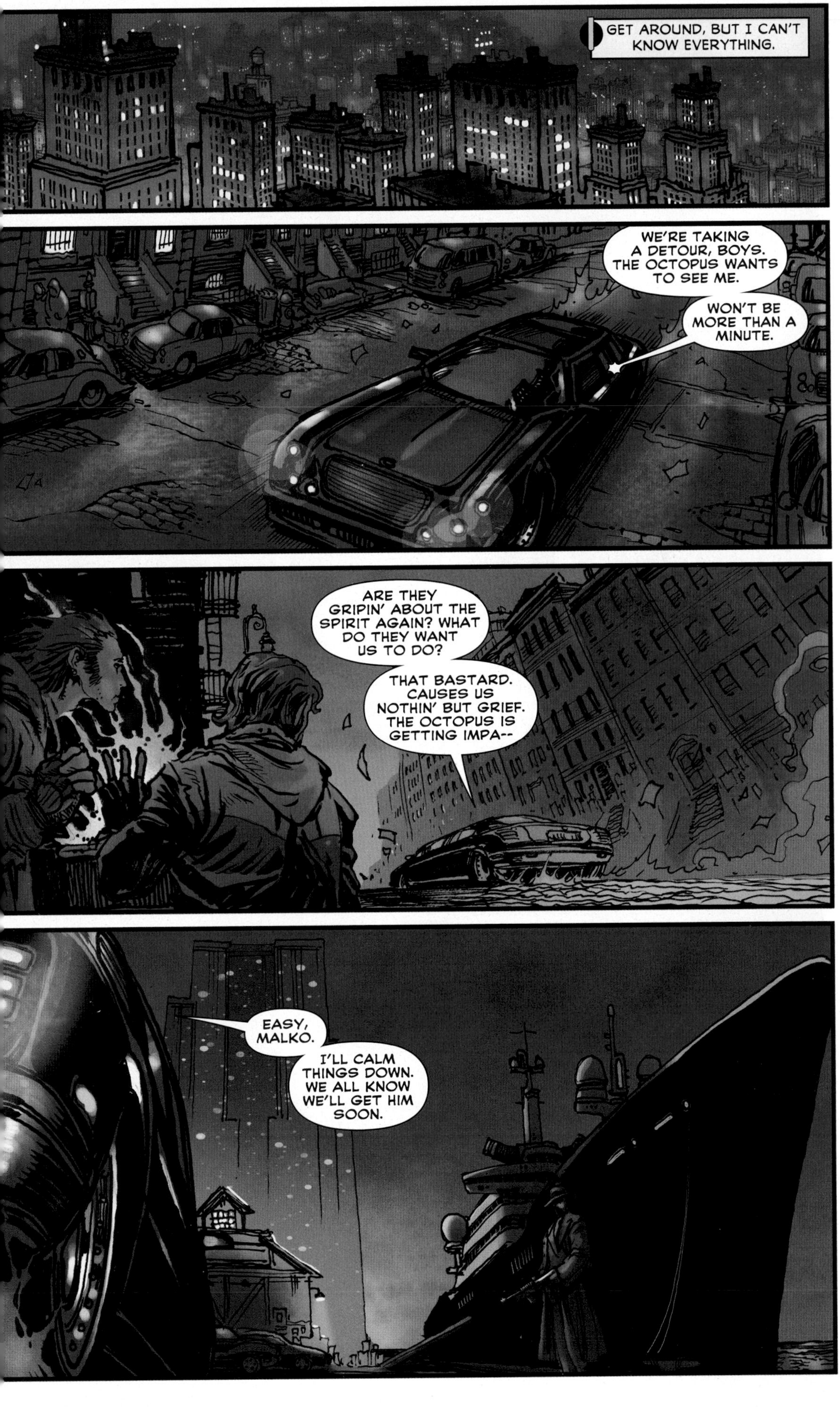
GET AROUND, BUT I CAN'T KNOW EVERYTHING.
WE'RE TAKING A DETOUR, BOYS. THE OCTOPUS WANTS TO SEE ME.
WON'T BE MORE THAN A MINUTE.
ARE THEY GRIPIN' ABOUT THE SPIRIT AGAIN? WHAT DO THEY WANT US TO DO?
THAT BASTARD. CAUSES US NOTHIN' BUT GRIEF. THE OCTOPUS IS GETTING IMPA--
EASY, MALKO.
I'LL CALM THINGS DOWN. WE ALL KNOW WE'LL GET HIM SOON.

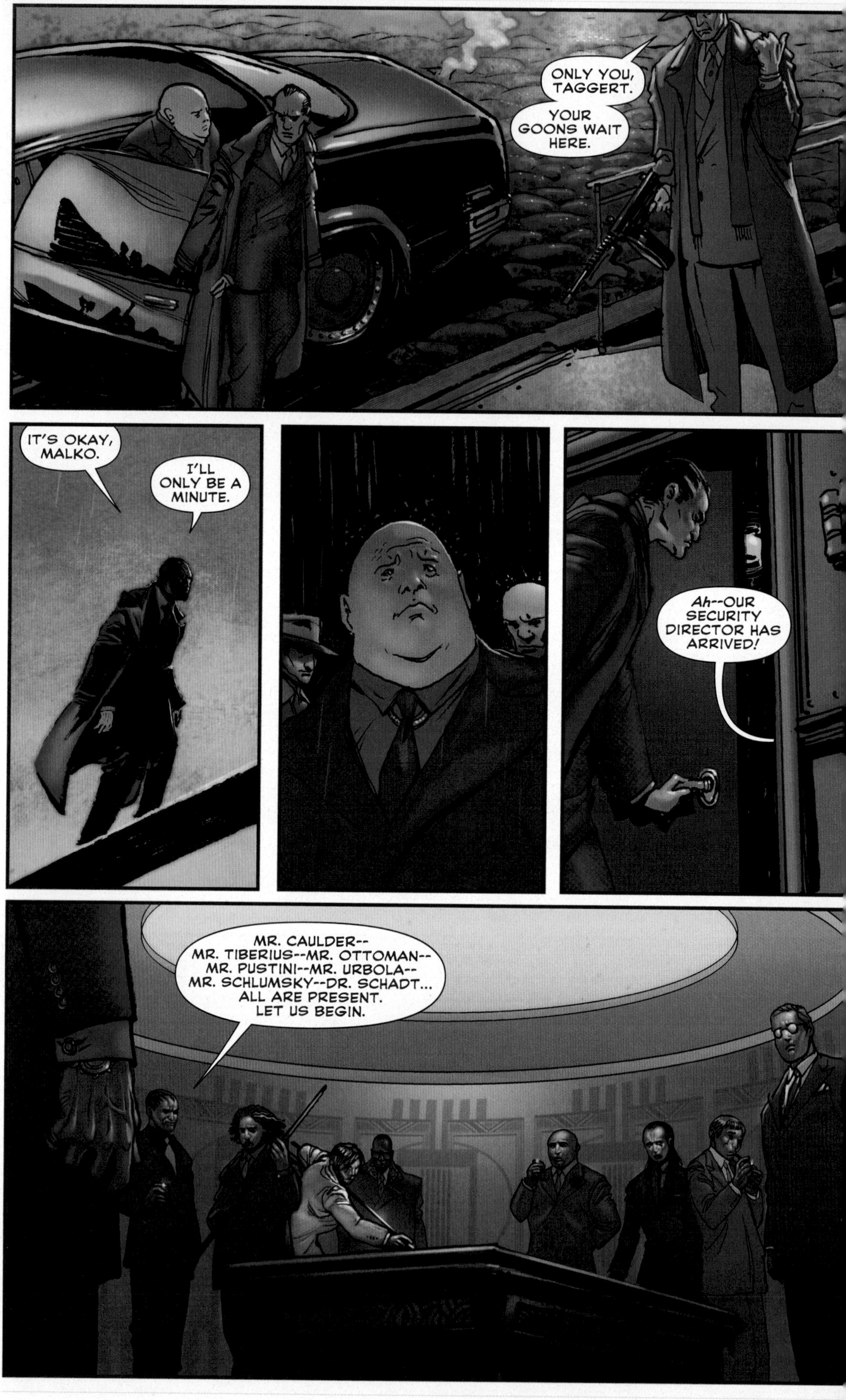
ONLY YOU, TAGGERT.
YOUR GOONS WAIT HERE.
IT'S OKAY, MALKO.
I'LL ONLY BE A MINUTE.
Ah--OUR SECURITY DIRECTOR HAS ARRIVED!
MR. CAULDER-- MR. TIBERIUS--MR. OTTOMAN-- MR. PUSTINI--MR. URBOLA-- MR. SCHLUMSKY--DR. SCHADT... ALL ARE PRESENT. LET US BEGIN.

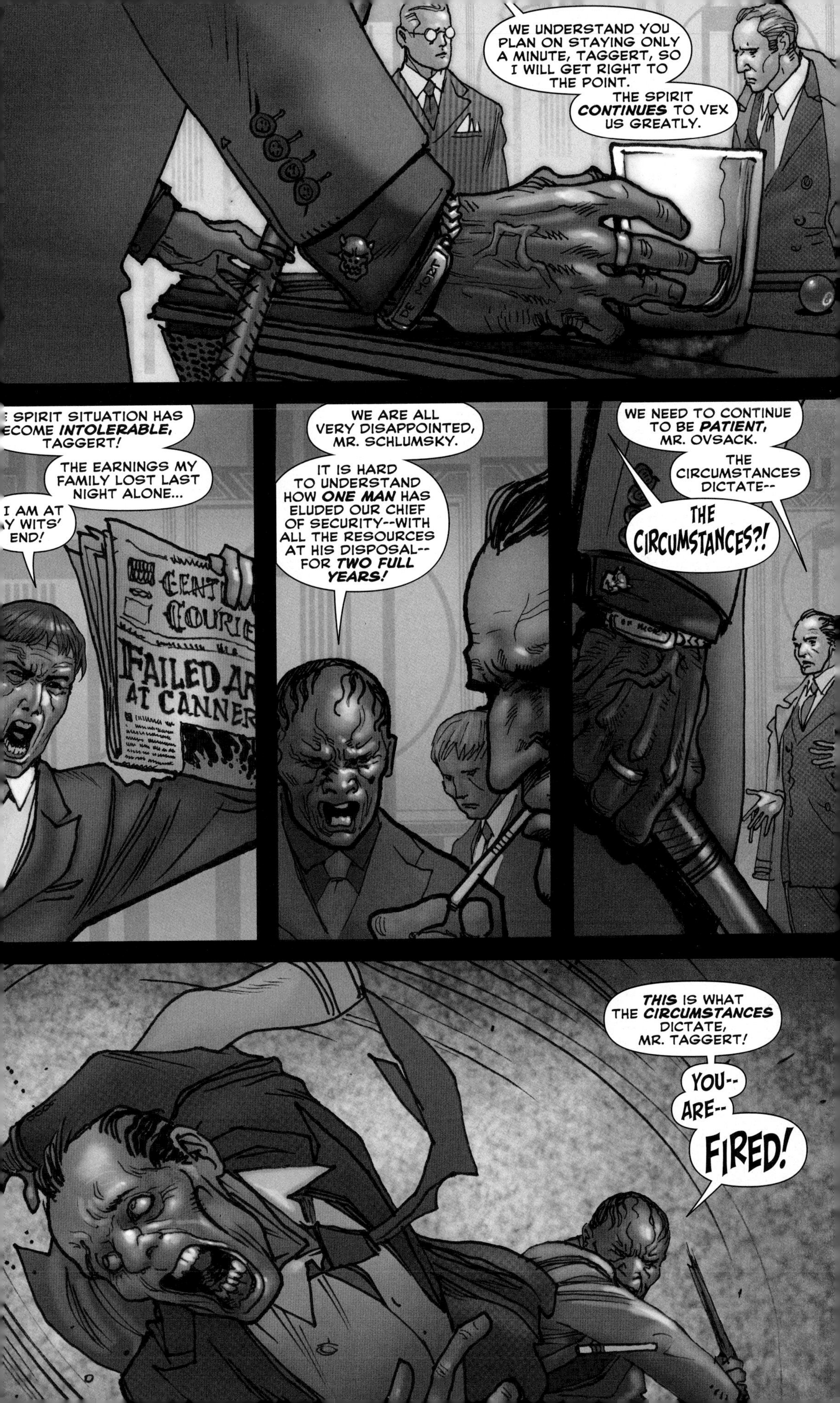
WE UNDERSTAND YOU PLAN ON STAYING ONLY A MINUTE, TAGGERT, SO I WILL GET RIGHT TO THE POINT.
THE SPIRIT CONTINUES TO VEX US GREATLY.
E SPIRIT SITUATION HAS ECOME INTOLERABLE, TAGGERT!
THE EARNINGS MY FAMILY LOST LAST NIGHT ALONE...
I AM AT Y WITS' END!
CENT COURIE
FAILED AR AT CANNER
WE ARE ALL VERY DISAPPOINTED, MR. SCHLUMSKY.
IT IS HARD TO UNDERSTAND HOW ONE MAN HAS ELUDED OUR CHIEF OF SECURITY--WITH ALL THE RESOURCES AT HIS DISPOSAL--FOR TWO FULL YEARS!
WE NEED TO CONTINUE TO BE PATIENT, MR. OVSACK.
THE CIRCUMSTANCES DICTATE--
THE CIRCUMSTANCES?!
THIS IS WHAT THE CIRCUMSTANCES DICTATE, MR. TAGGERT!
YOU--
ARE--
FIRED!

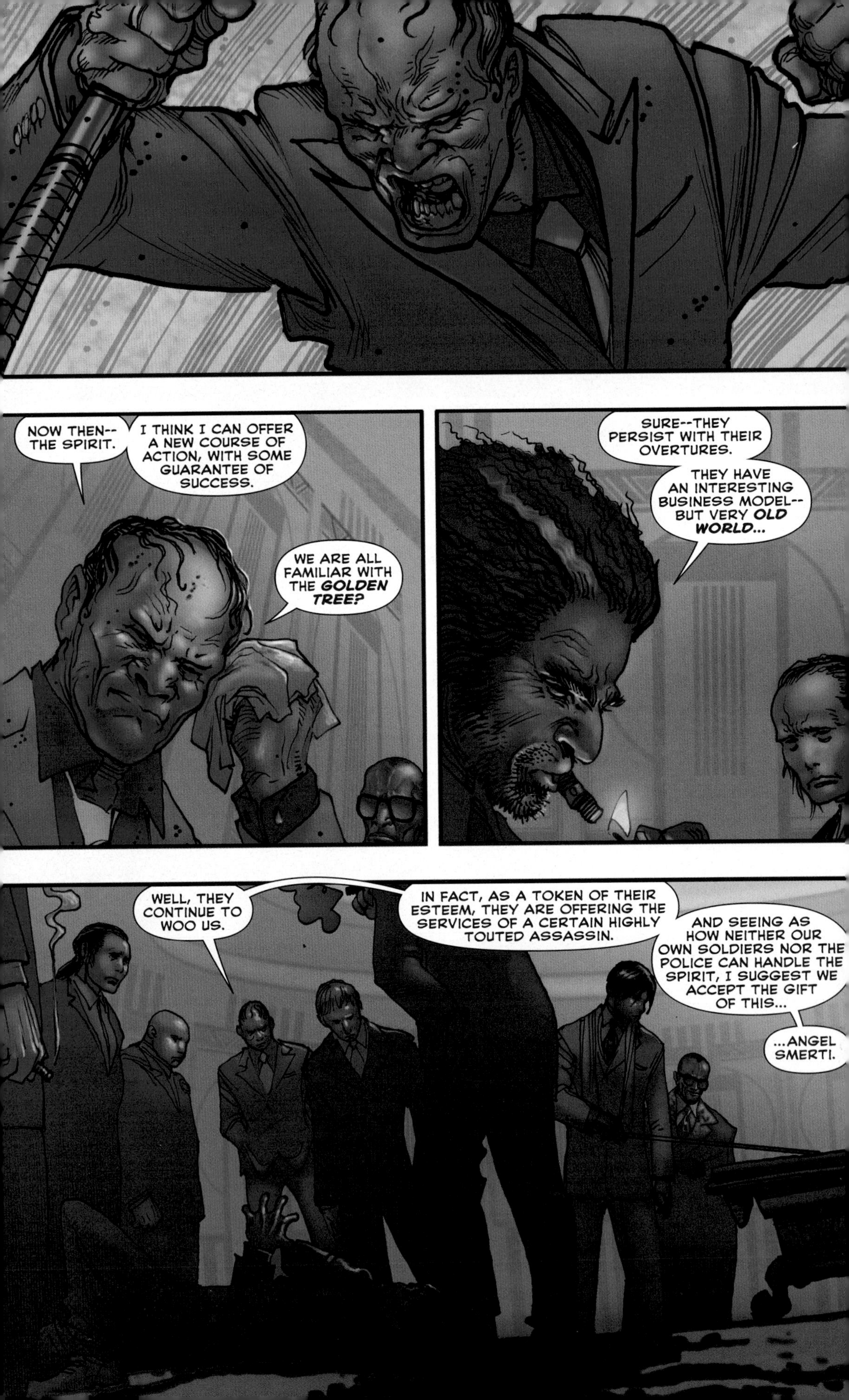
NOW THEN-- THE SPIRIT.
I THINK I CAN OFFER A NEW COURSE OF ACTION, WITH SOME GUARANTEE OF SUCCESS.
WE ARE ALL FAMILIAR WITH THE ***GOLDEN TREE?***
SURE--THEY PERSIST WITH THEIR OVERTURES.
THEY HAVE AN INTERESTING BUSINESS MODEL-- BUT VERY ***OLD WORLD...***
WELL, THEY CONTINUE TO WOO US.
IN FACT, AS A TOKEN OF THEIR ESTEEM, THEY ARE OFFERING THE SERVICES OF A CERTAIN HIGHLY TOUTED ASSASSIN.
AND SEEING AS HOW NEITHER OUR OWN SOLDIERS NOR THE POLICE CAN HANDLE THE SPIRIT, I SUGGEST WE ACCEPT THE GIFT OF THIS...
...ANGEL SMERTI.

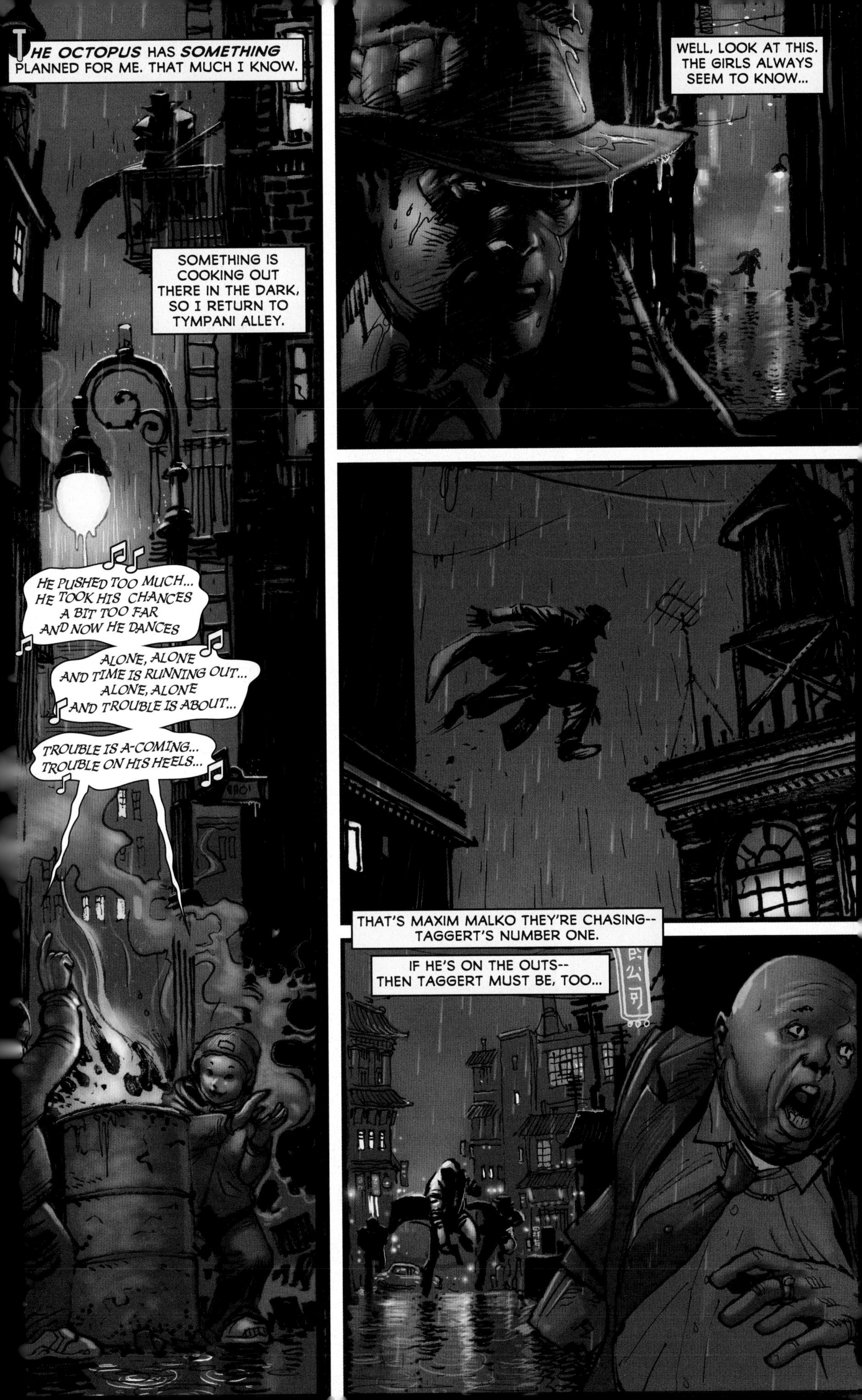
THE OCTOPUS HAS SOMETHING PLANNED FOR ME. THAT MUCH I KNOW.
SOMETHING IS COOKING OUT THERE IN THE DARK, SO I RETURN TO TYMPANI ALLEY.
HE PUSHED TOO MUCH... HE TOOK HIS CHANCES A BIT TOO FAR AND NOW HE DANCES
ALONE, ALONE AND TIME IS RUNNING OUT... ALONE, ALONE AND TROUBLE IS ABOUT...
TROUBLE IS A-COMING... TROUBLE ON HIS HEELS...
WELL, LOOK AT THIS. THE GIRLS ALWAYS SEEM TO KNOW...
THAT'S MAXIM MALKO THEY'RE CHASING-- TAGGERT'S NUMBER ONE.
IF HE'S ON THE OUTS-- THEN TAGGERT MUST BE, TOO...

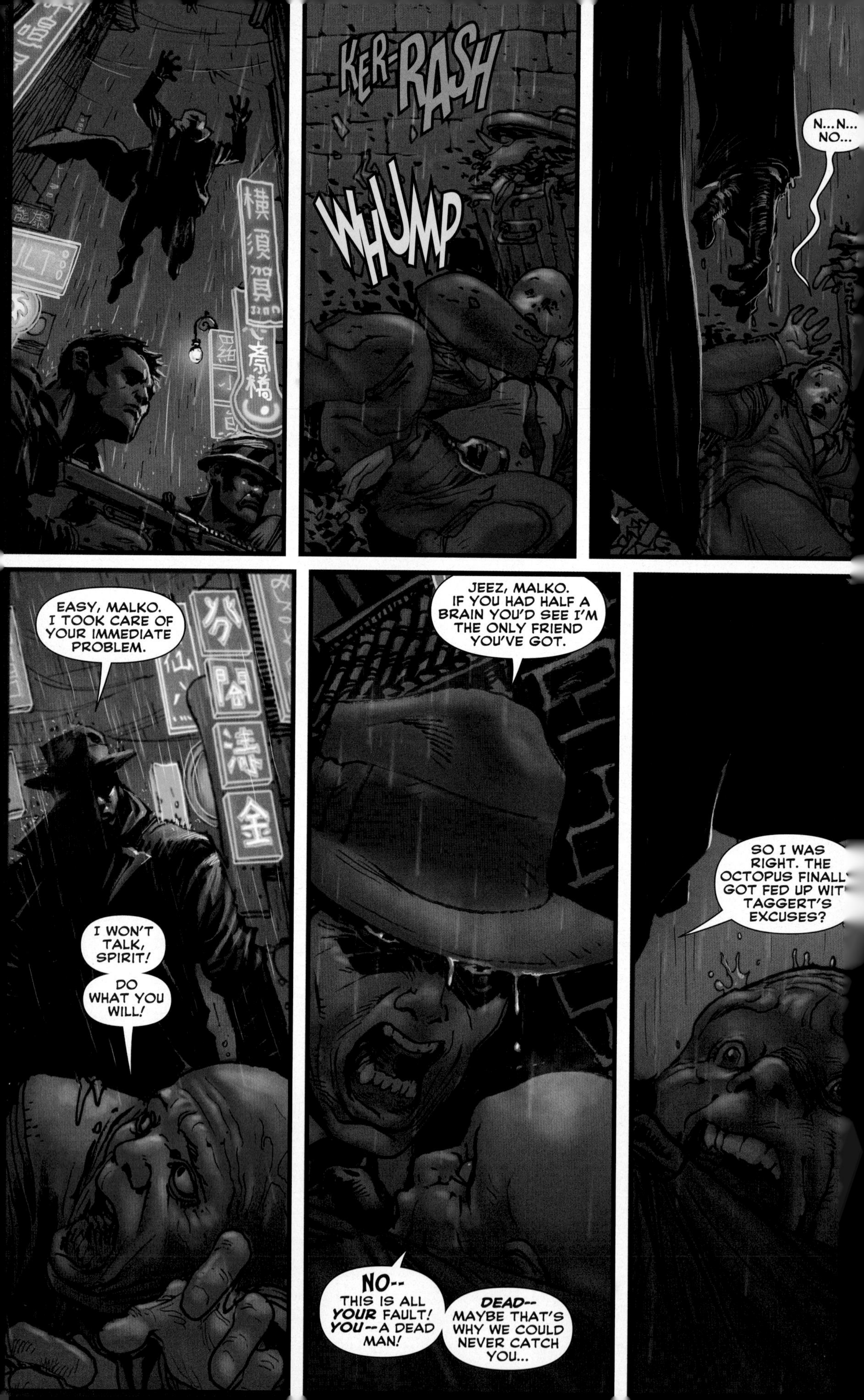
KER-RASH
WHUMP
N...N... NO...
EASY, MALKO. I TOOK CARE OF YOUR IMMEDIATE PROBLEM.
I WON'T TALK, SPIRIT!
DO WHAT YOU WILL!
JEEZ, MALKO. IF YOU HAD HALF A BRAIN YOU'D SEE I'M THE ONLY FRIEND YOU'VE GOT.
NO-- THIS IS ALL YOUR FAULT! YOU--A DEAD MAN!
DEAD-- MAYBE THAT'S WHY WE COULD NEVER CATCH YOU...
SO I WAS RIGHT. THE OCTOPUS FINALLY GOT FED UP WITH TAGGERT'S EXCUSES?

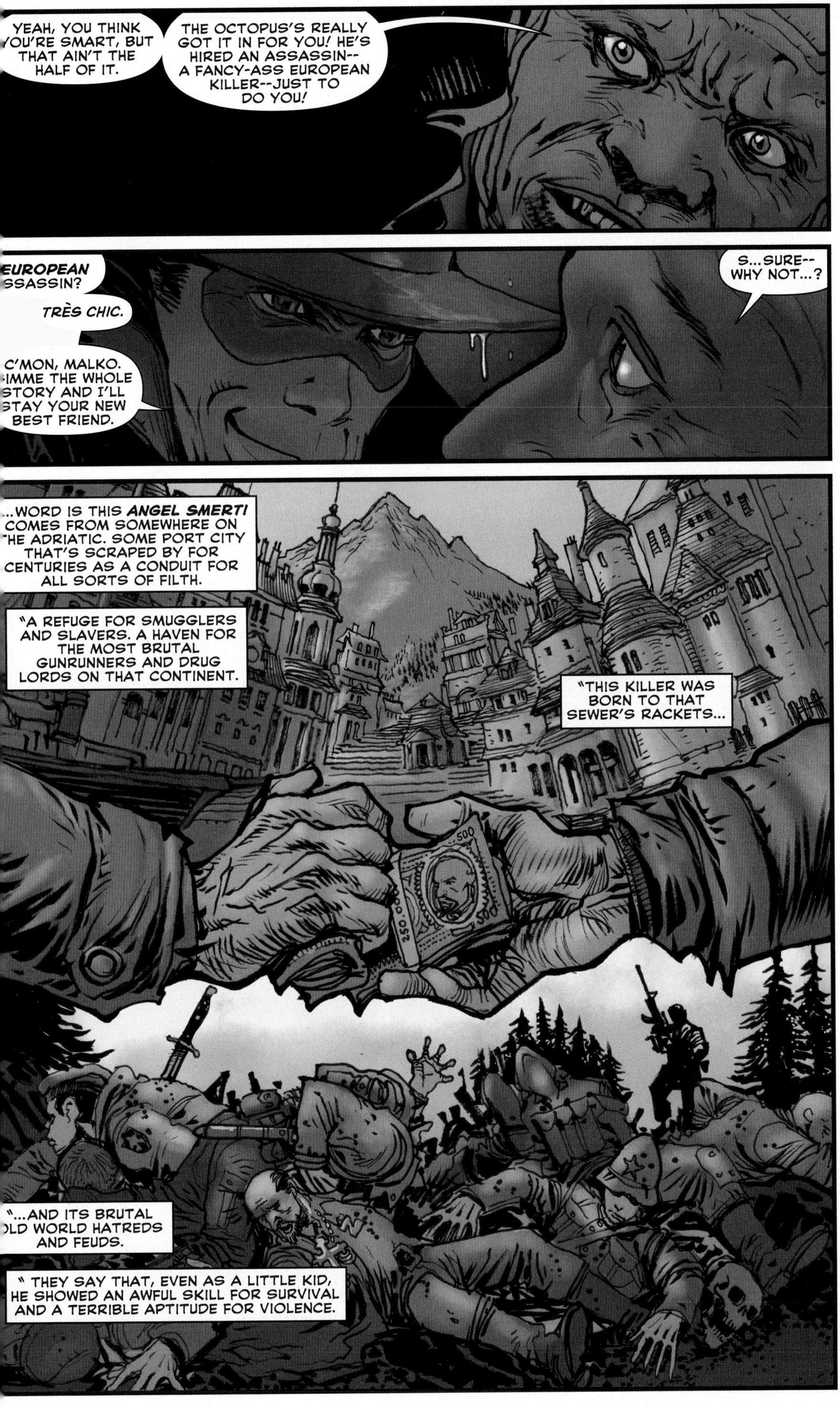

YEAH, YOU THINK YOU'RE SMART, BUT THAT AIN'T THE HALF OF IT.
THE OCTOPUS'S REALLY GOT IT IN FOR YOU! HE'S HIRED AN ASSASSIN-- A FANCY-ASS EUROPEAN KILLER--JUST TO DO YOU!
EUROPEAN ASSASSIN?
TRÈS CHIC.
C'MON, MALKO. GIMME THE WHOLE STORY AND I'LL STAY YOUR NEW BEST FRIEND.
S...SURE-- WHY NOT...?
...WORD IS THIS ANGEL SMERTI COMES FROM SOMEWHERE ON THE ADRIATIC. SOME PORT CITY THAT'S SCRAPED BY FOR CENTURIES AS A CONDUIT FOR ALL SORTS OF FILTH.
"A REFUGE FOR SMUGGLERS AND SLAVERS. A HAVEN FOR THE MOST BRUTAL GUNRUNNERS AND DRUG LORDS ON THAT CONTINENT.
"THIS KILLER WAS BORN TO THAT SEWER'S RACKETS...
"...AND ITS BRUTAL OLD WORLD HATREDS AND FEUDS.
" THEY SAY THAT, EVEN AS A LITTLE KID, HE SHOWED AN AWFUL SKILL FOR SURVIVAL AND A TERRIBLE APTITUDE FOR VIOLENCE.

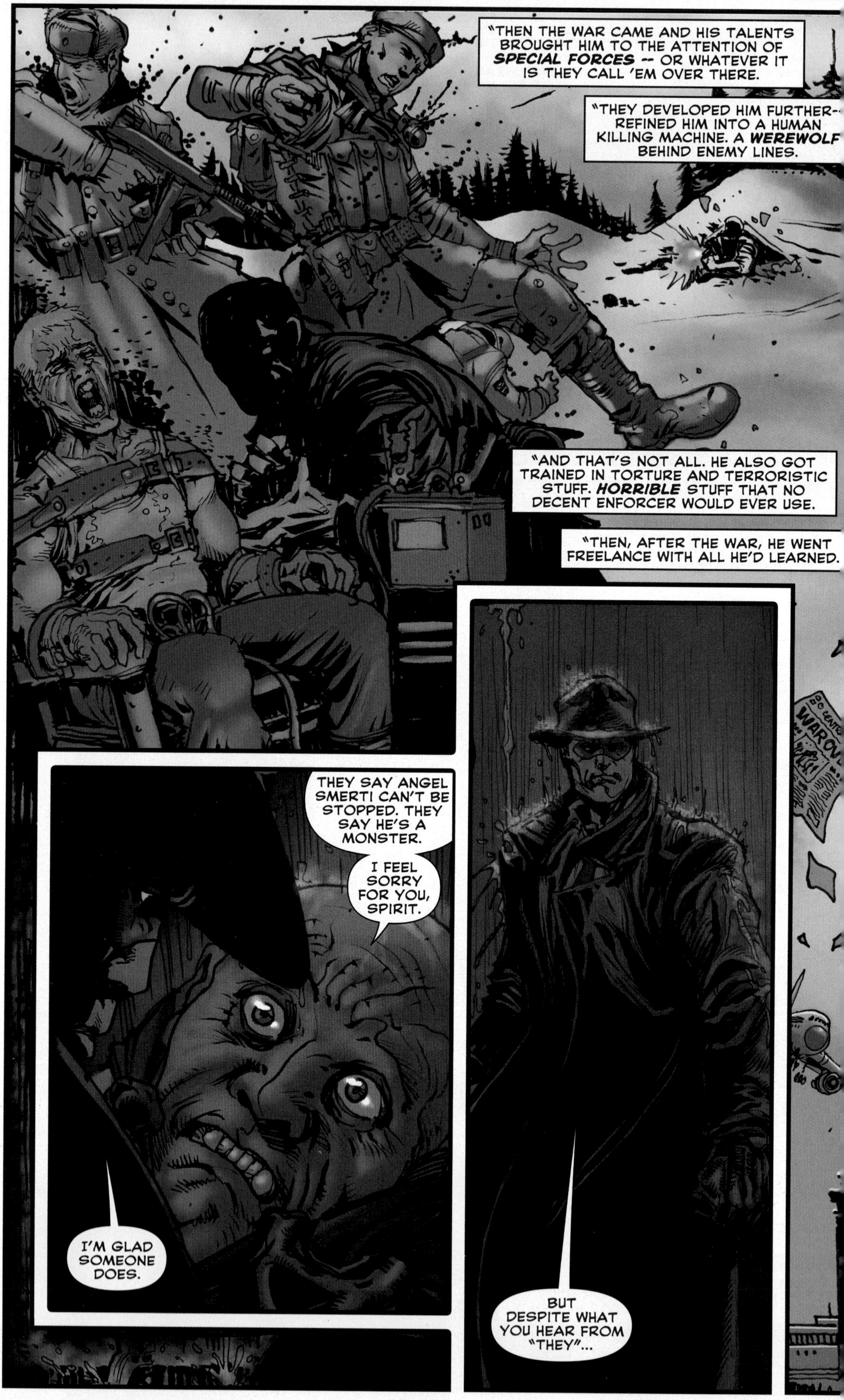
"THEN THE WAR CAME AND HIS TALENTS BROUGHT HIM TO THE ATTENTION OF ***SPECIAL FORCES*** -- OR WHATEVER IT IS THEY CALL 'EM OVER THERE.
"THEY DEVELOPED HIM FURTHER-- REFINED HIM INTO A HUMAN KILLING MACHINE. A ***WEREWOLF*** BEHIND ENEMY LINES.
"AND THAT'S NOT ALL. HE ALSO GOT TRAINED IN TORTURE AND TERRORISTIC STUFF. ***HORRIBLE*** STUFF THAT NO DECENT ENFORCER WOULD EVER USE.
"THEN, AFTER THE WAR, HE WENT FREELANCE WITH ALL HE'D LEARNED.
THEY SAY ANGEL SMERTI CAN'T BE STOPPED. THEY SAY HE'S A MONSTER.
I FEEL SORRY FOR YOU, SPIRIT.
I'M GLAD SOMEONE DOES.
BUT DESPITE WHAT YOU HEAR FROM "THEY"...

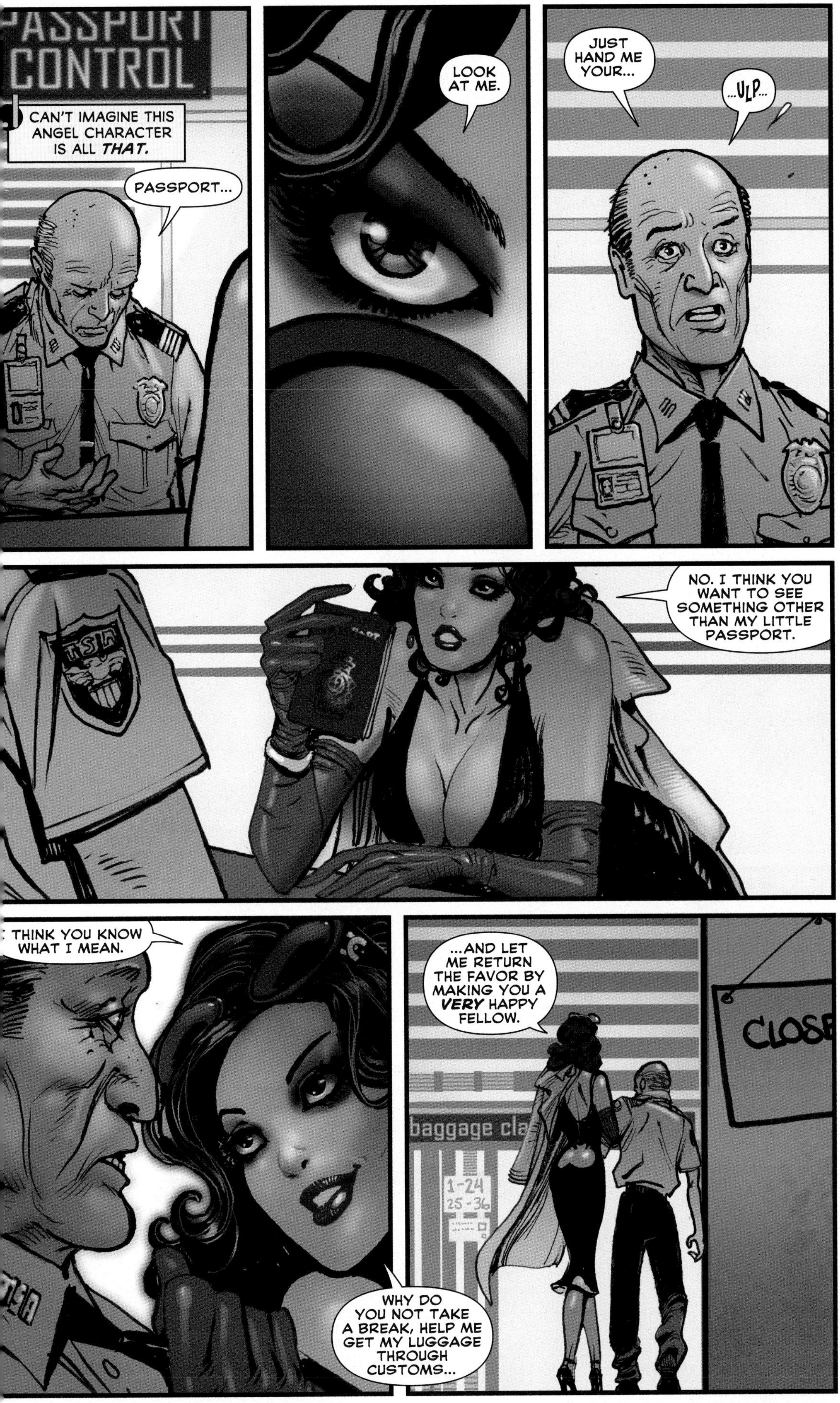
PASSPORT CONTROL
CAN'T IMAGINE THIS ANGEL CHARACTER IS ALL *THAT.*
PASSPORT...
LOOK AT ME.
JUST HAND ME YOUR...
...ULP...
NO. I THINK YOU WANT TO SEE SOMETHING OTHER THAN MY LITTLE PASSPORT.
THINK YOU KNOW WHAT I MEAN.
WHY DO YOU NOT TAKE A BREAK, HELP ME GET MY LUGGAGE THROUGH CUSTOMS...
...AND LET ME RETURN THE FAVOR BY MAKING YOU A *VERY* HAPPY FELLOW.
baggage cla
1-24
25-36
CLOSE

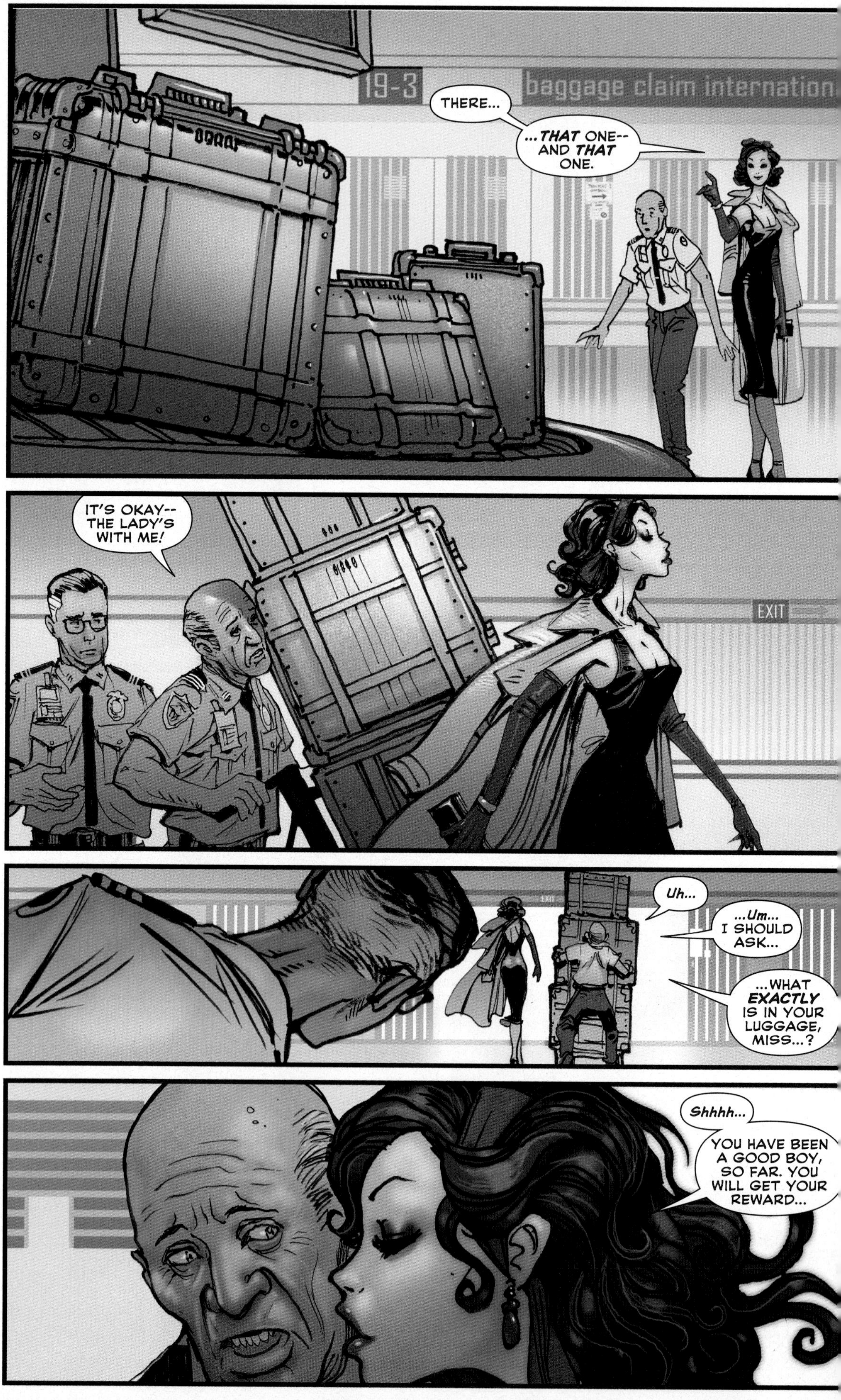
19-3
baggage claim internation
THERE...
...*THAT* ONE-- AND *THAT* ONE.
IT'S OKAY-- THE LADY'S WITH ME!
EXIT
EXIT
Uh...
...Um... I SHOULD ASK...
...WHAT *EXACTLY* IS IN YOUR LUGGAGE, MISS...?
Shhhh...
YOU HAVE BEEN A GOOD BOY, SO FAR. YOU WILL GET YOUR REWARD...

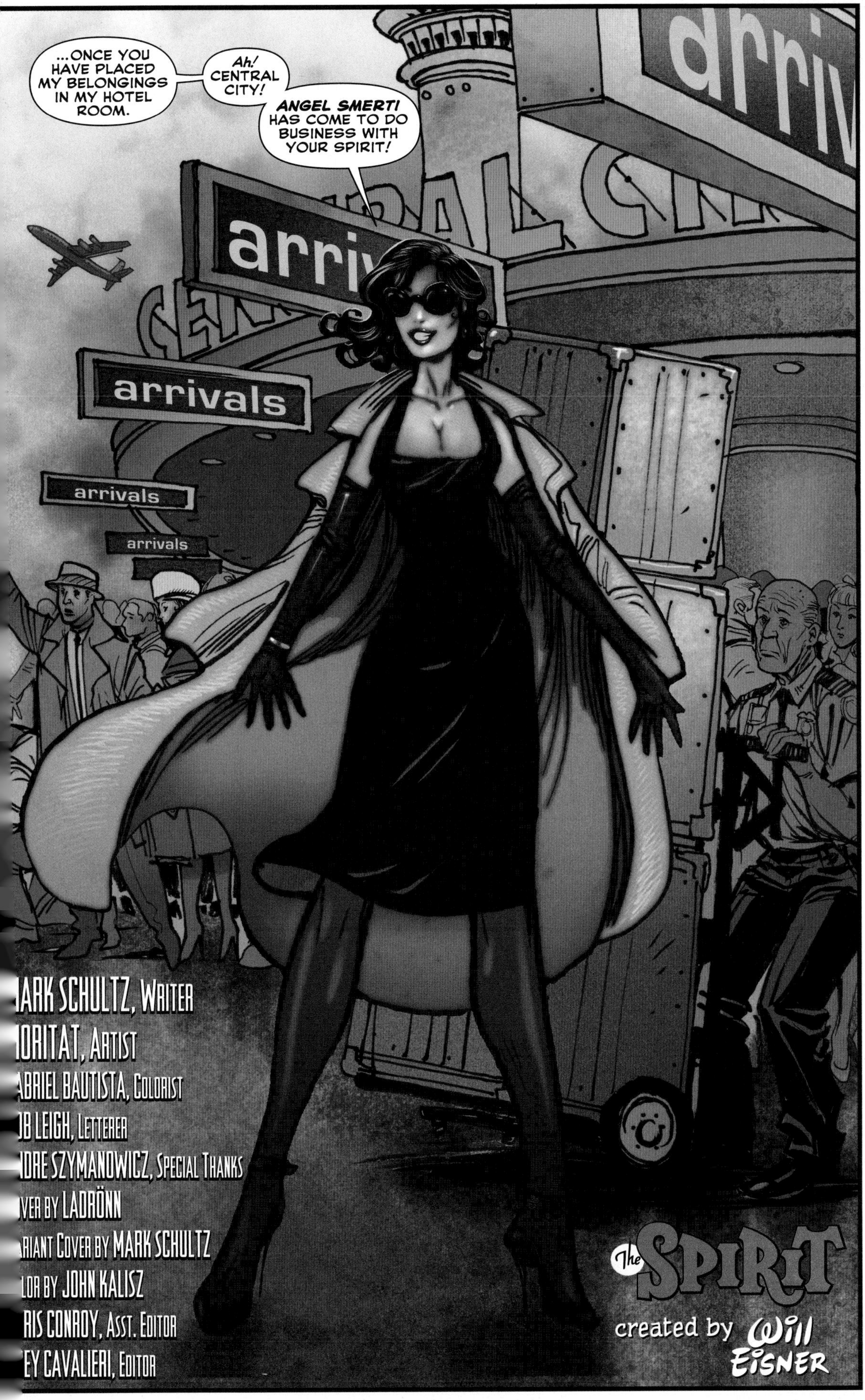

...ONCE YOU HAVE PLACED MY BELONGINGS IN MY HOTEL ROOM.
Ah! CENTRAL CITY!
ANGEL SMERT! HAS COME TO DO BUSINESS WITH YOUR SPIRIT!
arrivals
arrivals
arrivals
ARK SCHULTZ, WRITER
ORITAT, ARTIST
ABRIEL BAUTISTA, COLORIST
OB LEIGH, LETTERER
NDRE SZYMANOWICZ, SPECIAL THANKS
VER BY LADRÖNN
ARIANT COVER BY MARK SCHULTZ
LOR BY JOHN KALISZ
RIS CONROY, ASST. EDITOR
EY CAVALIERI, EDITOR
The SPIRIT
created by Will Eisner

ANGEL SMERTI **PART TWO**

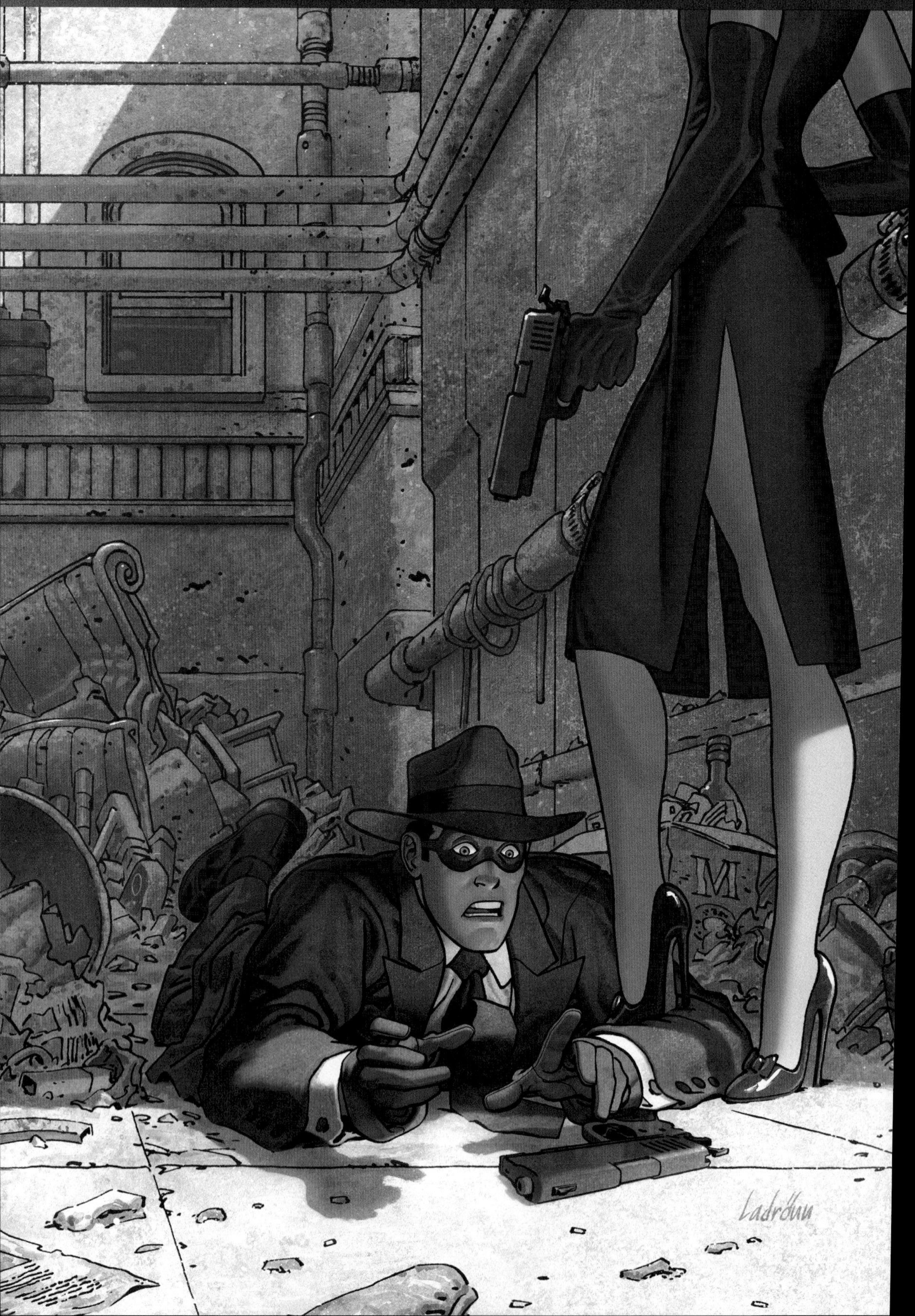

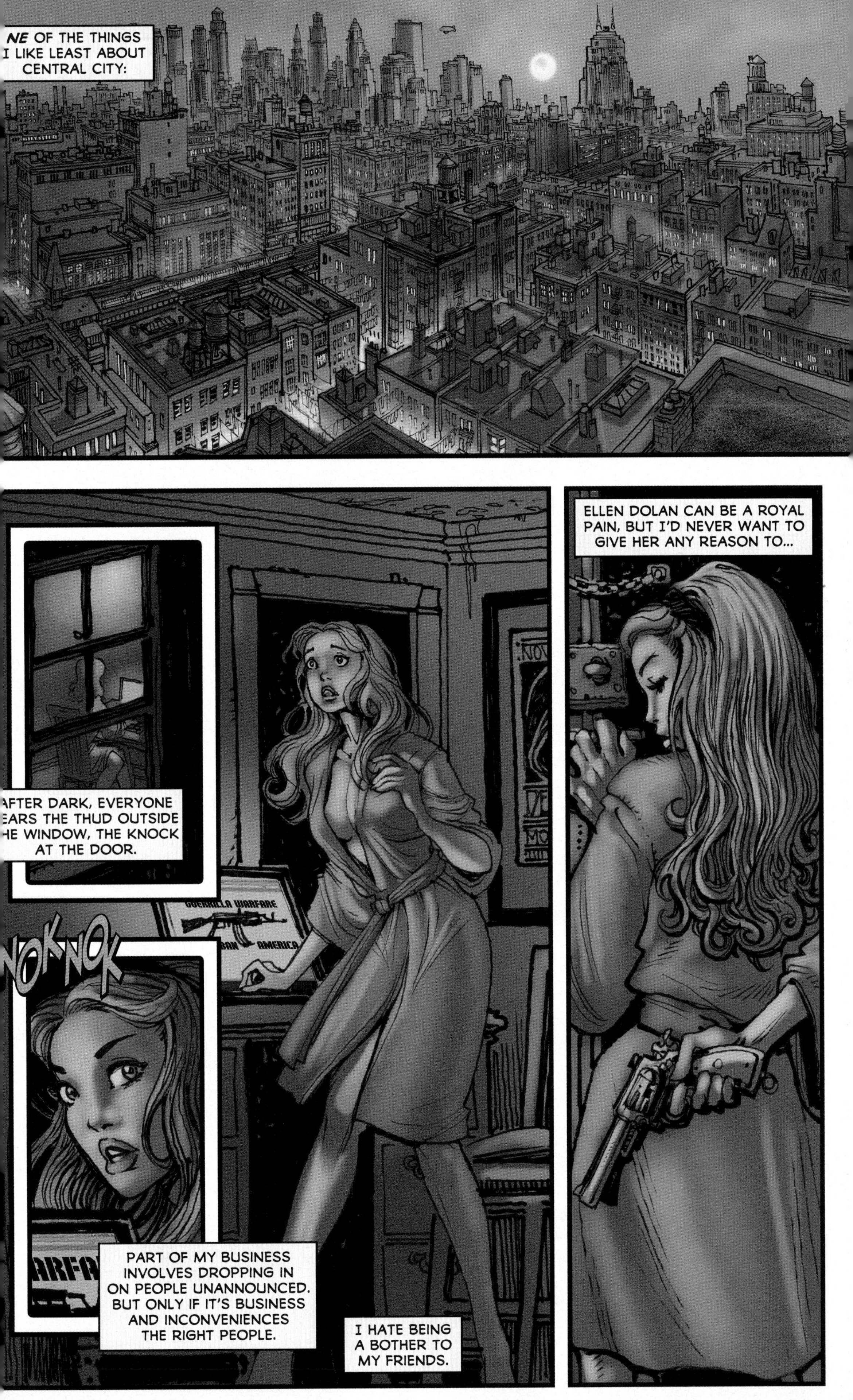
NE OF THE THINGS I LIKE LEAST ABOUT CENTRAL CITY:
AFTER DARK, EVERYONE EARS THE THUD OUTSIDE HE WINDOW, THE KNOCK AT THE DOOR.
NOK NOK
PART OF MY BUSINESS INVOLVES DROPPING IN ON PEOPLE UNANNOUNCED. BUT ONLY IF IT'S BUSINESS AND INCONVENIENCES THE RIGHT PEOPLE.
I HATE BEING A BOTHER TO MY FRIENDS.
ELLEN DOLAN CAN BE A ROYAL PAIN, BUT I'D NEVER WANT TO GIVE HER ANY REASON TO...

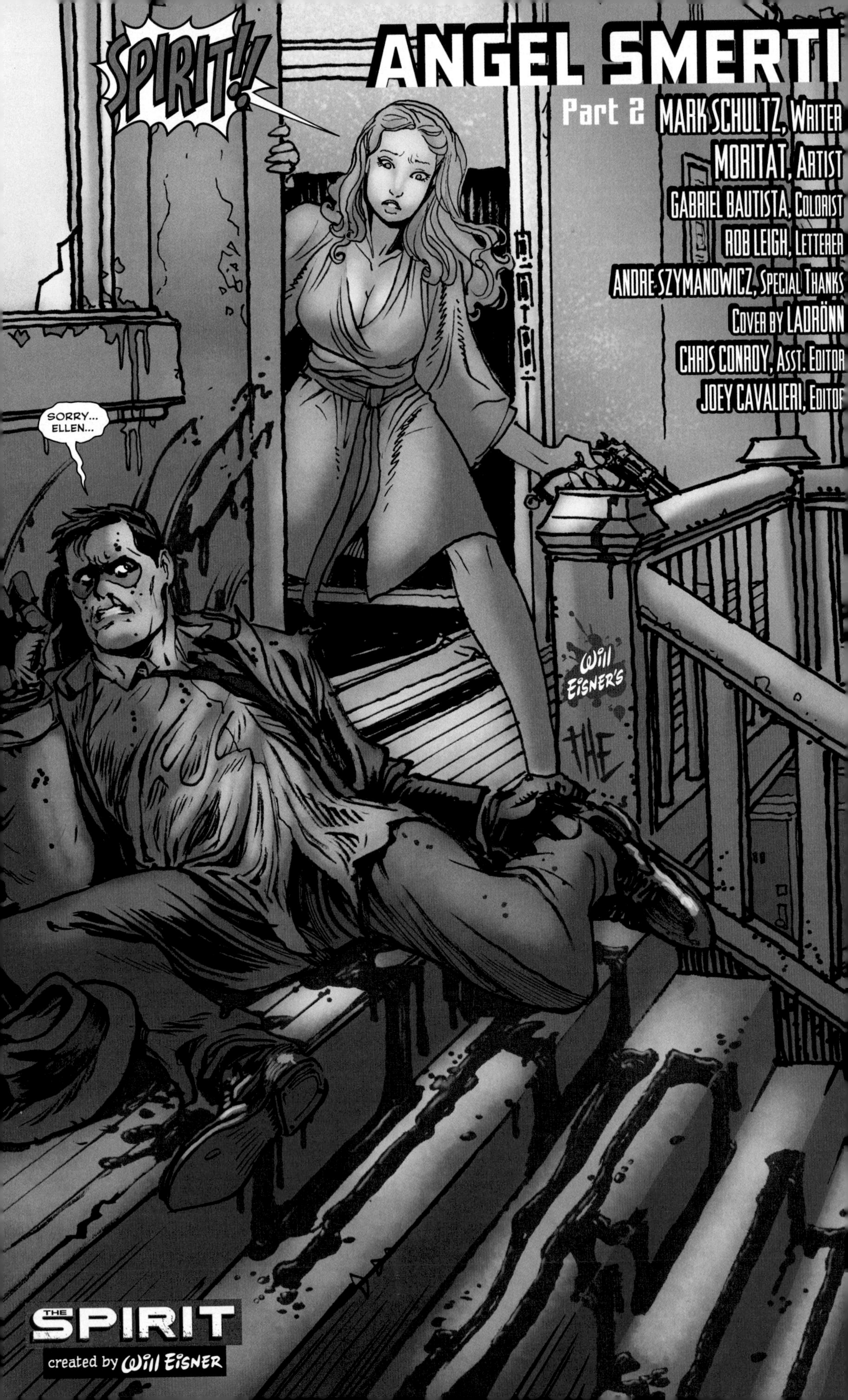
SPIRIT!!
ANGEL SMERTI
Part 2
MARK SCHULTZ, WRITER
MORITAT, ARTIST
GABRIEL BAUTISTA, COLORIST
ROB LEIGH, LETTERER
ANDRE SZYMANOWICZ, SPECIAL THANKS
COVER BY LADRÖNN
CHRIS CONROY, ASST. EDITOR
JOEY CAVALIERI, EDITOR
SORRY... ELLEN...
Will Eisner's THE
THE SPIRIT
created by Will Eisner

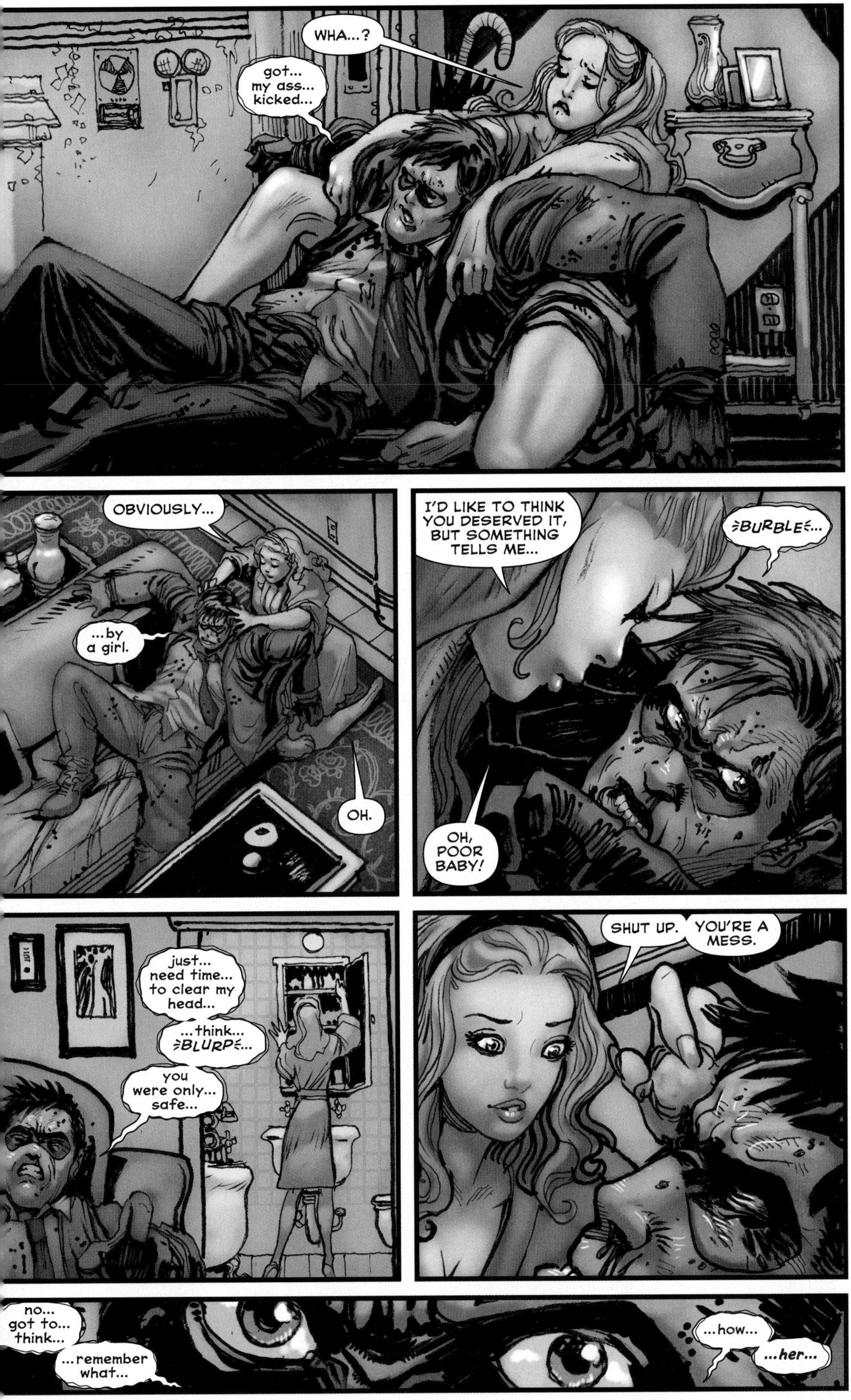
WHA...?
got... my ass... kicked...
OBVIOUSLY...
...by a girl.
OH.
I'D LIKE TO THINK YOU DESERVED IT, BUT SOMETHING TELLS ME...
BURBLE...
OH, POOR BABY!
just... need time... to clear my head...
...think... BLURP...
you were only... safe...
SHUT UP.
YOU'RE A MESS.
no... got to... think...
...remember what...
...how...
...her...

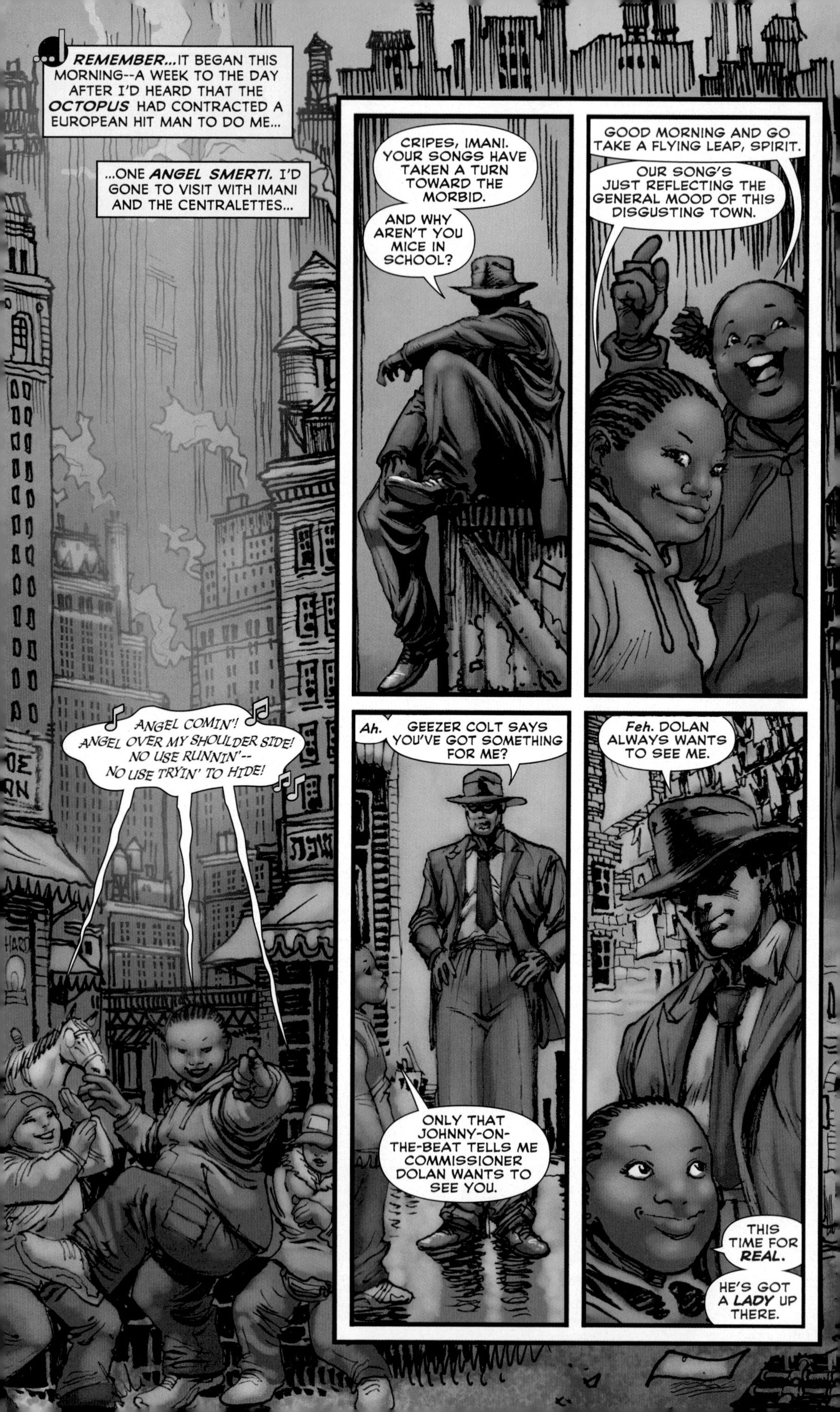
REMEMBER...IT BEGAN THIS MORNING--A WEEK TO THE DAY AFTER I'D HEARD THAT THE OCTOPUS HAD CONTRACTED A EUROPEAN HIT MAN TO DO ME...
...ONE ANGEL SMERTI. I'D GONE TO VISIT WITH IMANI AND THE CENTRALETTES...
ANGEL COMIN'! ANGEL OVER MY SHOULDER SIDE! NO USE RUNNIN'-- NO USE TRYIN' TO HIDE!
CRIPES, IMANI. YOUR SONGS HAVE TAKEN A TURN TOWARD THE MORBID.
AND WHY AREN'T YOU MICE IN SCHOOL?
GOOD MORNING AND GO TAKE A FLYING LEAP, SPIRIT.
OUR SONG'S JUST REFLECTING THE GENERAL MOOD OF THIS DISGUSTING TOWN.
Ah.
GEEZER COLT SAYS YOU'VE GOT SOMETHING FOR ME?
ONLY THAT JOHNNY-ON-THE-BEAT TELLS ME COMMISSIONER DOLAN WANTS TO SEE YOU.
Feh. DOLAN ALWAYS WANTS TO SEE ME.
THIS TIME FOR REAL.
HE'S GOT A LADY UP THERE.

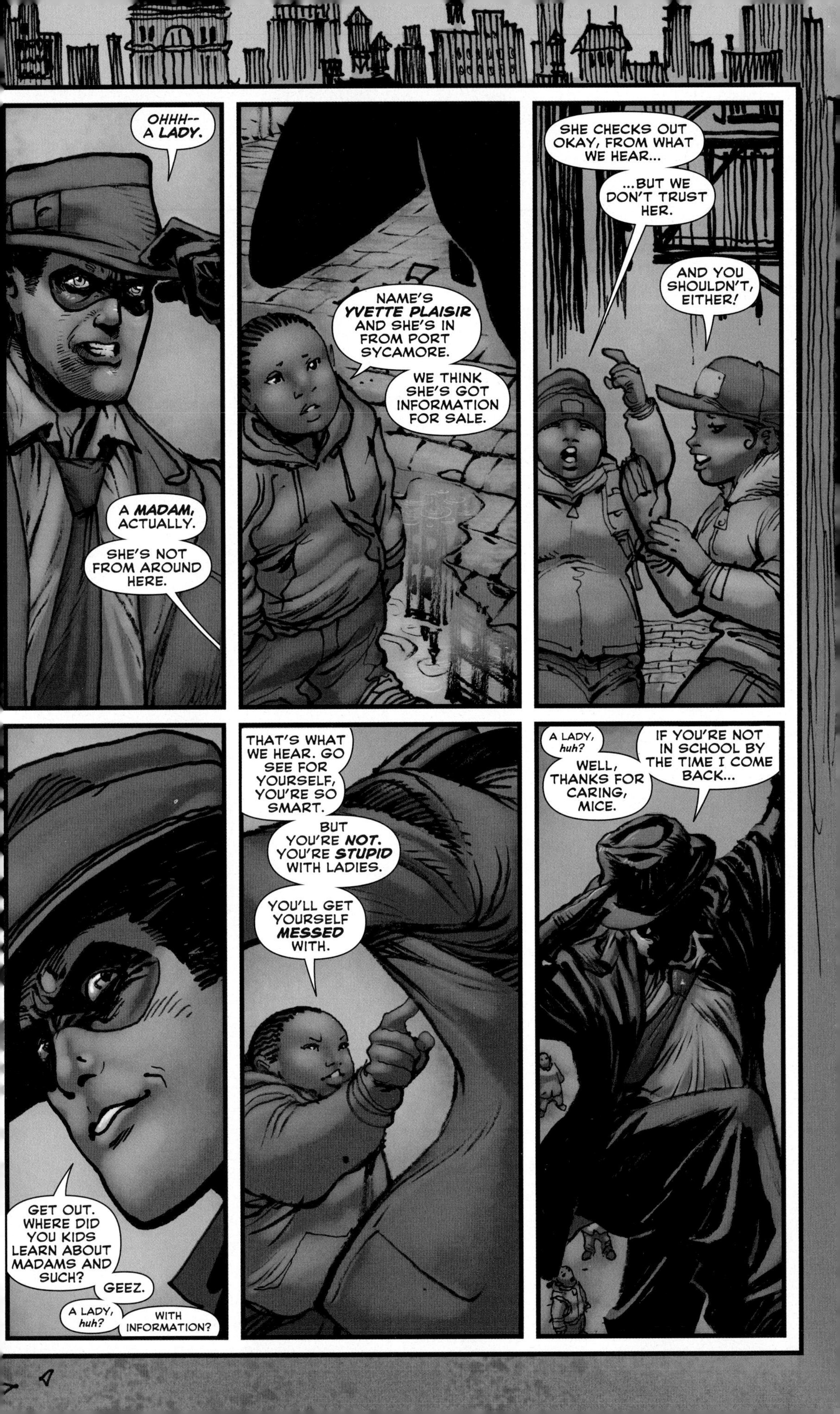
OHHH-- A *LADY.*
A *MADAM,* ACTUALLY.
SHE'S NOT FROM AROUND HERE.
NAME'S *YVETTE PLAISIR* AND SHE'S IN FROM PORT SYCAMORE.
WE THINK SHE'S GOT INFORMATION FOR SALE.
SHE CHECKS OUT OKAY, FROM WHAT WE HEAR...
...BUT WE DON'T TRUST HER.
AND YOU SHOULDN'T, EITHER!
GET OUT. WHERE DID YOU KIDS LEARN ABOUT MADAMS AND SUCH?
GEEZ.
A LADY, *huh?*
WITH INFORMATION?
THAT'S WHAT WE HEAR. GO SEE FOR YOURSELF, YOU'RE SO SMART.
BUT YOU'RE *NOT.* YOU'RE *STUPID* WITH LADIES.
YOU'LL GET YOURSELF *MESSED* WITH.
A LADY, *huh?*
WELL, THANKS FOR CARING, MICE.
IF YOU'RE NOT IN SCHOOL BY THE TIME I COME BACK...

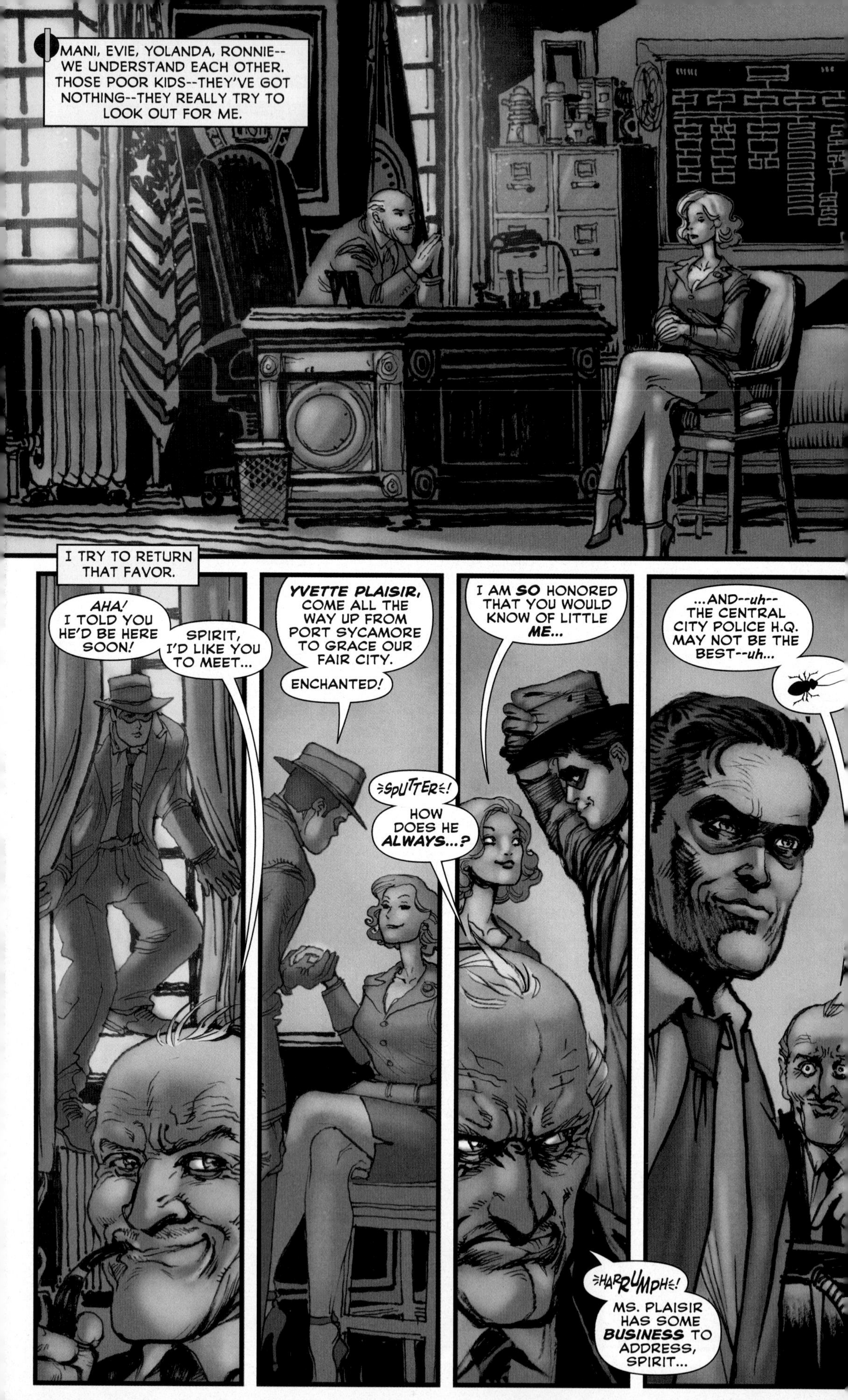
MANI, EVIE, YOLANDA, RONNIE--WE UNDERSTAND EACH OTHER. THOSE POOR KIDS--THEY'VE GOT NOTHING--THEY REALLY TRY TO LOOK OUT FOR ME.
I TRY TO RETURN THAT FAVOR.
AHA! I TOLD YOU HE'D BE HERE SOON!
SPIRIT, I'D LIKE YOU TO MEET...
YVETTE PLAISIR, COME ALL THE WAY UP FROM PORT SYCAMORE TO GRACE OUR FAIR CITY.
ENCHANTED!
SPUTTER!
HOW DOES HE ALWAYS...?
I AM SO HONORED THAT YOU WOULD KNOW OF LITTLE ME...
...AND--uh--THE CENTRAL CITY POLICE H.Q. MAY NOT BE THE BEST--uh...
HARRUMPH!
MS. PLAISIR HAS SOME BUSINESS TO ADDRESS, SPIRIT...

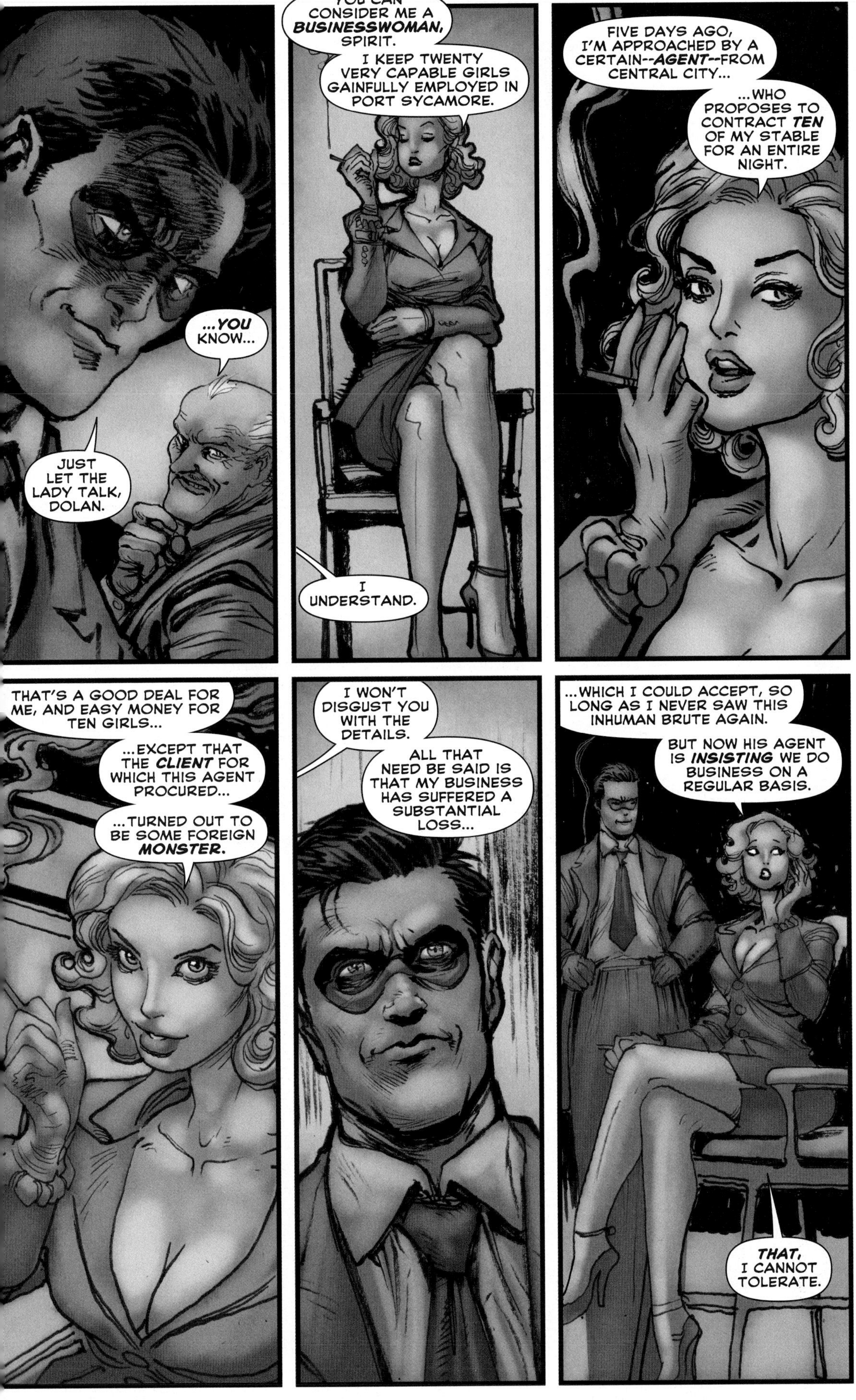

...YOU KNOW...
JUST LET THE LADY TALK, DOLAN.
YOU CAN CONSIDER ME A BUSINESSWOMAN, SPIRIT.
I KEEP TWENTY VERY CAPABLE GIRLS GAINFULLY EMPLOYED IN PORT SYCAMORE.
I UNDERSTAND.
FIVE DAYS AGO, I'M APPROACHED BY A CERTAIN--AGENT--FROM CENTRAL CITY...
...WHO PROPOSES TO CONTRACT TEN OF MY STABLE FOR AN ENTIRE NIGHT.
THAT'S A GOOD DEAL FOR ME, AND EASY MONEY FOR TEN GIRLS...
...EXCEPT THAT THE CLIENT FOR WHICH THIS AGENT PROCURED...
...TURNED OUT TO BE SOME FOREIGN MONSTER.
I WON'T DISGUST YOU WITH THE DETAILS.
ALL THAT NEED BE SAID IS THAT MY BUSINESS HAS SUFFERED A SUBSTANTIAL LOSS...
...WHICH I COULD ACCEPT, SO LONG AS I NEVER SAW THIS INHUMAN BRUTE AGAIN.
BUT NOW HIS AGENT IS INSISTING WE DO BUSINESS ON A REGULAR BASIS.
THAT, I CANNOT TOLERATE.

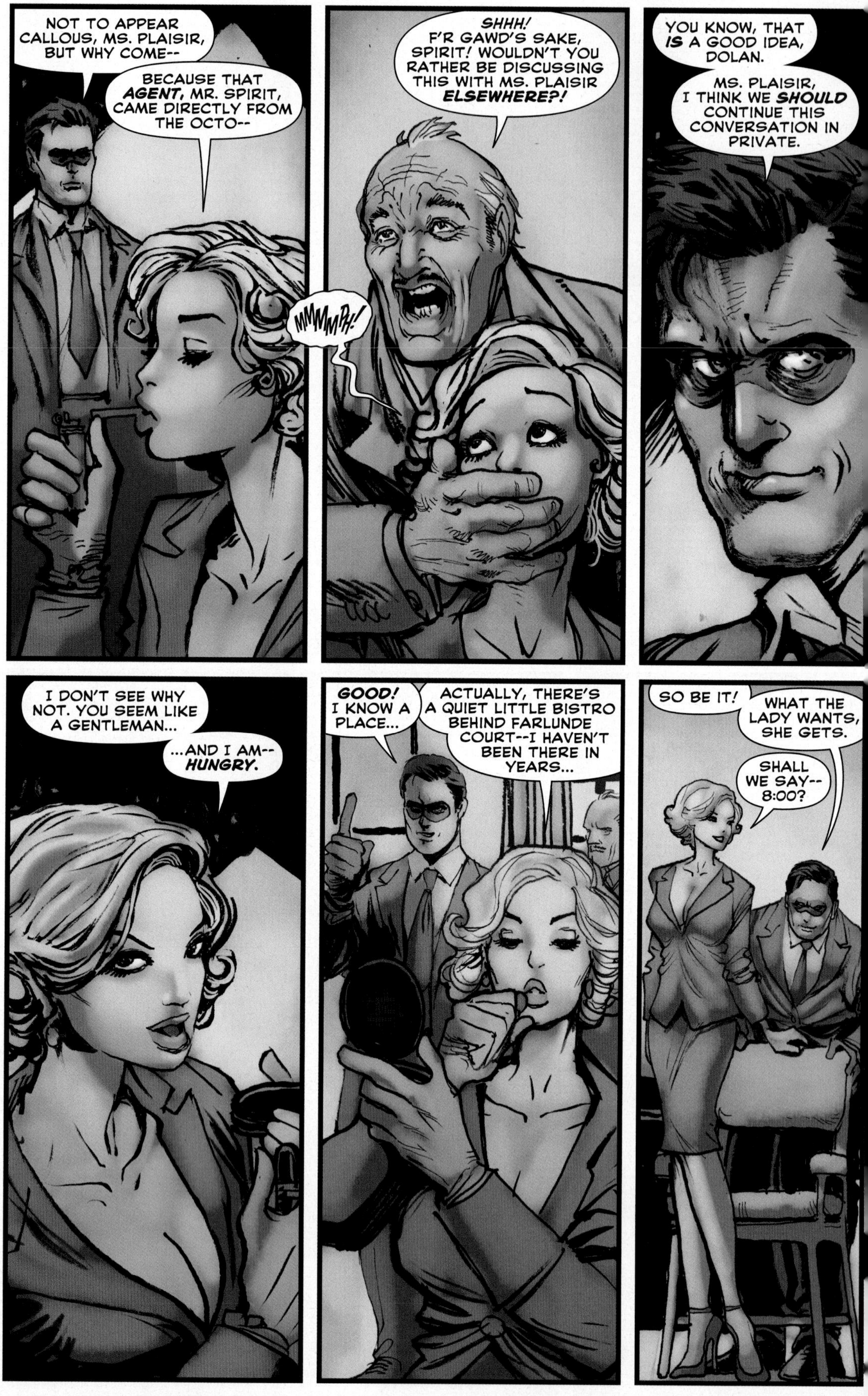

NOT TO APPEAR CALLOUS, MS. PLAISIR, BUT WHY COME--
BECAUSE THAT AGENT, MR. SPIRIT, CAME DIRECTLY FROM THE OCTO--
SHHH! F'R GAWD'S SAKE, SPIRIT! WOULDN'T YOU RATHER BE DISCUSSING THIS WITH MS. PLAISIR ELSEWHERE?!
MMMMPH!
YOU KNOW, THAT IS A GOOD IDEA, DOLAN.
MS. PLAISIR, I THINK WE SHOULD CONTINUE THIS CONVERSATION IN PRIVATE.
I DON'T SEE WHY NOT. YOU SEEM LIKE A GENTLEMAN...
...AND I AM-- HUNGRY.
GOOD! I KNOW A PLACE...
ACTUALLY, THERE'S A QUIET LITTLE BISTRO BEHIND FARLUNDE COURT--I HAVEN'T BEEN THERE IN YEARS...
SO BE IT!
WHAT THE LADY WANTS, SHE GETS.
SHALL WE SAY-- 8:00?

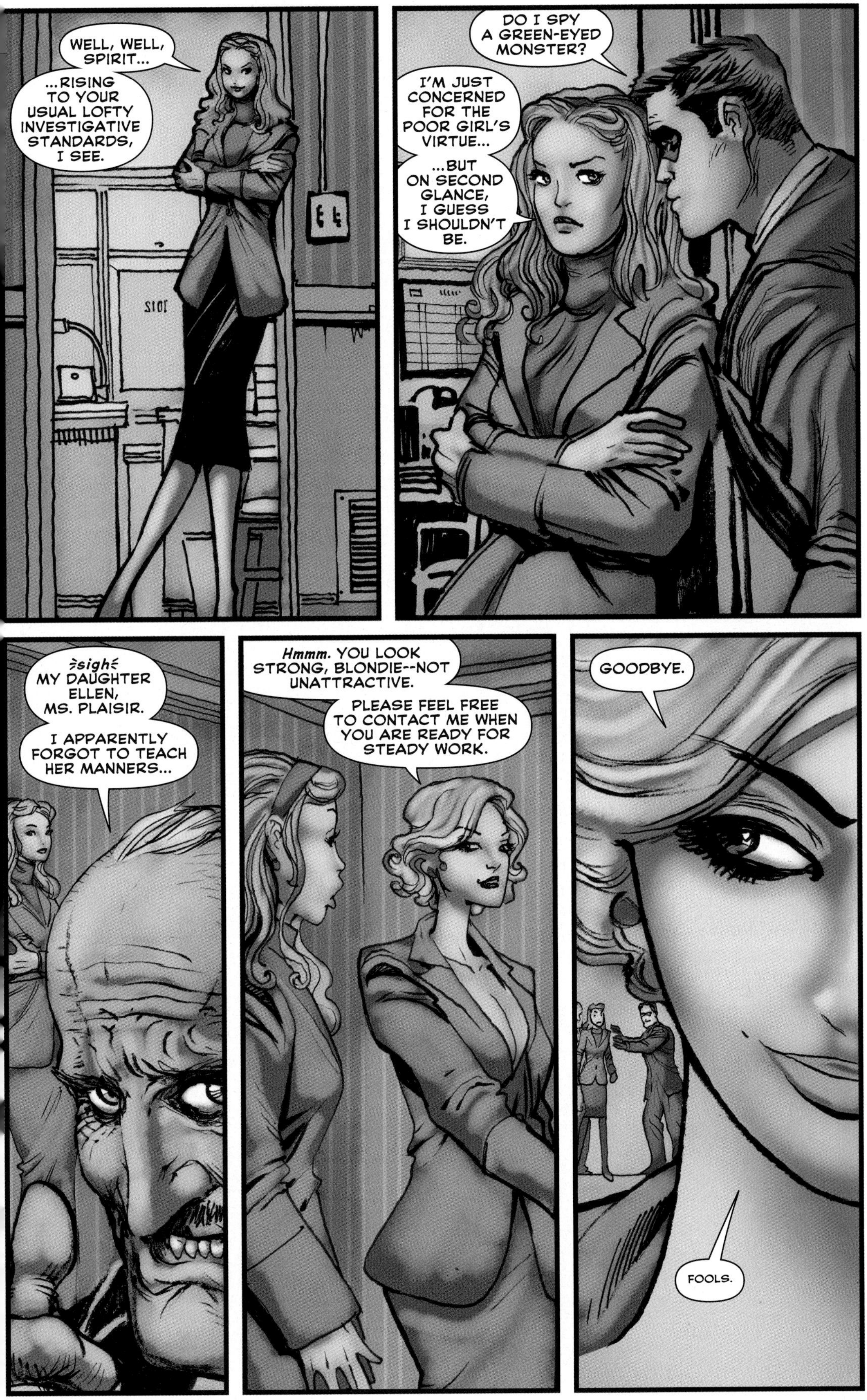
WELL, WELL, SPIRIT...
...RISING TO YOUR USUAL LOFTY INVESTIGATIVE STANDARDS, I SEE.
DO I SPY A GREEN-EYED MONSTER?
I'M JUST CONCERNED FOR THE POOR GIRL'S VIRTUE...
...BUT ON SECOND GLANCE, I GUESS I SHOULDN'T BE.
sigh
MY DAUGHTER ELLEN, MS. PLAISIR.
I APPARENTLY FORGOT TO TEACH HER MANNERS...
Hmmm. YOU LOOK STRONG, BLONDIE--NOT UNATTRACTIVE.
PLEASE FEEL FREE TO CONTACT ME WHEN YOU ARE READY FOR STEADY WORK.
GOODBYE.
FOOLS.

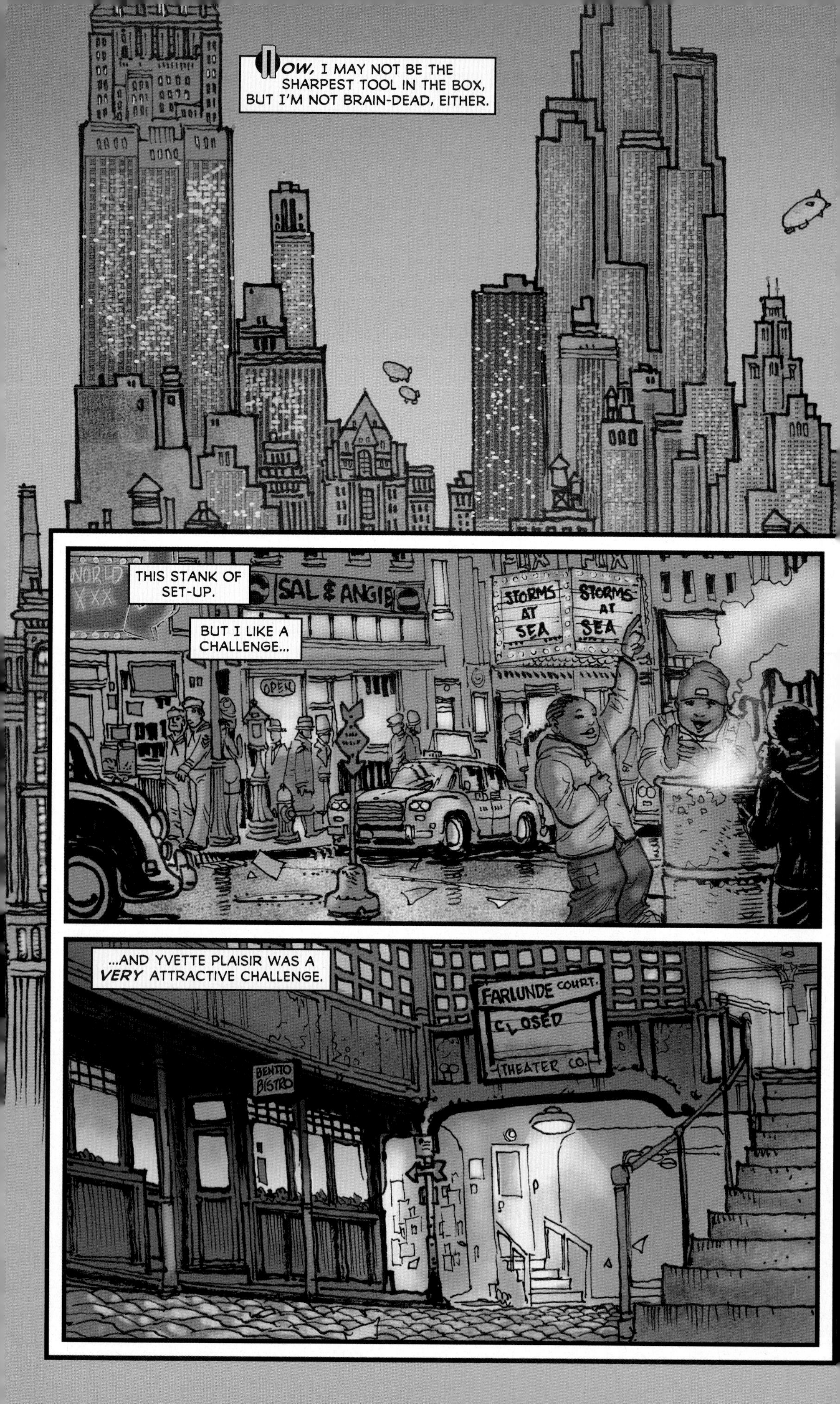
NOW, I MAY NOT BE THE SHARPEST TOOL IN THE BOX, BUT I'M NOT BRAIN-DEAD, EITHER.
WORLD XXX
THIS STANK OF SET-UP.
SAL & ANGI
BUT I LIKE A CHALLENGE...
STORMS AT SEA
STORMS AT SEA
OPEN
...AND YVETTE PLAISIR WAS A *VERY* ATTRACTIVE CHALLENGE.
FARLUNDE COURT.
CLOSED
THEATER CO.
BENITO BISTRO

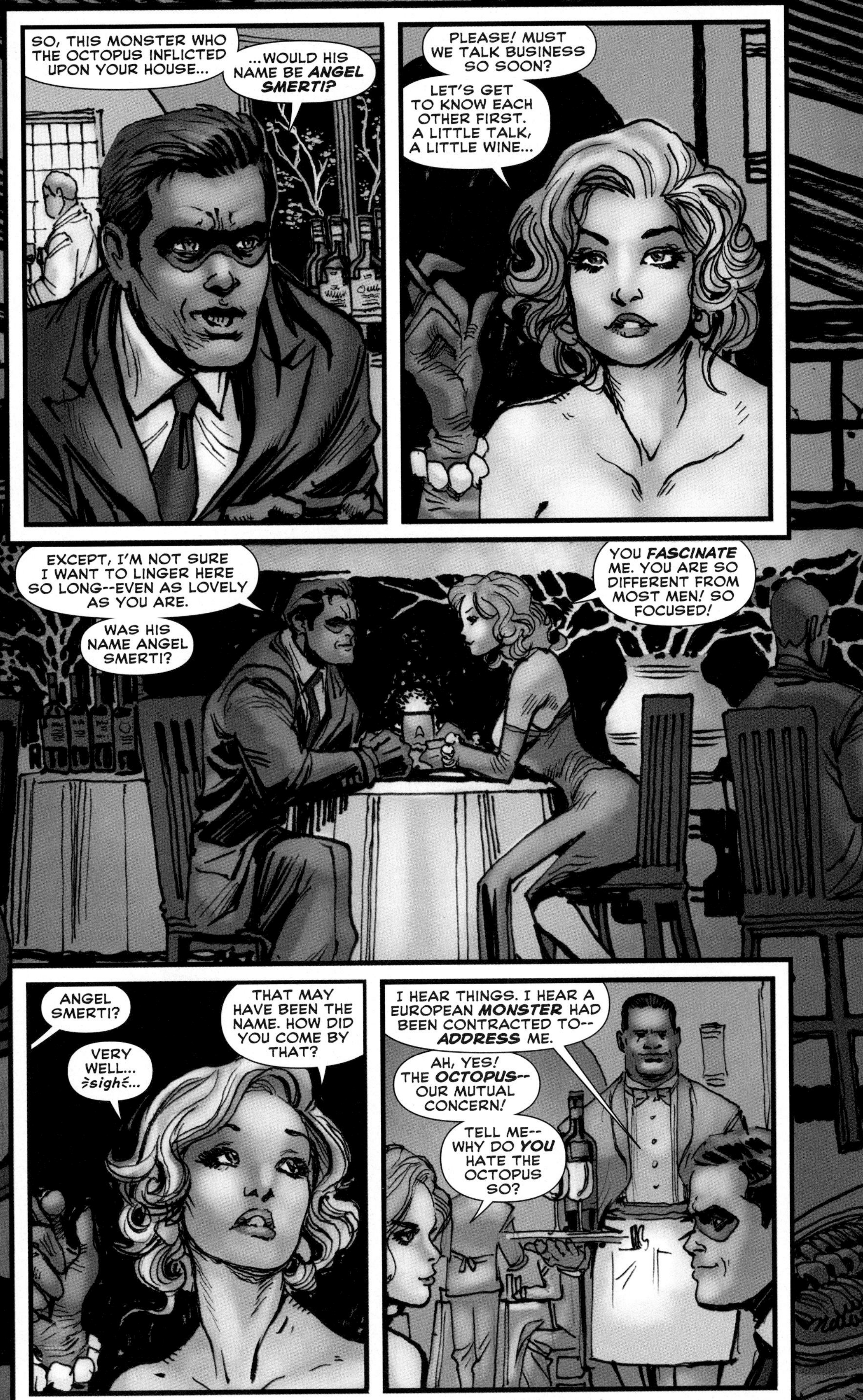
SO, THIS MONSTER WHO THE OCTOPUS INFLICTED UPON YOUR HOUSE...
...WOULD HIS NAME BE ANGEL SMERTI?
PLEASE! MUST WE TALK BUSINESS SO SOON?
LET'S GET TO KNOW EACH OTHER FIRST. A LITTLE TALK, A LITTLE WINE...
EXCEPT, I'M NOT SURE I WANT TO LINGER HERE SO LONG--EVEN AS LOVELY AS YOU ARE.
WAS HIS NAME ANGEL SMERTI?
YOU FASCINATE ME. YOU ARE SO DIFFERENT FROM MOST MEN! SO FOCUSED!
ANGEL SMERTI?
VERY WELL... ≶sigh≷...
THAT MAY HAVE BEEN THE NAME. HOW DID YOU COME BY THAT?
I HEAR THINGS. I HEAR A EUROPEAN MONSTER HAD BEEN CONTRACTED TO-- ADDRESS ME.
AH, YES! THE OCTOPUS-- OUR MUTUAL CONCERN!
TELL ME-- WHY DO YOU HATE THE OCTOPUS SO?

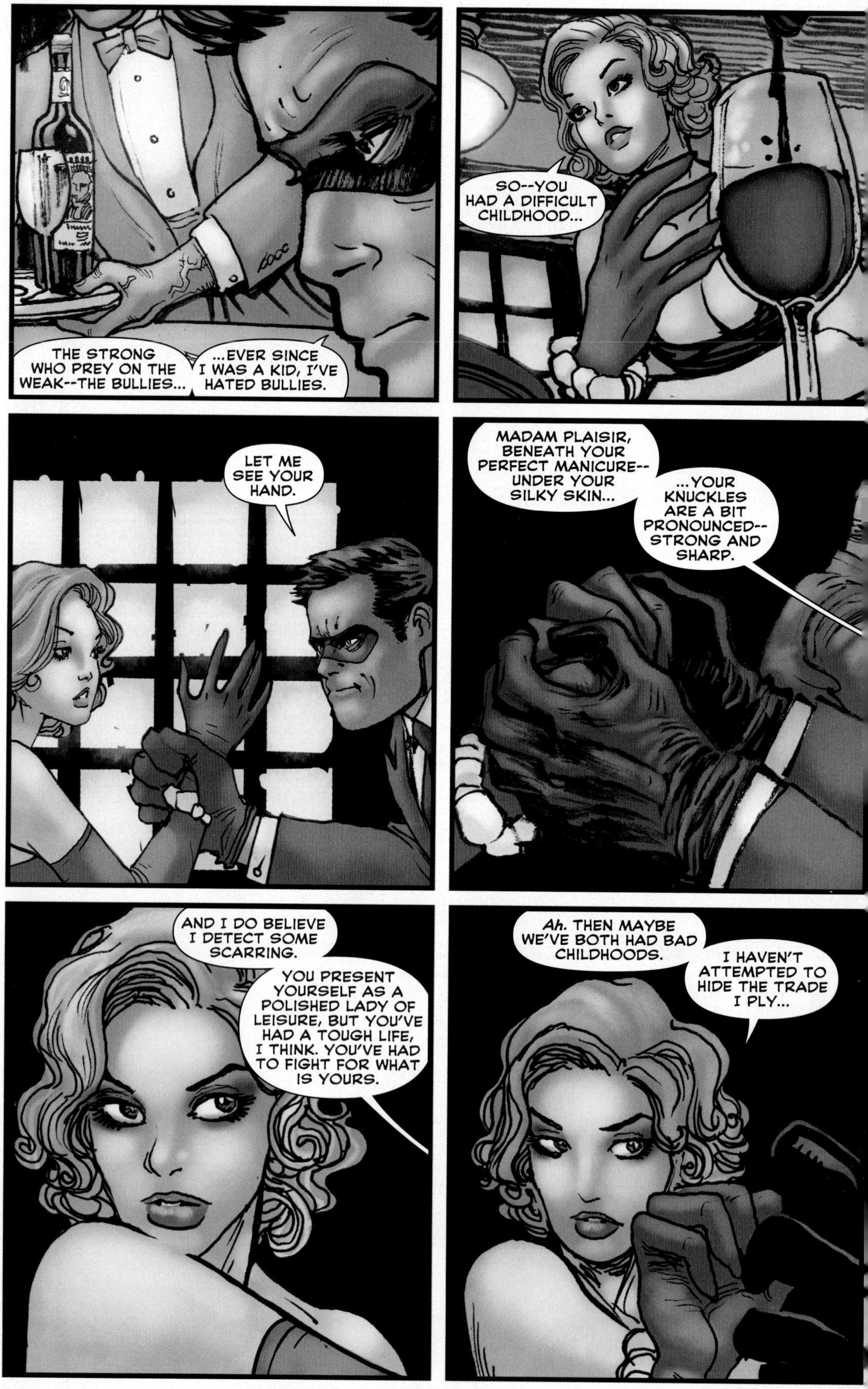
THE STRONG WHO PREY ON THE WEAK--THE BULLIES...
...EVER SINCE I WAS A KID, I'VE HATED BULLIES.
SO--YOU HAD A DIFFICULT CHILDHOOD...
LET ME SEE YOUR HAND.
MADAM PLAISIR, BENEATH YOUR PERFECT MANICURE-- UNDER YOUR SILKY SKIN...
...YOUR KNUCKLES ARE A BIT PRONOUNCED-- STRONG AND SHARP.
AND I DO BELIEVE I DETECT SOME SCARRING.
YOU PRESENT YOURSELF AS A POLISHED LADY OF LEISURE, BUT YOU'VE HAD A TOUGH LIFE, I THINK. YOU'VE HAD TO FIGHT FOR WHAT IS YOURS.
Ah. THEN MAYBE WE'VE BOTH HAD BAD CHILDHOODS.
I HAVEN'T ATTEMPTED TO HIDE THE TRADE I PLY...

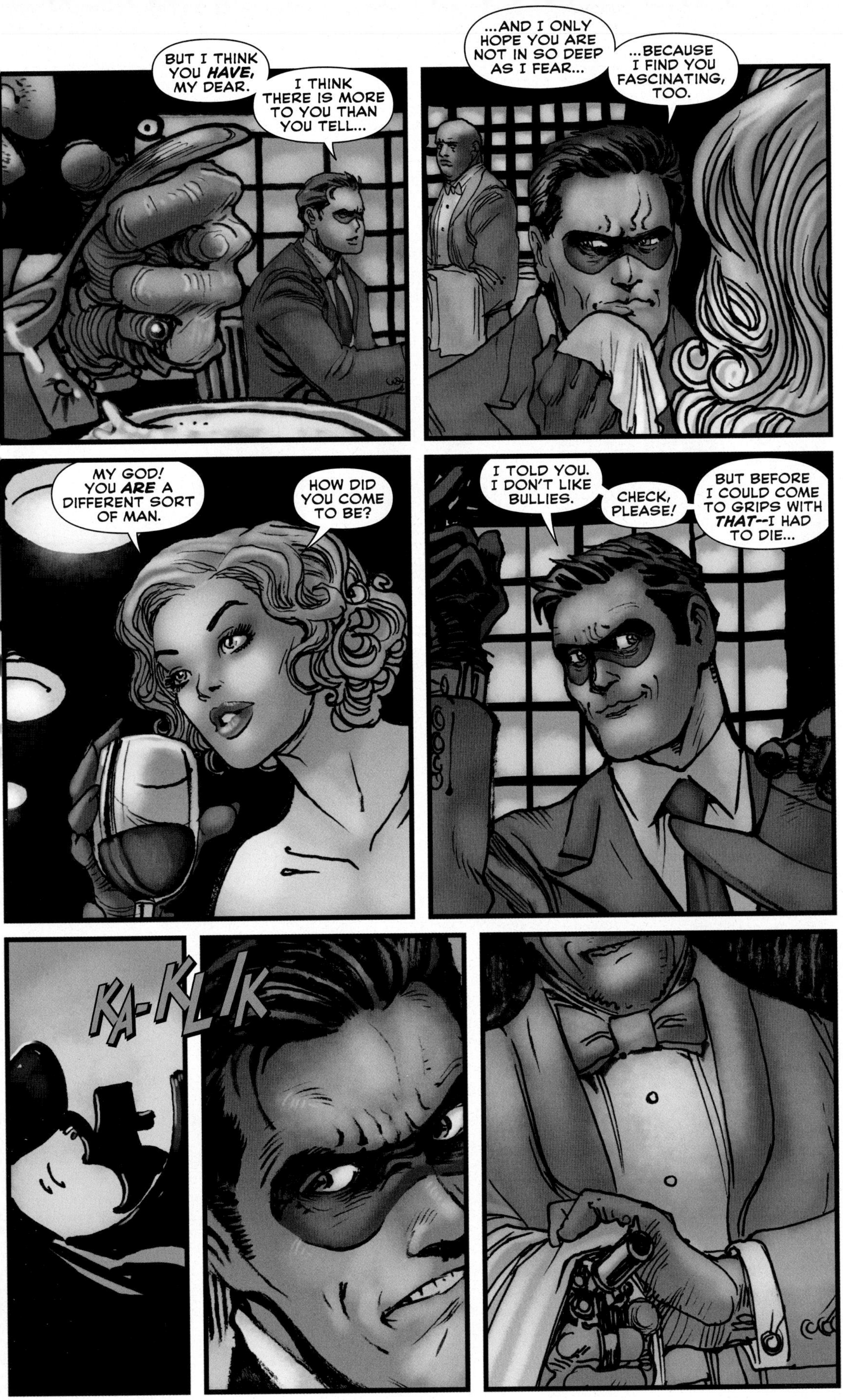
BUT I THINK YOU *HAVE,* MY DEAR.
I THINK THERE IS MORE TO YOU THAN YOU TELL...
...AND I ONLY HOPE YOU ARE NOT IN SO DEEP AS I FEAR...
...BECAUSE I FIND YOU FASCINATING, TOO.
MY GOD! YOU *ARE* A DIFFERENT SORT OF MAN.
HOW DID YOU COME TO BE?
I TOLD YOU. I DON'T LIKE BULLIES.
CHECK, PLEASE!
BUT BEFORE I COULD COME TO GRIPS WITH *THAT*--I HAD TO DIE...
KA-KLIK

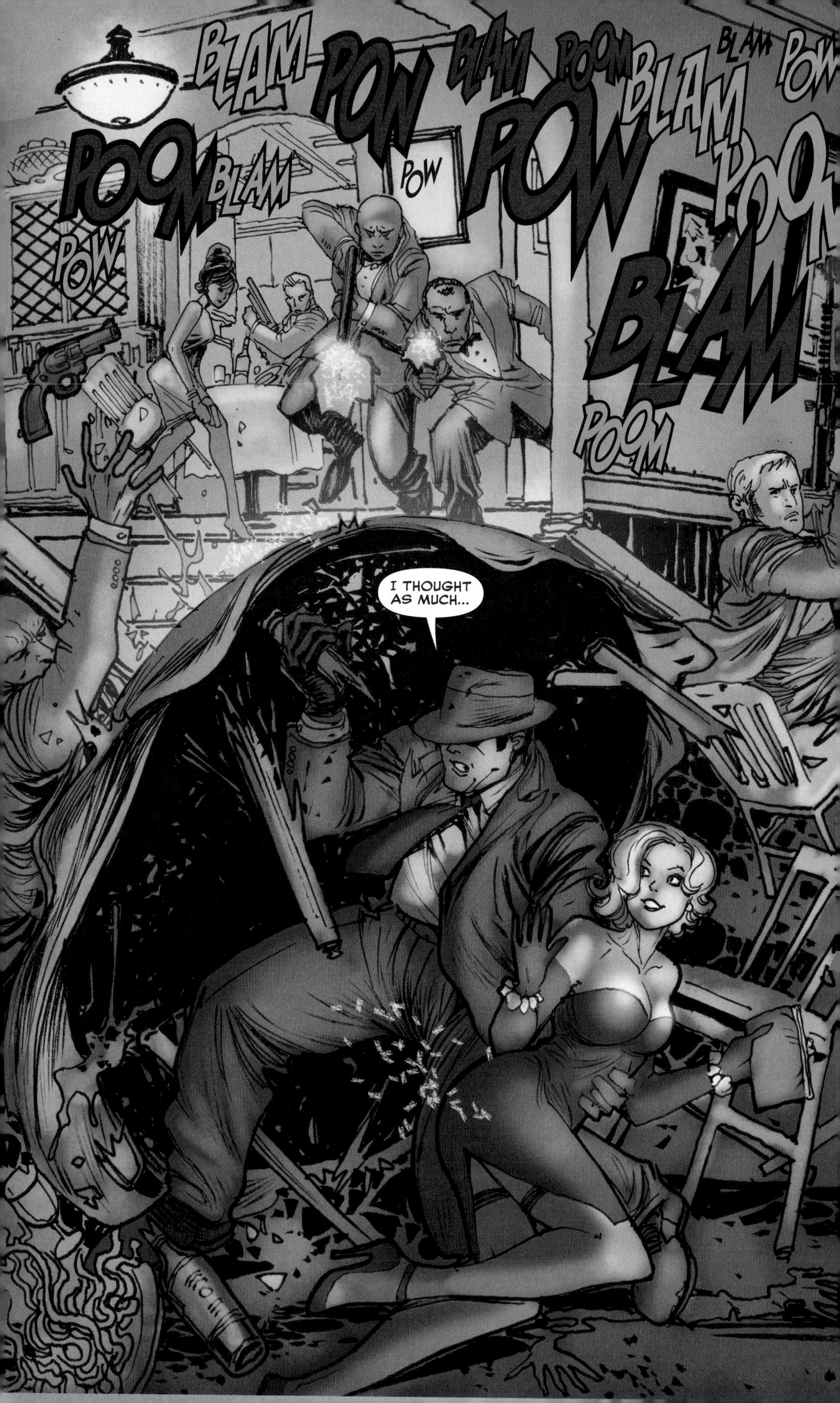
BLAM
POW
BLAM
POOM
BLAM
BLAM
POW
POOM
BLAM
POW
POW
POW
POOM
BLAM
POOM
I THOUGHT AS MUCH...

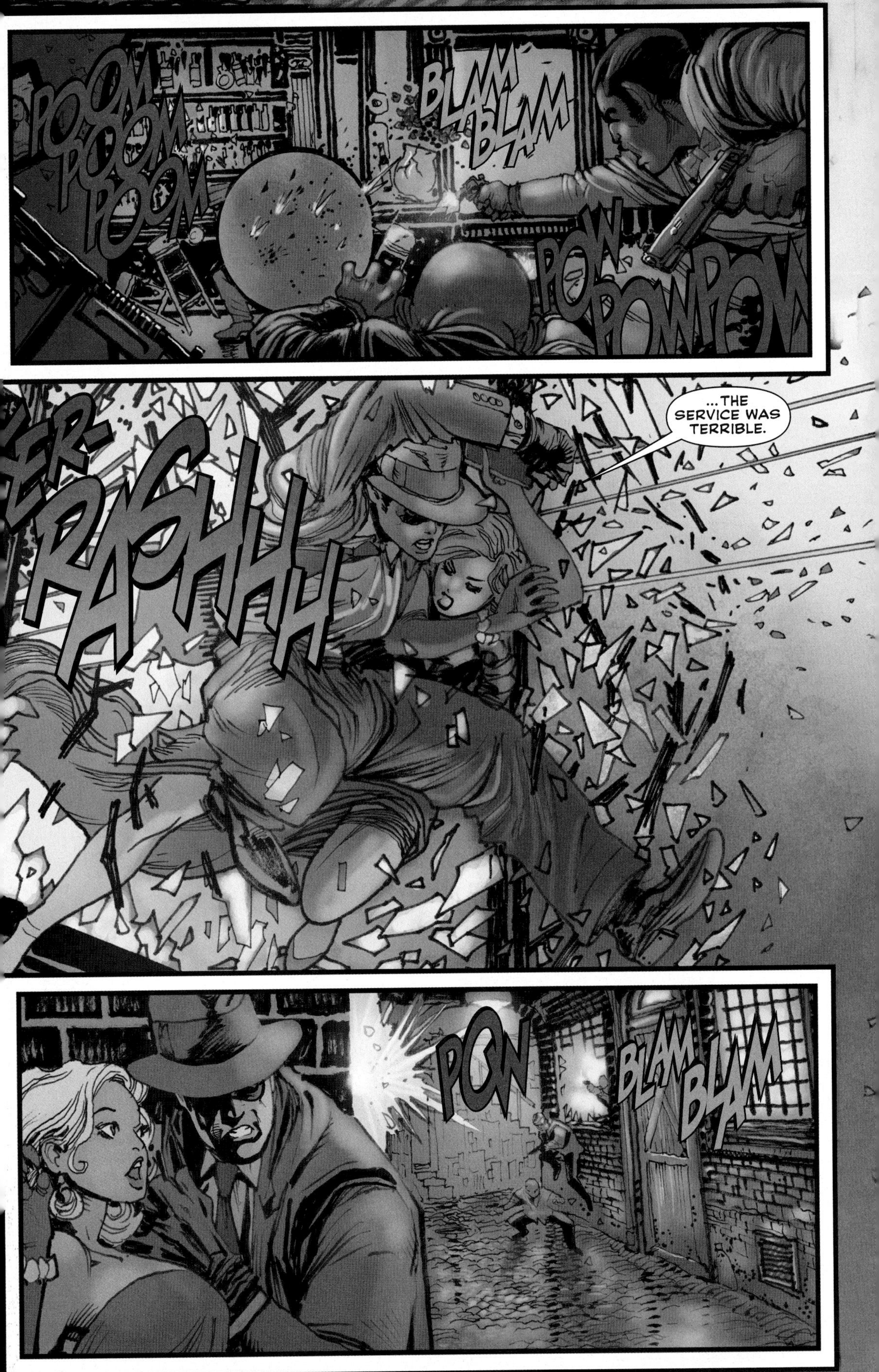
POOM POOM POOM
BLAM BLAM
POW POW POW
ER-RASHHH
...THE SERVICE WAS TERRIBLE.
POW
BLAM BLAM

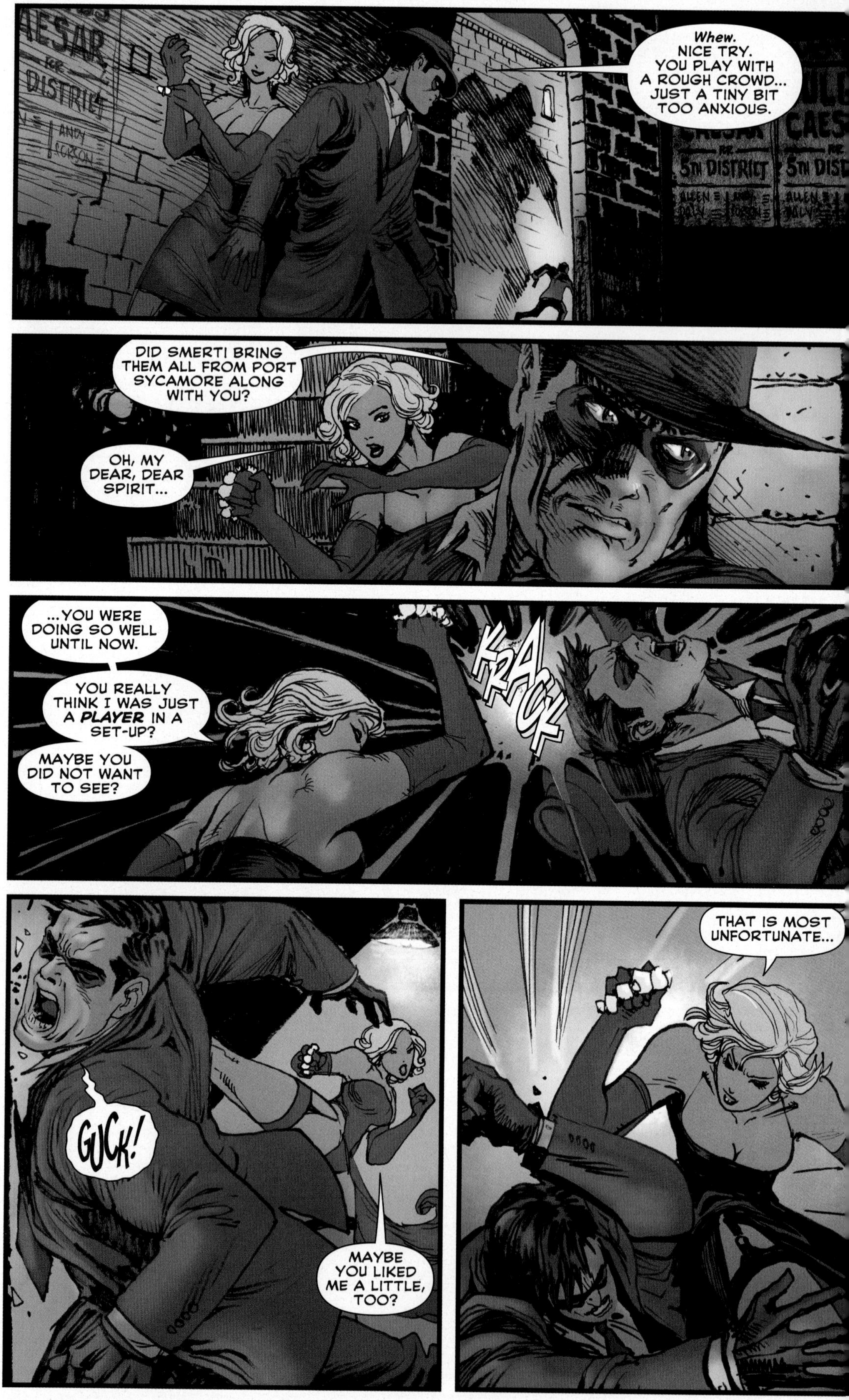
Whew. NICE TRY. YOU PLAY WITH A ROUGH CROWD... JUST A TINY BIT TOO ANXIOUS.
DID SMERTI BRING THEM ALL FROM PORT SYCAMORE ALONG WITH YOU?
OH, MY DEAR, DEAR SPIRIT...
...YOU WERE DOING SO WELL UNTIL NOW.
YOU REALLY THINK I WAS JUST A PLAYER IN A SET-UP?
MAYBE YOU DID NOT WANT TO SEE?
KRACK
GUCK!
MAYBE YOU LIKED ME A LITTLE, TOO?
THAT IS MOST UNFORTUNATE...

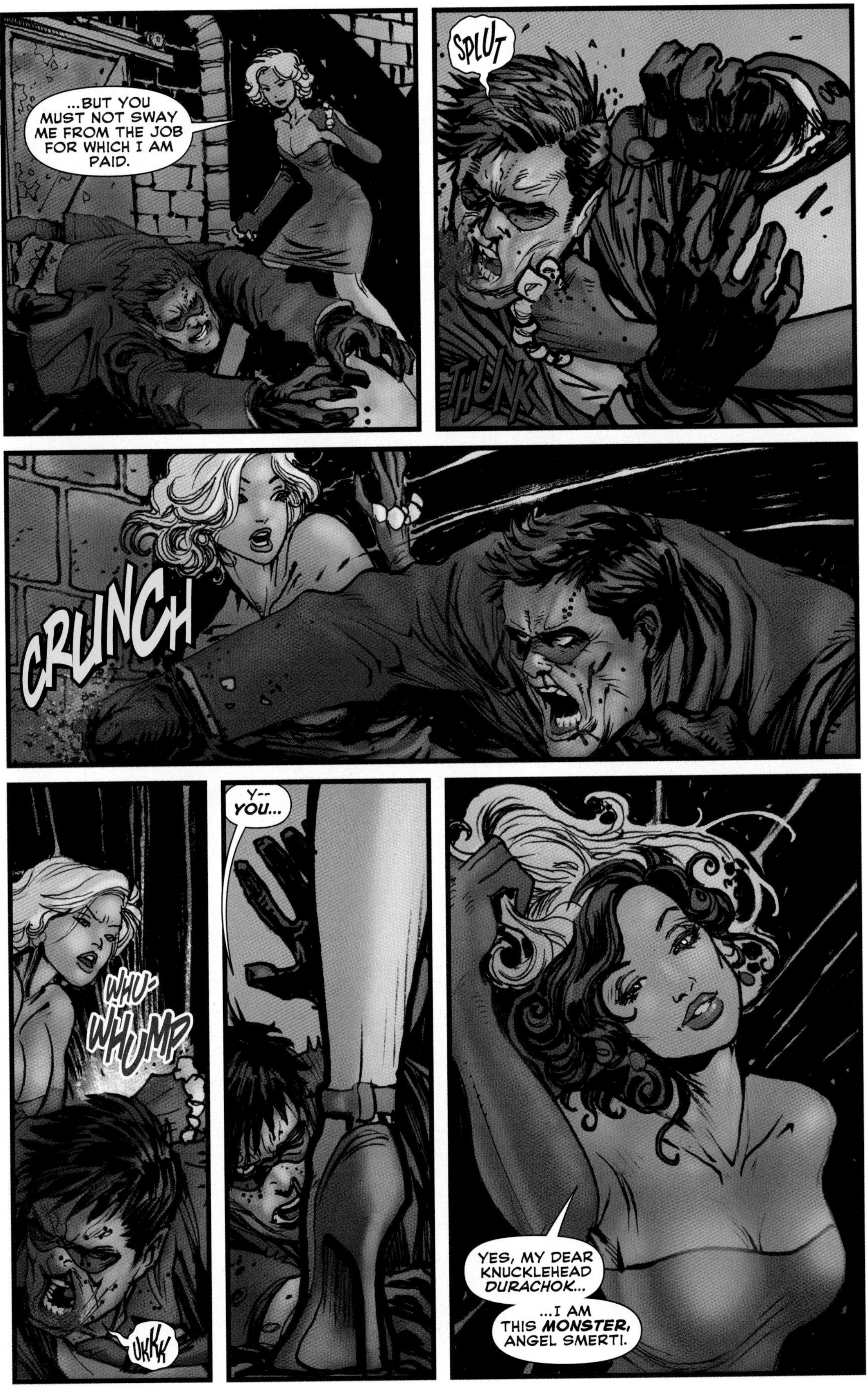
...BUT YOU MUST NOT SWAY ME FROM THE JOB FOR WHICH I AM PAID.
SPLUT
THUNK
CRUNCH
WHU-WHUMP
UKKK
Y-- *YOU...*
YES, MY DEAR KNUCKLEHEAD *DURACHOK...*
...I AM THIS *MONSTER,* ANGEL SMERTI.

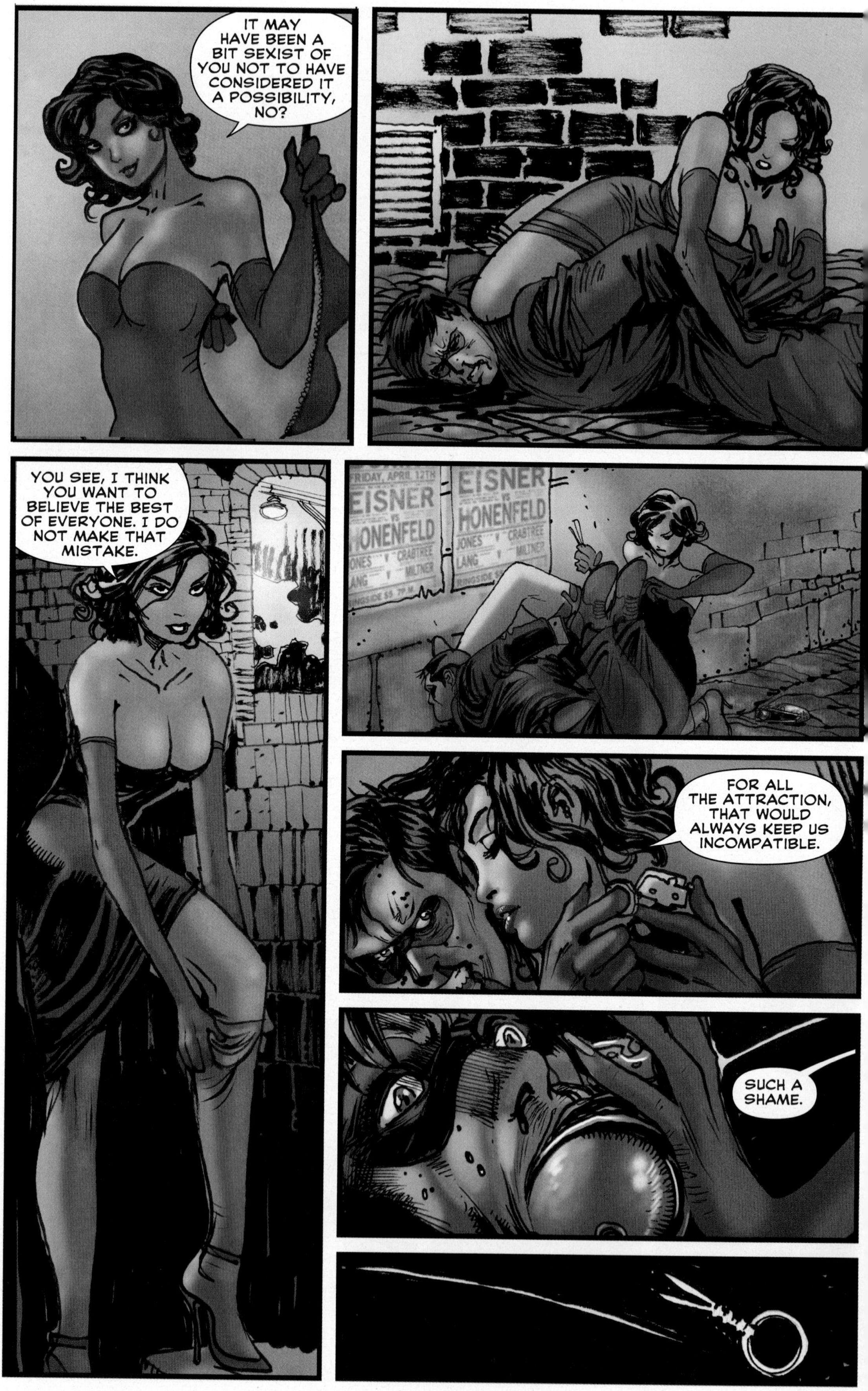
IT MAY HAVE BEEN A BIT SEXIST OF YOU NOT TO HAVE CONSIDERED IT A POSSIBILITY, NO?
YOU SEE, I THINK YOU WANT TO BELIEVE THE BEST OF EVERYONE. I DO NOT MAKE THAT MISTAKE.
FRIDAY, APRIL 12TH
EISNER
HONENFELD
JONES
CRABTREE
LANG
MILTNER
FOR ALL THE ATTRACTION, THAT WOULD ALWAYS KEEP US INCOMPATIBLE.
SUCH A SHAME.

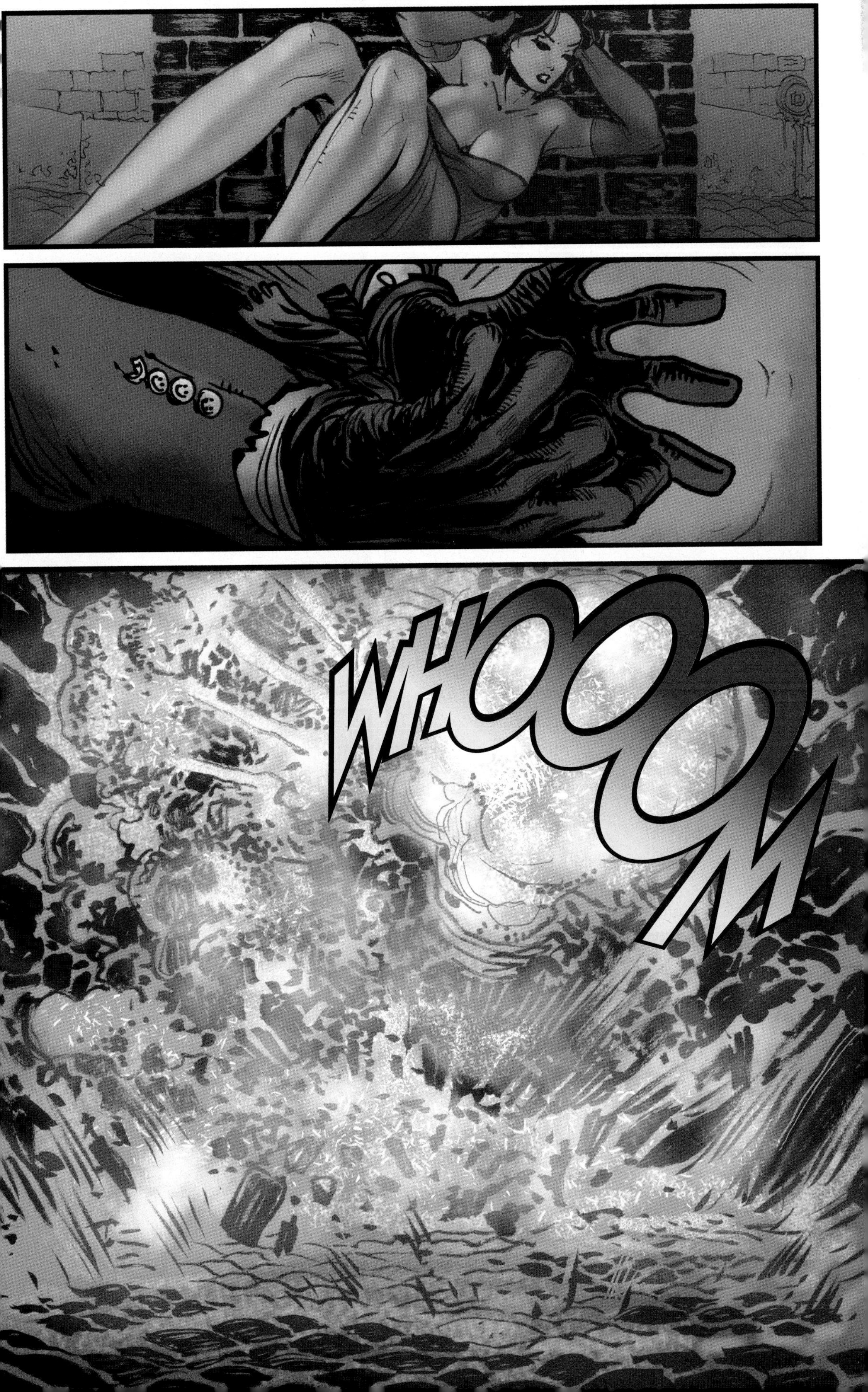
WHOOOOM

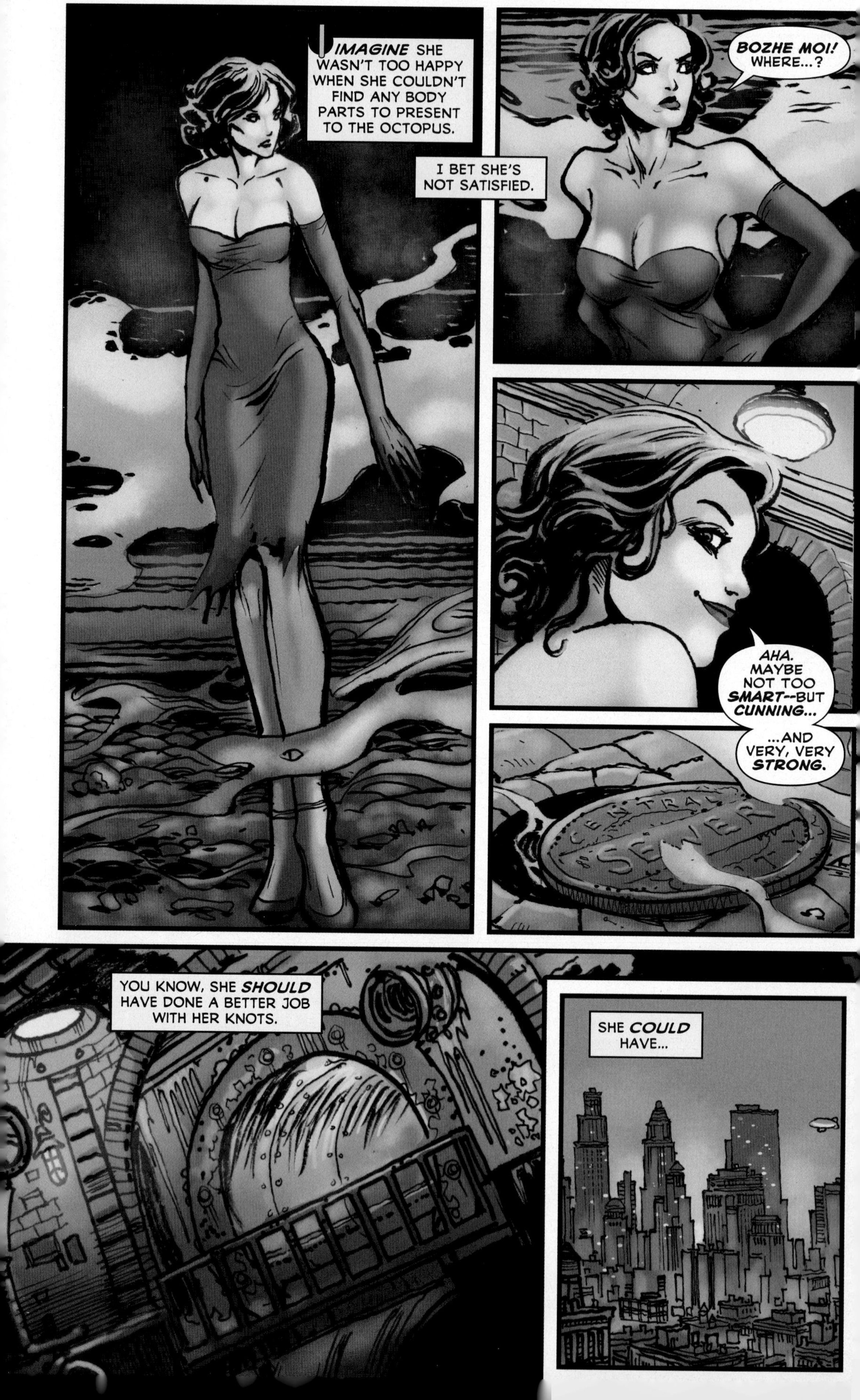
I IMAGINE SHE WASN'T TOO HAPPY WHEN SHE COULDN'T FIND ANY BODY PARTS TO PRESENT TO THE OCTOPUS.
I BET SHE'S NOT SATISFIED.
BOZHE MOI! WHERE...?
AHA. MAYBE NOT TOO SMART--BUT CUNNING...
...AND VERY, VERY STRONG.
CENTRAL SEWER
YOU KNOW, SHE SHOULD HAVE DONE A BETTER JOB WITH HER KNOTS.
SHE COULD HAVE...

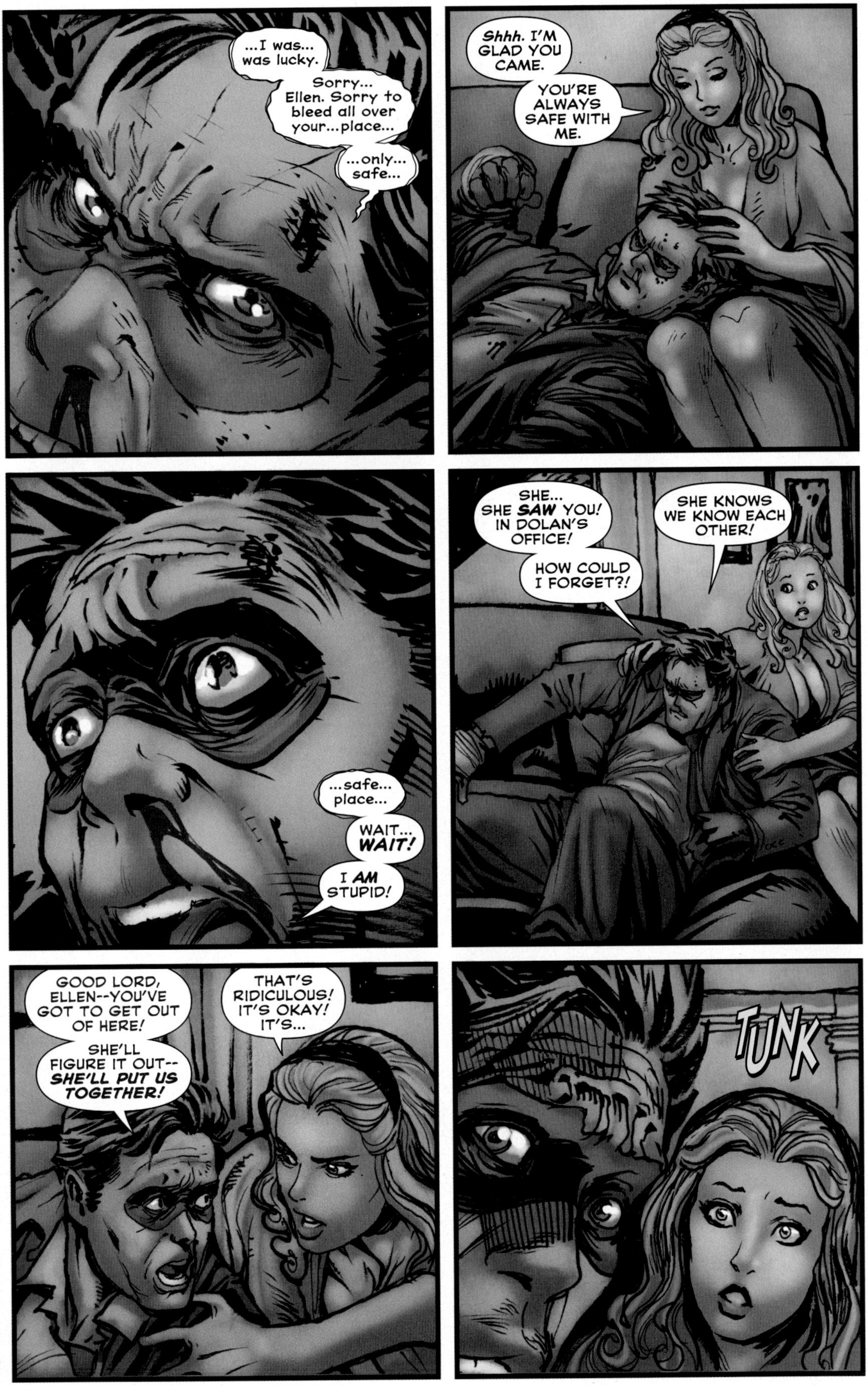
...I was...
was lucky.
Sorry...
Ellen. Sorry to
bleed all over
your...place...
...only...
safe...
Shhh. I'M
GLAD YOU
CAME.
YOU'RE
ALWAYS
SAFE WITH
ME.
...safe...
place...
WAIT...
WAIT!
I ***AM***
STUPID!
SHE...
SHE ***SAW*** YOU!
IN DOLAN'S
OFFICE!
HOW COULD
I FORGET?!
SHE KNOWS
WE KNOW EACH
OTHER!
GOOD LORD,
ELLEN--YOU'VE
GOT TO GET OUT
OF HERE!
SHE'LL
FIGURE IT OUT--
SHE'LL PUT US
TOGETHER!
THAT'S
RIDICULOUS!
IT'S OKAY!
IT'S...
TUNK

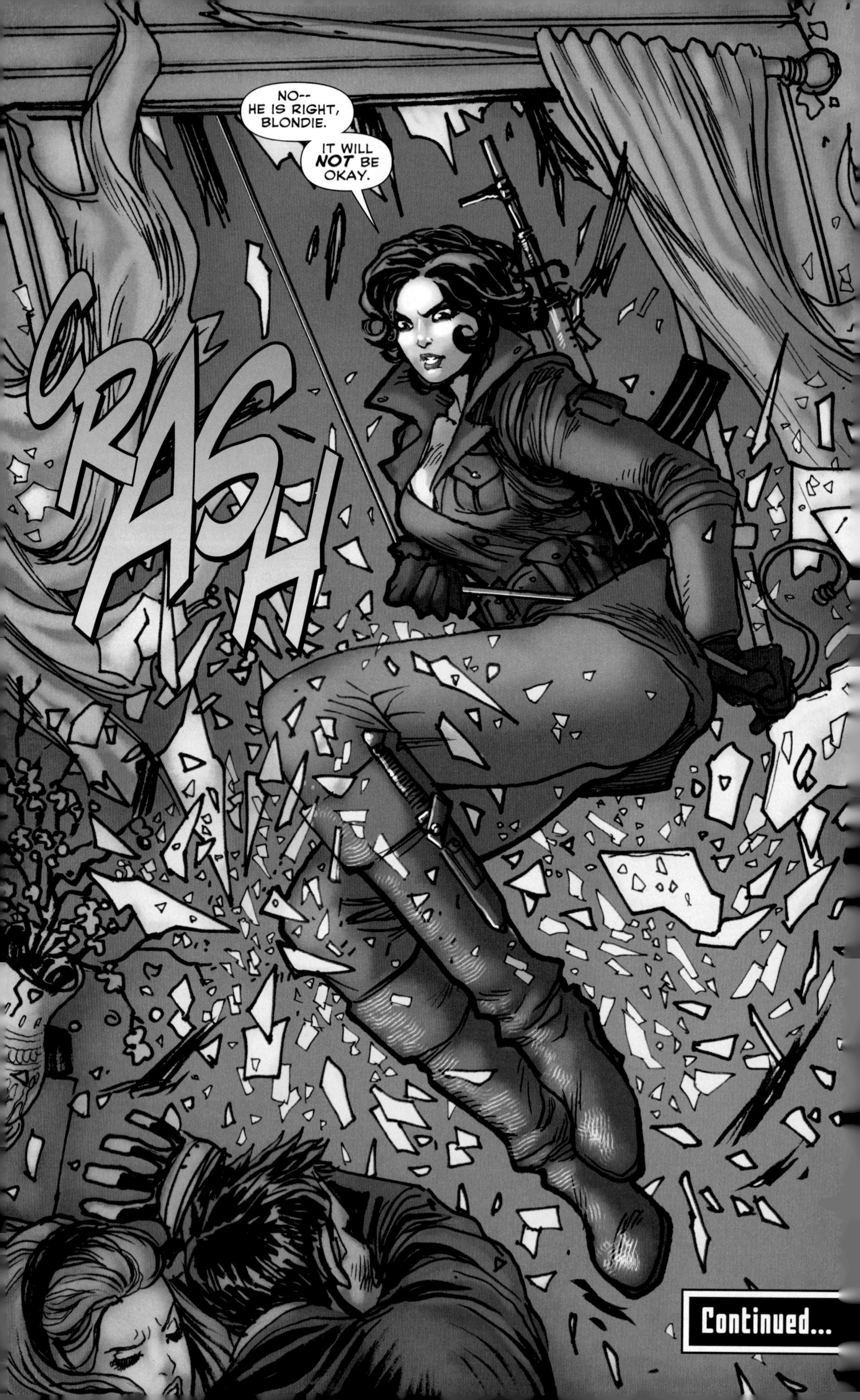
NO-- HE IS RIGHT, BLONDIE.
IT WILL *NOT* BE OKAY.
CRASH
Continued...

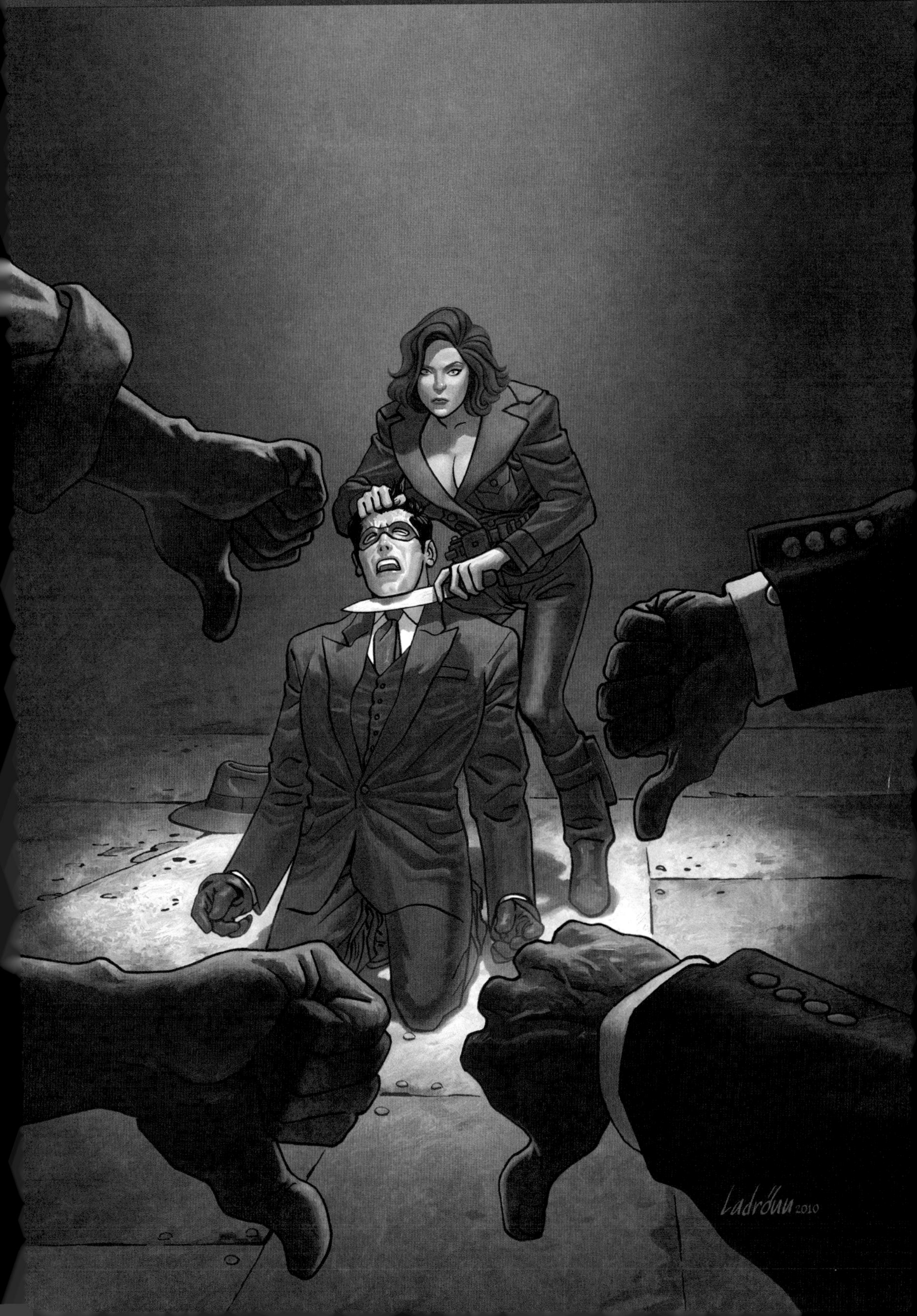
Ladrönn 2010

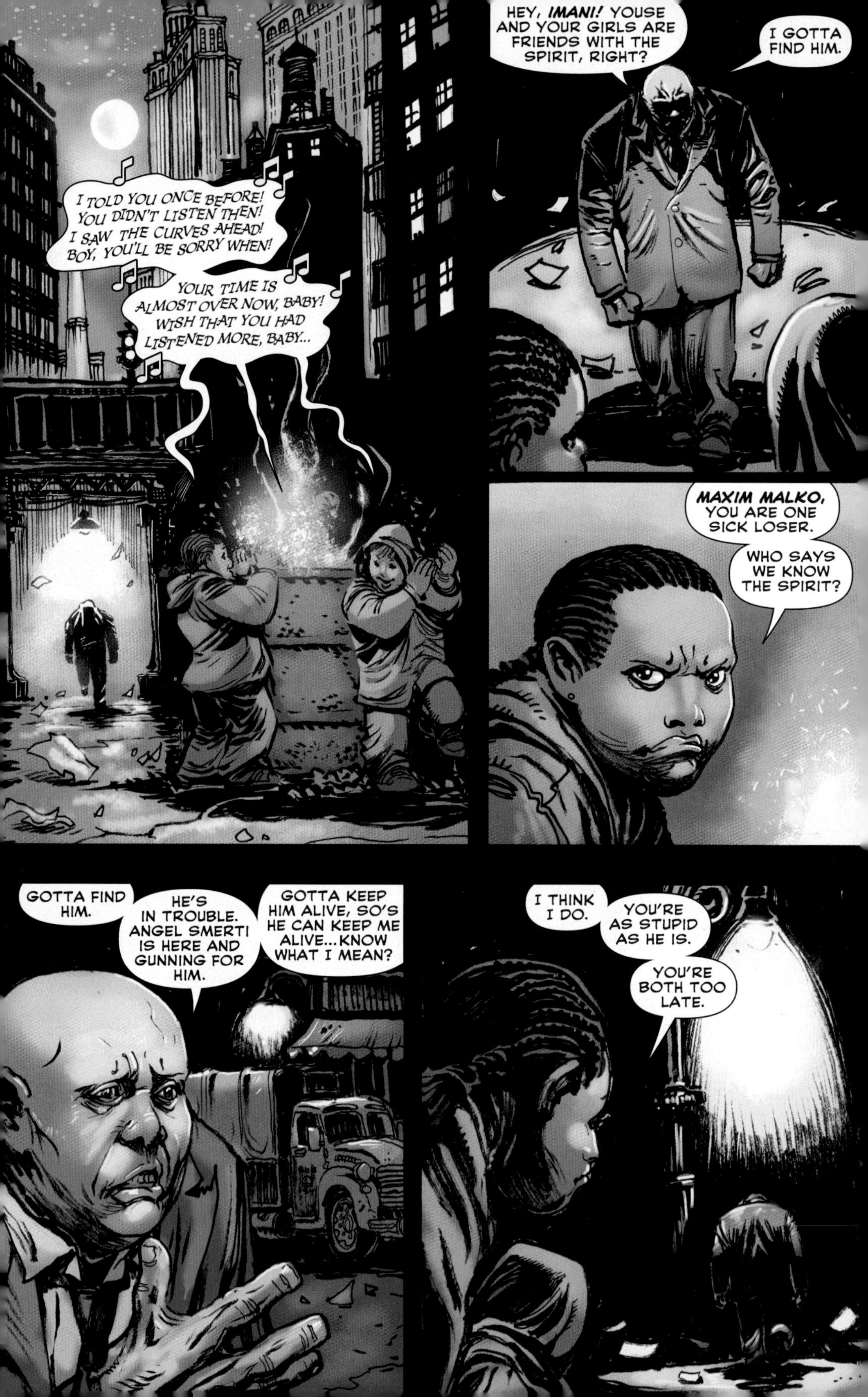
I TOLD YOU ONCE BEFORE! YOU DIDN'T LISTEN THEN! I SAW THE CURVES AHEAD! BOY, YOU'LL BE SORRY WHEN!
YOUR TIME IS ALMOST OVER NOW, BABY! WISH THAT YOU HAD LISTENED MORE, BABY...
HEY, IMANI! YOUSE AND YOUR GIRLS ARE FRIENDS WITH THE SPIRIT, RIGHT?
I GOTTA FIND HIM.
MAXIM MALKO, YOU ARE ONE SICK LOSER.
WHO SAYS WE KNOW THE SPIRIT?
GOTTA FIND HIM.
HE'S IN TROUBLE. ANGEL SMERTI IS HERE AND GUNNING FOR HIM.
GOTTA KEEP HIM ALIVE, SO'S HE CAN KEEP ME ALIVE...KNOW WHAT I MEAN?
I THINK I DO.
YOU'RE AS STUPID AS HE IS.
YOU'RE BOTH TOO LATE.

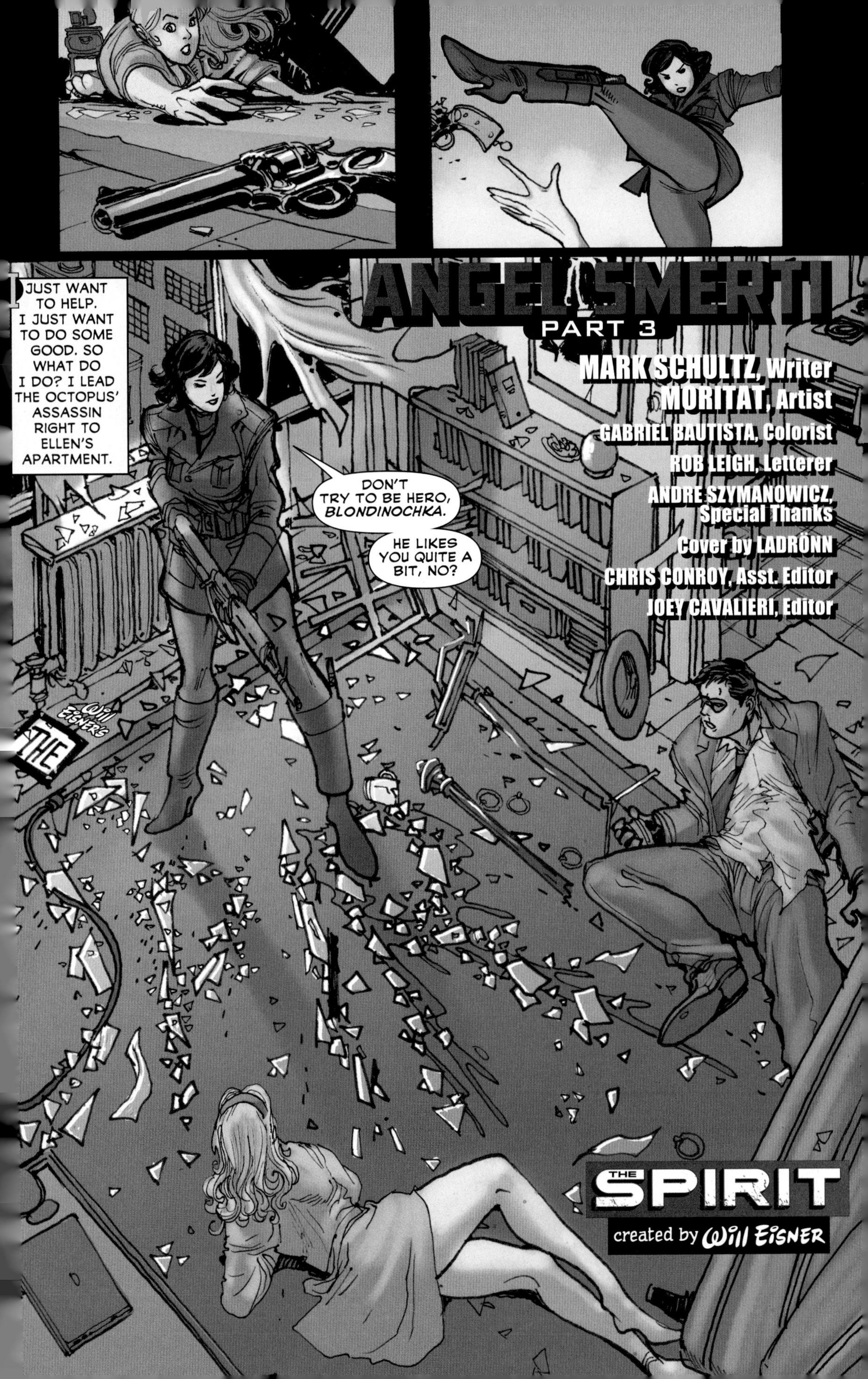

I JUST WANT TO HELP. I JUST WANT TO DO SOME GOOD. SO WHAT DO I DO? I LEAD THE OCTOPUS' ASSASSIN RIGHT TO ELLEN'S APARTMENT.
ANGEL SMERTI
PART 3
MARK SCHULTZ, Writer
MORITAT, Artist
GABRIEL BAUTISTA, Colorist
ROB LEIGH, Letterer
ANDRE SZYMANOWICZ, Special Thanks
Cover by LADRÖNN
CHRIS CONROY, Asst. Editor
JOEY CAVALIERI, Editor
DON'T TRY TO BE HERO, *BLONDINOCHKA.*
HE LIKES YOU QUITE A BIT, NO?
WILL EISNER'S THE
THE SPIRIT
created by WILL EISNER

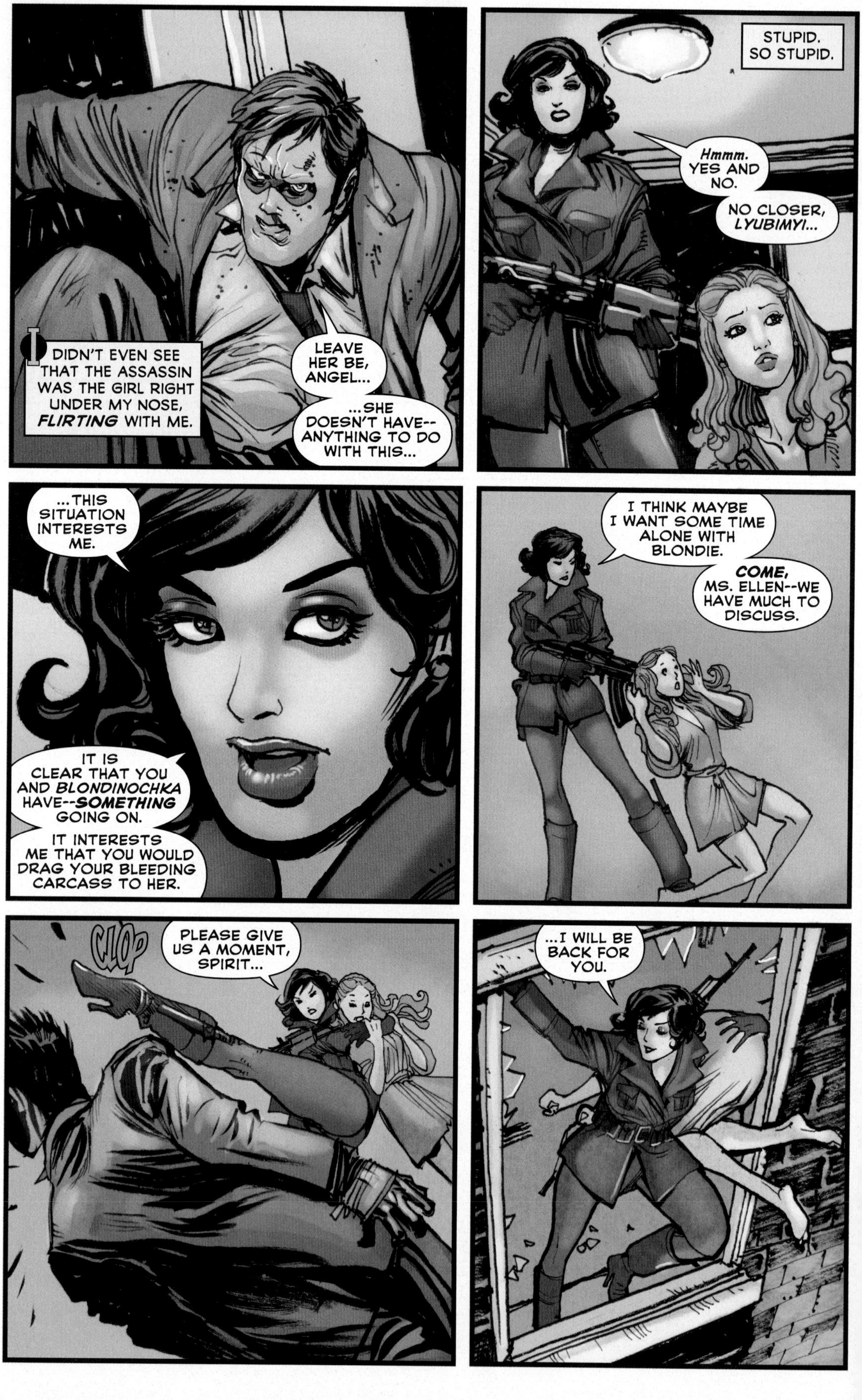
I DIDN'T EVEN SEE THAT THE ASSASSIN WAS THE GIRL RIGHT UNDER MY NOSE, *FLIRTING* WITH ME.
LEAVE HER BE, ANGEL...
...SHE DOESN'T HAVE-- ANYTHING TO DO WITH THIS...
STUPID. SO STUPID.
Hmmm. YES AND NO.
NO CLOSER, *LYUBIMYI*...
...THIS SITUATION INTERESTS ME.
IT IS CLEAR THAT YOU AND *BLONDINOCHKA* HAVE--*SOMETHING* GOING ON.
IT INTERESTS ME THAT YOU WOULD DRAG YOUR BLEEDING CARCASS TO HER.
I THINK MAYBE I WANT SOME TIME ALONE WITH BLONDIE.
COME, MS. ELLEN--WE HAVE MUCH TO DISCUSS.
CLOP
PLEASE GIVE US A MOMENT, SPIRIT...
...I WILL BE BACK FOR YOU.

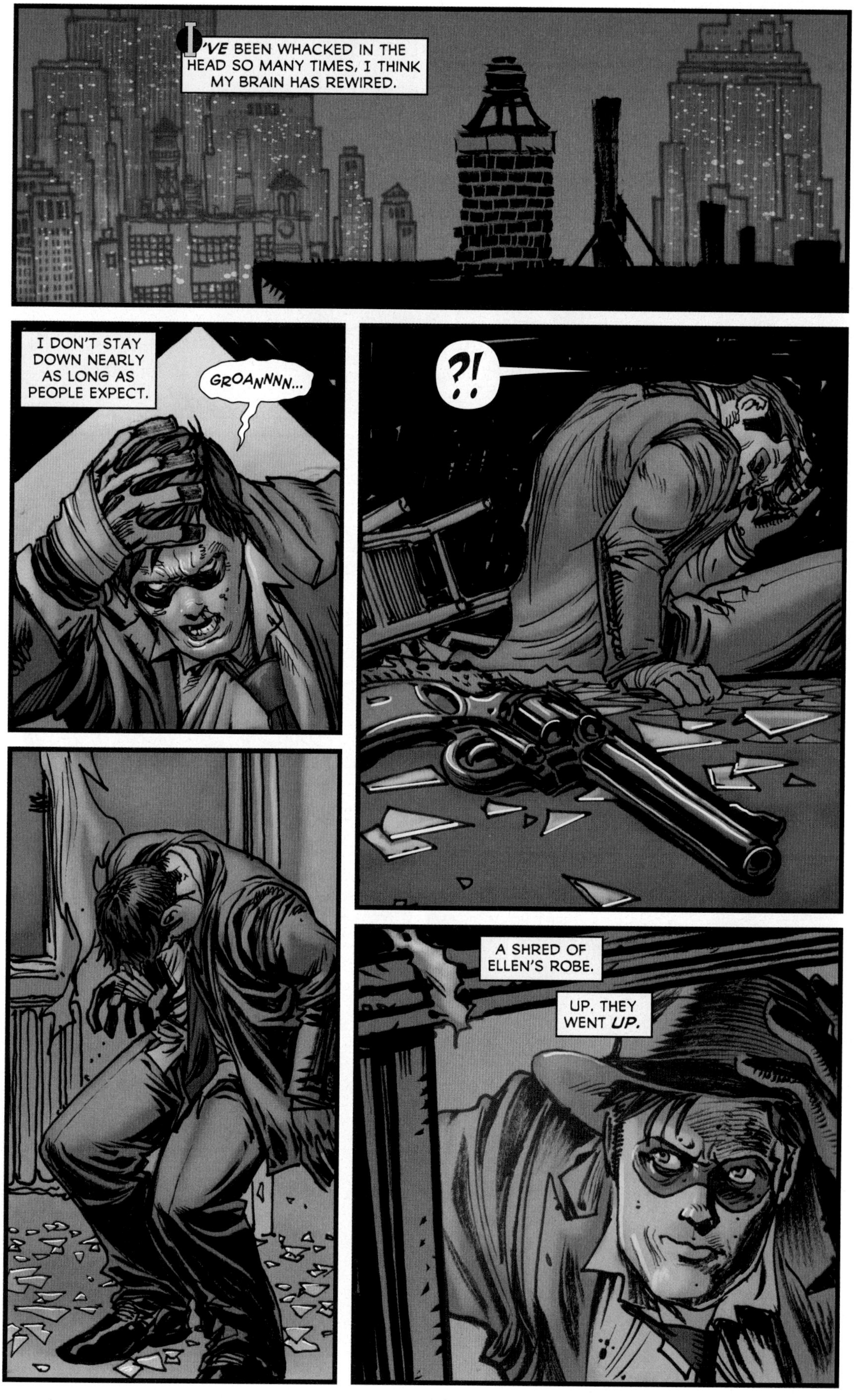
I'VE BEEN WHACKED IN THE HEAD SO MANY TIMES, I THINK MY BRAIN HAS REWIRED.
I DON'T STAY DOWN NEARLY AS LONG AS PEOPLE EXPECT.
GROANNNN...
?!
A SHRED OF ELLEN'S ROBE.
UP. THEY WENT *UP.*

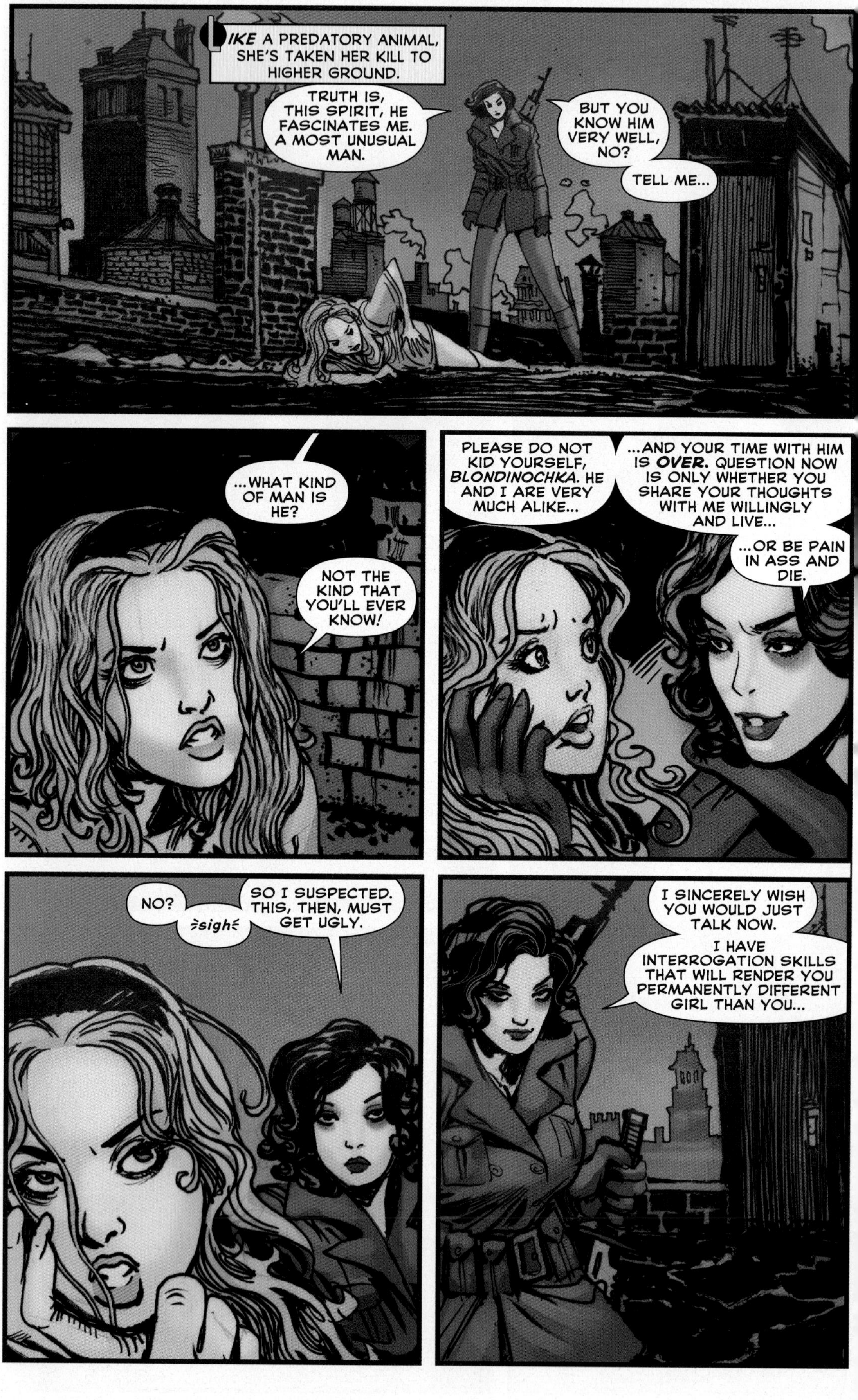
LIKE A PREDATORY ANIMAL, SHE'S TAKEN HER KILL TO HIGHER GROUND.
TRUTH IS, THIS SPIRIT, HE FASCINATES ME. A MOST UNUSUAL MAN.
BUT YOU KNOW HIM VERY WELL, NO?
TELL ME...
...WHAT KIND OF MAN IS HE?
NOT THE KIND THAT YOU'LL EVER KNOW!
PLEASE DO NOT KID YOURSELF, BLONDINOCHKA. HE AND I ARE VERY MUCH ALIKE...
...AND YOUR TIME WITH HIM IS OVER. QUESTION NOW IS ONLY WHETHER YOU SHARE YOUR THOUGHTS WITH ME WILLINGLY AND LIVE...
...OR BE PAIN IN ASS AND DIE.
NO?
sigh
SO I SUSPECTED. THIS, THEN, MUST GET UGLY.
I SINCERELY WISH YOU WOULD JUST TALK NOW.
I HAVE INTERROGATION SKILLS THAT WILL RENDER YOU PERMANENTLY DIFFERENT GIRL THAN YOU...

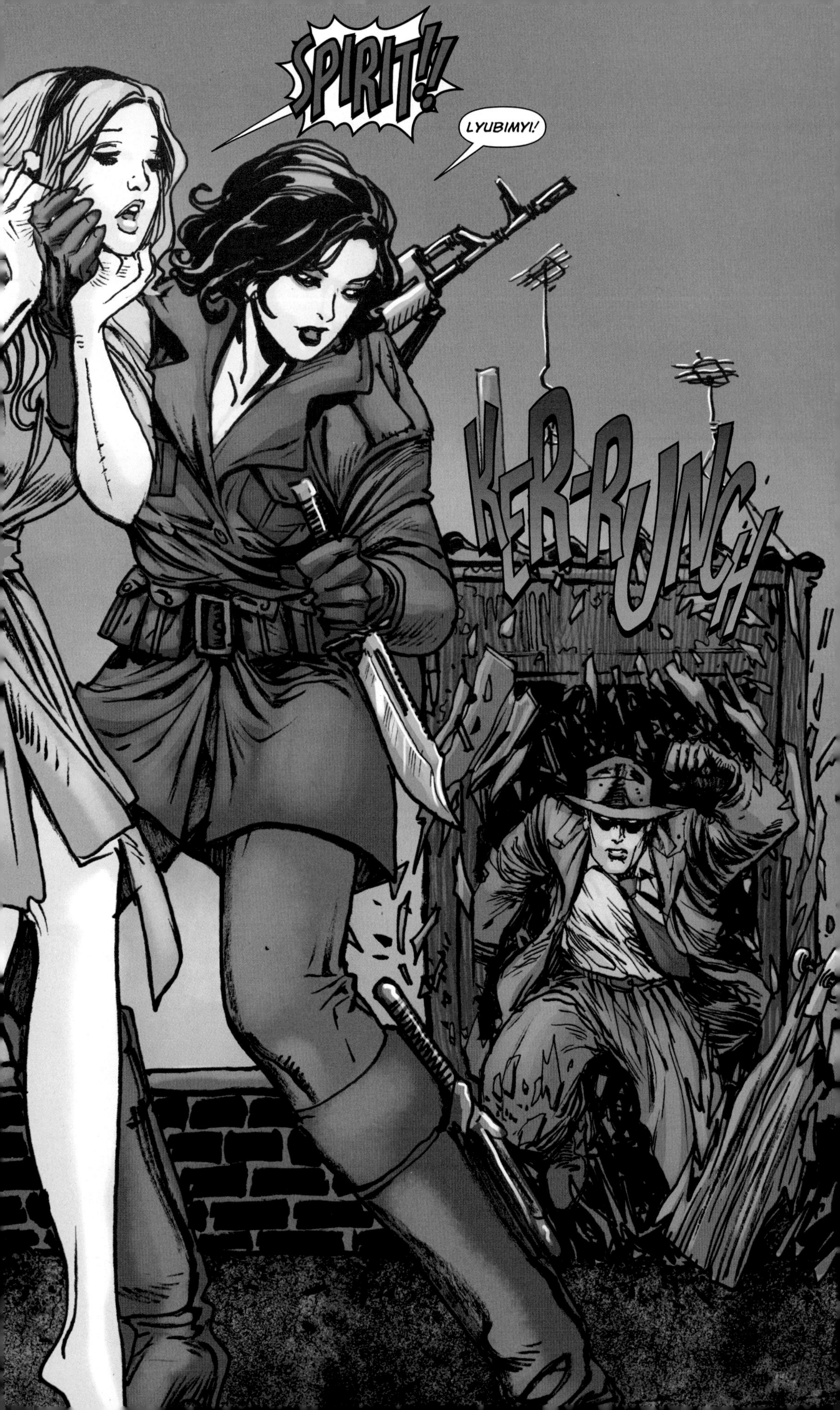
SPIRIT!!
LYUBIMYI!
KER-RUNCH

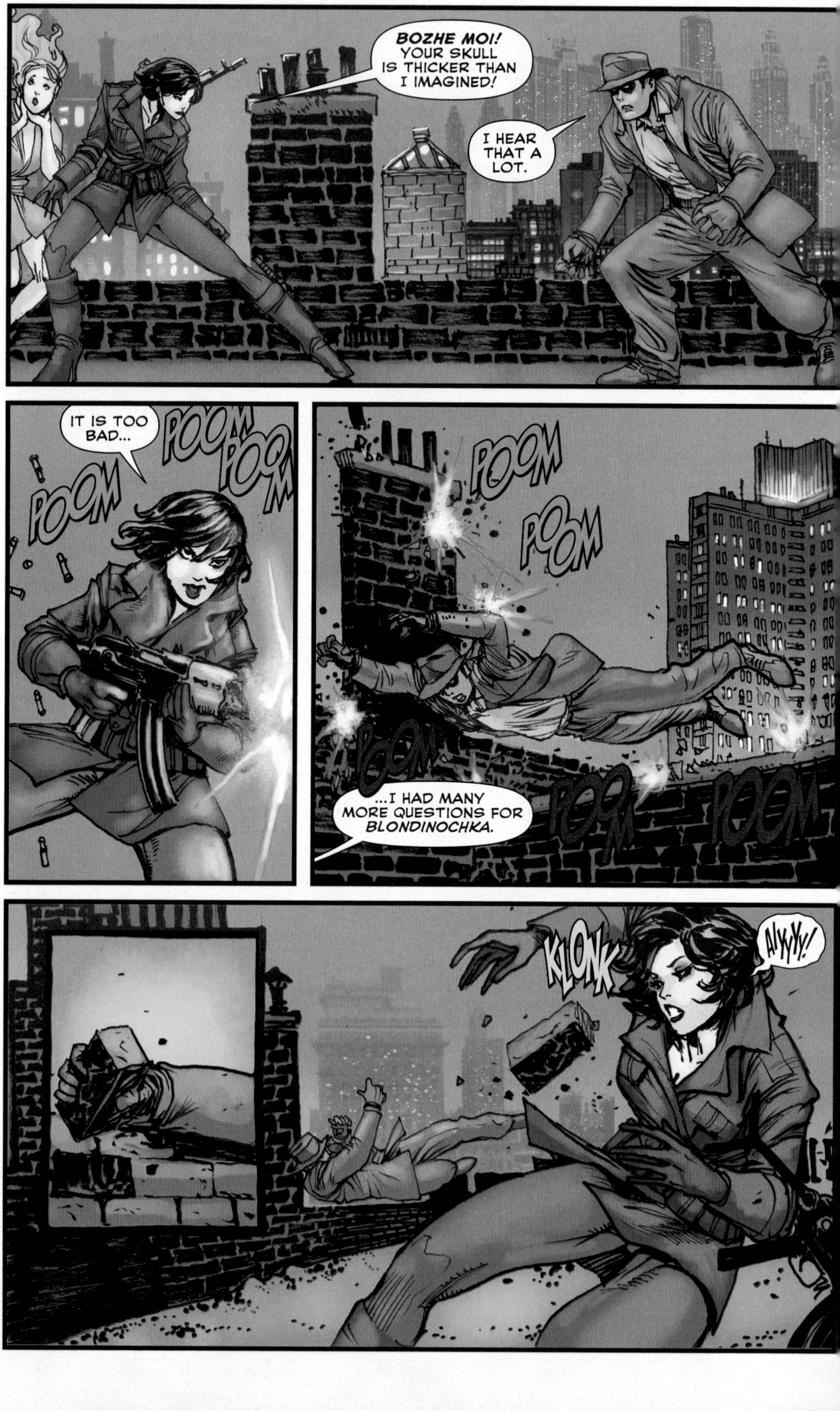
BOZHE MOI! YOUR SKULL IS THICKER THAN I IMAGINED!
I HEAR THAT A LOT.
IT IS TOO BAD...
POOM
POOM POOM
POOM
POOM
POOM
...I HAD MANY MORE QUESTIONS FOR BLONDINOCHKA.
POOM
POOM
KLONK
AIYYYY!

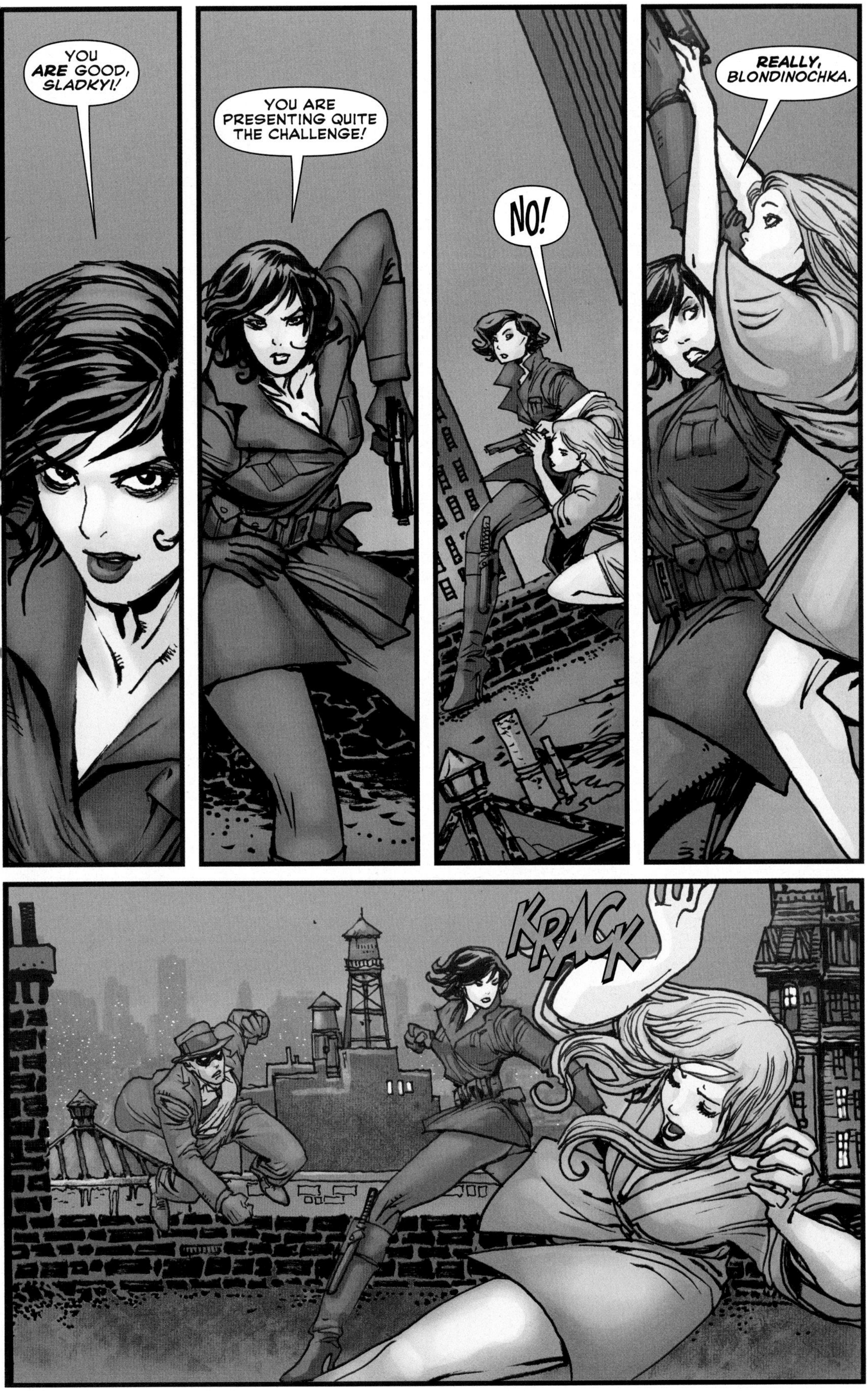
YOU ARE GOOD, SLADKY!!
YOU ARE PRESENTING QUITE THE CHALLENGE!
NO!
REALLY, BLONDINOCHKA.
KRACK

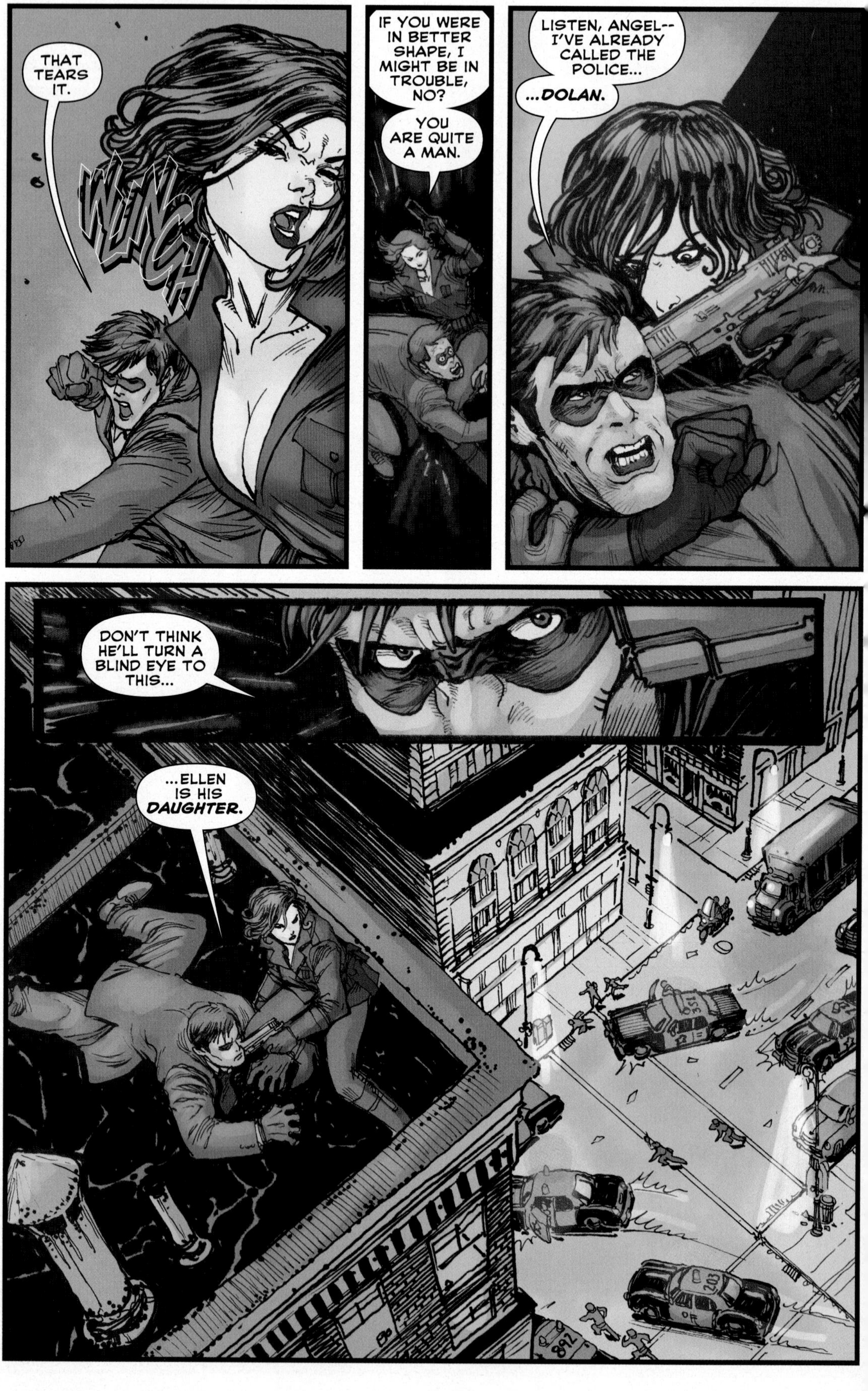

THAT TEARS IT.
WUNCH
IF YOU WERE IN BETTER SHAPE, I MIGHT BE IN TROUBLE, NO?
YOU ARE QUITE A MAN.
LISTEN, ANGEL-- I'VE ALREADY CALLED THE POLICE...
...DOLAN.
DON'T THINK HE'LL TURN A BLIND EYE TO THIS...
...ELLEN IS HIS DAUGHTER.

YOU ARE RIGHT. THIS MUST END SOONER THAN I WISHED.
FIRST-- *BLONDINOCHKA.* MAYBE YOU ARE TOO DANGEROUS TO LET LI--
OOF!

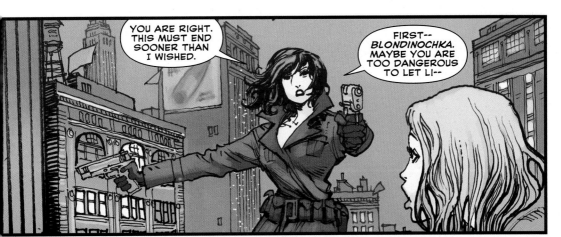

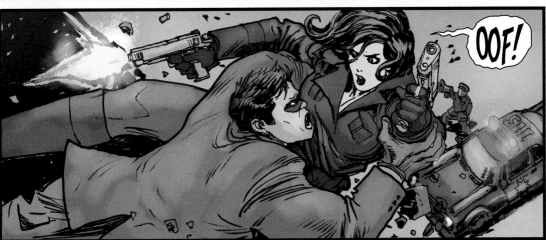

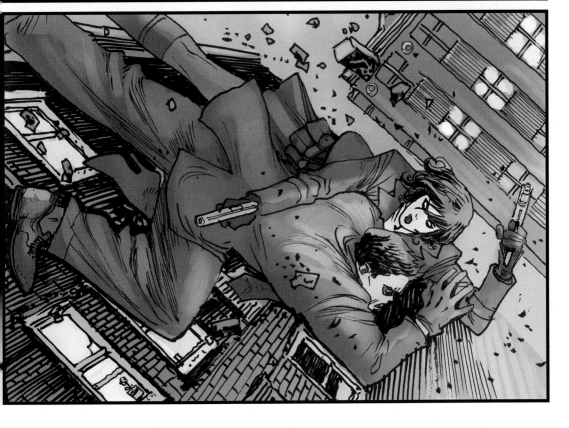

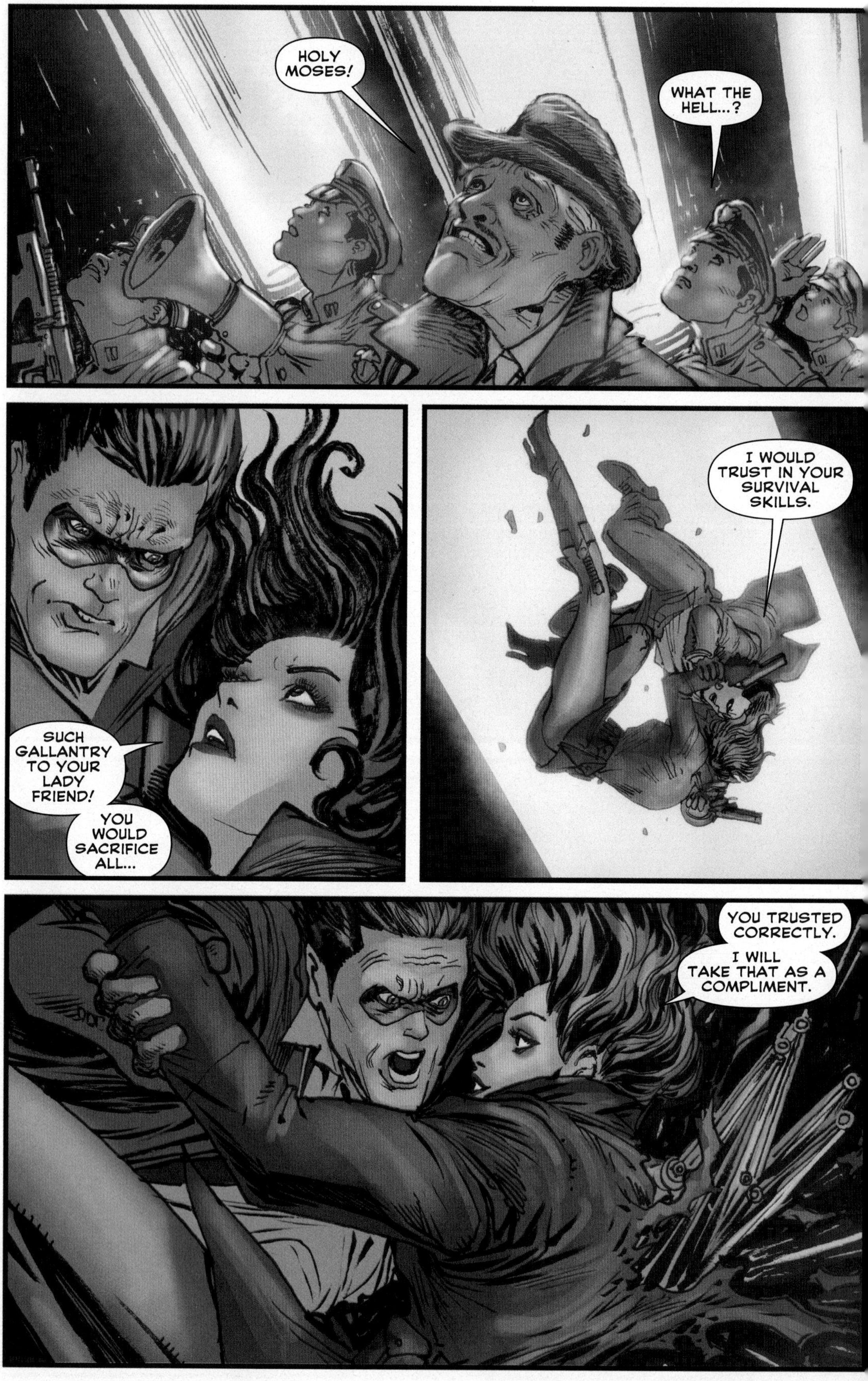
HOLY MOSES!
WHAT THE HELL...?
SUCH GALLANTRY TO YOUR LADY FRIEND!
YOU WOULD SACRIFICE ALL...
I WOULD TRUST IN YOUR SURVIVAL SKILLS.
YOU TRUSTED CORRECTLY.
I WILL TAKE THAT AS A COMPLIMENT.

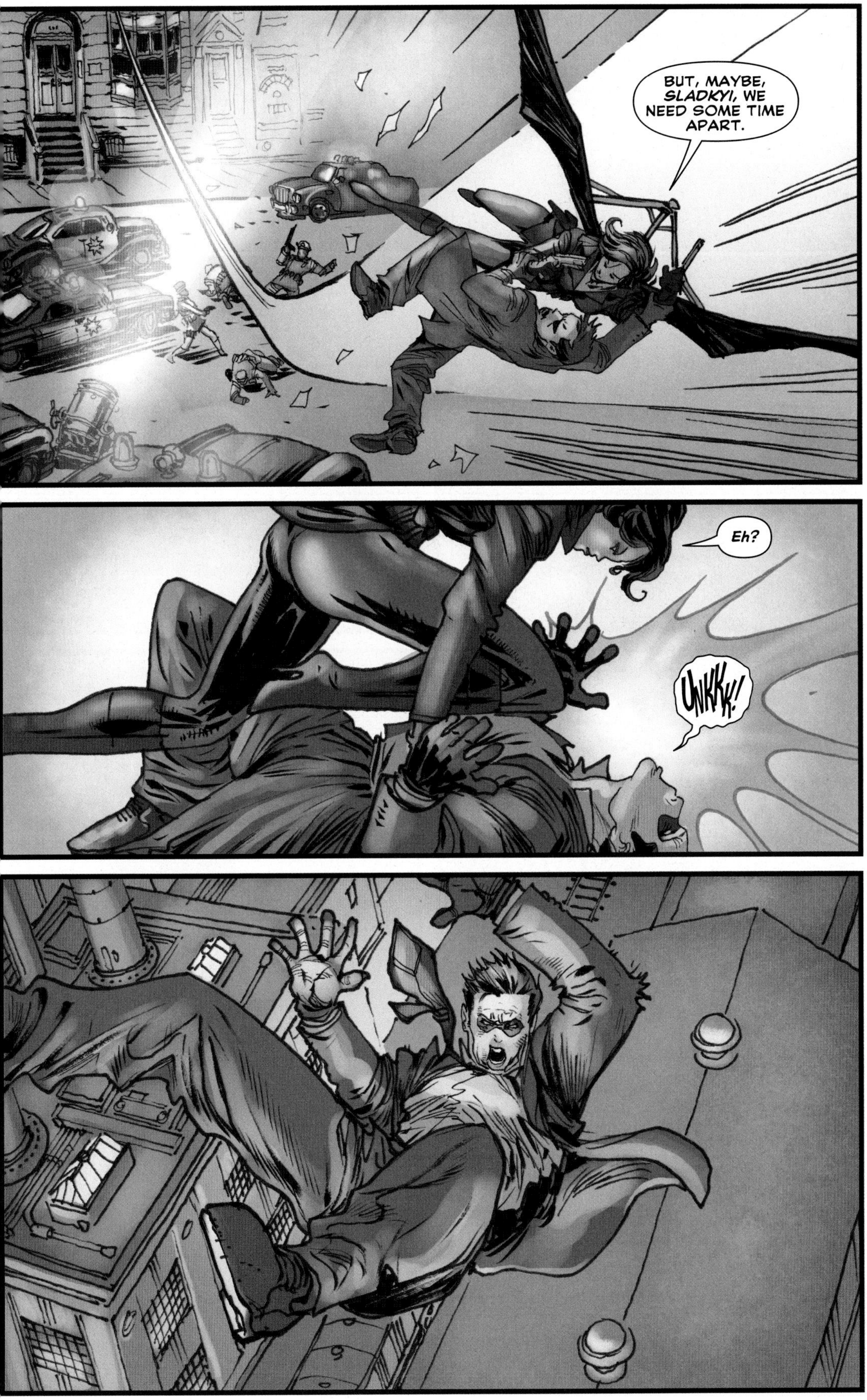
BUT, MAYBE, SLADKYI, WE NEED SOME TIME APART.
Eh?
UNKKK!

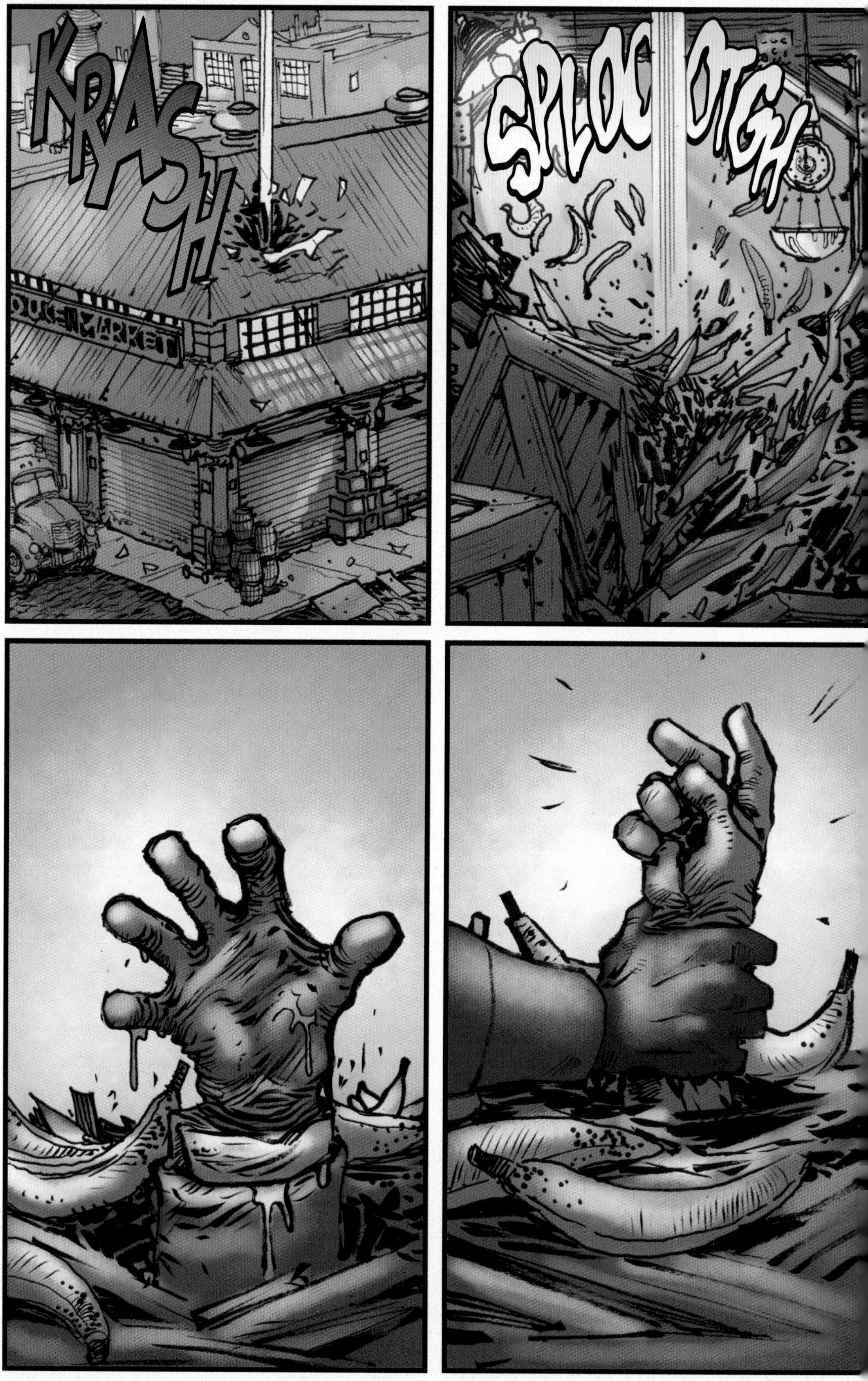
KRASH
SPLOOOTGH

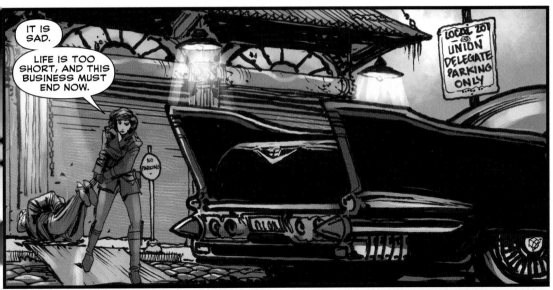

IT IS SAD.

LIFE IS TOO SHORT, AND THIS BUSINESS MUST END NOW.

LOCAL 267
UNION DELEGATE PARKING ONLY

NO PARKING

KRUNKLE

YOU CAUSED ME SOME EMBARRASSMENT WHEN YOU ESCAPED EARLIER.

I HAD TO CALL OCTOPUS AND RESCHEDULE MY *PRESENTATION.*

ZZZ

ZZT

VROOOOM

THIS TIME, I MAKE NO MISTAKE. I DELIVER YOU ALIVE.

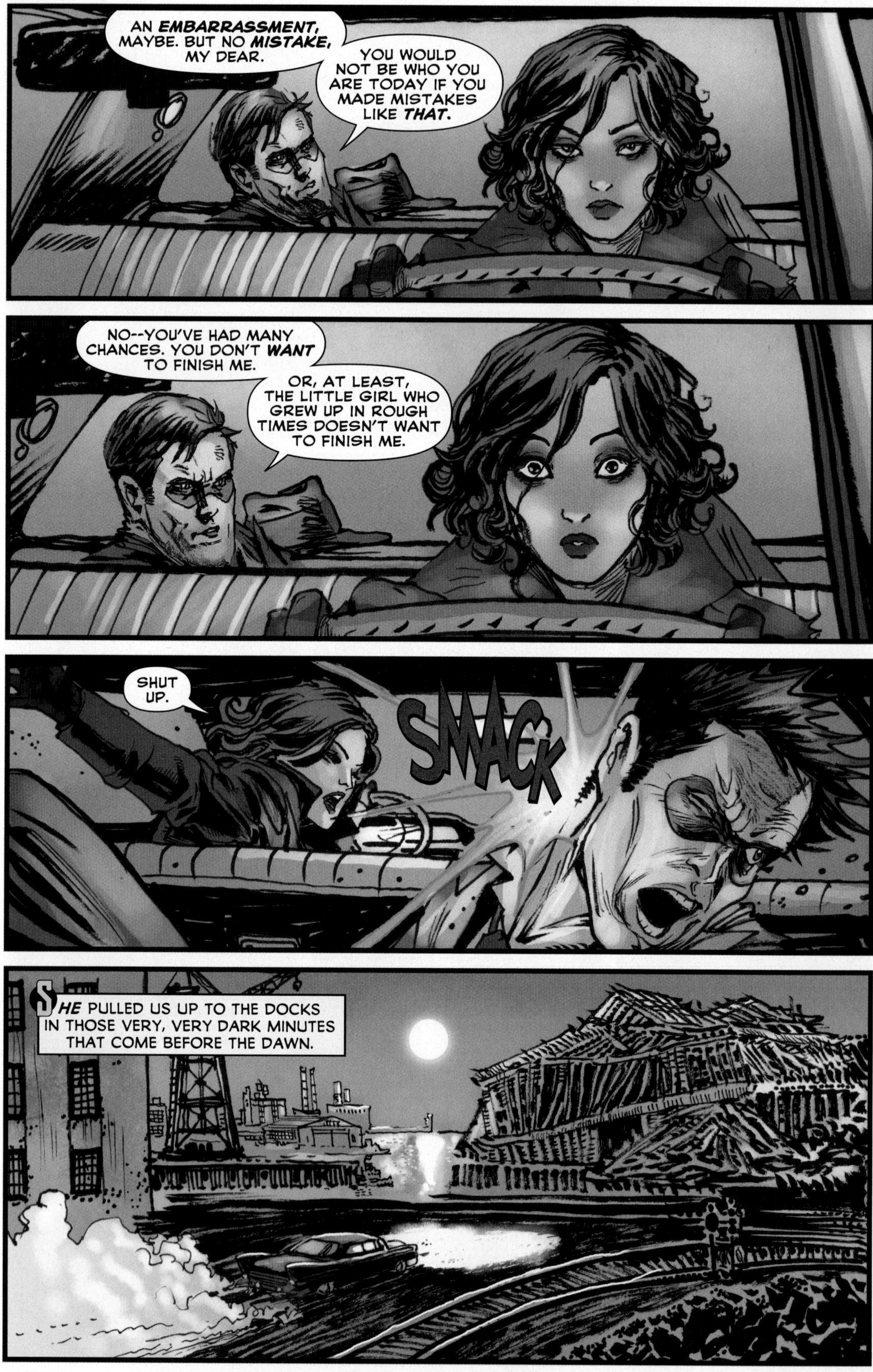

AN **EMBARRASSMENT,** MAYBE. BUT NO **MISTAKE,** MY DEAR.
YOU WOULD NOT BE WHO YOU ARE TODAY IF YOU MADE MISTAKES LIKE **THAT.**
NO--YOU'VE HAD MANY CHANCES. YOU DON'T **WANT** TO FINISH ME.
OR, AT LEAST, THE LITTLE GIRL WHO GREW UP IN ROUGH TIMES DOESN'T WANT TO FINISH ME.
SHUT UP.
SMACK
S**HE** PULLED US UP TO THE DOCKS IN THOSE VERY, VERY DARK MINUTES THAT COME BEFORE THE DAWN.

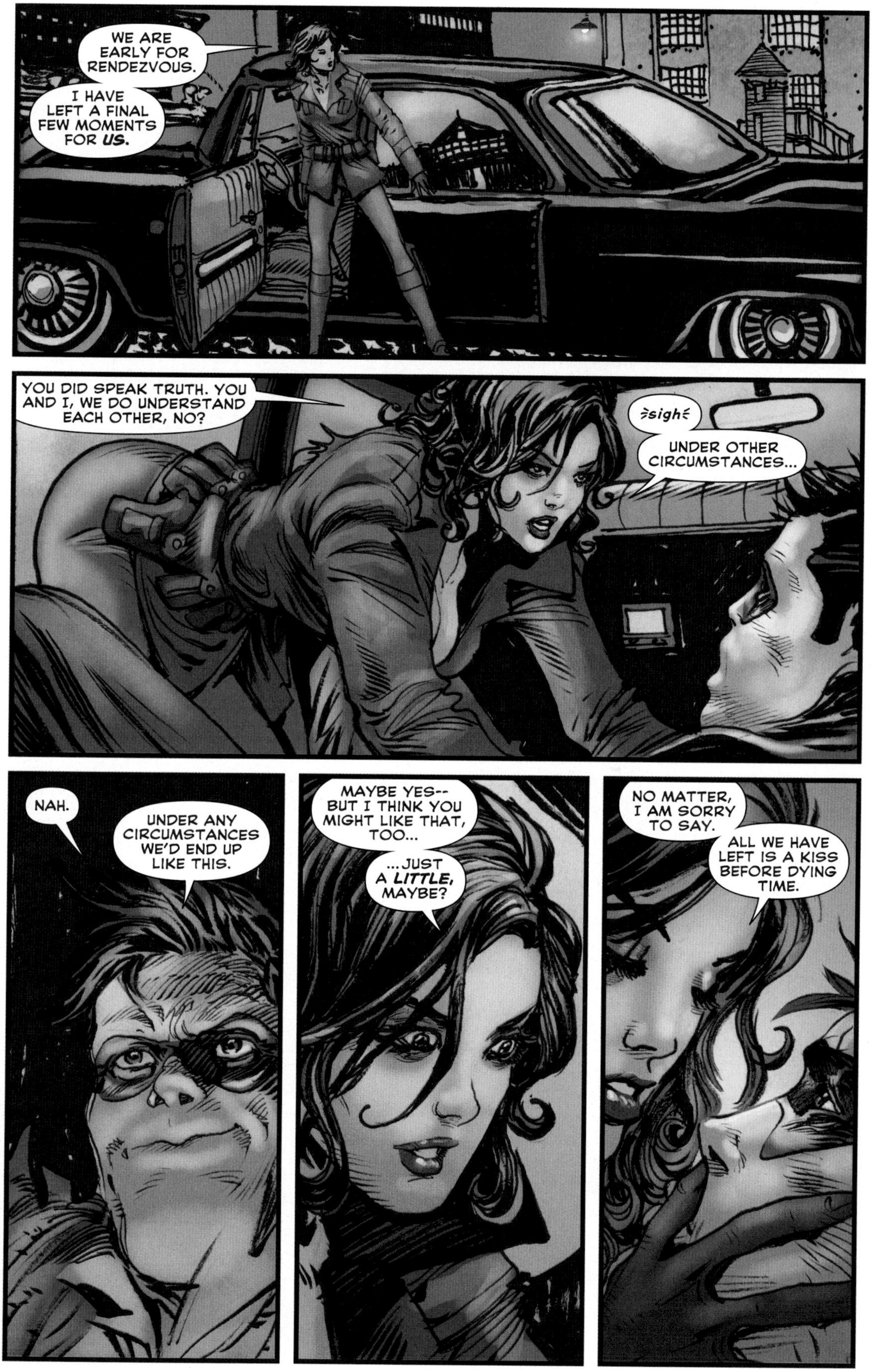
WE ARE EARLY FOR RENDEZVOUS.
I HAVE LEFT A FINAL FEW MOMENTS FOR *US.*
YOU DID SPEAK TRUTH. YOU AND I, WE DO UNDERSTAND EACH OTHER, NO?
sigh
UNDER OTHER CIRCUMSTANCES...
NAH.
UNDER ANY CIRCUMSTANCES WE'D END UP LIKE THIS.
MAYBE YES-- BUT I THINK YOU MIGHT LIKE THAT, TOO...
...JUST A *LITTLE,* MAYBE?
NO MATTER, I AM SORRY TO SAY.
ALL WE HAVE LEFT IS A KISS BEFORE DYING TIME.

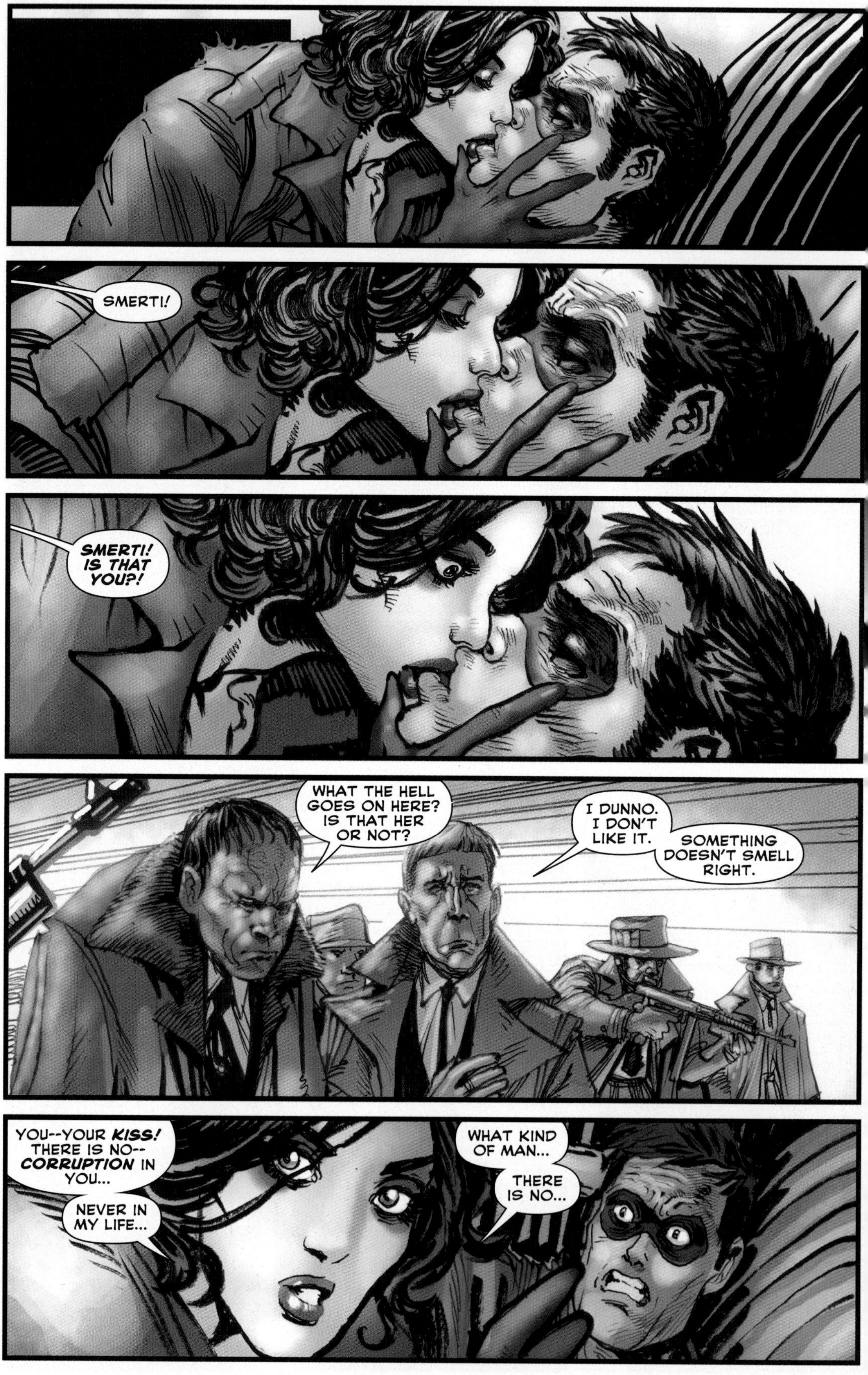
SMERTI!
SMERTI! IS THAT YOU?!
WHAT THE HELL GOES ON HERE? IS THAT HER OR NOT?
I DUNNO. I DON'T LIKE IT.
SOMETHING DOESN'T SMELL RIGHT.
YOU--YOUR KISS! THERE IS NO-- CORRUPTION IN YOU...
NEVER IN MY LIFE...
WHAT KIND OF MAN...
THERE IS NO...

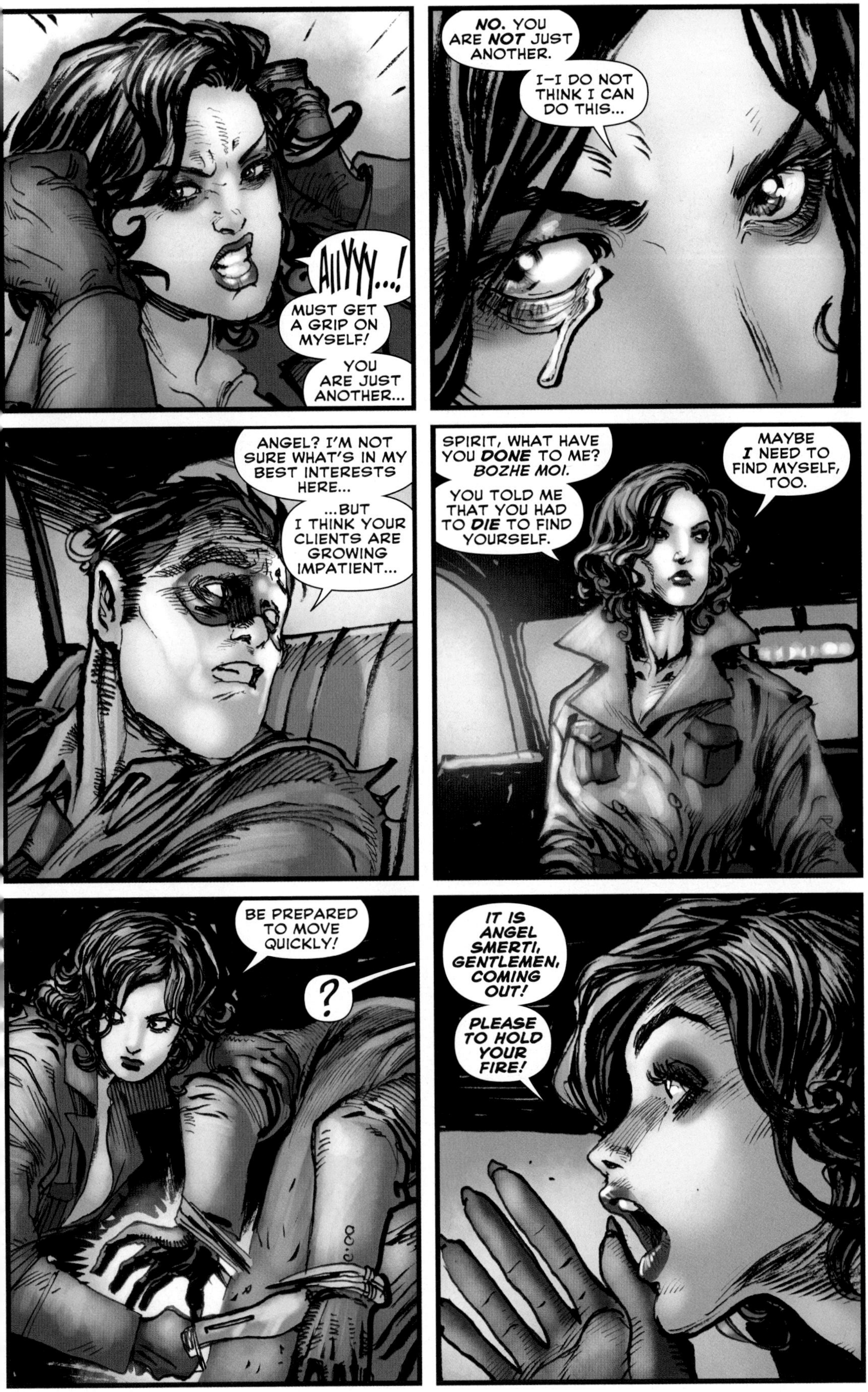
AIIYYY...!
MUST GET A GRIP ON MYSELF!
YOU ARE JUST ANOTHER...
NO. YOU ARE NOT JUST ANOTHER.
I—I DO NOT THINK I CAN DO THIS...
ANGEL? I'M NOT SURE WHAT'S IN MY BEST INTERESTS HERE...
...BUT I THINK YOUR CLIENTS ARE GROWING IMPATIENT...
SPIRIT, WHAT HAVE YOU DONE TO ME? BOZHE MOI.
YOU TOLD ME THAT YOU HAD TO DIE TO FIND YOURSELF.
MAYBE I NEED TO FIND MYSELF, TOO.
BE PREPARED TO MOVE QUICKLY!
?
IT IS ANGEL SMERTI, GENTLEMEN, COMING OUT!
PLEASE TO HOLD YOUR FIRE!

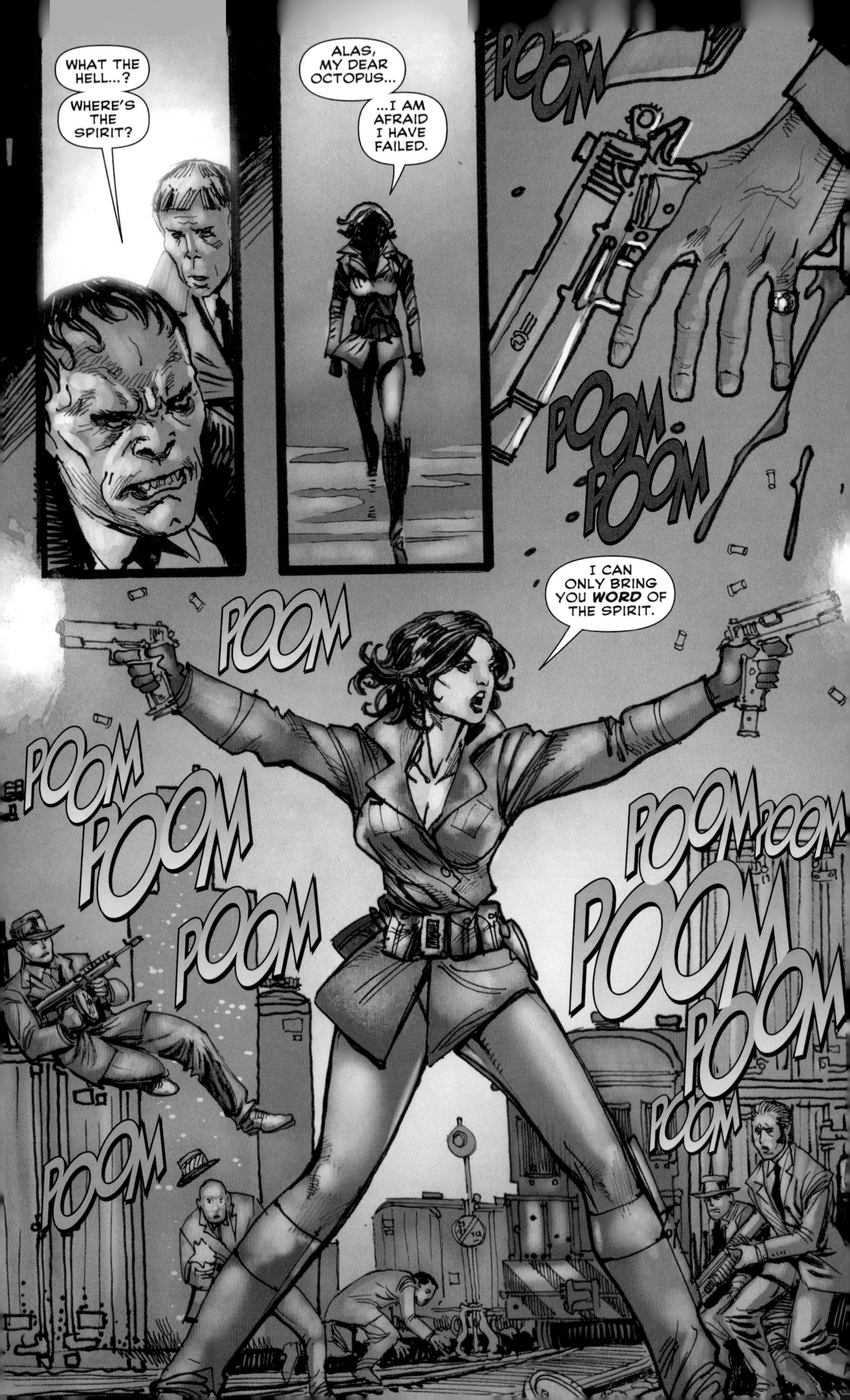
WHAT THE HELL...?
WHERE'S THE SPIRIT?
ALAS, MY DEAR OCTOPUS...
...I AM AFRAID I HAVE FAILED.
POOM
POOM POOM
I CAN ONLY BRING YOU ***WORD*** OF THE SPIRIT.
POOM
POOM POOM POOM
POOM POOM POOM POOM POOM
POOM

POOM
POOM
POOM
GO!
GO!!

POOM
POOM
POOM
ANGEL!

REMEMBER THE MONSTER ANGEL SMERTI, YOU SONS OF--
POOM
POOM
POOM
POOM
POOM
POOM

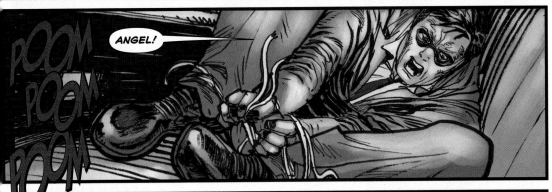

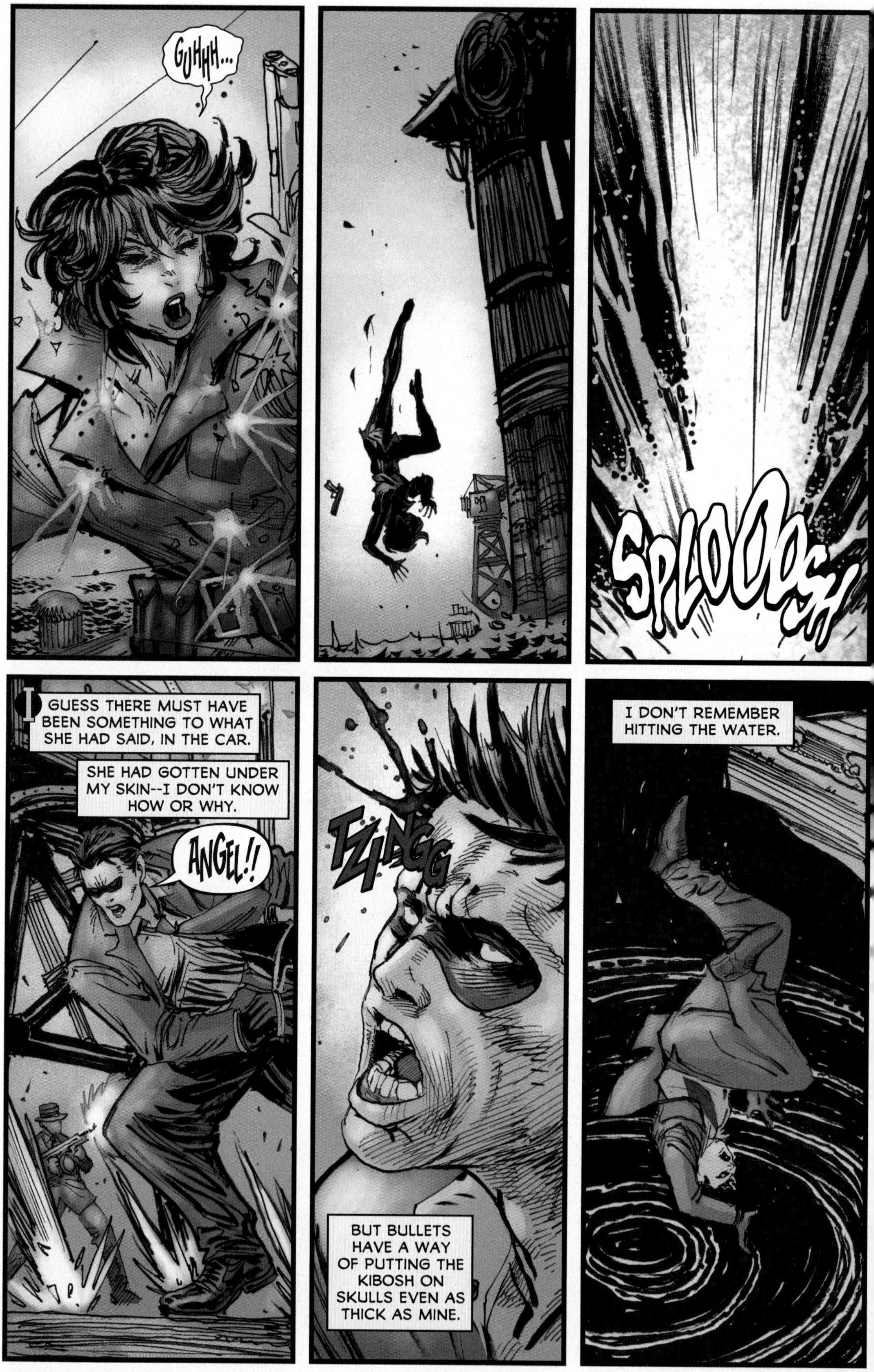
GUHHH...
SPLOOOSH
I GUESS THERE MUST HAVE BEEN SOMETHING TO WHAT SHE HAD SAID, IN THE CAR.
SHE HAD GOTTEN UNDER MY SKIN--I DON'T KNOW HOW OR WHY.
ANGEL!!
TZINGG
BUT BULLETS HAVE A WAY OF PUTTING THE KIBOSH ON SKULLS EVEN AS THICK AS MINE.
I DON'T REMEMBER HITTING THE WATER.

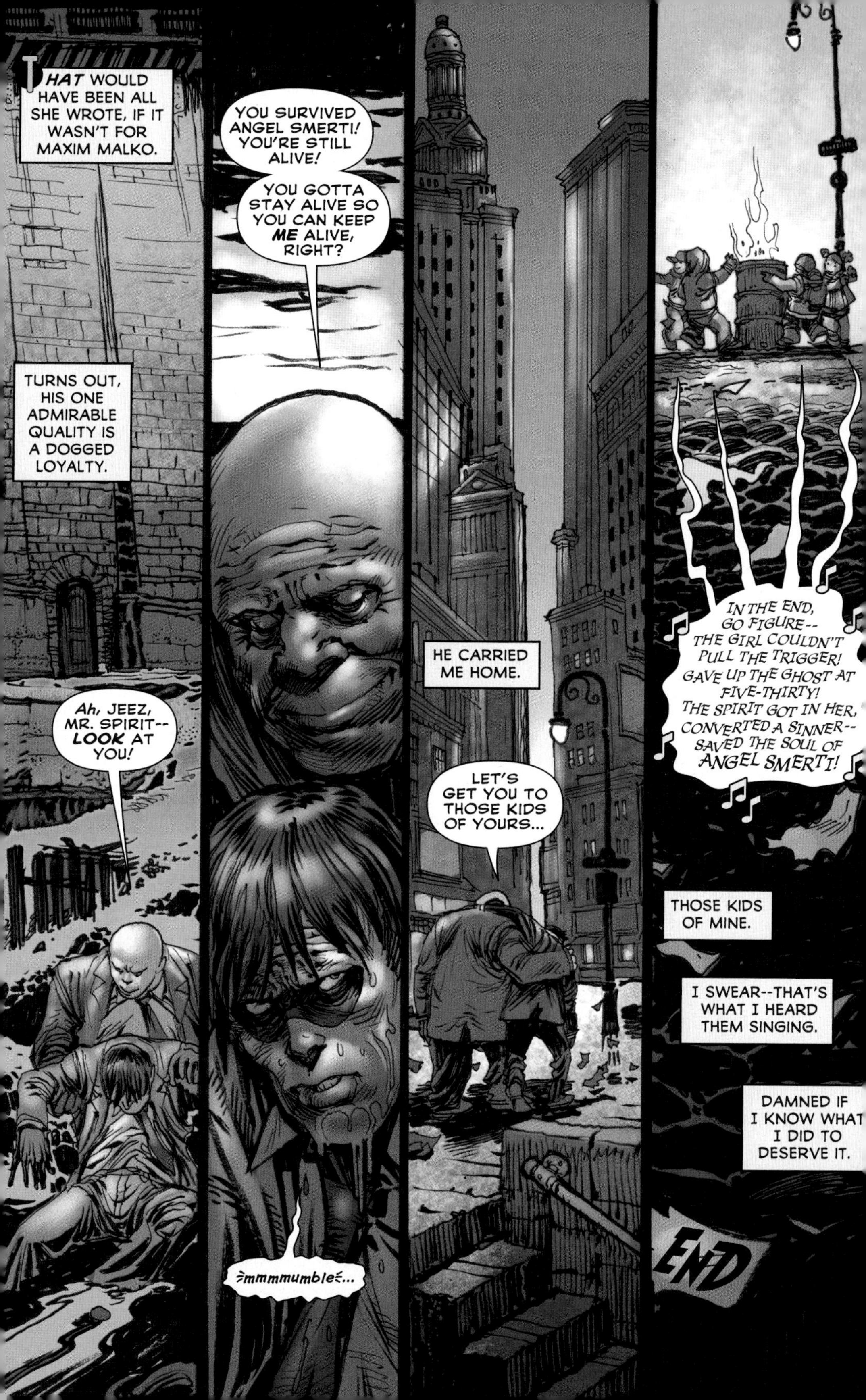
THAT WOULD HAVE BEEN ALL SHE WROTE, IF IT WASN'T FOR MAXIM MALKO.
TURNS OUT, HIS ONE ADMIRABLE QUALITY IS A DOGGED LOYALTY.
Ah, JEEZ, MR. SPIRIT--LOOK AT YOU!
YOU SURVIVED ANGEL SMERTI! YOU'RE STILL ALIVE!
YOU GOTTA STAY ALIVE SO YOU CAN KEEP ME ALIVE, RIGHT?
≷mmmmumble≷...
HE CARRIED ME HOME.
LET'S GET YOU TO THOSE KIDS OF YOURS...
IN THE END, GO FIGURE-- THE GIRL COULDN'T PULL THE TRIGGER! GAVE UP THE GHOST AT FIVE-THIRTY! THE SPIRIT GOT IN HER, CONVERTED A SINNER-- SAVED THE SOUL OF ANGEL SMERTI!
THOSE KIDS OF MINE.
I SWEAR--THAT'S WHAT I HEARD THEM SINGING.
DAMNED IF I KNOW WHAT I DID TO DESERVE IT.
END

FROST BITE **PART ONE**

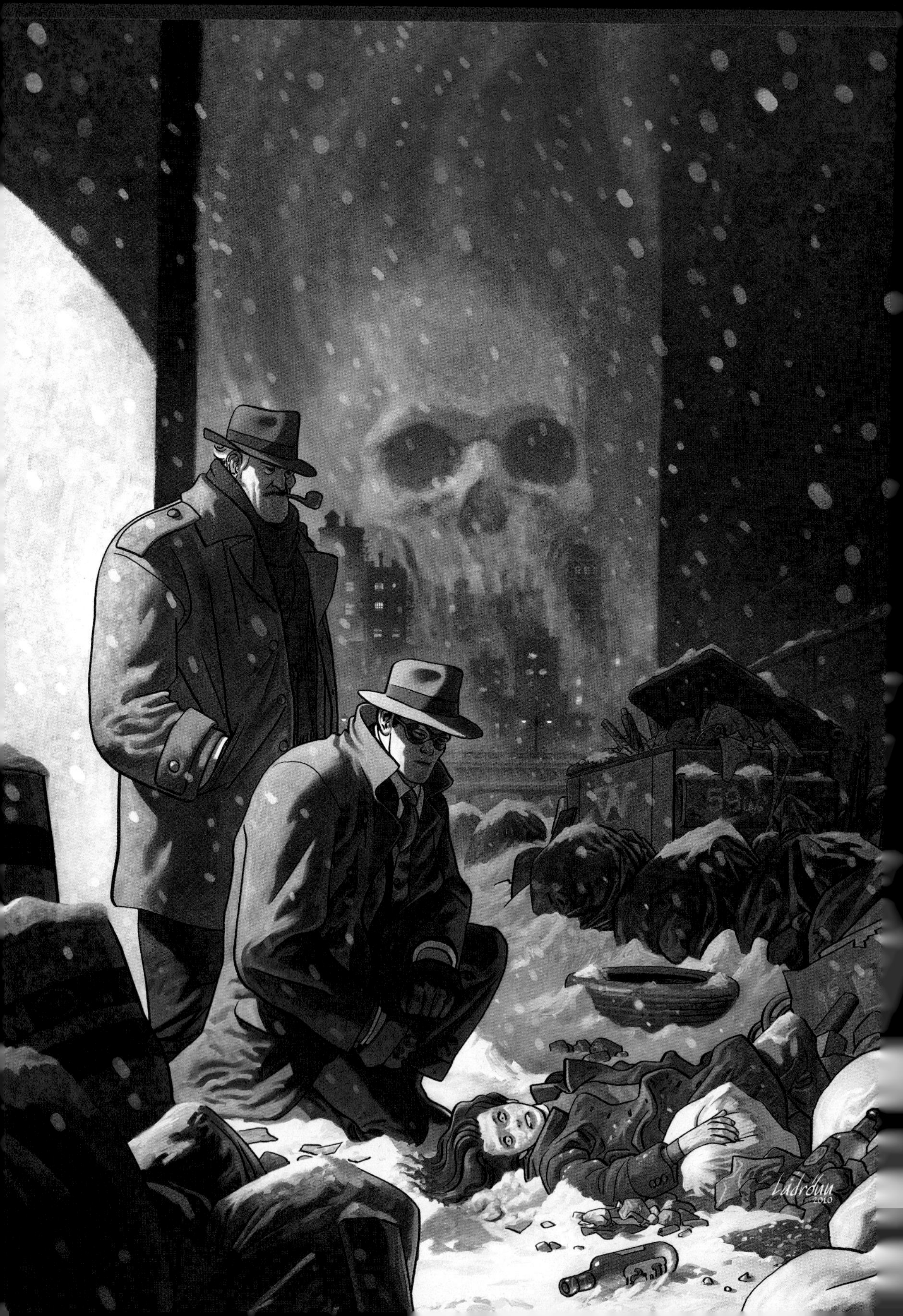

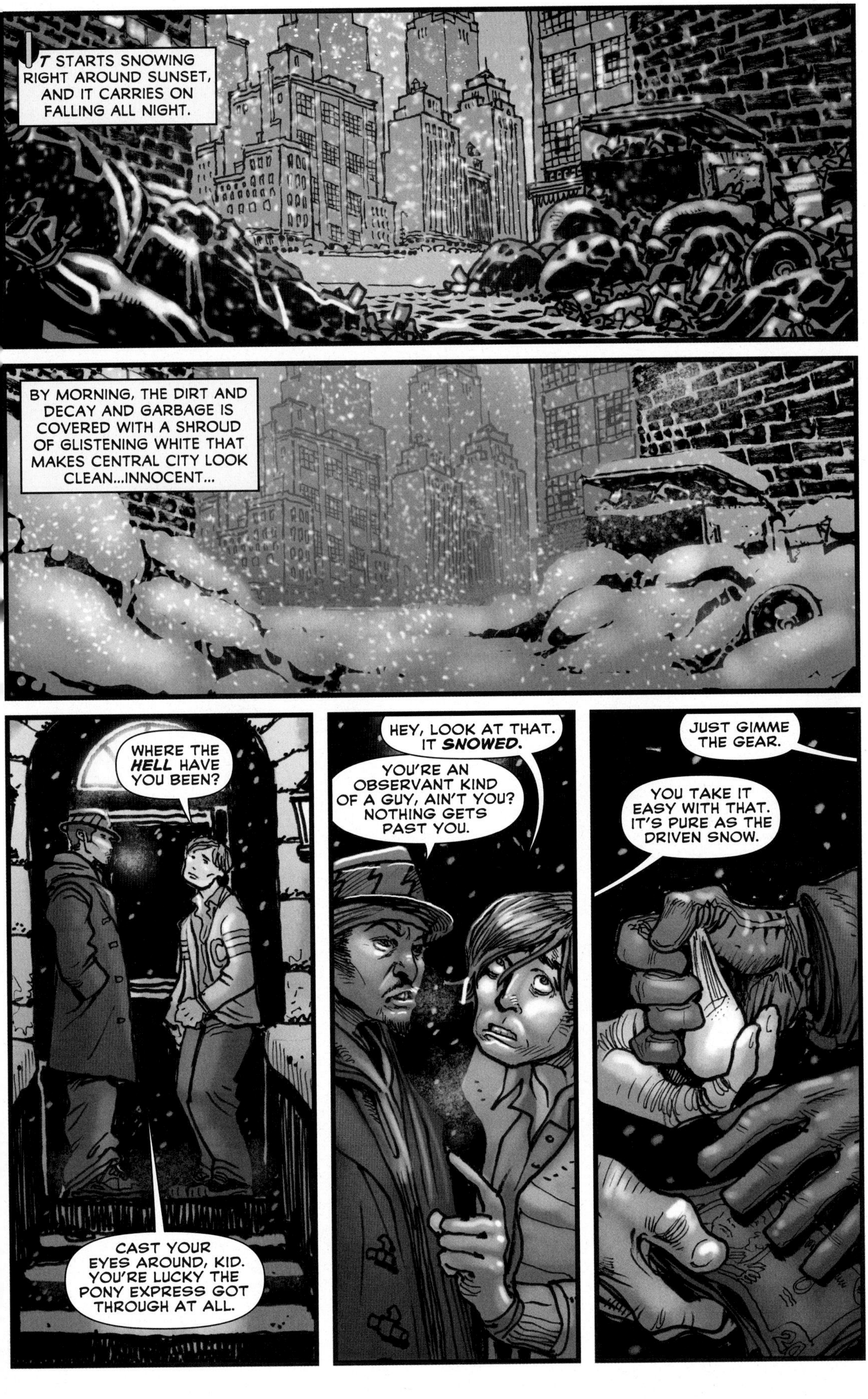
IT STARTS SNOWING RIGHT AROUND SUNSET, AND IT CARRIES ON FALLING ALL NIGHT.
BY MORNING, THE DIRT AND DECAY AND GARBAGE IS COVERED WITH A SHROUD OF GLISTENING WHITE THAT MAKES CENTRAL CITY LOOK CLEAN...INNOCENT...
WHERE THE HELL HAVE YOU BEEN?
CAST YOUR EYES AROUND, KID. YOU'RE LUCKY THE PONY EXPRESS GOT THROUGH AT ALL.
HEY, LOOK AT THAT. IT SNOWED.
YOU'RE AN OBSERVANT KIND OF A GUY, AIN'T YOU? NOTHING GETS PAST YOU.
JUST GIMME THE GEAR.
YOU TAKE IT EASY WITH THAT. IT'S PURE AS THE DRIVEN SNOW.

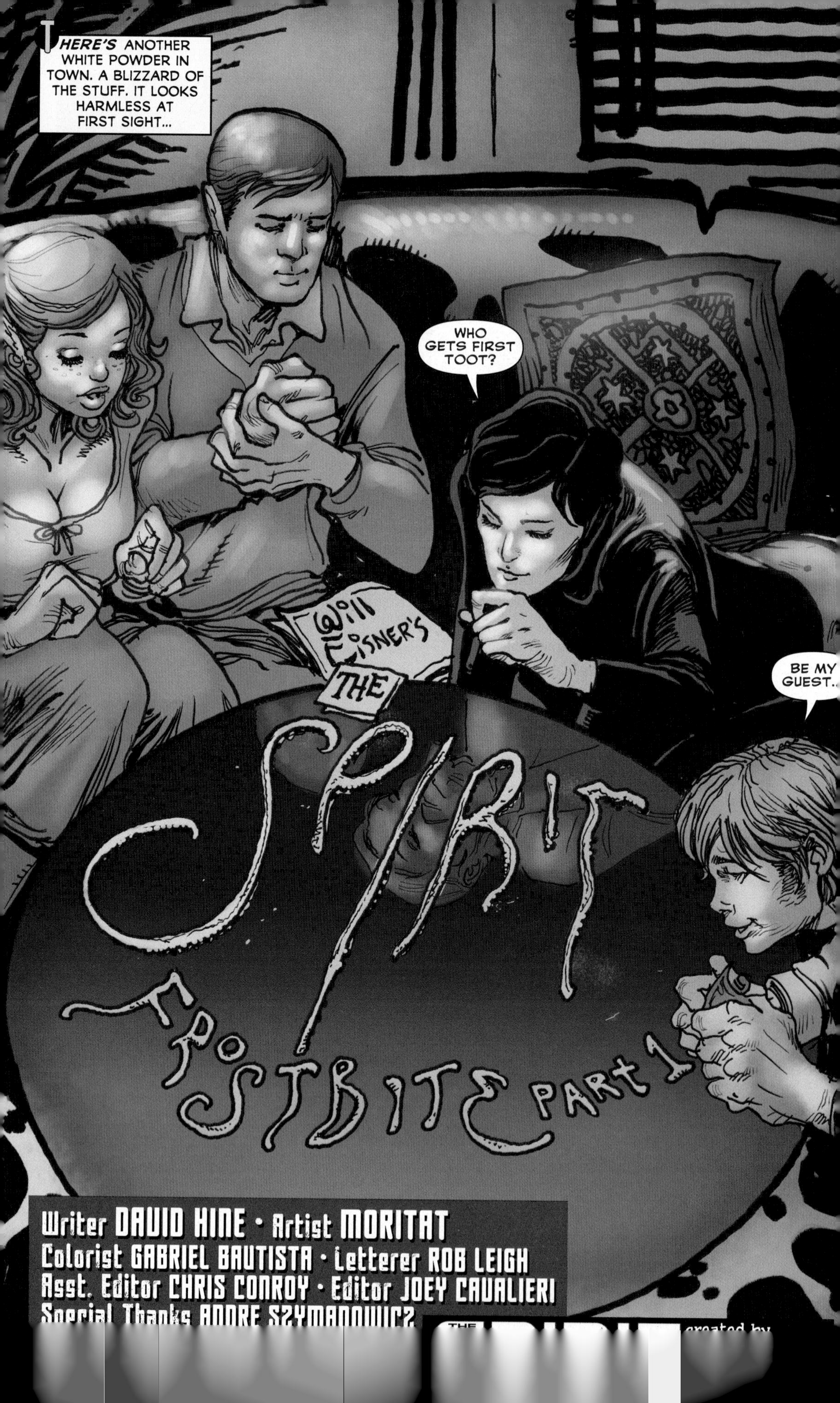
THERE'S ANOTHER WHITE POWDER IN TOWN. A BLIZZARD OF THE STUFF. IT LOOKS HARMLESS AT FIRST SIGHT...
WHO GETS FIRST TOOT?
BE MY GUEST...
Will Eisner's THE SPIRIT
FROSTBITE PART 1
Writer DAVID HINE • Artist MORITAT
Colorist GABRIEL BAUTISTA • Letterer ROB LEIGH
Asst. Editor CHRIS CONROY • Editor JOEY CAVALIERI

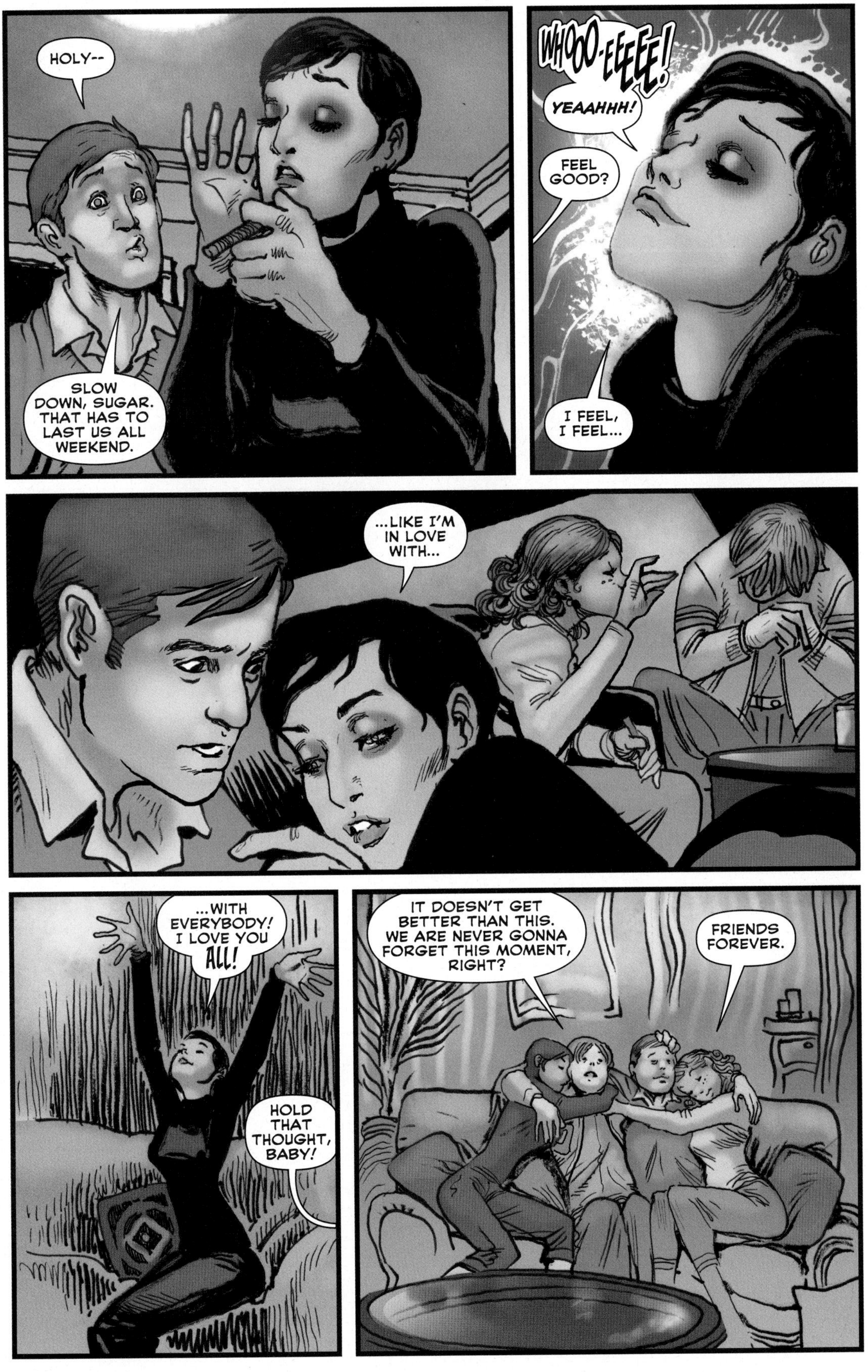
HOLY--
SLOW DOWN, SUGAR. THAT HAS TO LAST US ALL WEEKEND.
WHOOO-EEEEE!
YEAAHHH!
FEEL GOOD?
I FEEL, I FEEL...
...LIKE I'M IN LOVE WITH...
...WITH EVERYBODY! I LOVE YOU ALL!
HOLD THAT THOUGHT, BABY!
IT DOESN'T GET BETTER THAN THIS. WE ARE NEVER GONNA FORGET THIS MOMENT, RIGHT?
FRIENDS FOREVER.

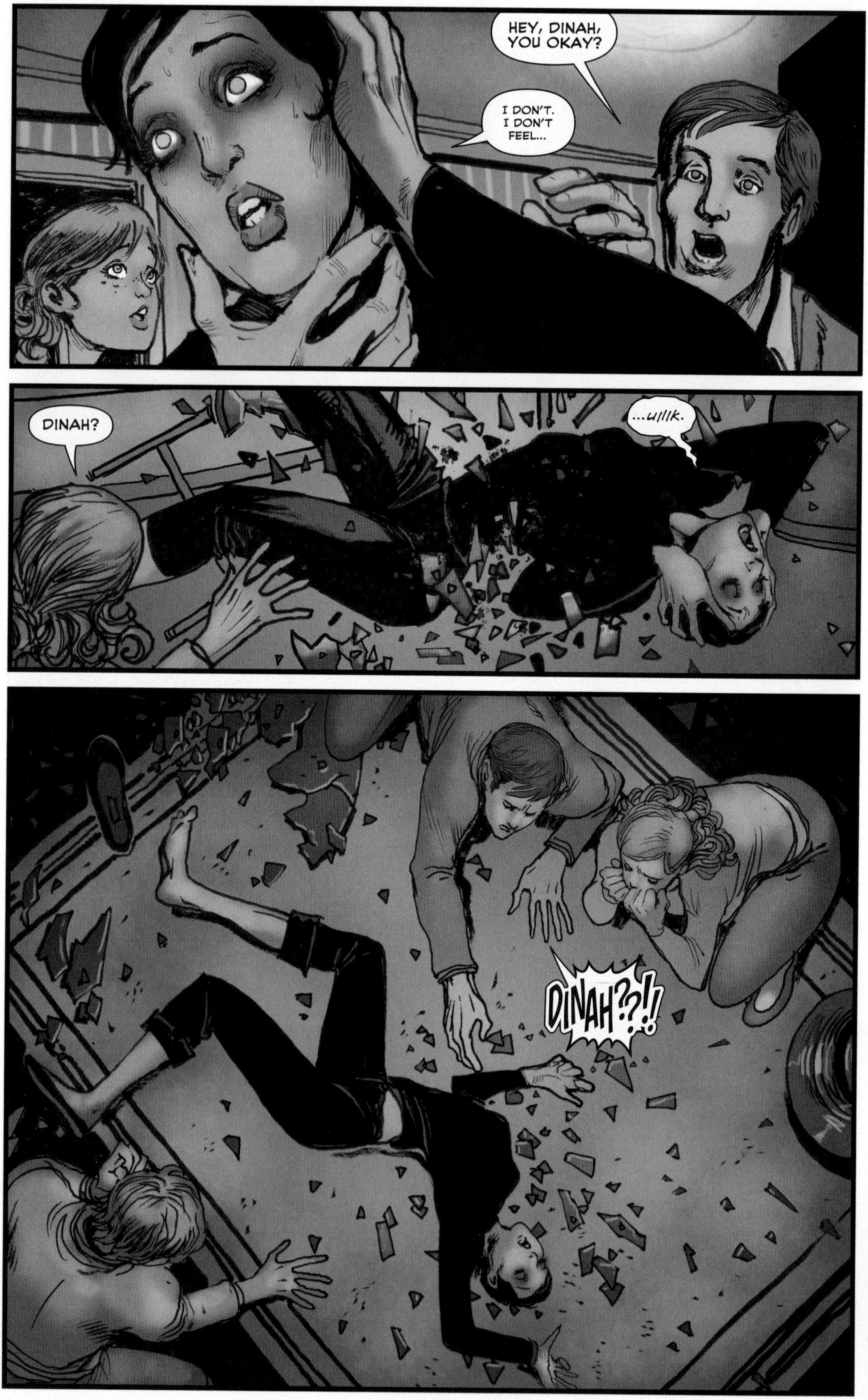
HEY, DINAH, YOU OKAY?
I DON'T. I DON'T FEEL...
DINAH?
...ULLK.
DINAH?!?!

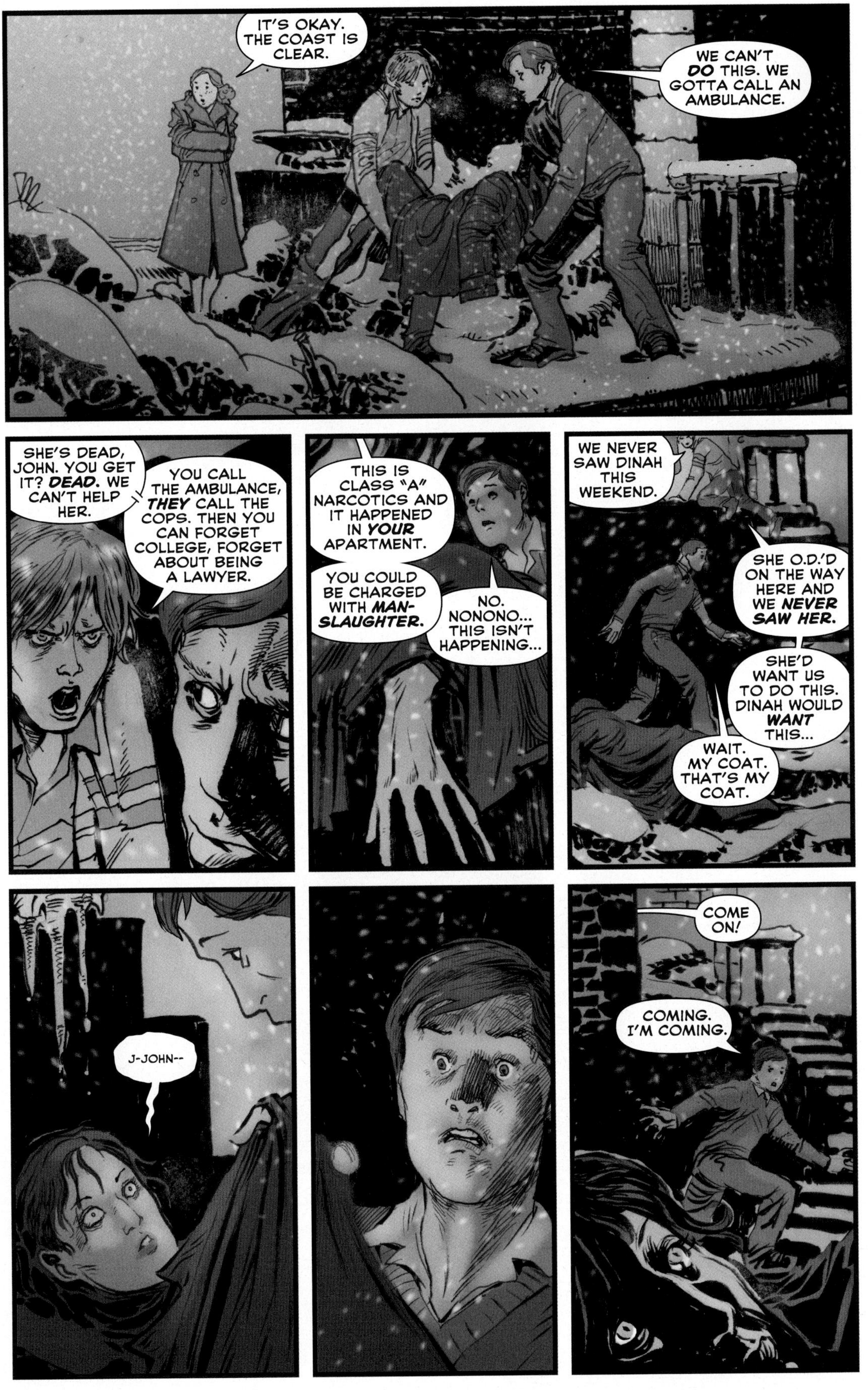
IT'S OKAY. THE COAST IS CLEAR.
WE CAN'T DO THIS. WE GOTTA CALL AN AMBULANCE.
SHE'S DEAD, JOHN. YOU GET IT? DEAD. WE CAN'T HELP HER.
YOU CALL THE AMBULANCE, THEY CALL THE COPS. THEN YOU CAN FORGET COLLEGE, FORGET ABOUT BEING A LAWYER.
THIS IS CLASS "A" NARCOTICS AND IT HAPPENED IN YOUR APARTMENT.
YOU COULD BE CHARGED WITH MAN-SLAUGHTER.
NO. NONONO... THIS ISN'T HAPPENING...
WE NEVER SAW DINAH THIS WEEKEND.
SHE O.D.'D ON THE WAY HERE AND WE NEVER SAW HER.
SHE'D WANT US TO DO THIS. DINAH WOULD WANT THIS...
WAIT. MY COAT. THAT'S MY COAT.
J-JOHN--
COME ON!
COMING. I'M COMING.

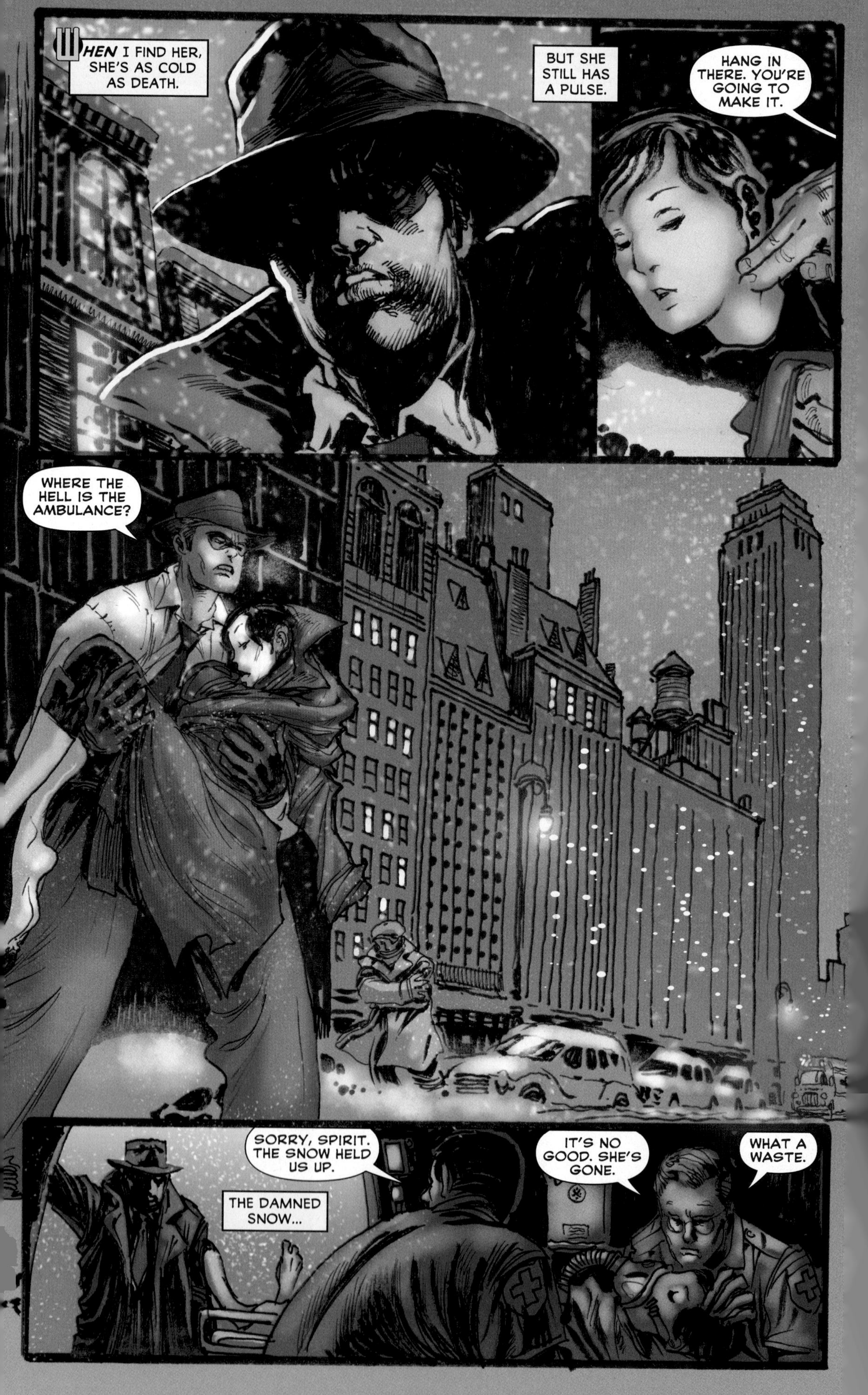
WHEN I FIND HER, SHE'S AS COLD AS DEATH.
BUT SHE STILL HAS A PULSE.
HANG IN THERE. YOU'RE GOING TO MAKE IT.
WHERE THE HELL IS THE AMBULANCE?
SORRY, SPIRIT. THE SNOW HELD US UP.
THE DAMNED SNOW...
IT'S NO GOOD. SHE'S GONE.
WHAT A WASTE.

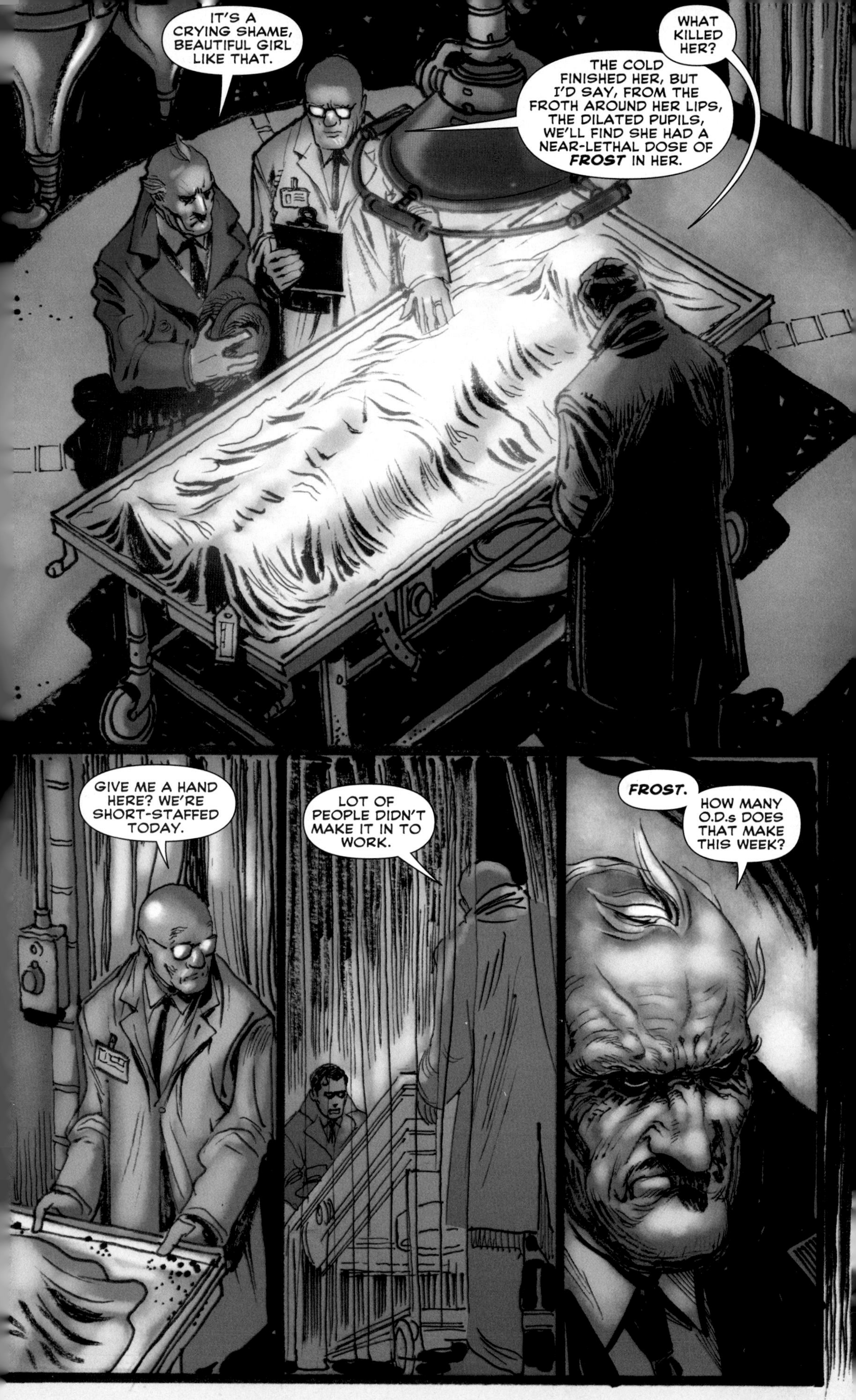

IT'S A CRYING SHAME, BEAUTIFUL GIRL LIKE THAT.
WHAT KILLED HER?
THE COLD FINISHED HER, BUT I'D SAY, FROM THE FROTH AROUND HER LIPS, THE DILATED PUPILS, WE'LL FIND SHE HAD A NEAR-LETHAL DOSE OF *FROST* IN HER.
GIVE ME A HAND HERE? WE'RE SHORT-STAFFED TODAY.
LOT OF PEOPLE DIDN'T MAKE IT IN TO WORK.
FROST.
HOW MANY O.D.s DOES THAT MAKE THIS WEEK?

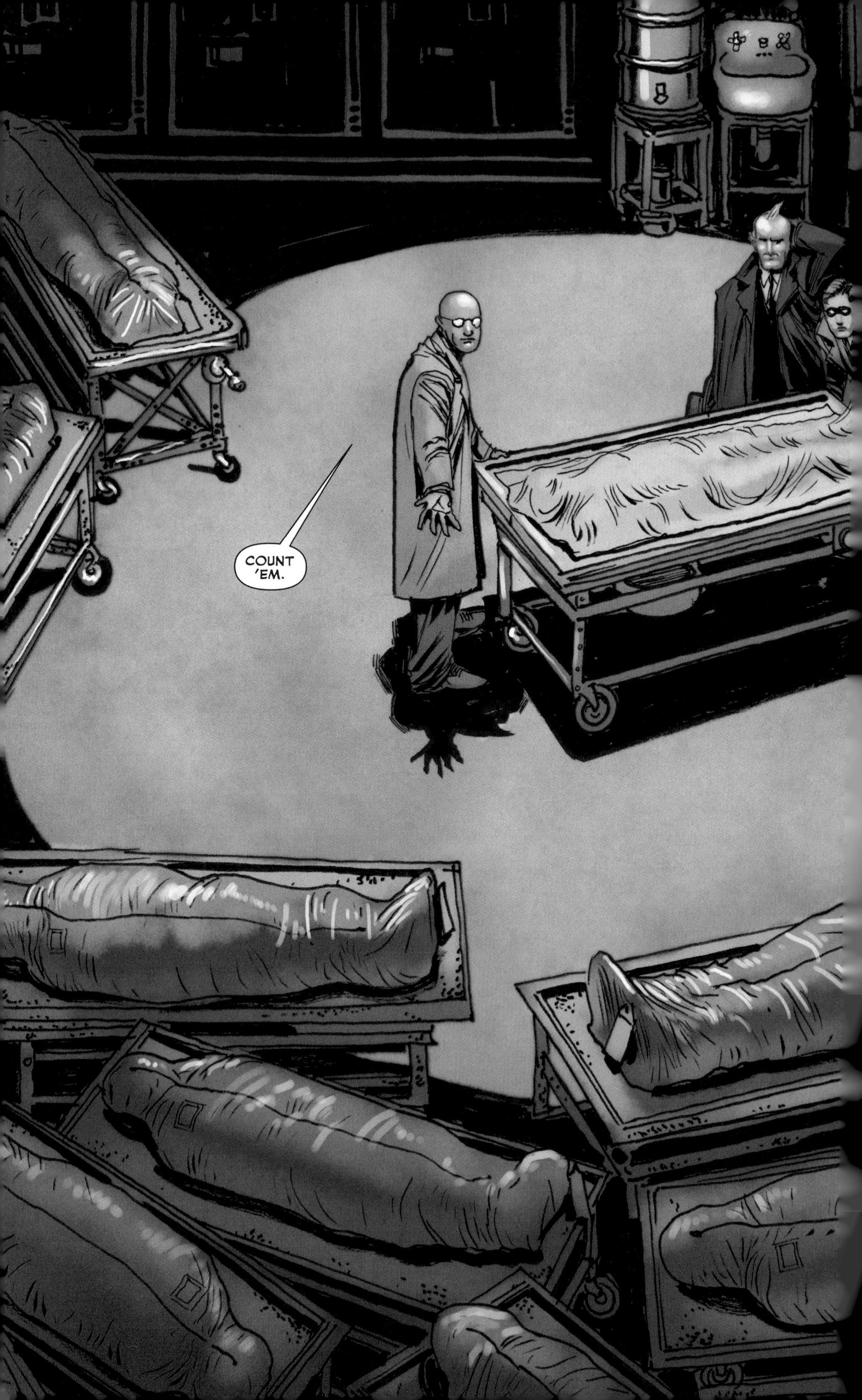
COUNT 'EM.

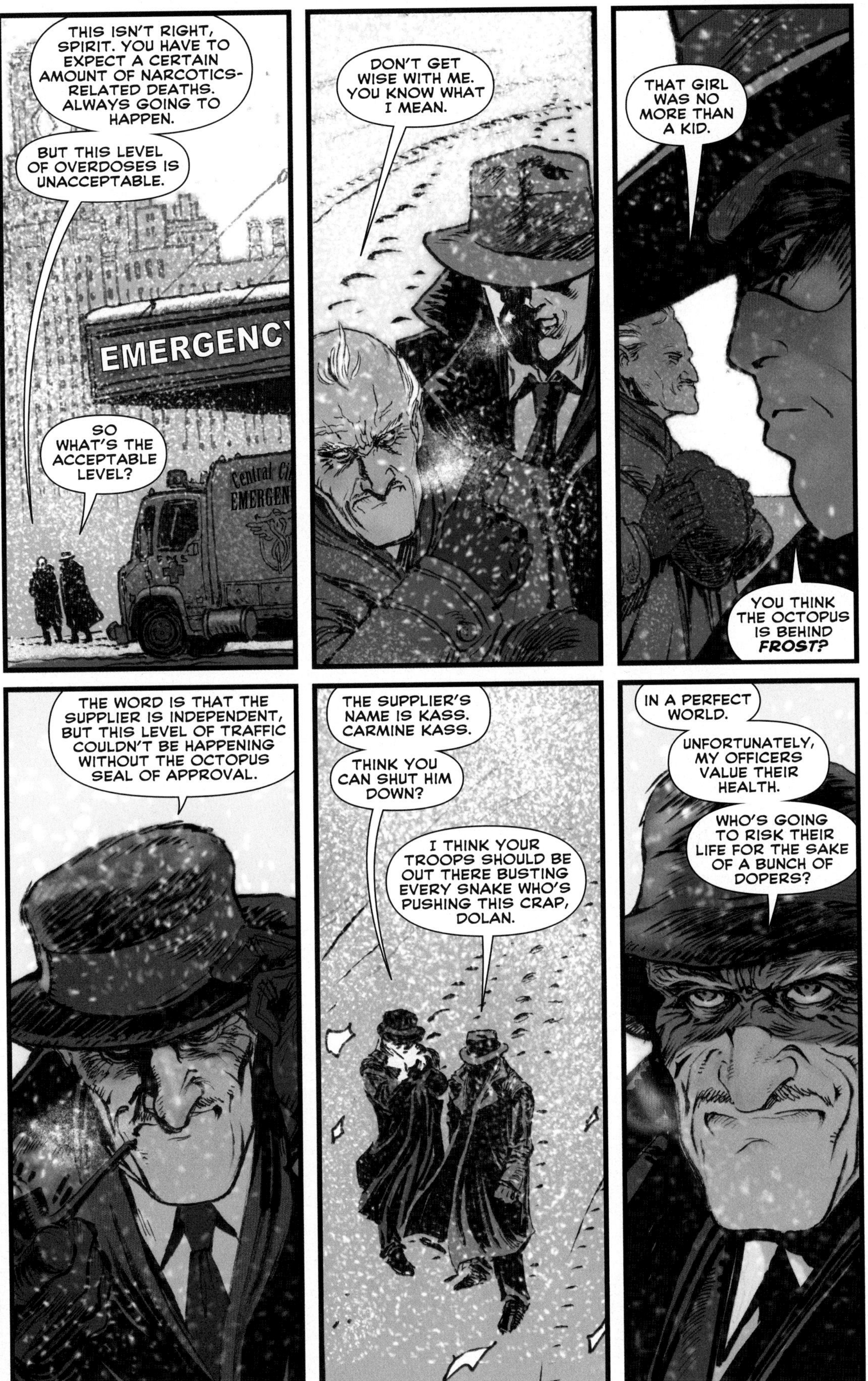
THIS ISN'T RIGHT, SPIRIT. YOU HAVE TO EXPECT A CERTAIN AMOUNT OF NARCOTICS-RELATED DEATHS. ALWAYS GOING TO HAPPEN.
BUT THIS LEVEL OF OVERDOSES IS UNACCEPTABLE.
EMERGENCY
SO WHAT'S THE ACCEPTABLE LEVEL?
DON'T GET WISE WITH ME. YOU KNOW WHAT I MEAN.
THAT GIRL WAS NO MORE THAN A KID.
YOU THINK THE OCTOPUS IS BEHIND ***FROST?***
THE WORD IS THAT THE SUPPLIER IS INDEPENDENT, BUT THIS LEVEL OF TRAFFIC COULDN'T BE HAPPENING WITHOUT THE OCTOPUS SEAL OF APPROVAL.
THE SUPPLIER'S NAME IS KASS. CARMINE KASS.
THINK YOU CAN SHUT HIM DOWN?
I THINK YOUR TROOPS SHOULD BE OUT THERE BUSTING EVERY SNAKE WHO'S PUSHING THIS CRAP, DOLAN.
IN A PERFECT WORLD.
UNFORTUNATELY, MY OFFICERS VALUE THEIR HEALTH.
WHO'S GOING TO RISK THEIR LIFE FOR THE SAKE OF A BUNCH OF DOPERS?

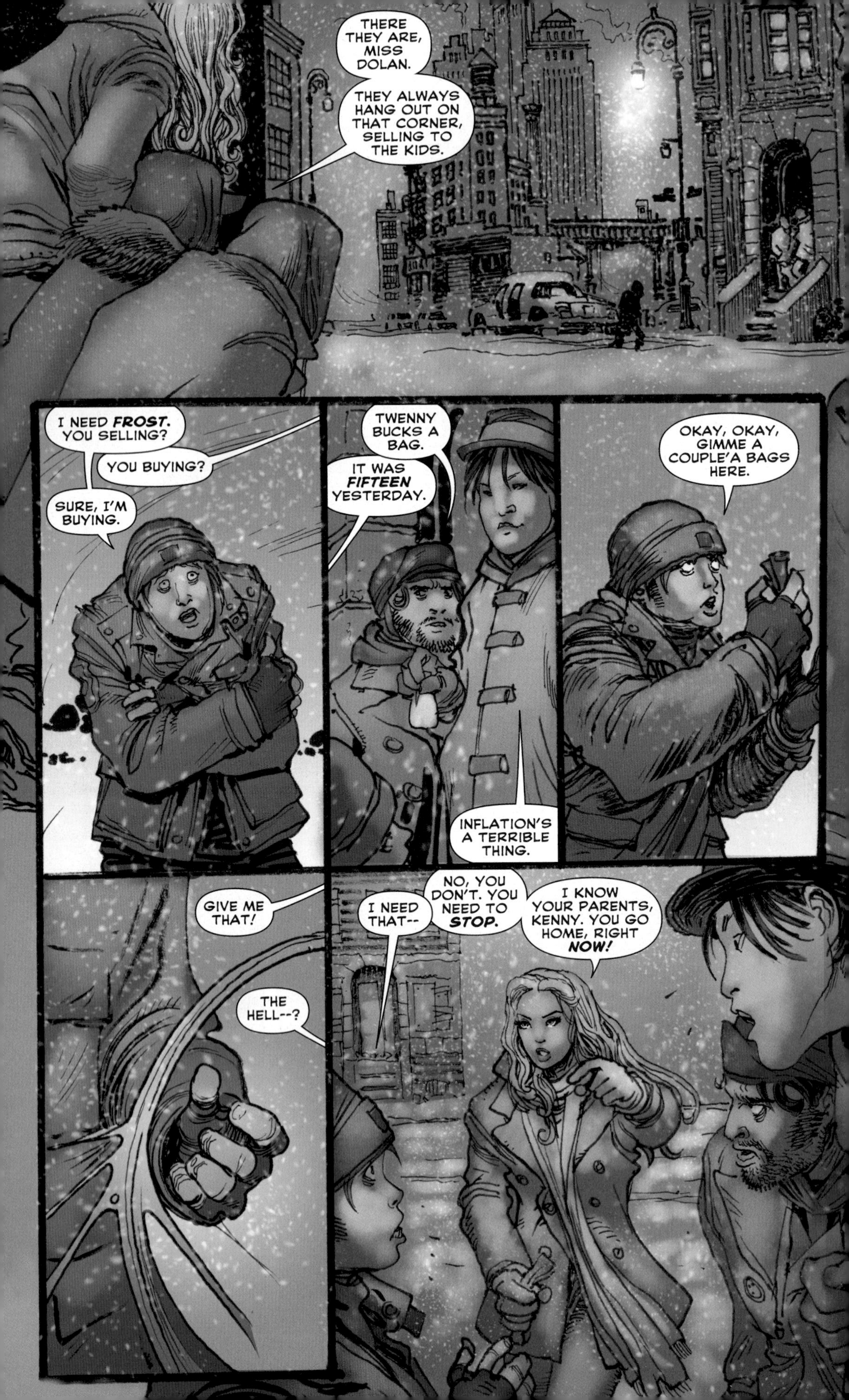
THERE THEY ARE, MISS DOLAN.
THEY ALWAYS HANG OUT ON THAT CORNER, SELLING TO THE KIDS.
I NEED **FROST.** YOU SELLING?
YOU BUYING?
SURE, I'M BUYING.
TWENNY BUCKS A BAG.
IT WAS **FIFTEEN** YESTERDAY.
INFLATION'S A TERRIBLE THING.
OKAY, OKAY, GIMME A COUPLE'A BAGS HERE.
GIVE ME THAT!
THE HELL--?
I NEED THAT--
NO, YOU DON'T. YOU NEED TO **STOP.**
I KNOW YOUR PARENTS, KENNY. YOU GO HOME, RIGHT **NOW!**

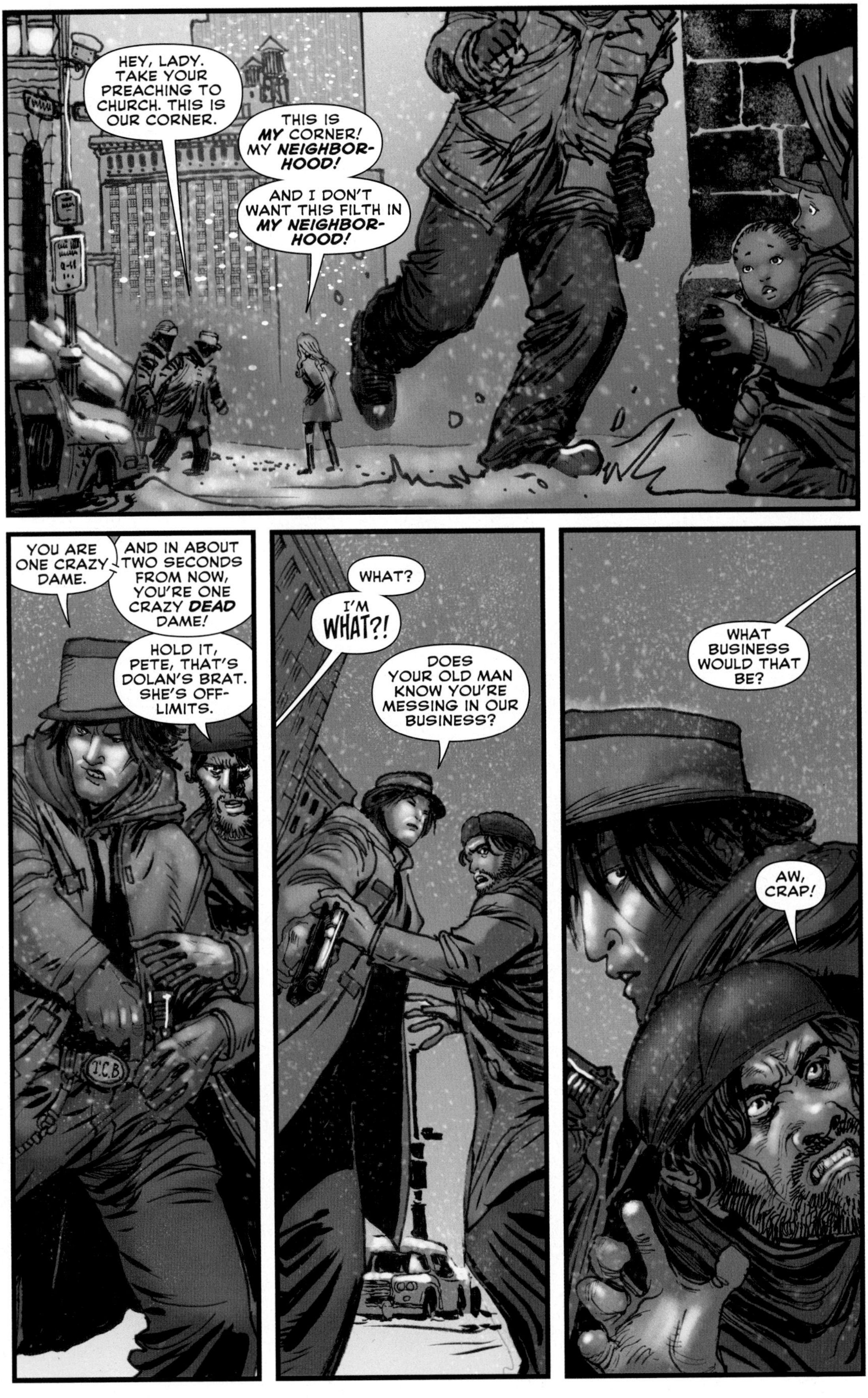
HEY, LADY. TAKE YOUR PREACHING TO CHURCH. THIS IS OUR CORNER.
THIS IS MY CORNER! MY NEIGHBOR-HOOD!
AND I DON'T WANT THIS FILTH IN MY NEIGHBOR-HOOD!
YOU ARE ONE CRAZY DAME.
AND IN ABOUT TWO SECONDS FROM NOW, YOU'RE ONE CRAZY DEAD DAME!
HOLD IT, PETE, THAT'S DOLAN'S BRAT. SHE'S OFF-LIMITS.
WHAT?
I'M WHAT?!
DOES YOUR OLD MAN KNOW YOU'RE MESSING IN OUR BUSINESS?
WHAT BUSINESS WOULD THAT BE?
AW, CRAP!

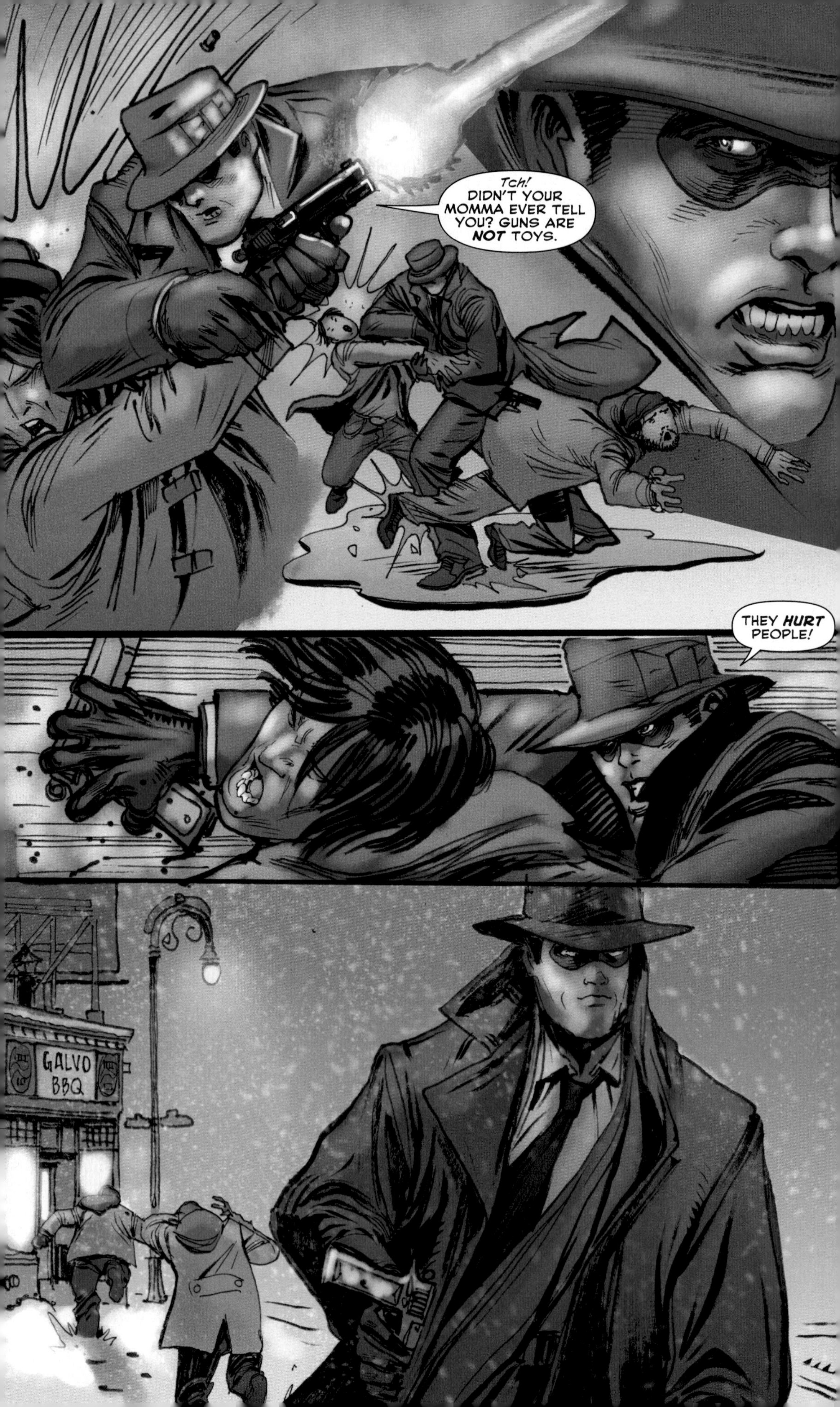
Tch! DIDN'T YOUR MOMMA EVER TELL YOU? GUNS ARE NOT TOYS.
THEY HURT PEOPLE!
GALVO BBQ

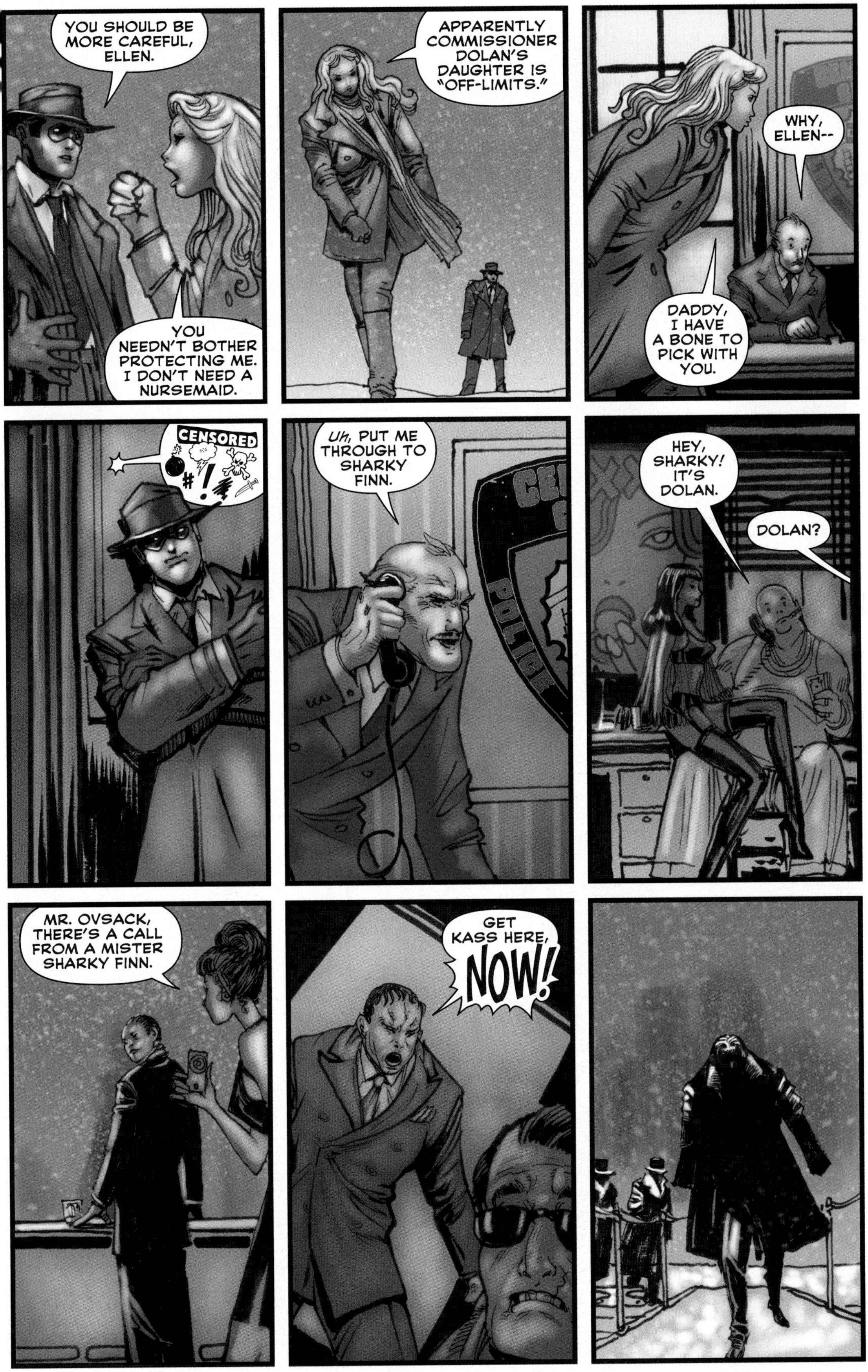
YOU SHOULD BE MORE CAREFUL, ELLEN.
YOU NEEDN'T BOTHER PROTECTING ME. I DON'T NEED A NURSEMAID.
APPARENTLY COMMISSIONER DOLAN'S DAUGHTER IS "OFF-LIMITS."
WHY, ELLEN--
DADDY, I HAVE A BONE TO PICK WITH YOU.
CENSORED
#!
Uh, PUT ME THROUGH TO SHARKY FINN.
POLICE
HEY, SHARKY! IT'S DOLAN.
DOLAN?
MR. OVSACK, THERE'S A CALL FROM A MISTER SHARKY FINN.
GET KASS HERE, NOW!

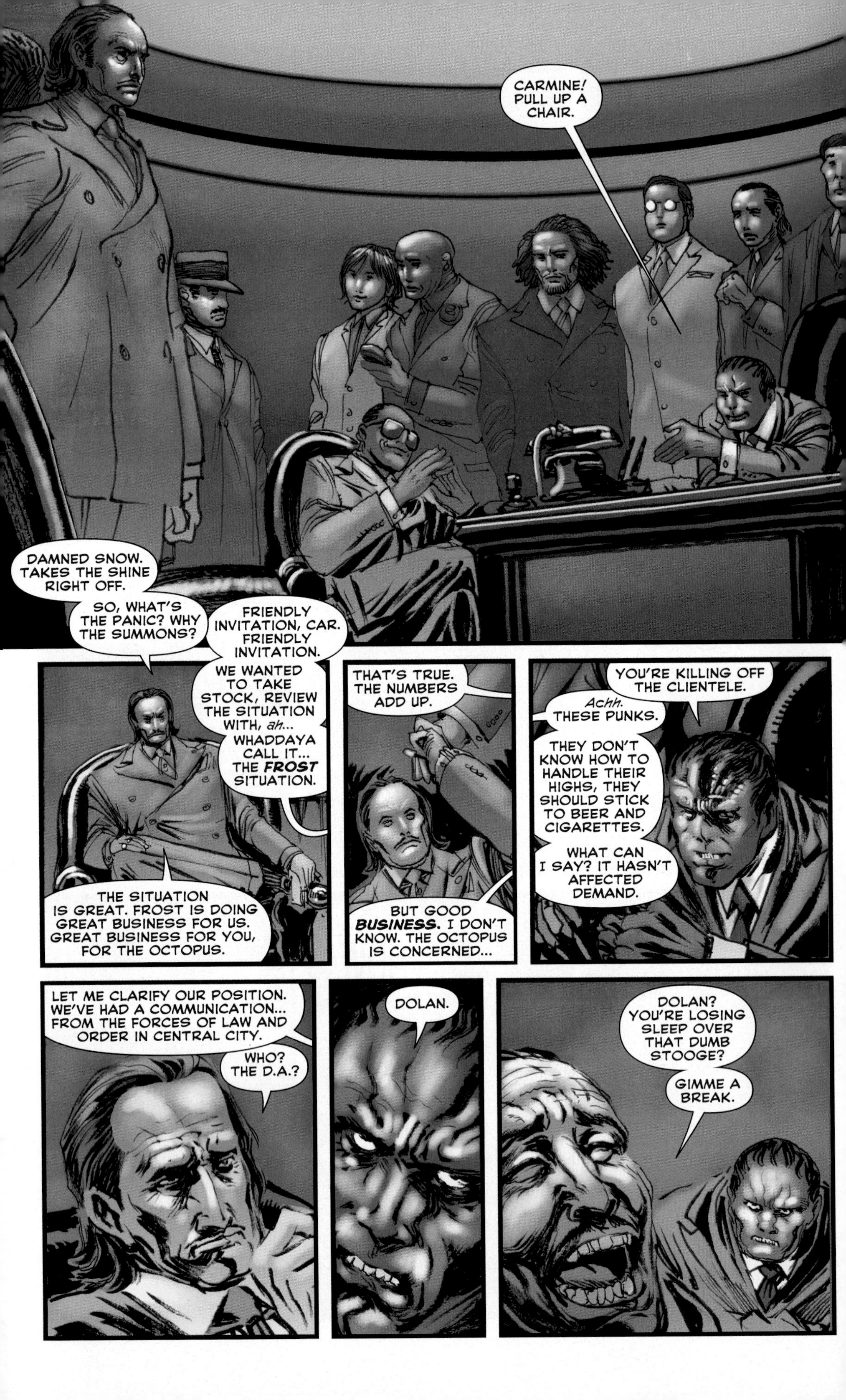
CARMINE! PULL UP A CHAIR.
DAMNED SNOW. TAKES THE SHINE RIGHT OFF.
SO, WHAT'S THE PANIC? WHY THE SUMMONS?
FRIENDLY INVITATION, CAR. FRIENDLY INVITATION.
WE WANTED TO TAKE STOCK, REVIEW THE SITUATION WITH, *ah*... WHADDAYA CALL IT... THE ***FROST*** SITUATION.
THE SITUATION IS GREAT. FROST IS DOING GREAT BUSINESS FOR US. GREAT BUSINESS FOR YOU, FOR THE OCTOPUS.
THAT'S TRUE. THE NUMBERS ADD UP.
BUT GOOD ***BUSINESS.*** I DON'T KNOW. THE OCTOPUS IS CONCERNED...
YOU'RE KILLING OFF THE CLIENTELE.
Achh. THESE PUNKS.
THEY DON'T KNOW HOW TO HANDLE THEIR HIGHS, THEY SHOULD STICK TO BEER AND CIGARETTES.
WHAT CAN I SAY? IT HASN'T AFFECTED DEMAND.
LET ME CLARIFY OUR POSITION. WE'VE HAD A COMMUNICATION... FROM THE FORCES OF LAW AND ORDER IN CENTRAL CITY.
WHO? THE D.A.?
DOLAN.
DOLAN? YOU'RE LOSING SLEEP OVER THAT DUMB STOOGE?
GIMME A BREAK.

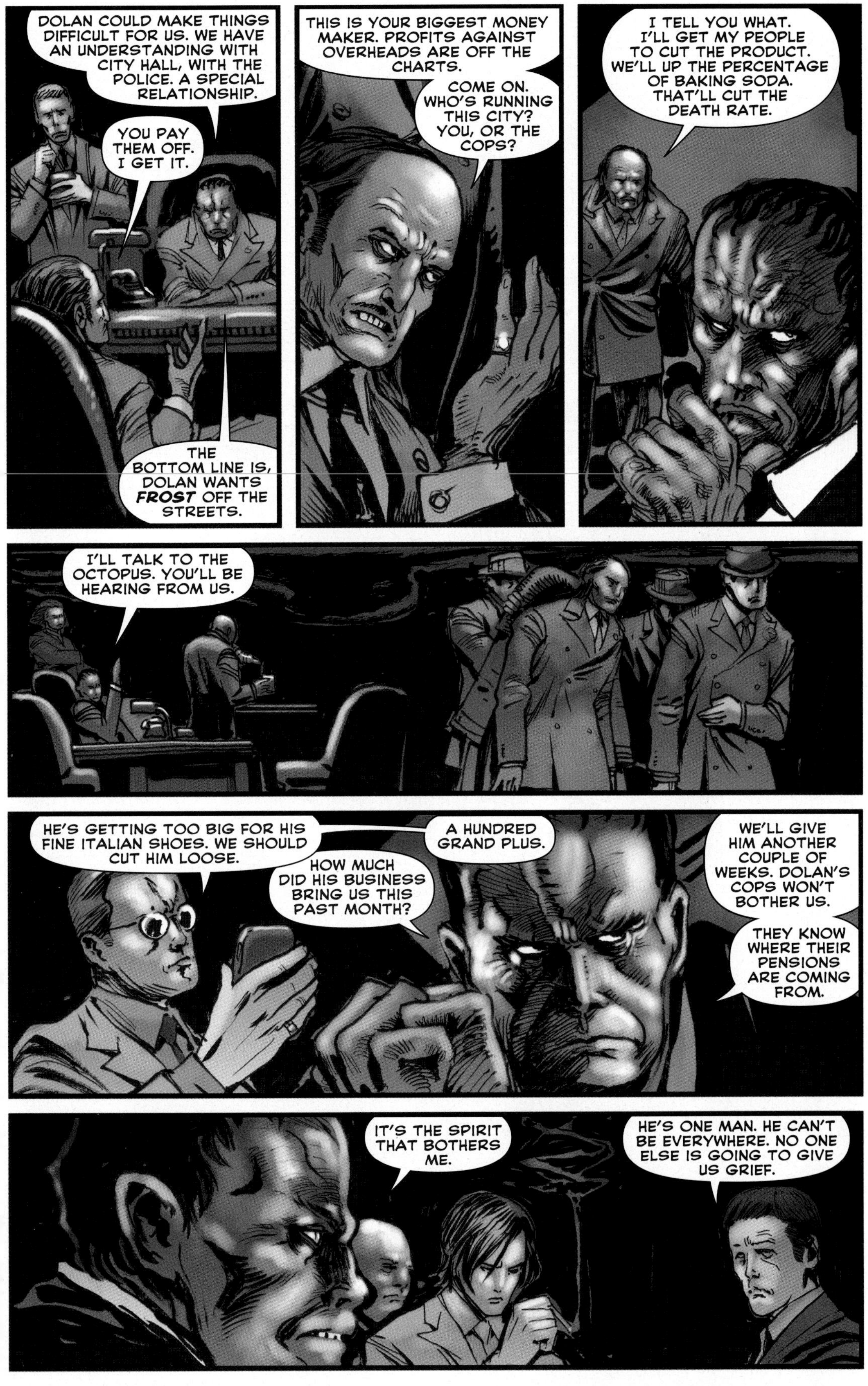
DOLAN COULD MAKE THINGS DIFFICULT FOR US. WE HAVE AN UNDERSTANDING WITH CITY HALL, WITH THE POLICE. A SPECIAL RELATIONSHIP.
YOU PAY THEM OFF. I GET IT.
THE BOTTOM LINE IS, DOLAN WANTS FROST OFF THE STREETS.
THIS IS YOUR BIGGEST MONEY MAKER. PROFITS AGAINST OVERHEADS ARE OFF THE CHARTS.
COME ON. WHO'S RUNNING THIS CITY? YOU, OR THE COPS?
I TELL YOU WHAT. I'LL GET MY PEOPLE TO CUT THE PRODUCT. WE'LL UP THE PERCENTAGE OF BAKING SODA. THAT'LL CUT THE DEATH RATE.
I'LL TALK TO THE OCTOPUS. YOU'LL BE HEARING FROM US.
HE'S GETTING TOO BIG FOR HIS FINE ITALIAN SHOES. WE SHOULD CUT HIM LOOSE.
HOW MUCH DID HIS BUSINESS BRING US THIS PAST MONTH?
A HUNDRED GRAND PLUS.
WE'LL GIVE HIM ANOTHER COUPLE OF WEEKS. DOLAN'S COPS WON'T BOTHER US.
THEY KNOW WHERE THEIR PENSIONS ARE COMING FROM.
IT'S THE SPIRIT THAT BOTHERS ME.
HE'S ONE MAN. HE CAN'T BE EVERYWHERE. NO ONE ELSE IS GOING TO GIVE US GRIEF.

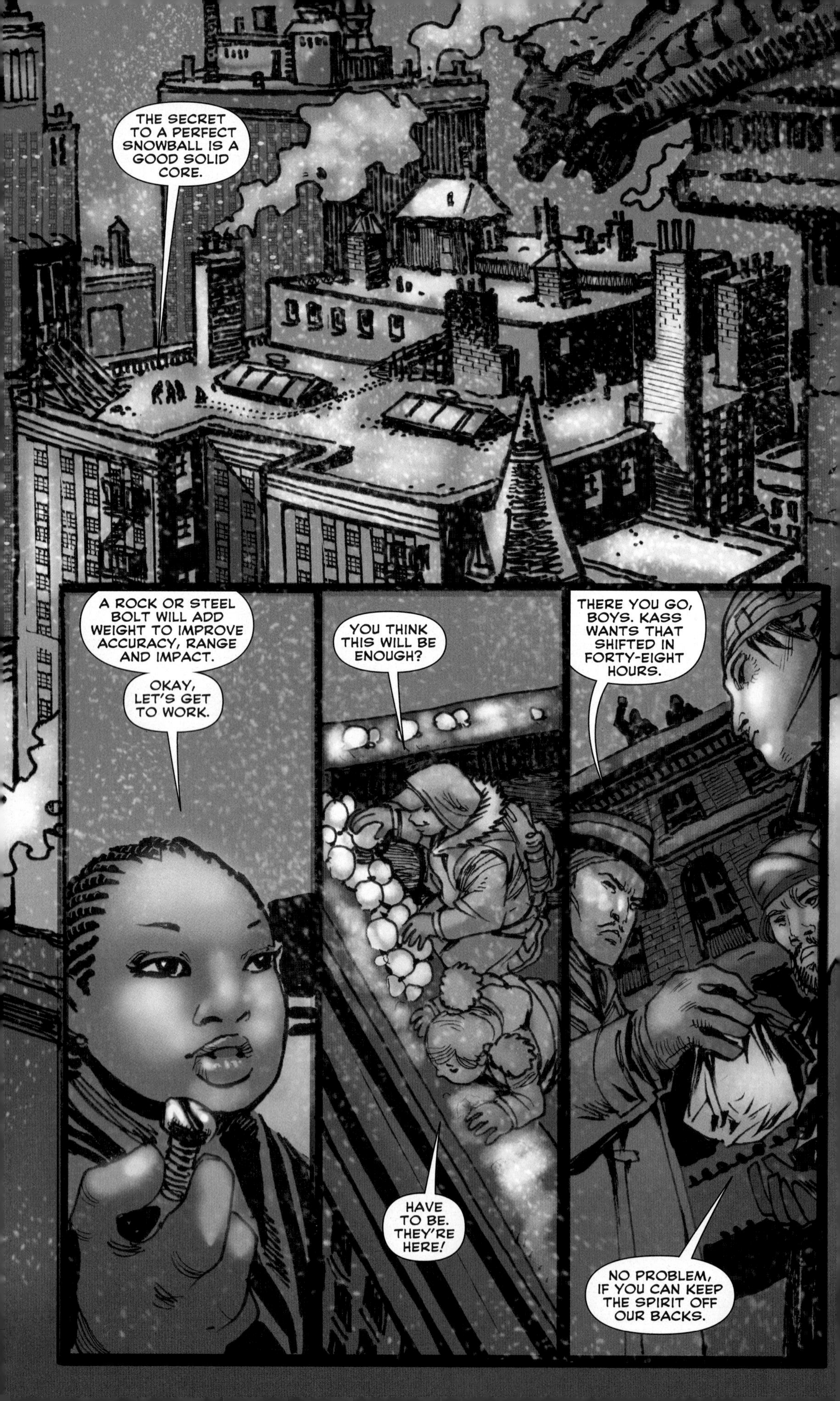
THE SECRET TO A PERFECT SNOWBALL IS A GOOD SOLID CORE.
A ROCK OR STEEL BOLT WILL ADD WEIGHT TO IMPROVE ACCURACY, RANGE AND IMPACT.
OKAY, LET'S GET TO WORK.
YOU THINK THIS WILL BE ENOUGH?
HAVE TO BE. THEY'RE HERE!
THERE YOU GO, BOYS. KASS WANTS THAT SHIFTED IN FORTY-EIGHT HOURS.
NO PROBLEM, IF YOU CAN KEEP THE SPIRIT OFF OUR BACKS.

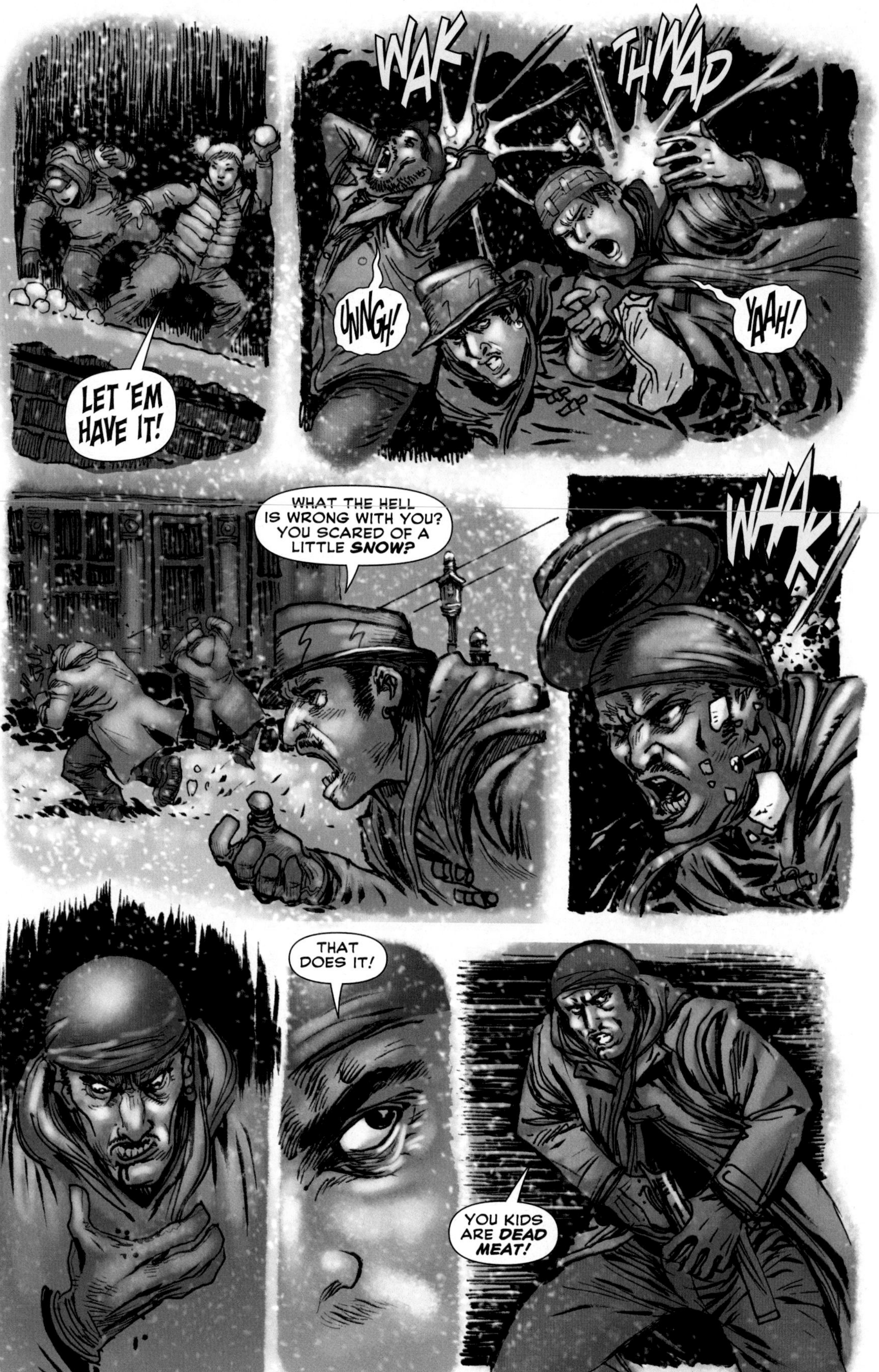
LET 'EM HAVE IT!
WAK
THWAP
UNNGH!
YAAH!
WHAT THE HELL IS WRONG WITH YOU? YOU SCARED OF A LITTLE SNOW?
WHAK
THAT DOES IT!
YOU KIDS ARE DEAD MEAT!

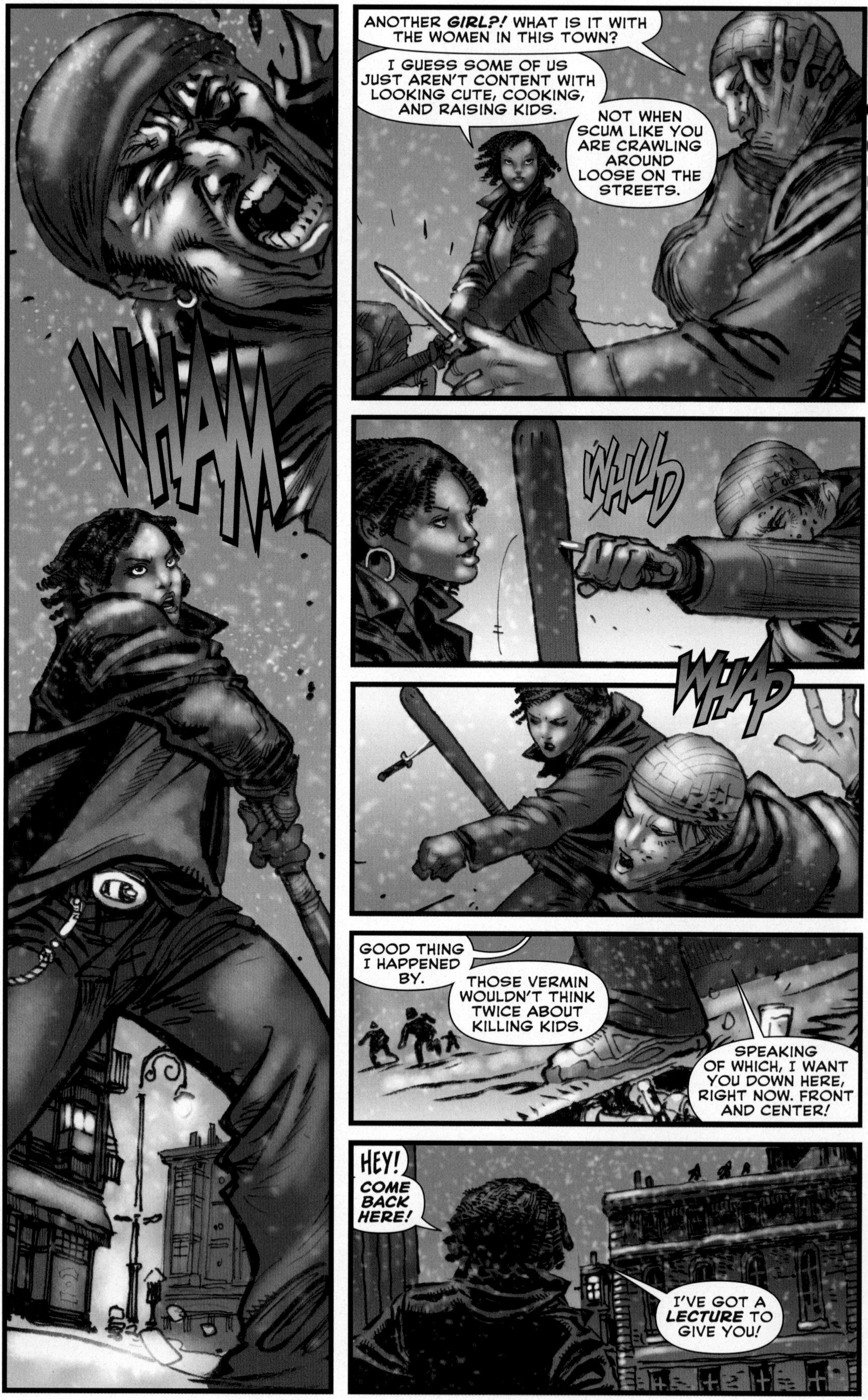
WHAM
ANOTHER GIRL?! WHAT IS IT WITH THE WOMEN IN THIS TOWN?
I GUESS SOME OF US JUST AREN'T CONTENT WITH LOOKING CUTE, COOKING, AND RAISING KIDS.
NOT WHEN SCUM LIKE YOU ARE CRAWLING AROUND LOOSE ON THE STREETS.
WHUD
WHAP
GOOD THING I HAPPENED BY.
THOSE VERMIN WOULDN'T THINK TWICE ABOUT KILLING KIDS.
SPEAKING OF WHICH, I WANT YOU DOWN HERE, RIGHT NOW. FRONT AND CENTER!
HEY! COME BACK HERE!
I'VE GOT A LECTURE TO GIVE YOU!

DIDJA SEE HIS FACE?

"A LITTLE SNOW AIN'T GONNA HURT YA!"

EVERY TIME THEY SHOW UP IN THE NEIGHBORHOOD, WE HIT THEM.

NOBODY KNOWS THESE STREETS LIKE US. THEY NEVER GONNA CATCH US.

KRAASSSHH

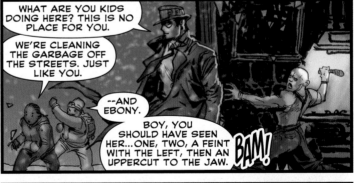

WHAT ARE YOU KIDS DOING HERE? THIS IS NO PLACE FOR YOU.

WE'RE CLEANING THE GARBAGE OFF THE STREETS. JUST LIKE YOU.

--AND EBONY.

BOY, YOU SHOULD HAVE SEEN HER...ONE, TWO, A FEINT WITH THE LEFT, THEN AN UPPERCUT TO THE JAW.

BAM!

WHERE *IS* EBONY? SHE WAS SUPPOSED TO MEET ME HERE.

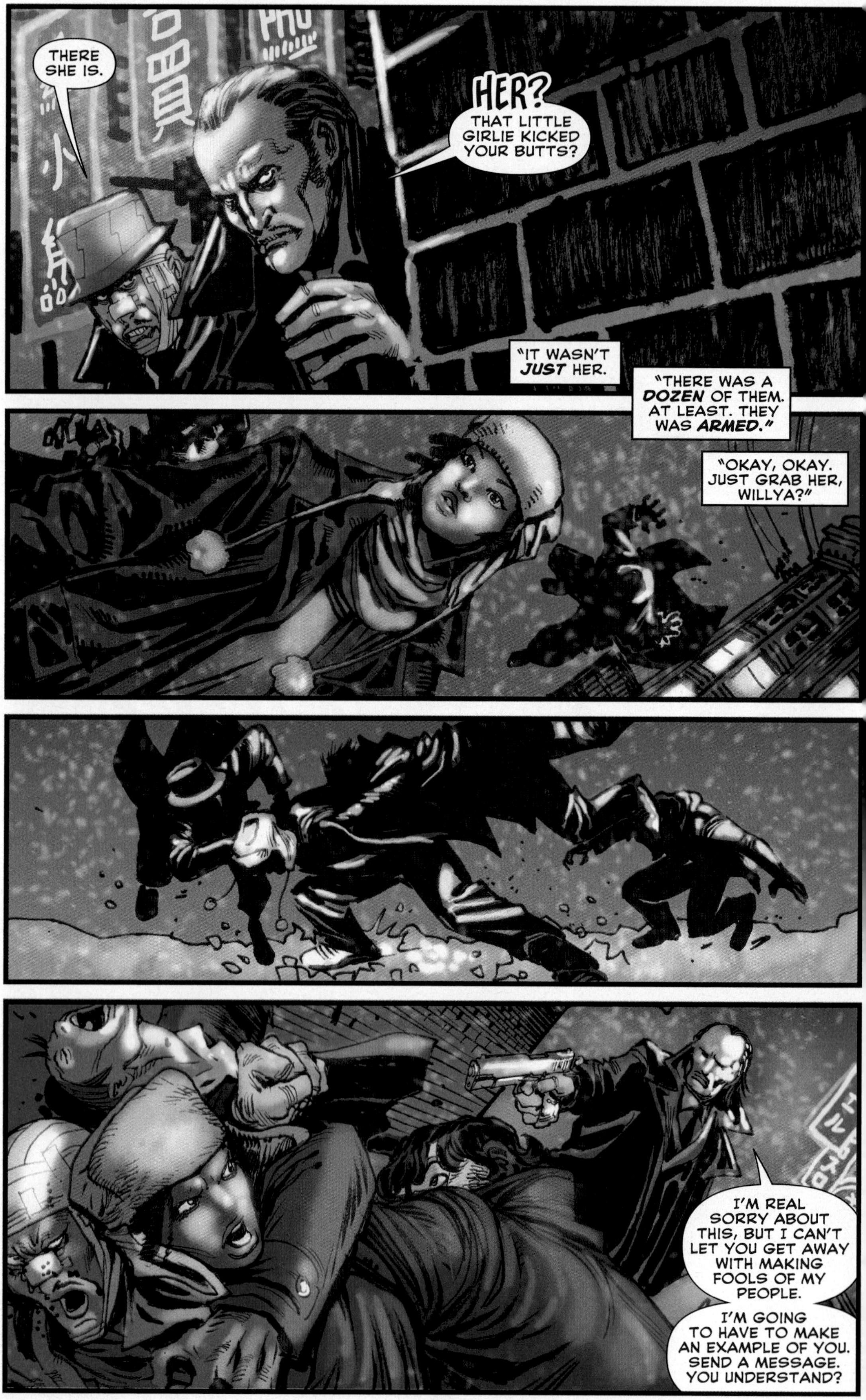

THERE SHE IS.
HER? THAT LITTLE GIRLIE KICKED YOUR BUTTS?
"IT WASN'T JUST HER.
"THERE WAS A DOZEN OF THEM. AT LEAST. THEY WAS ARMED."
"OKAY, OKAY. JUST GRAB HER, WILLYA?"
PHO
I'M REAL SORRY ABOUT THIS, BUT I CAN'T LET YOU GET AWAY WITH MAKING FOOLS OF MY PEOPLE.
I'M GOING TO HAVE TO MAKE AN EXAMPLE OF YOU. SEND A MESSAGE. YOU UNDERSTAND?

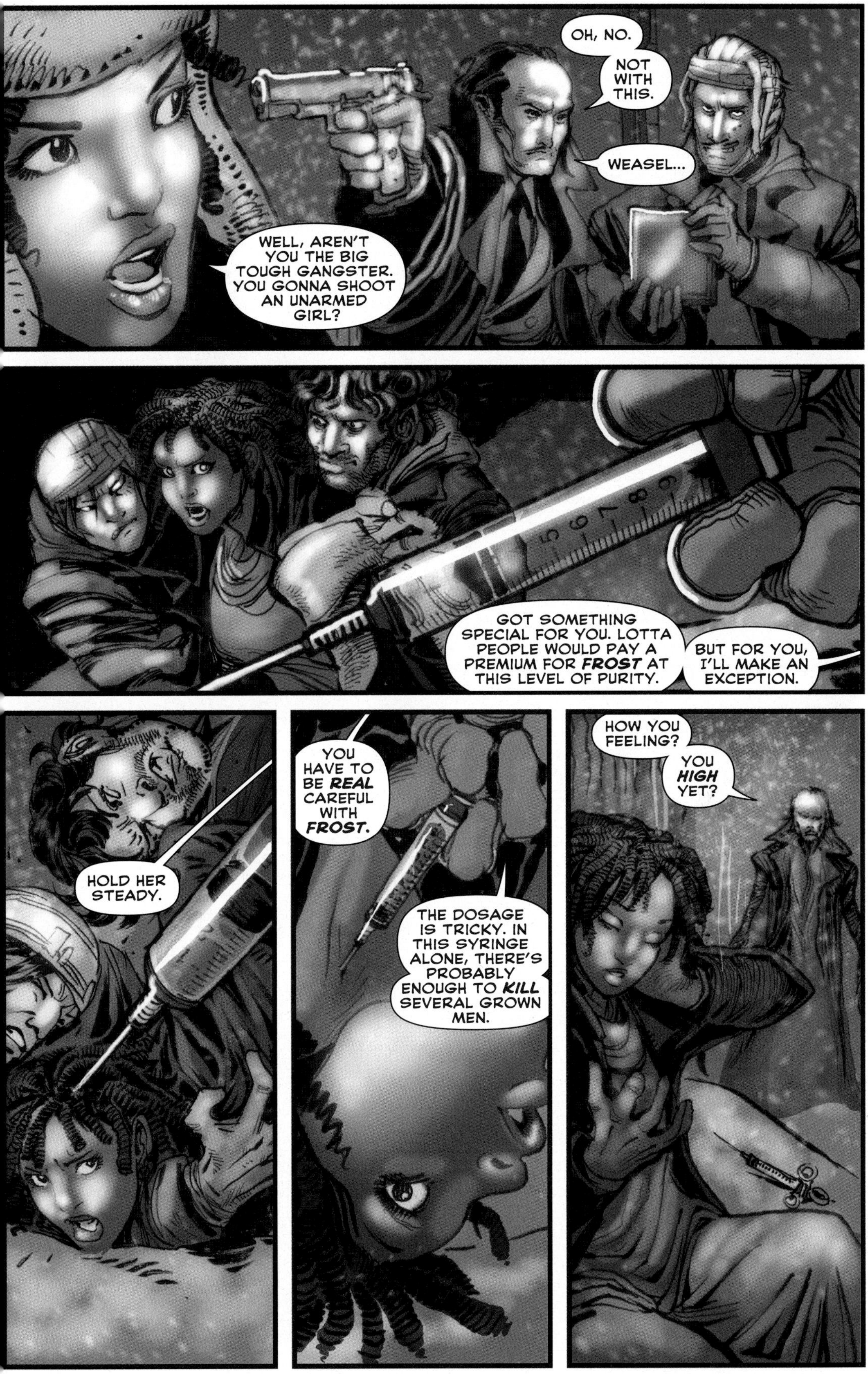
OH, NO.
NOT WITH THIS.
WEASEL...
WELL, AREN'T YOU THE BIG TOUGH GANGSTER. YOU GONNA SHOOT AN UNARMED GIRL?
GOT SOMETHING SPECIAL FOR YOU. LOTTA PEOPLE WOULD PAY A PREMIUM FOR FROST AT THIS LEVEL OF PURITY.
BUT FOR YOU, I'LL MAKE AN EXCEPTION.
HOLD HER STEADY.
YOU HAVE TO BE REAL CAREFUL WITH FROST.
THE DOSAGE IS TRICKY. IN THIS SYRINGE ALONE, THERE'S PROBABLY ENOUGH TO KILL SEVERAL GROWN MEN.
HOW YOU FEELING?
YOU HIGH YET?

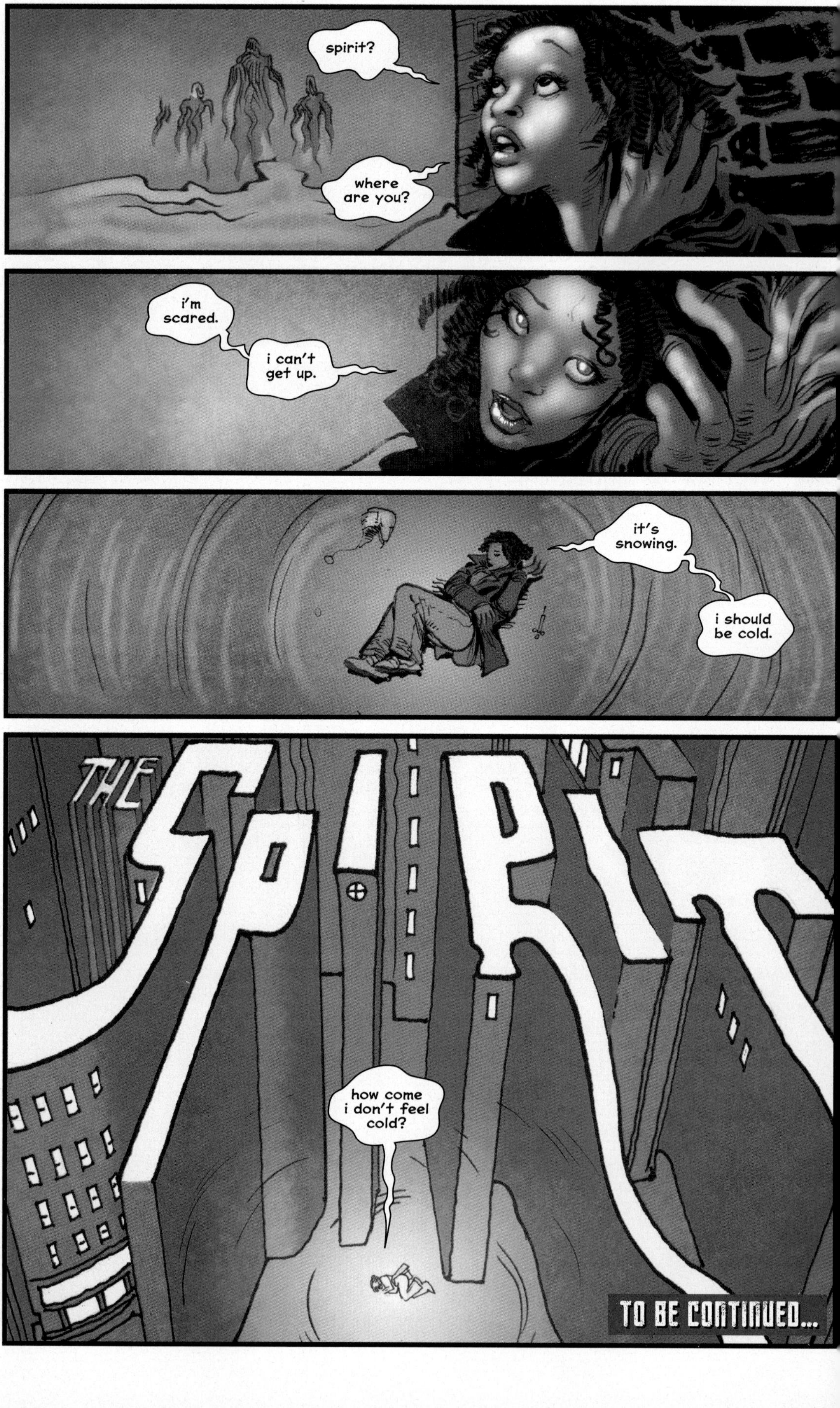
spirit?
where are you?
i'm scared.
i can't get up.
it's snowing.
i should be cold.
THE SPIRIT
how come i don't feel cold?
TO BE CONTINUED...

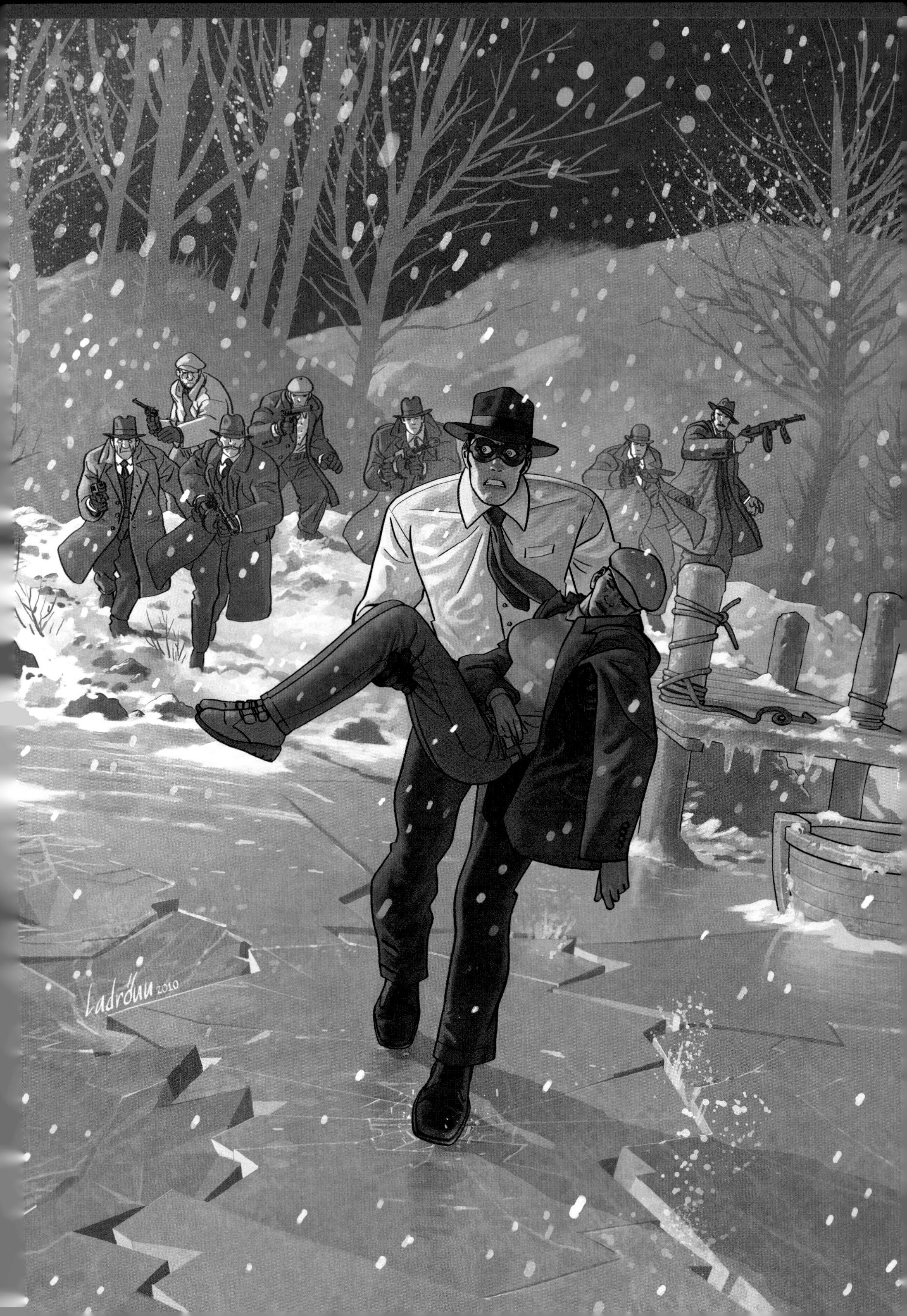
Ladrönn 2010

so tired...
have to take
a rest...

...no no no...that's
what the others did...
the ones who died...

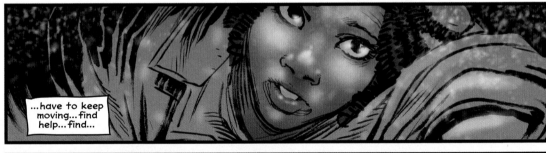

...have to keep
moving...find
help...find...

...okay...that's not real...
that's the dope...making
me see things...

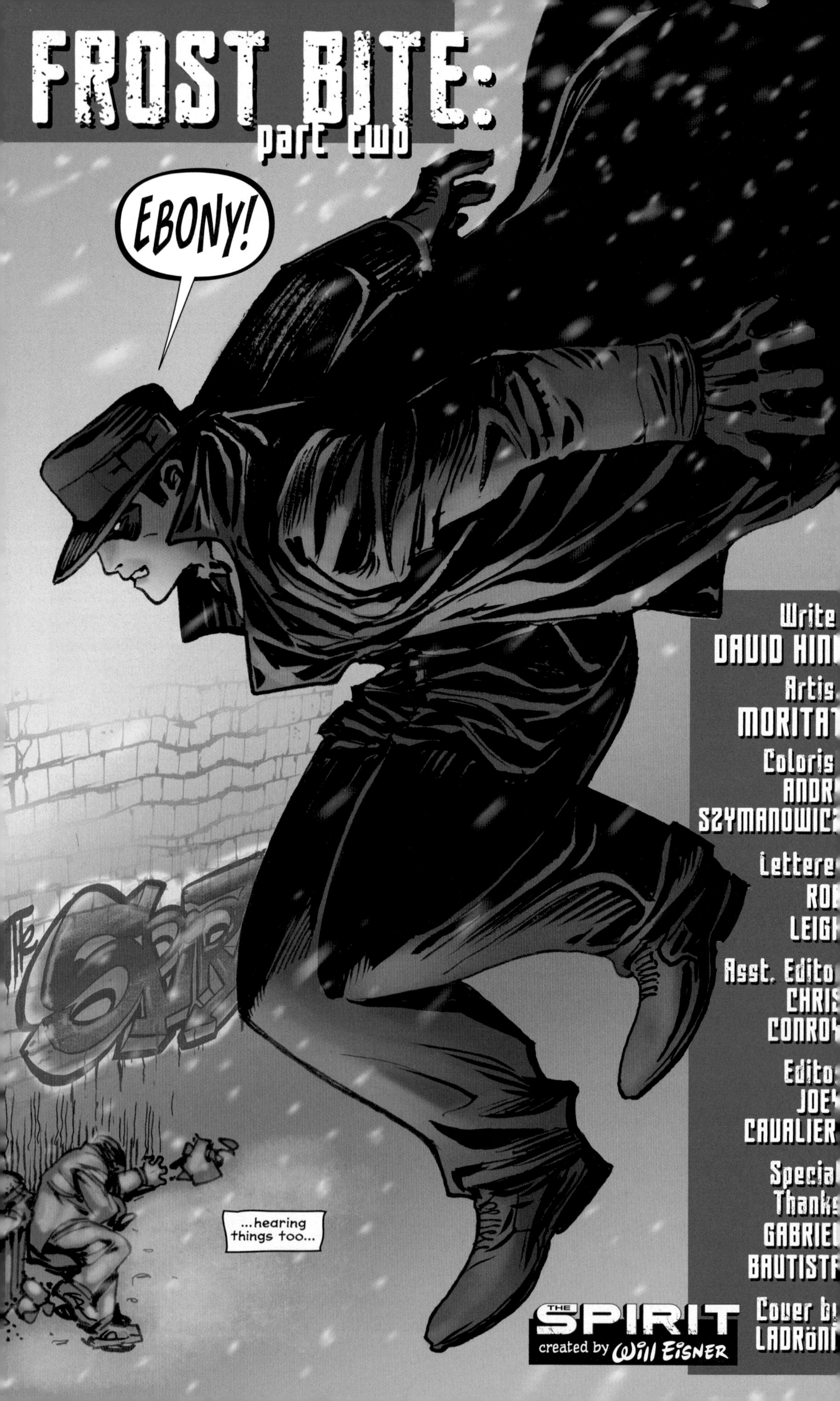
FROST BITE:
part two
EBONY!
...hearing things too...
Write
DAVID HIN
Artis
MORITAT
Coloris
ANDR
SZYMANOWIC
Lettere
RO
LEIG
Asst. Edito
CHRIS
CONRO
Edito
JOE
CAVALIER
Special
Thank
GABRIE
BAUTIST
THE SPIRIT
created by Will Eisner
Cover b
LADRÖN

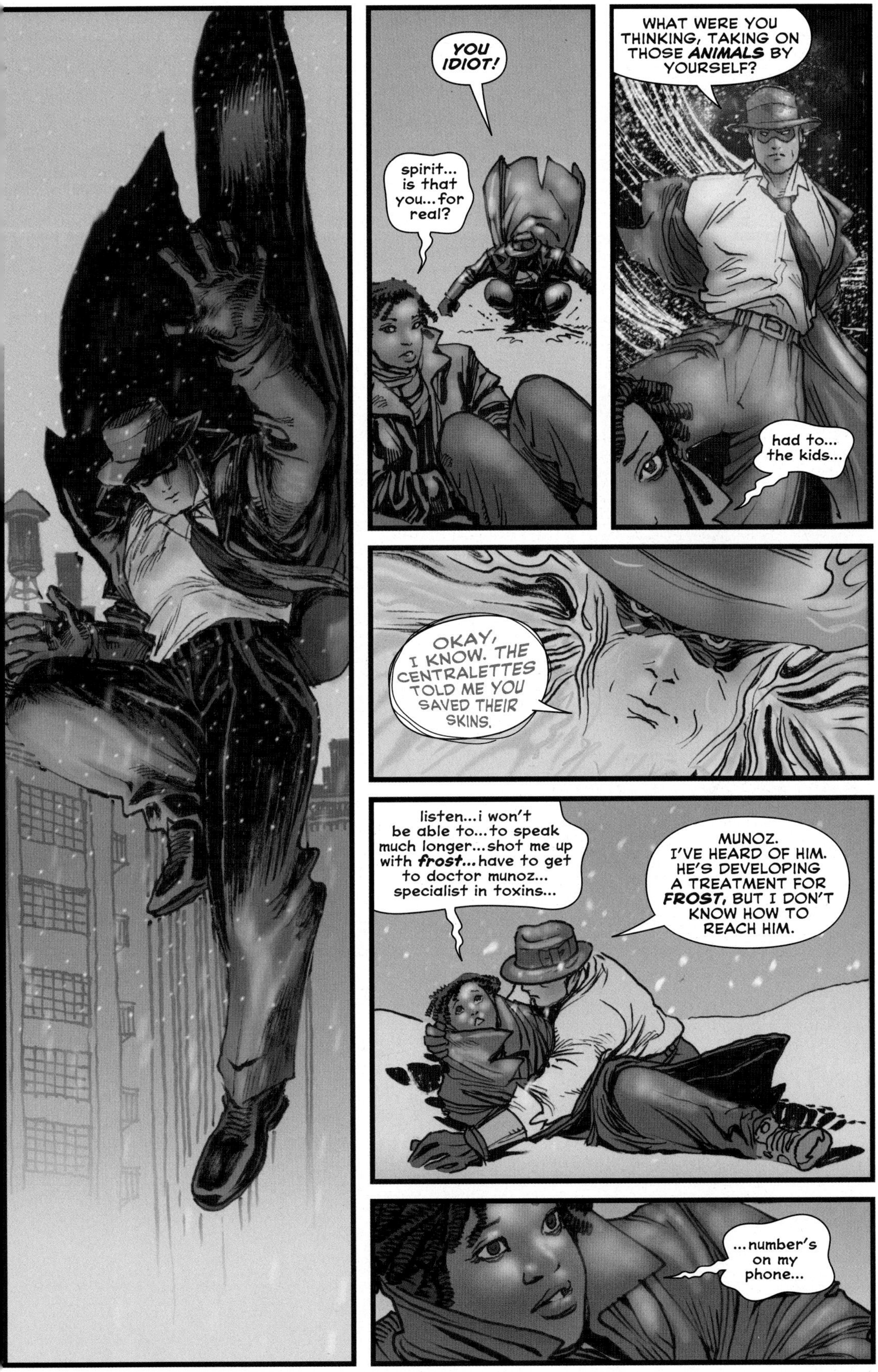

YOU IDIOT!
spirit... is that you...for real?
WHAT WERE YOU THINKING, TAKING ON THOSE ANIMALS BY YOURSELF?
had to... the kids...
OKAY, I KNOW. THE CENTRALETTES TOLD ME YOU SAVED THEIR SKINS.
listen...i won't be able to...to speak much longer...shot me up with frost...have to get to doctor munoz... specialist in toxins...
MUNOZ. I'VE HEARD OF HIM. HE'S DEVELOPING A TREATMENT FOR FROST, BUT I DON'T KNOW HOW TO REACH HIM.
...number's on my phone...

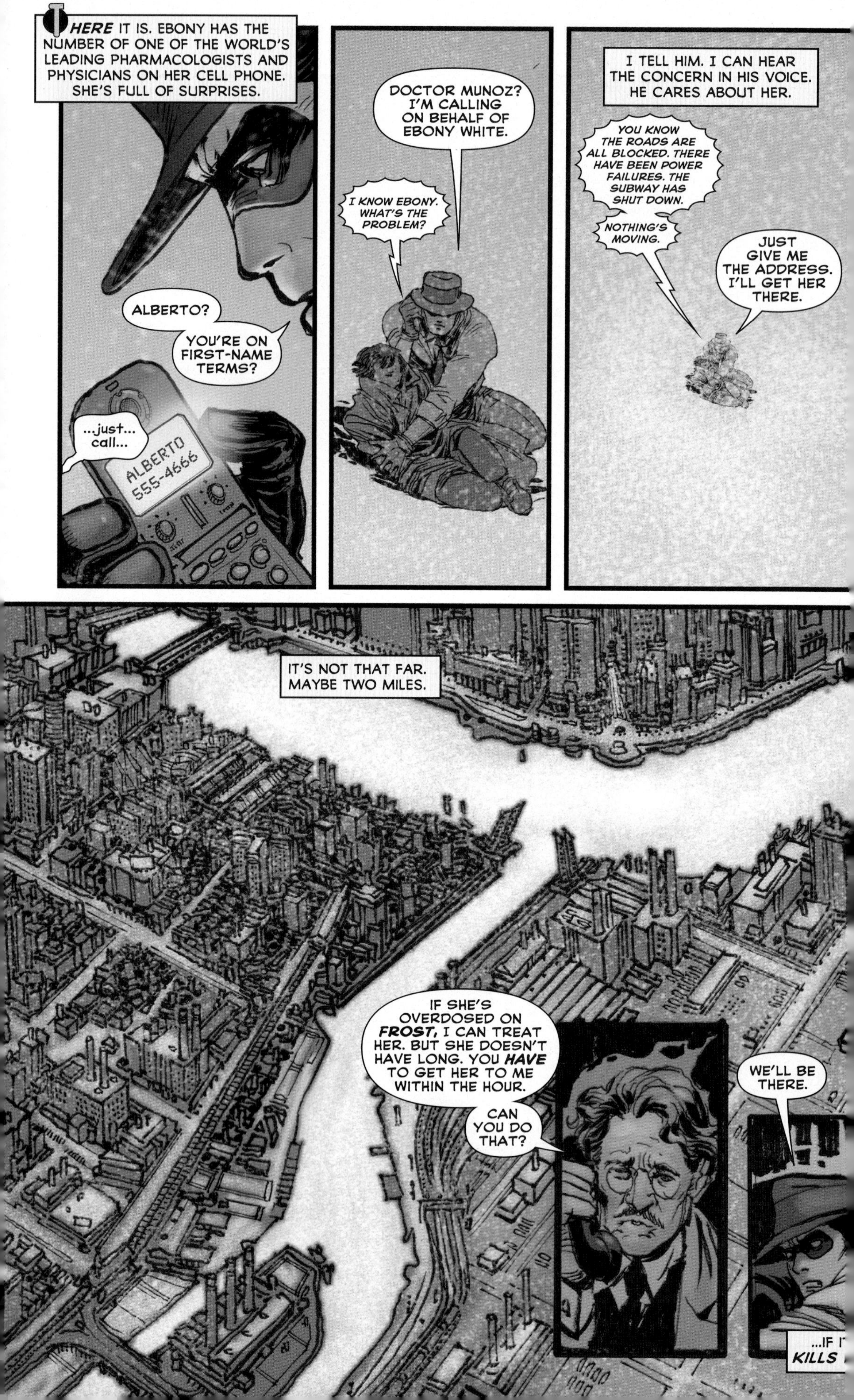
THERE IT IS. EBONY HAS THE NUMBER OF ONE OF THE WORLD'S LEADING PHARMACOLOGISTS AND PHYSICIANS ON HER CELL PHONE. SHE'S FULL OF SURPRISES.
ALBERTO?
YOU'RE ON FIRST-NAME TERMS?
...just... call...
ALBERTO 555-4666
DOCTOR MUNOZ? I'M CALLING ON BEHALF OF EBONY WHITE.
I KNOW EBONY. WHAT'S THE PROBLEM?
I TELL HIM. I CAN HEAR THE CONCERN IN HIS VOICE. HE CARES ABOUT HER.
YOU KNOW THE ROADS ARE ALL BLOCKED. THERE HAVE BEEN POWER FAILURES. THE SUBWAY HAS SHUT DOWN.
NOTHING'S MOVING.
JUST GIVE ME THE ADDRESS. I'LL GET HER THERE.
IT'S NOT THAT FAR. MAYBE TWO MILES.
IF SHE'S OVERDOSED ON FROST, I CAN TREAT HER. BUT SHE DOESN'T HAVE LONG. YOU HAVE TO GET HER TO ME WITHIN THE HOUR.
CAN YOU DO THAT?
WE'LL BE THERE.
...IF I
KILLS

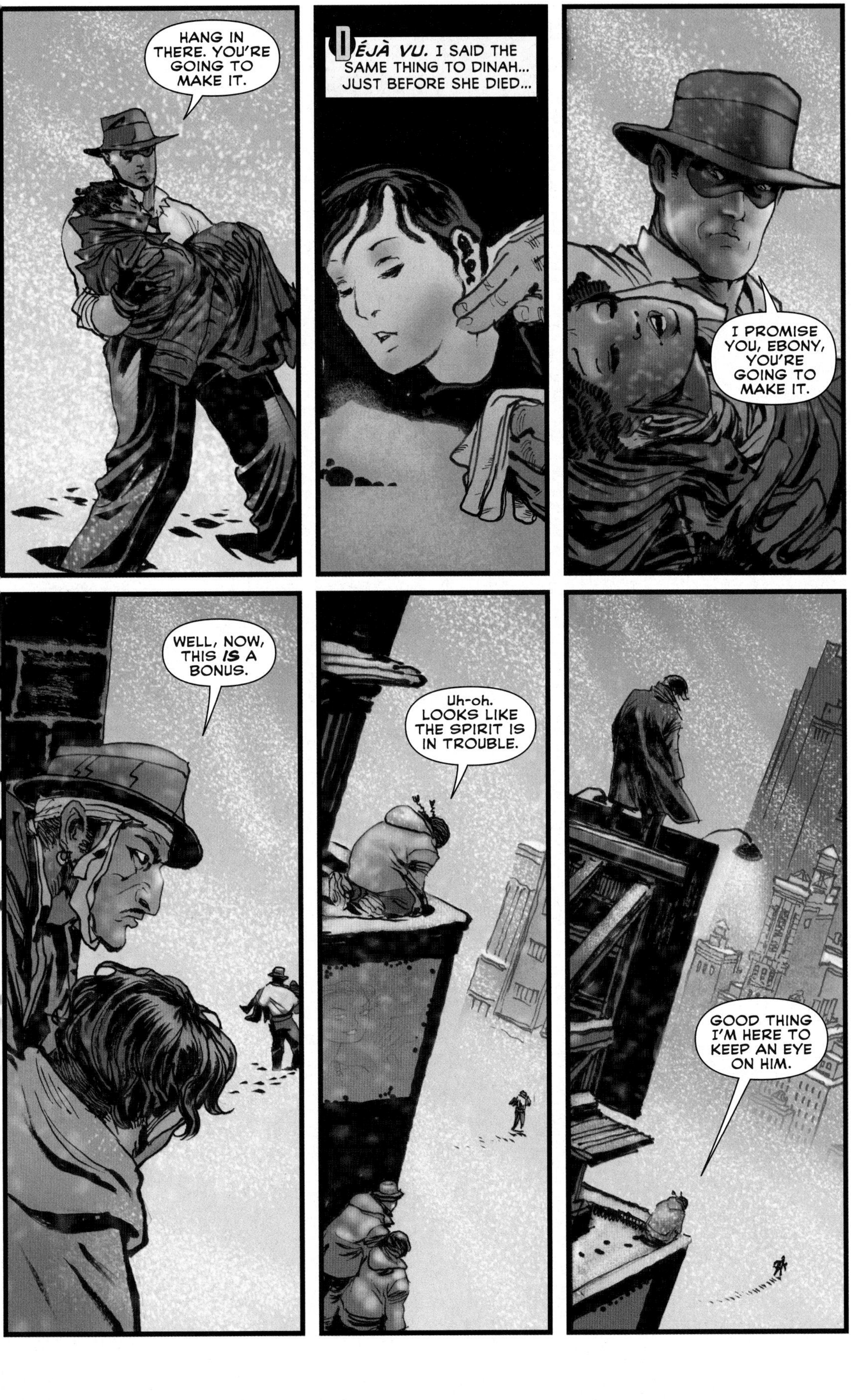
HANG IN THERE. YOU'RE GOING TO MAKE IT.
DÉJÀ VU. I SAID THE SAME THING TO DINAH... JUST BEFORE SHE DIED...
I PROMISE YOU, EBONY, YOU'RE GOING TO MAKE IT.
WELL, NOW, THIS IS A BONUS.
Uh-oh. LOOKS LIKE THE SPIRIT IS IN TROUBLE.
GOOD THING I'M HERE TO KEEP AN EYE ON HIM.

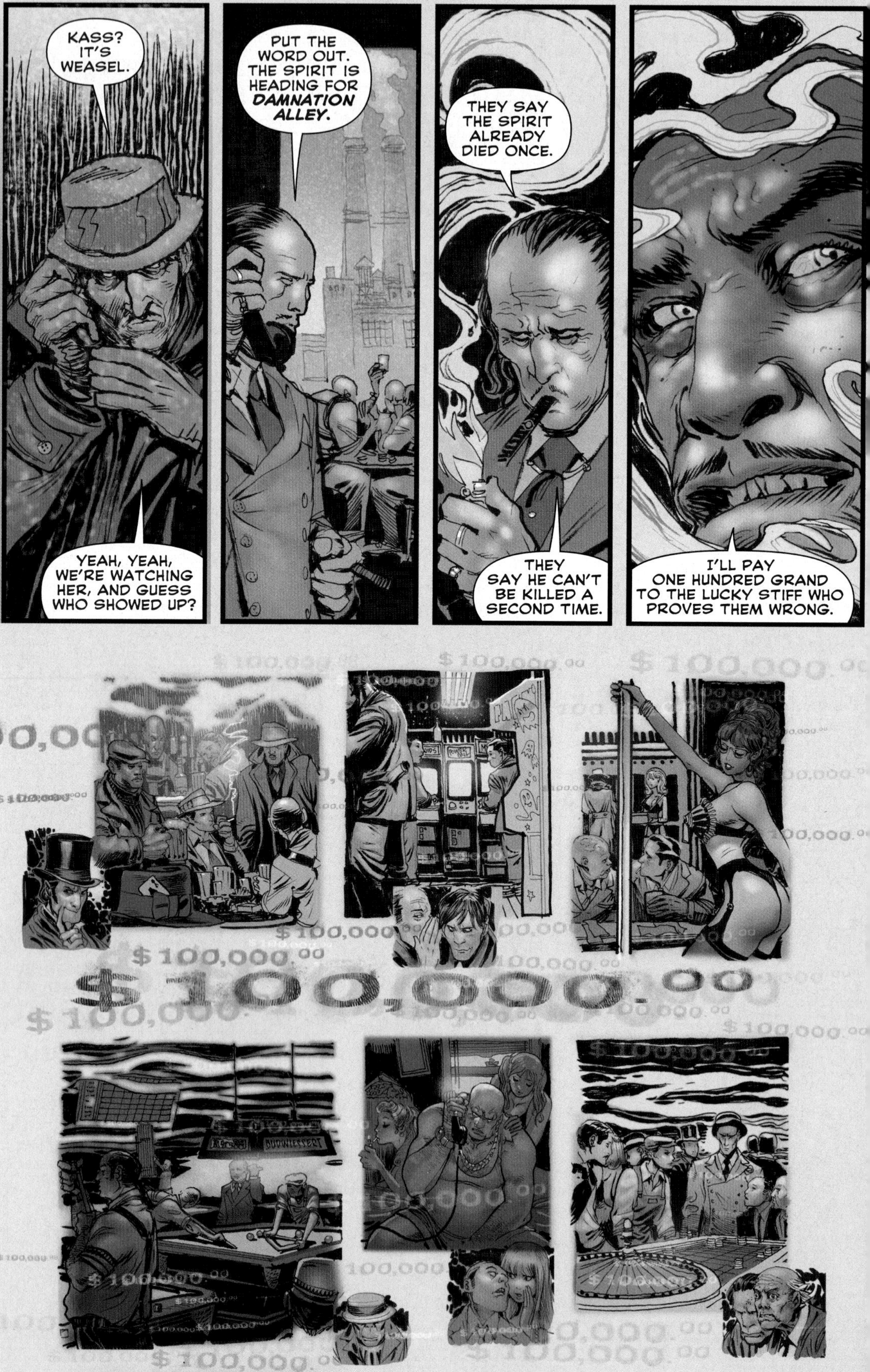
KASS? IT'S WEASEL.
YEAH, YEAH, WE'RE WATCHING HER, AND GUESS WHO SHOWED UP?
PUT THE WORD OUT. THE SPIRIT IS HEADING FOR *DAMNATION ALLEY.*
THEY SAY THE SPIRIT ALREADY DIED ONCE.
THEY SAY HE CAN'T BE KILLED A SECOND TIME.
I'LL PAY ONE HUNDRED GRAND TO THE LUCKY STIFF WHO PROVES THEM WRONG.
$100,000.00

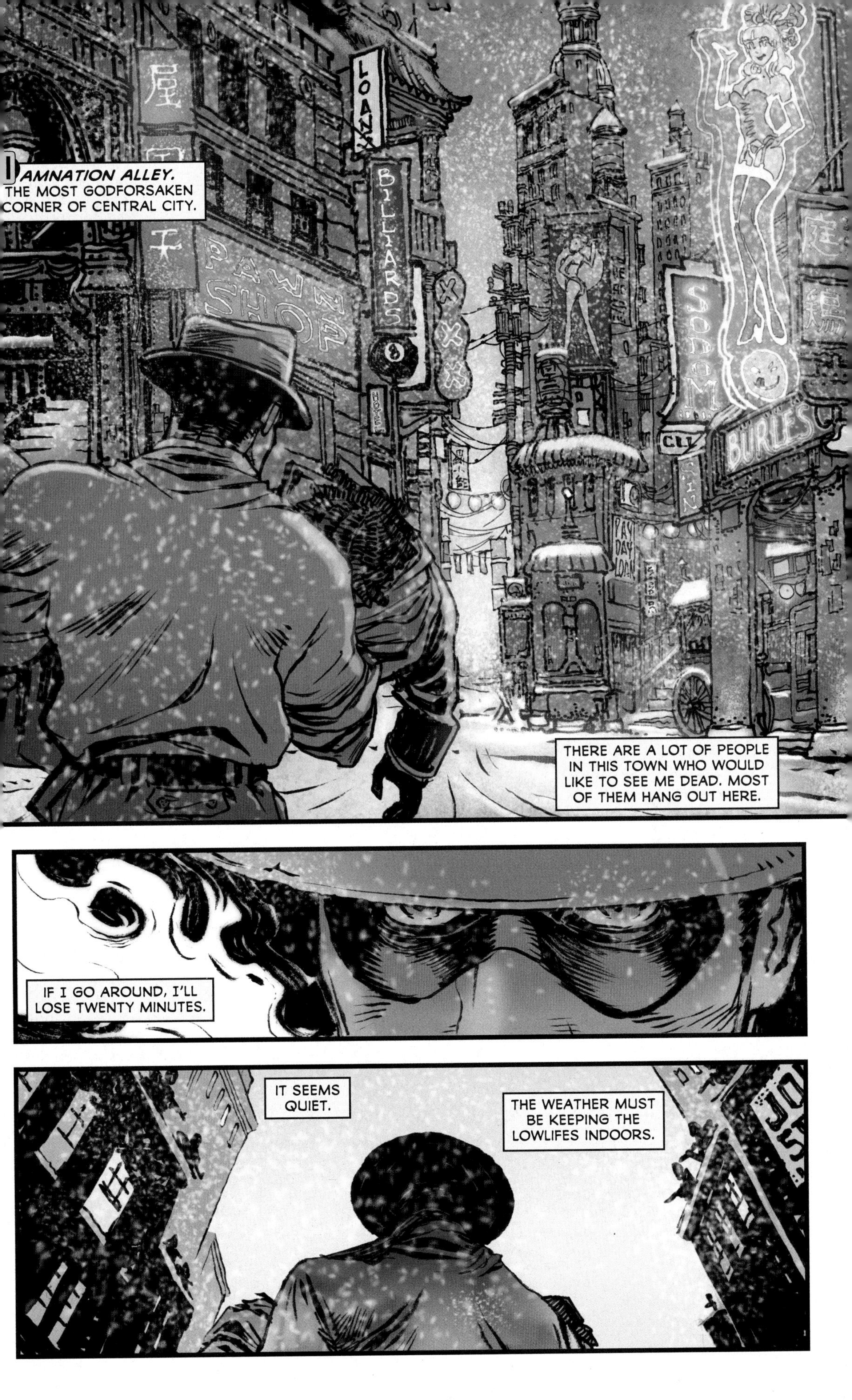
DAMNATION ALLEY.
THE MOST GODFORSAKEN CORNER OF CENTRAL CITY.
LOANS
BILLIARDS
PAWN SHOP
HOTEL
PAY DAY LOAN
SODOM
BURLES
THERE ARE A LOT OF PEOPLE IN THIS TOWN WHO WOULD LIKE TO SEE ME DEAD. MOST OF THEM HANG OUT HERE.
IF I GO AROUND, I'LL LOSE TWENTY MINUTES.
IT SEEMS QUIET.
THE WEATHER MUST BE KEEPING THE LOWLIFES INDOORS.

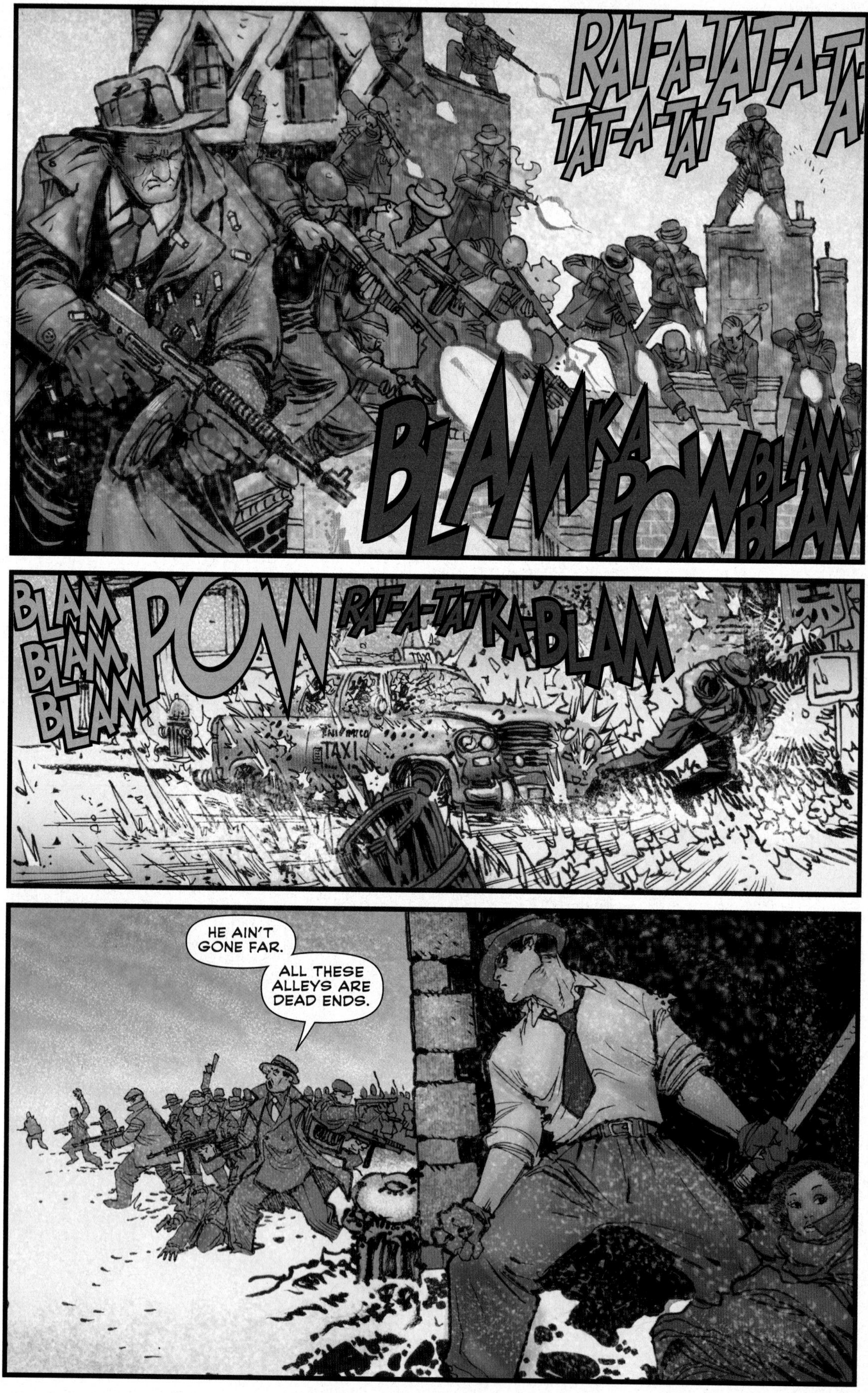
RAT-A-TAT-A-TAT-A
TAT-A-TAT-A-TAT
BLAMKAPOW BLAM BLAM
BLAM BLAM BLAM
POW
RAT-A-TATKA-BLAM
TAXI
HE AIN'T GONE FAR.
ALL THESE ALLEYS ARE DEAD ENDS.

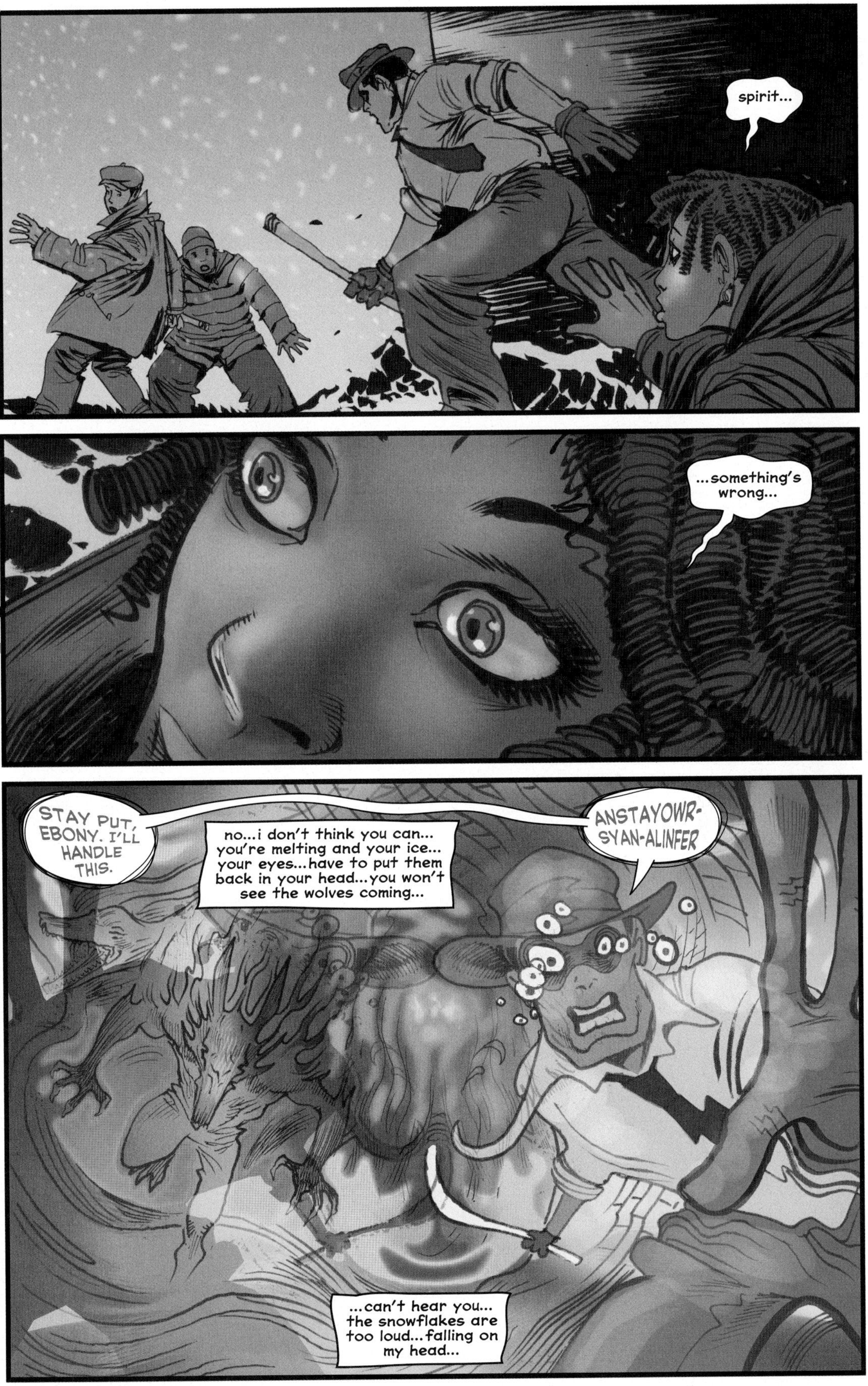
spirit...
...something's wrong...
STAY PUT, EBONY. I'LL HANDLE THIS.
ANSTAYOWR-SYAN-ALINFER
no...i don't think you can... you're melting and your ice... your eyes...have to put them back in your head...you won't see the wolves coming...
...can't hear you... the snowflakes are too loud...falling on my head...

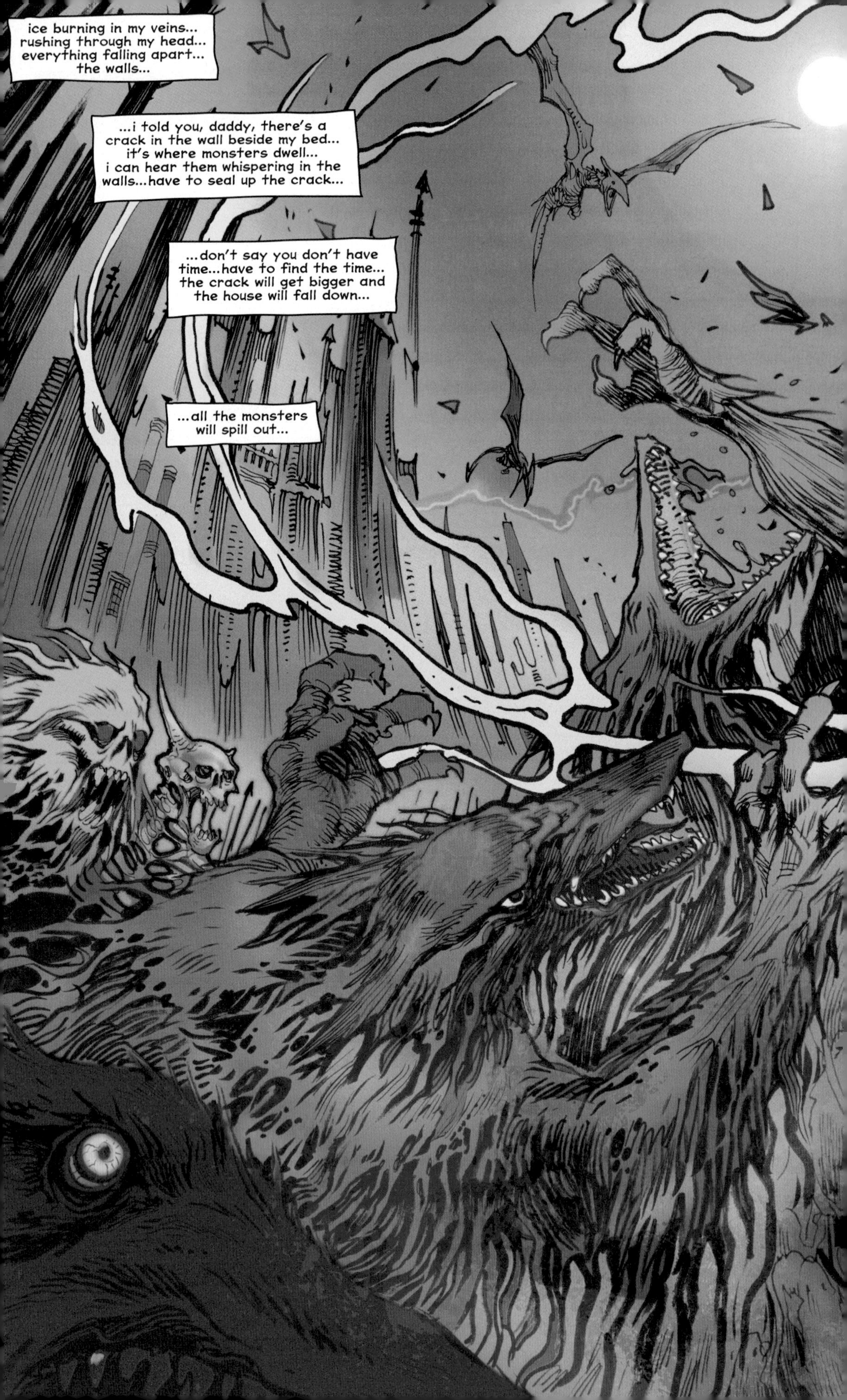
ice burning in my veins... rushing through my head... everything falling apart... the walls...
...i told you, daddy, there's a crack in the wall beside my bed... it's where monsters dwell... i can hear them whispering in the walls...have to seal up the crack...
...don't say you don't have time...have to find the time... the crack will get bigger and the house will fall down...
...all the monsters will spill out...

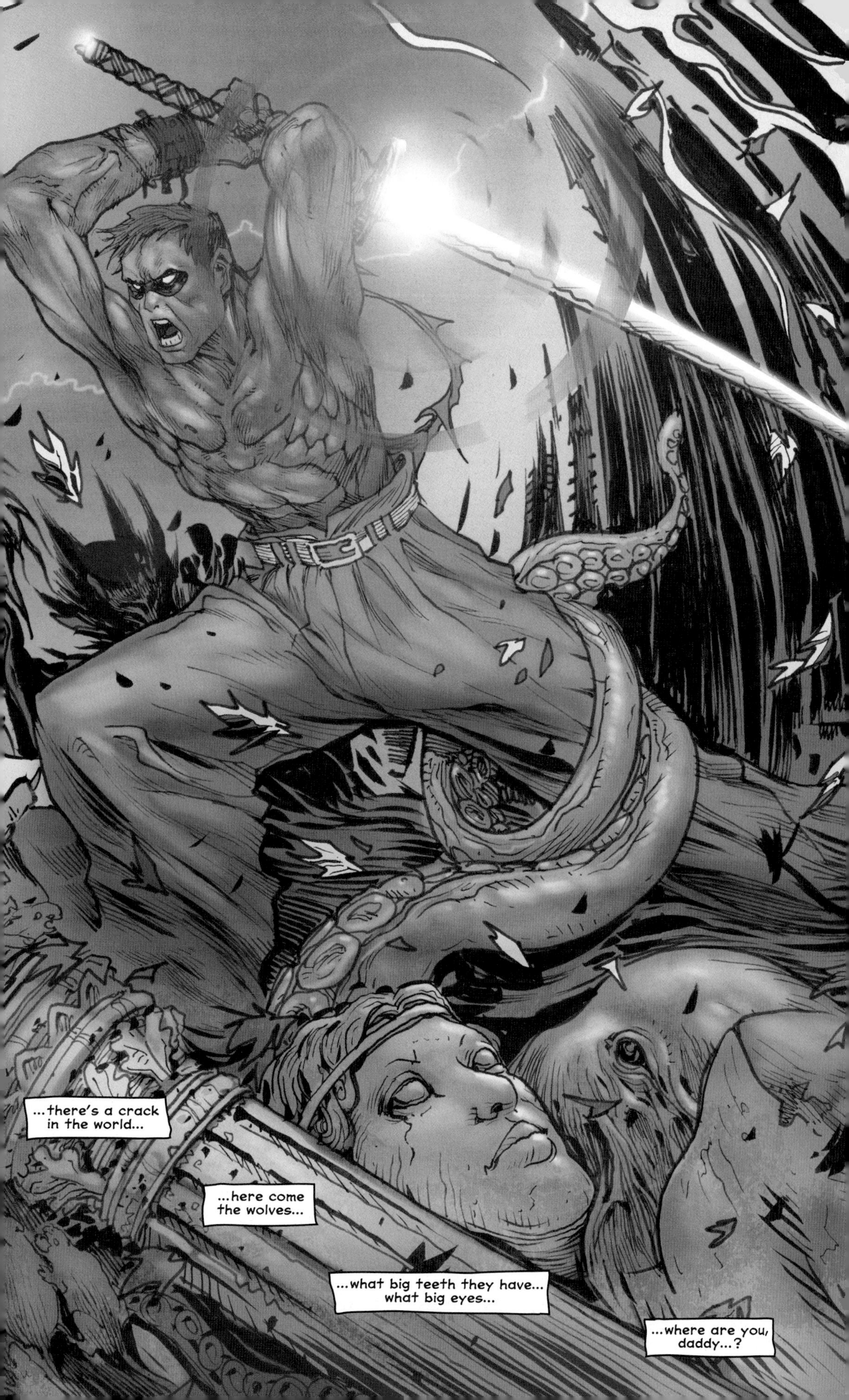
...there's a crack in the world...
...here come the wolves...
...what big teeth they have... what big eyes...
...where are you, daddy...?

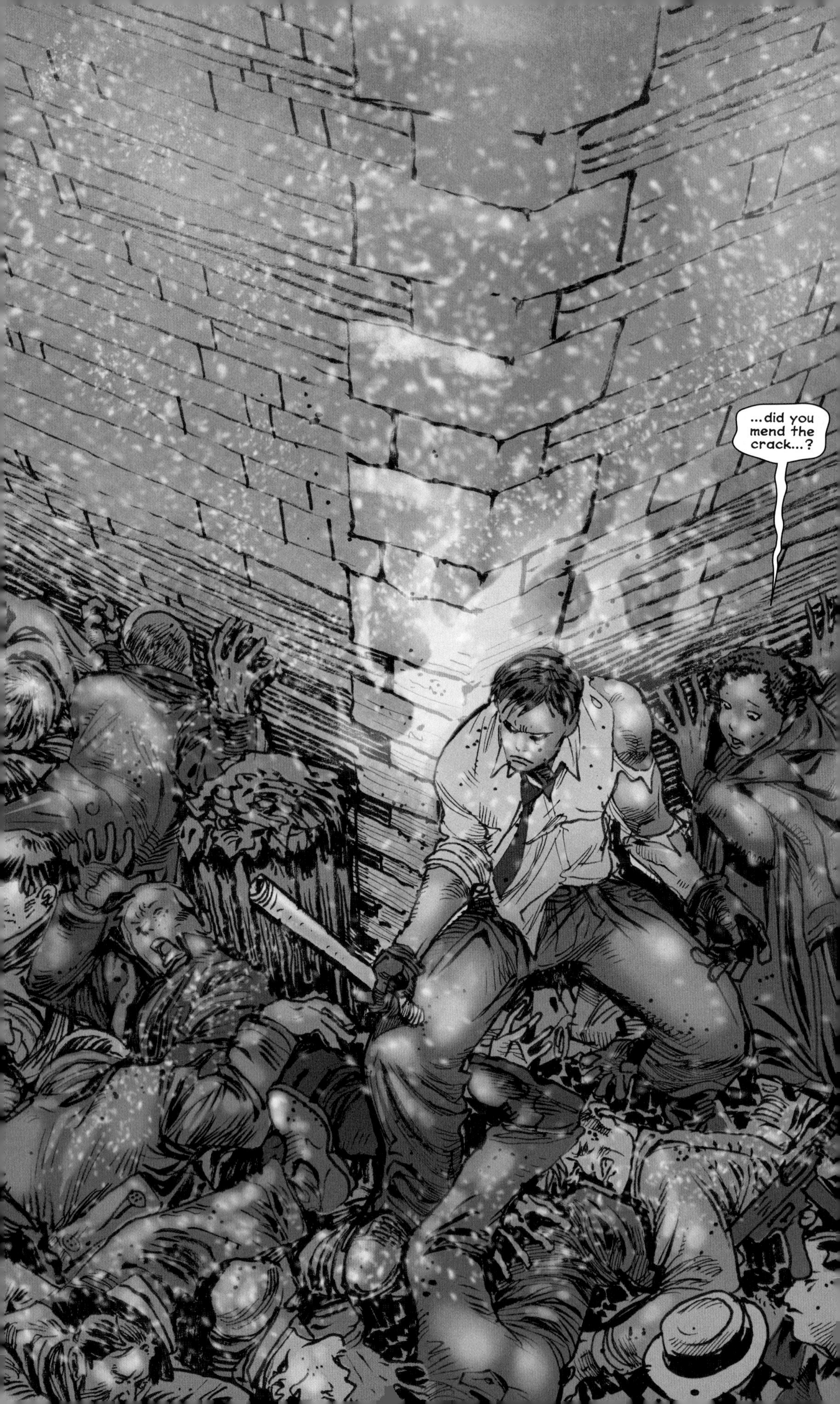
...did you mend the crack...?

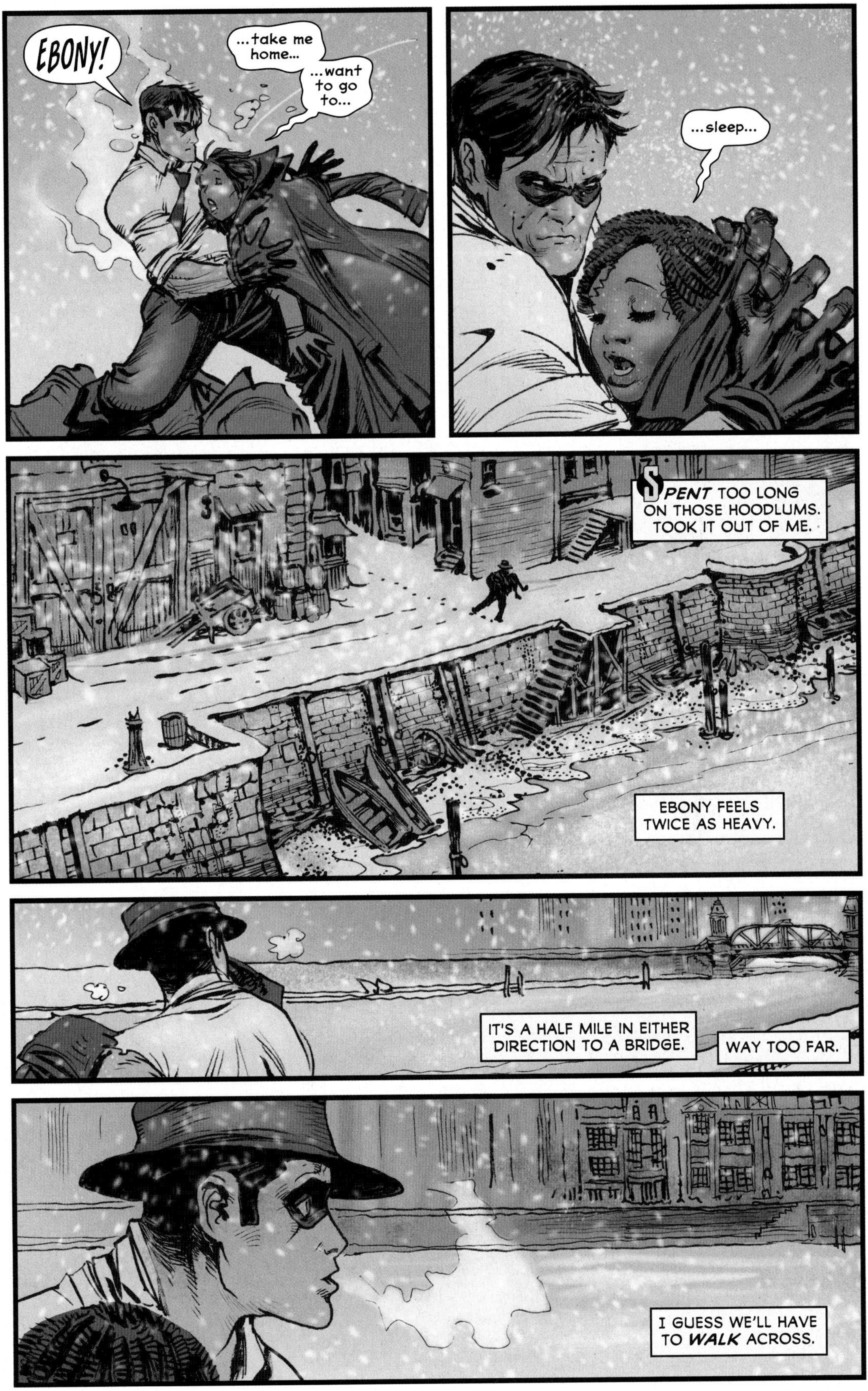
EBONY!
...take me home...
...want to go to...
...sleep...
SPENT TOO LONG ON THOSE HOODLUMS. TOOK IT OUT OF ME.
EBONY FEELS TWICE AS HEAVY.
IT'S A HALF MILE IN EITHER DIRECTION TO A BRIDGE.
WAY TOO FAR.
I GUESS WE'LL HAVE TO WALK ACROSS.

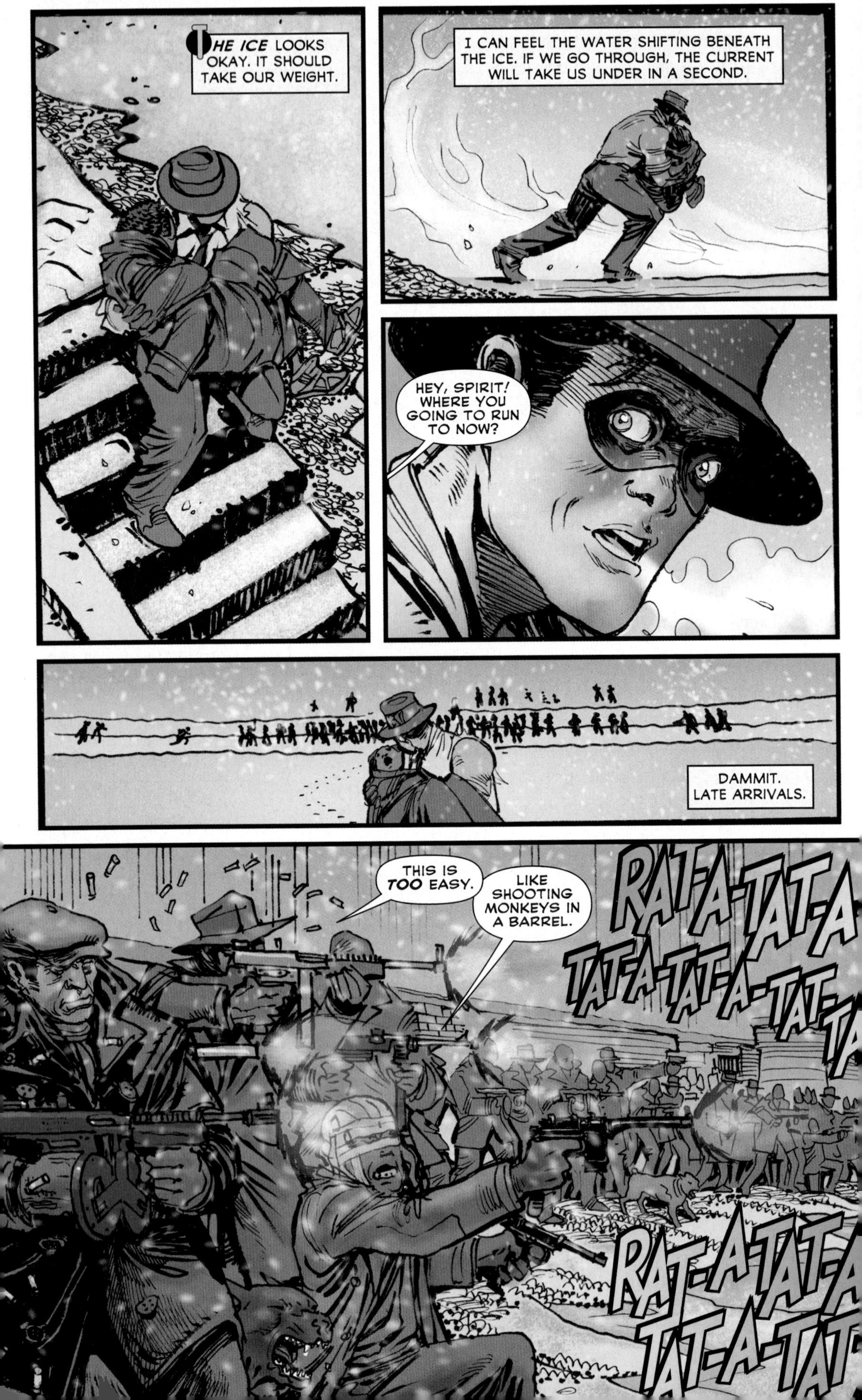

THE ICE LOOKS OKAY. IT SHOULD TAKE OUR WEIGHT.
I CAN FEEL THE WATER SHIFTING BENEATH THE ICE. IF WE GO THROUGH, THE CURRENT WILL TAKE US UNDER IN A SECOND.
HEY, SPIRIT! WHERE YOU GOING TO RUN TO NOW?
DAMMIT. LATE ARRIVALS.
THIS IS TOO EASY.
LIKE SHOOTING MONKEYS IN A BARREL.
RAT-A-TAT-A TAT-A-TAT-A-TAT-TA
RAT-A-TAT-A TAT-A-TAT

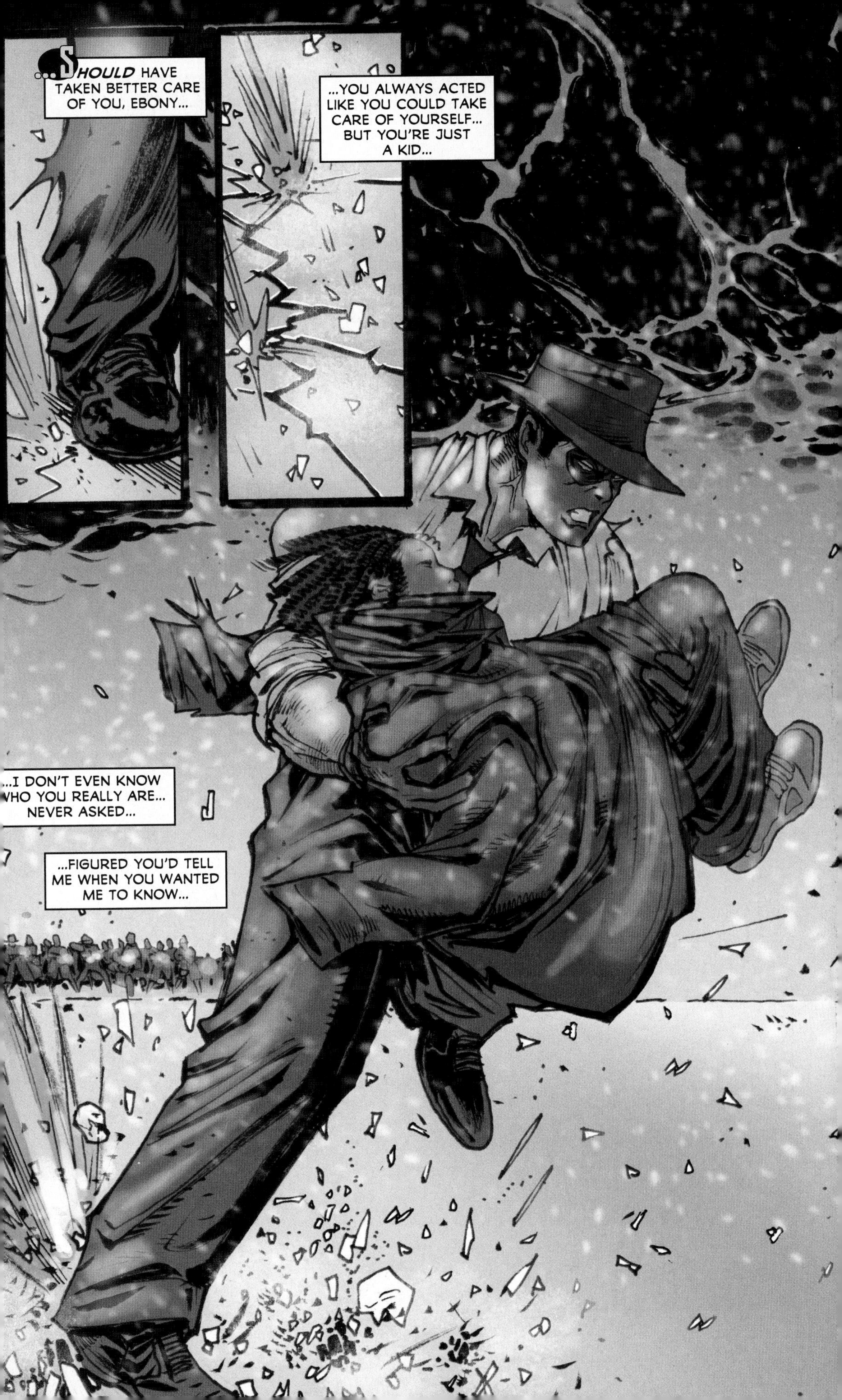
...SHOULD HAVE TAKEN BETTER CARE OF YOU, EBONY...
...YOU ALWAYS ACTED LIKE YOU COULD TAKE CARE OF YOURSELF... BUT YOU'RE JUST A KID...
...I DON'T EVEN KNOW WHO YOU REALLY ARE... NEVER ASKED...
...FIGURED YOU'D TELL ME WHEN YOU WANTED ME TO KNOW...

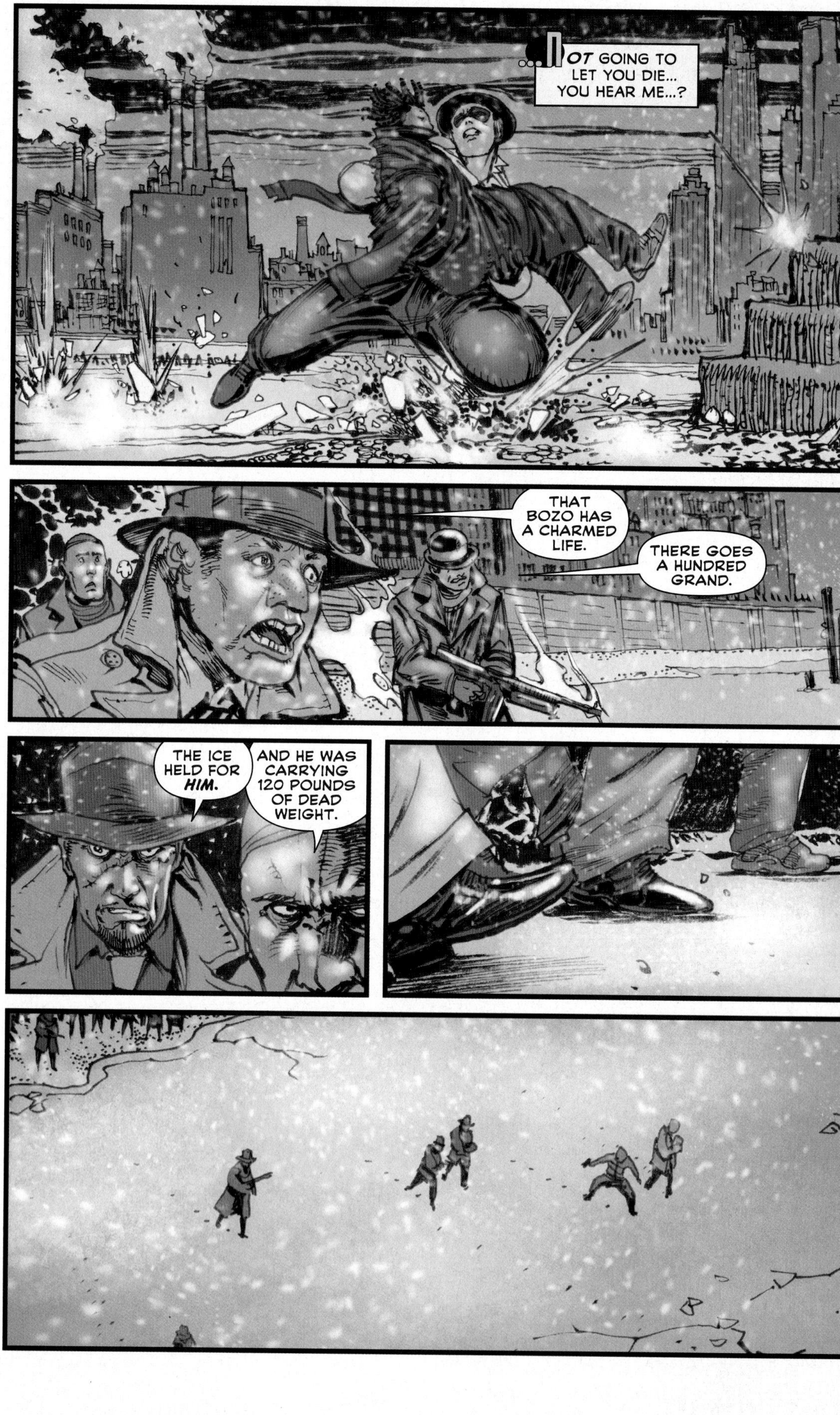
...NOT GOING TO LET YOU DIE... YOU HEAR ME...?
THAT BOZO HAS A CHARMED LIFE.
THERE GOES A HUNDRED GRAND.
THE ICE HELD FOR *HIM*.
AND HE WAS CARRYING 120 POUNDS OF DEAD WEIGHT.

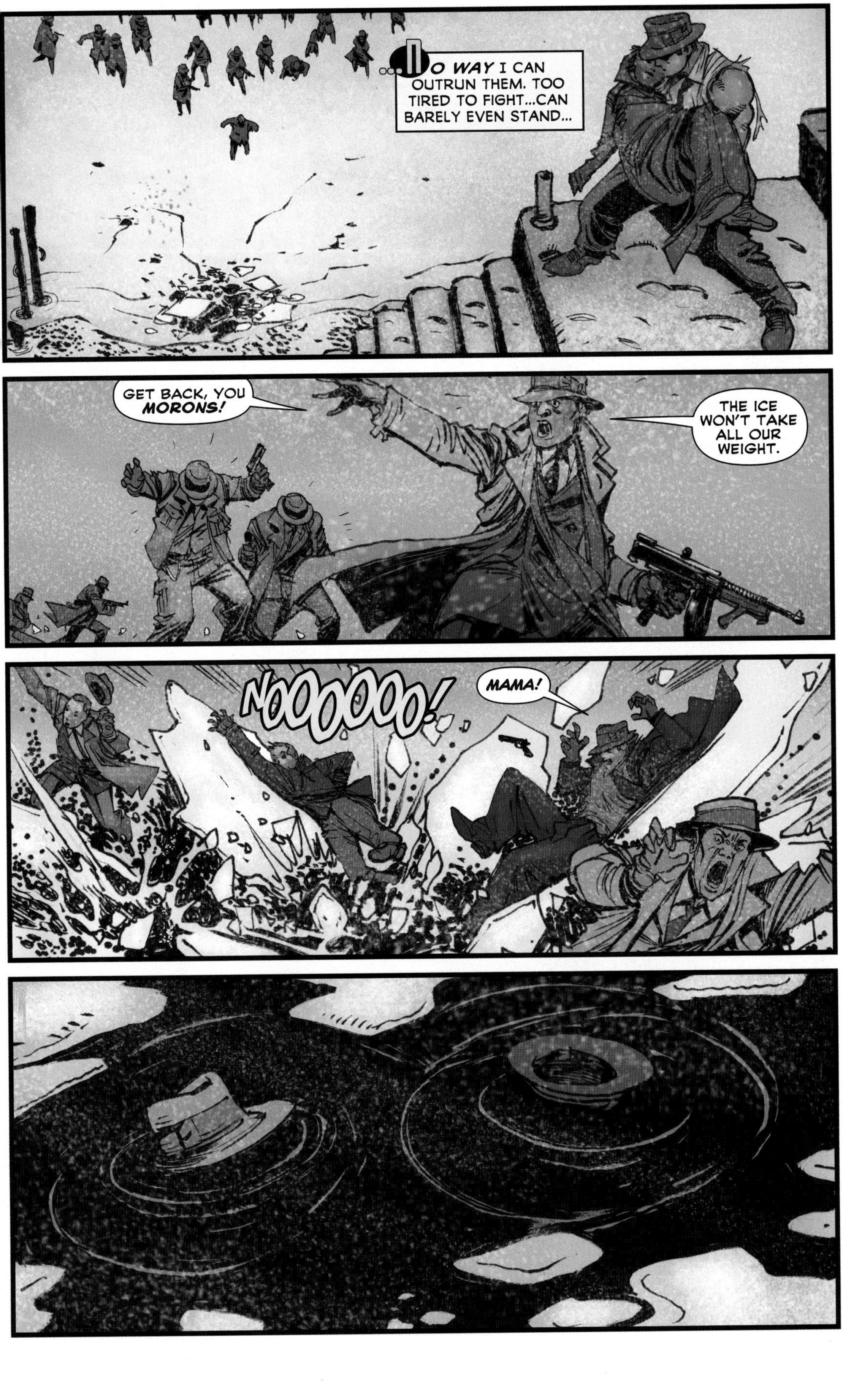
...NO WAY I CAN OUTRUN THEM. TOO TIRED TO FIGHT...CAN BARELY EVEN STAND...
GET BACK, YOU MORONS!
THE ICE WON'T TAKE ALL OUR WEIGHT.
NOOOOOO!
MAMA!

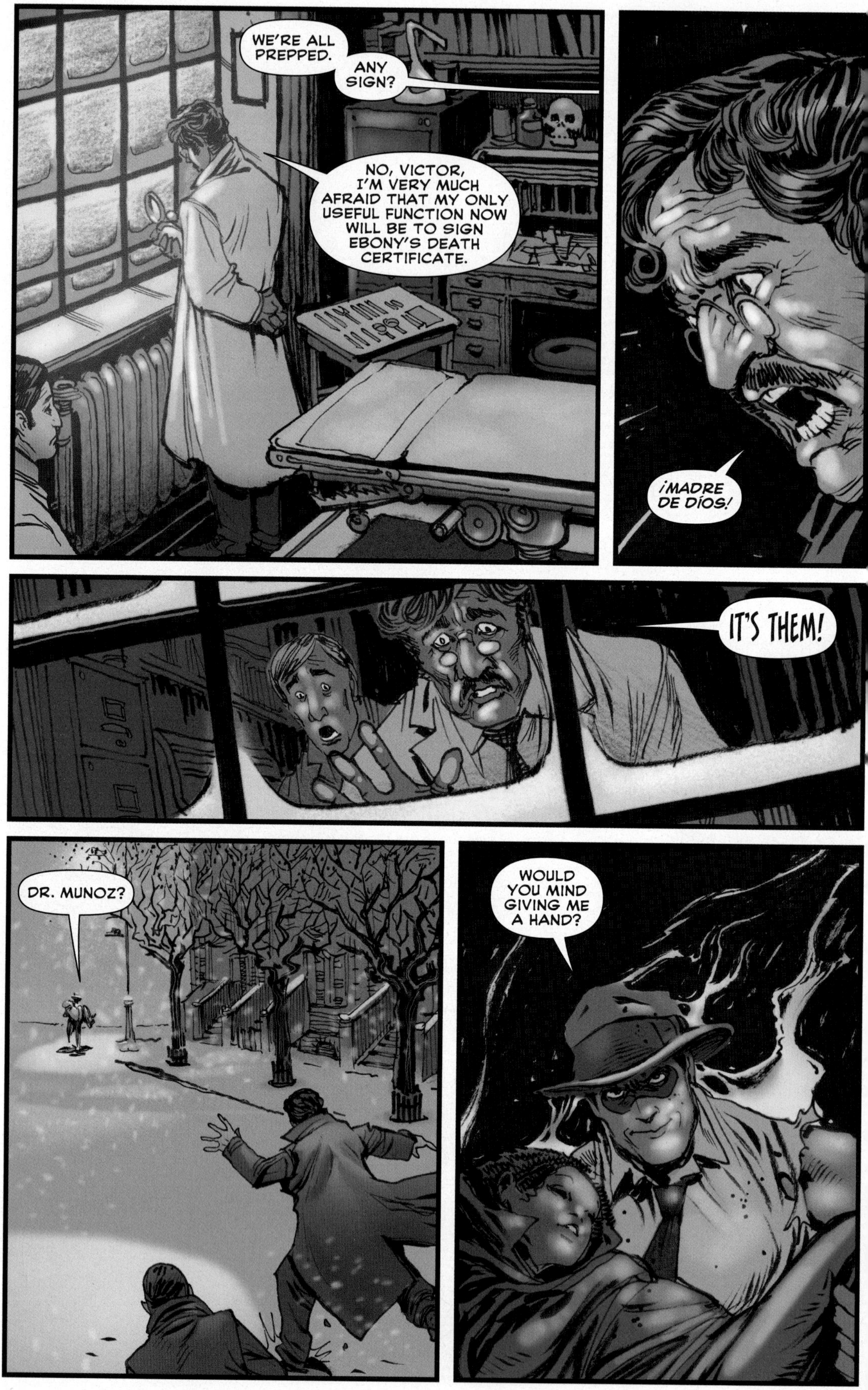
WE'RE ALL PREPPED.
ANY SIGN?
NO, VICTOR, I'M VERY MUCH AFRAID THAT MY ONLY USEFUL FUNCTION NOW WILL BE TO SIGN EBONY'S DEATH CERTIFICATE.
¡MADRE DE DÍOS!
IT'S THEM!
DR. MUNOZ?
WOULD YOU MIND GIVING ME A HAND?

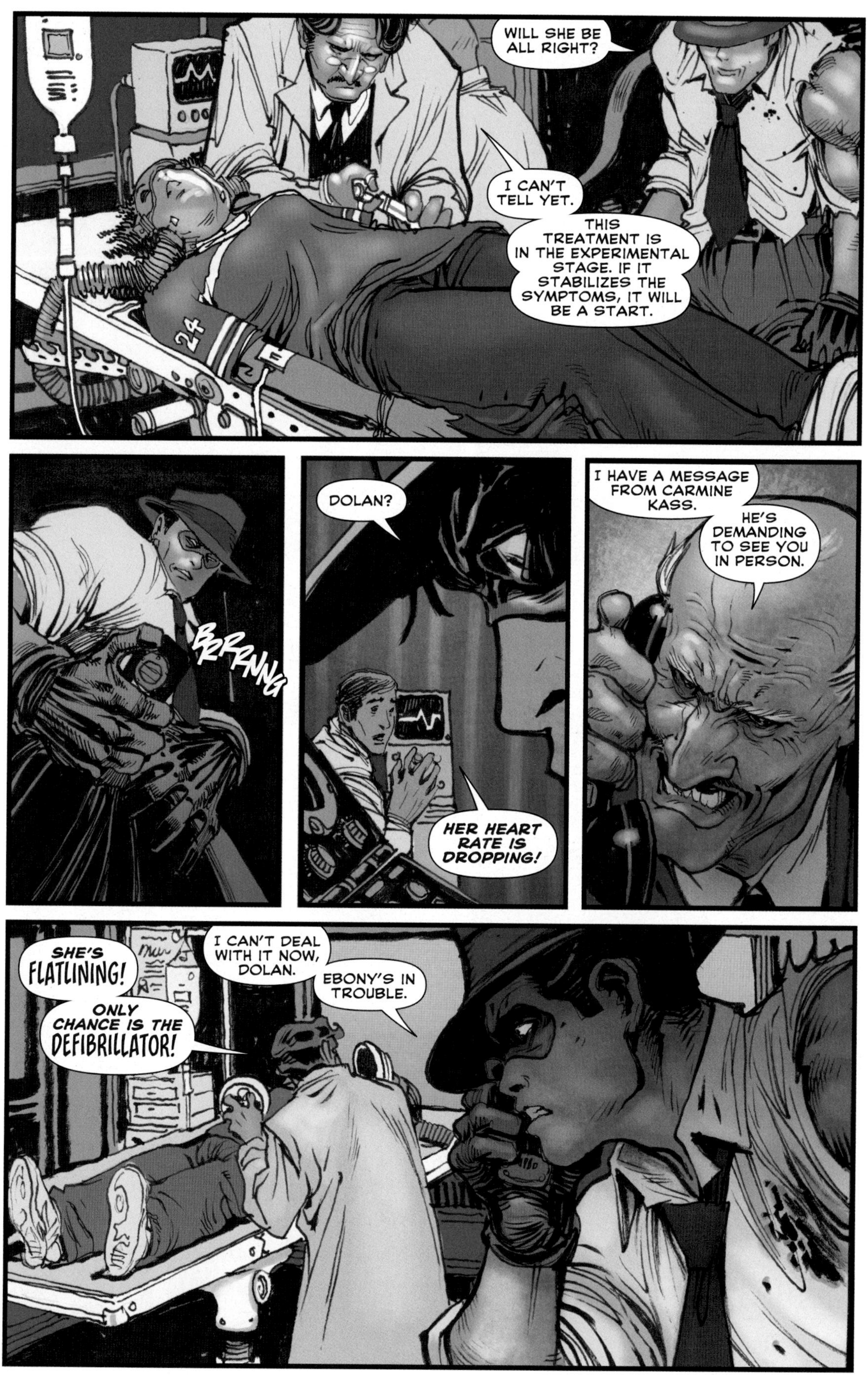
WILL SHE BE ALL RIGHT?
I CAN'T TELL YET.
THIS TREATMENT IS IN THE EXPERIMENTAL STAGE. IF IT STABILIZES THE SYMPTOMS, IT WILL BE A START.
BRRRNNG
DOLAN?
HER HEART RATE IS DROPPING!
I HAVE A MESSAGE FROM CARMINE KASS.
HE'S DEMANDING TO SEE YOU IN PERSON.
SHE'S FLATLINING!
ONLY CHANCE IS THE DEFIBRILLATOR!
I CAN'T DEAL WITH IT NOW, DOLAN.
EBONY'S IN TROUBLE.

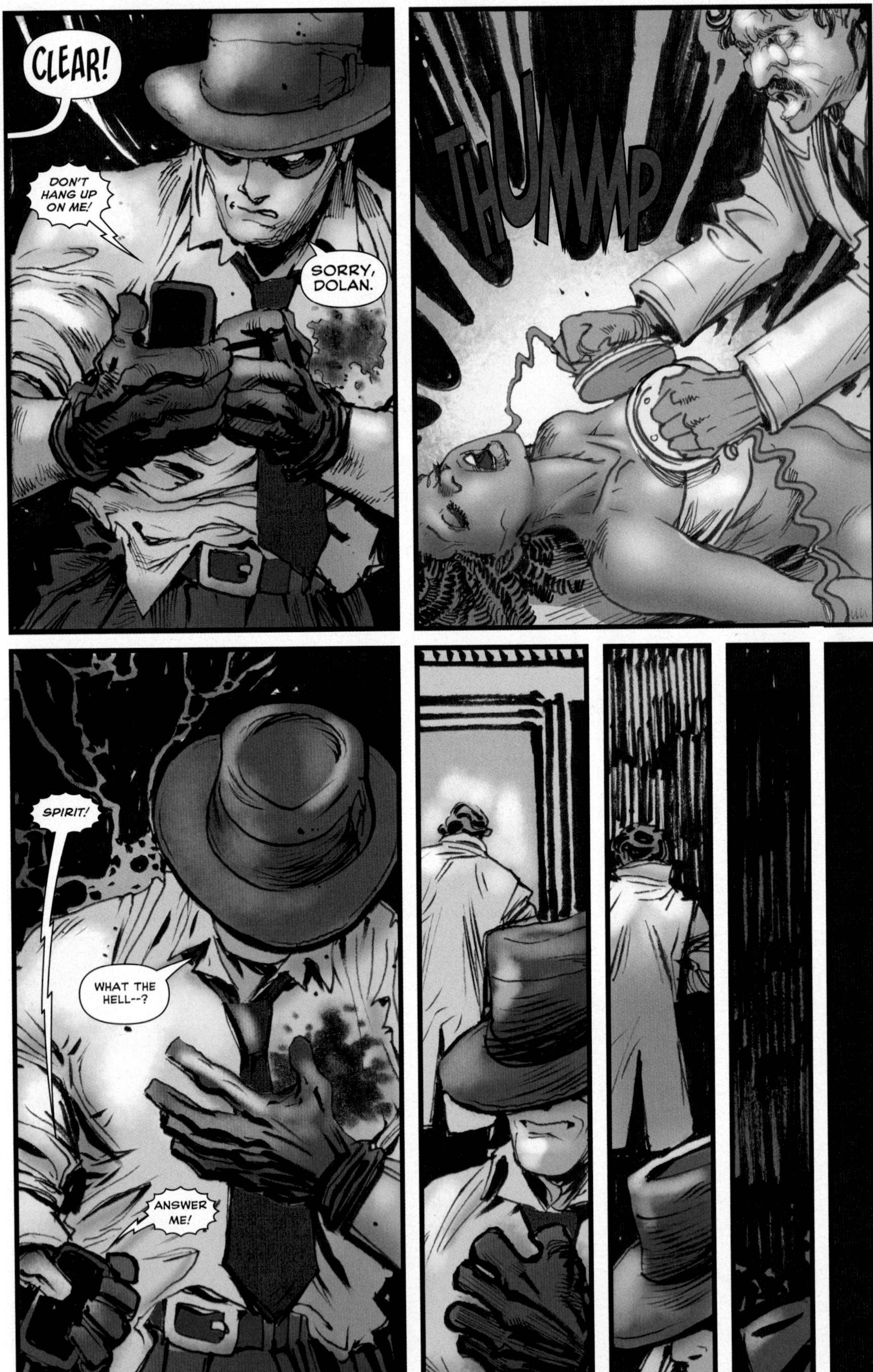
CLEAR!
DON'T HANG UP ON ME!
SORRY, DOLAN.
THUMMP
SPIRIT!
WHAT THE HELL--?
ANSWER ME!

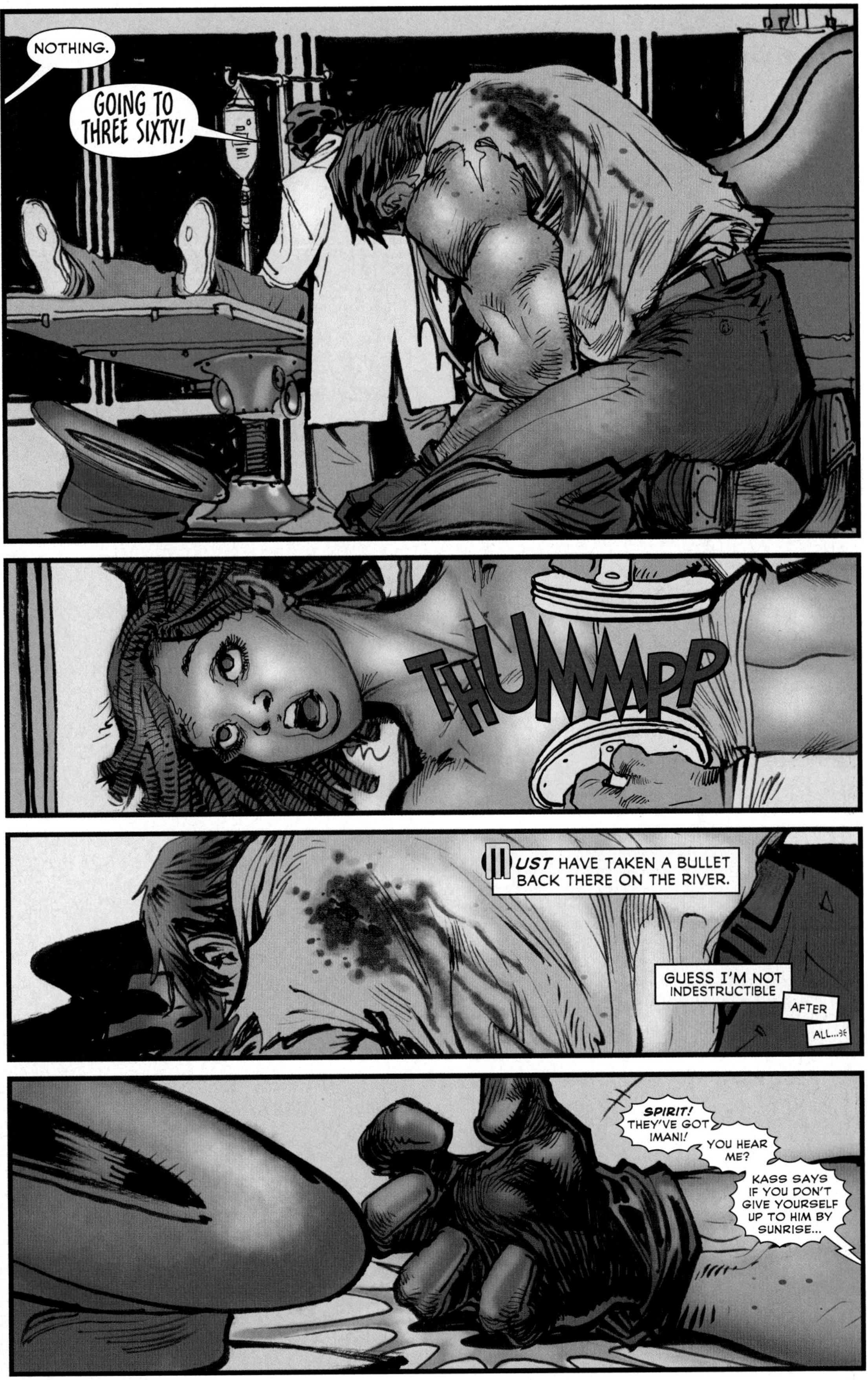
NOTHING.
GOING TO THREE SIXTY!
THUMMPP
MUST HAVE TAKEN A BULLET BACK THERE ON THE RIVER.
GUESS I'M NOT INDESTRUCTIBLE
AFTER
ALL...
SPIRIT! THEY'VE GOT IMANI!
YOU HEAR ME?
KASS SAYS IF YOU DON'T GIVE YOURSELF UP TO HIM BY SUNRISE...

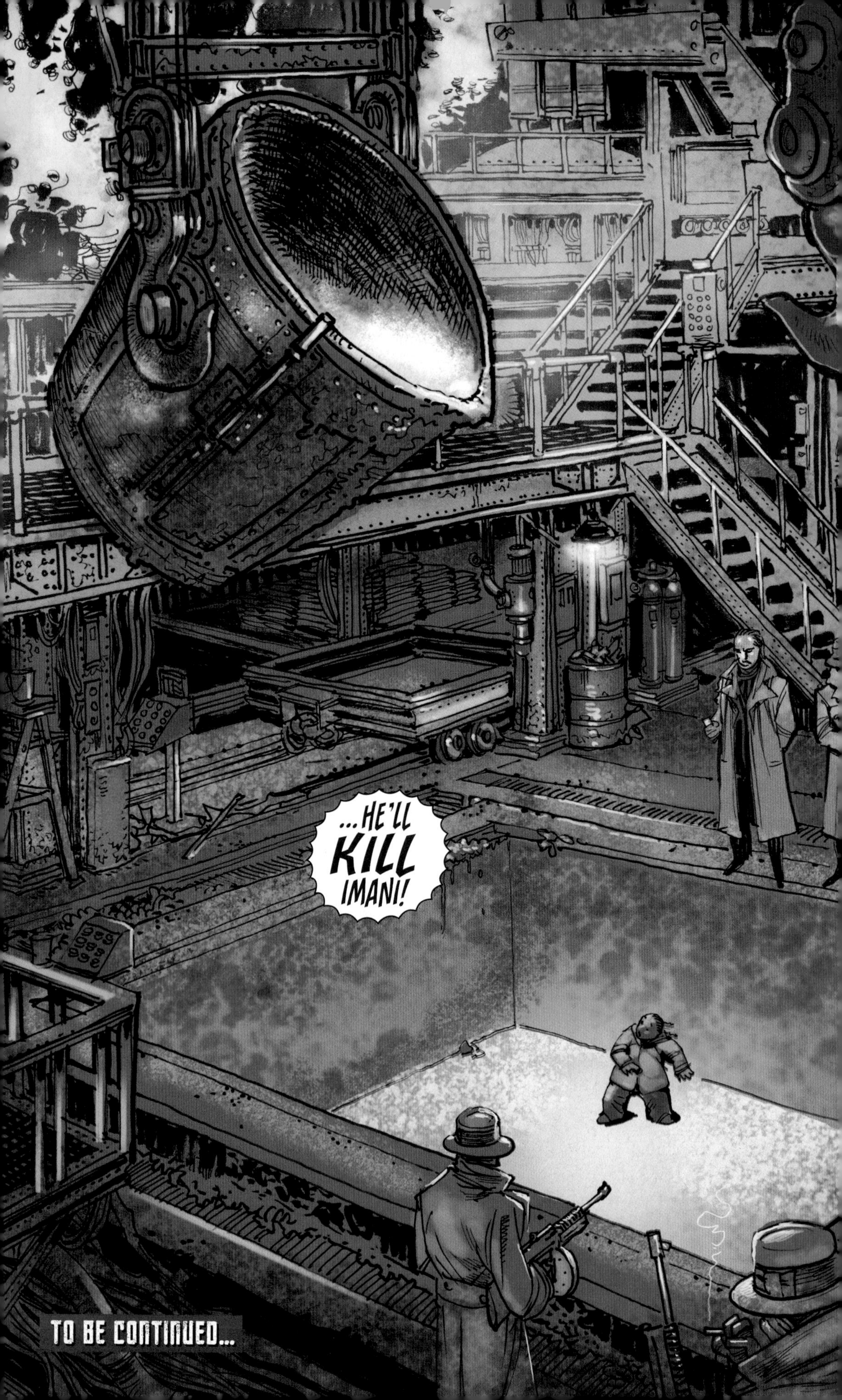
...HE'LL KILL IMANI!
TO BE CONTINUED...

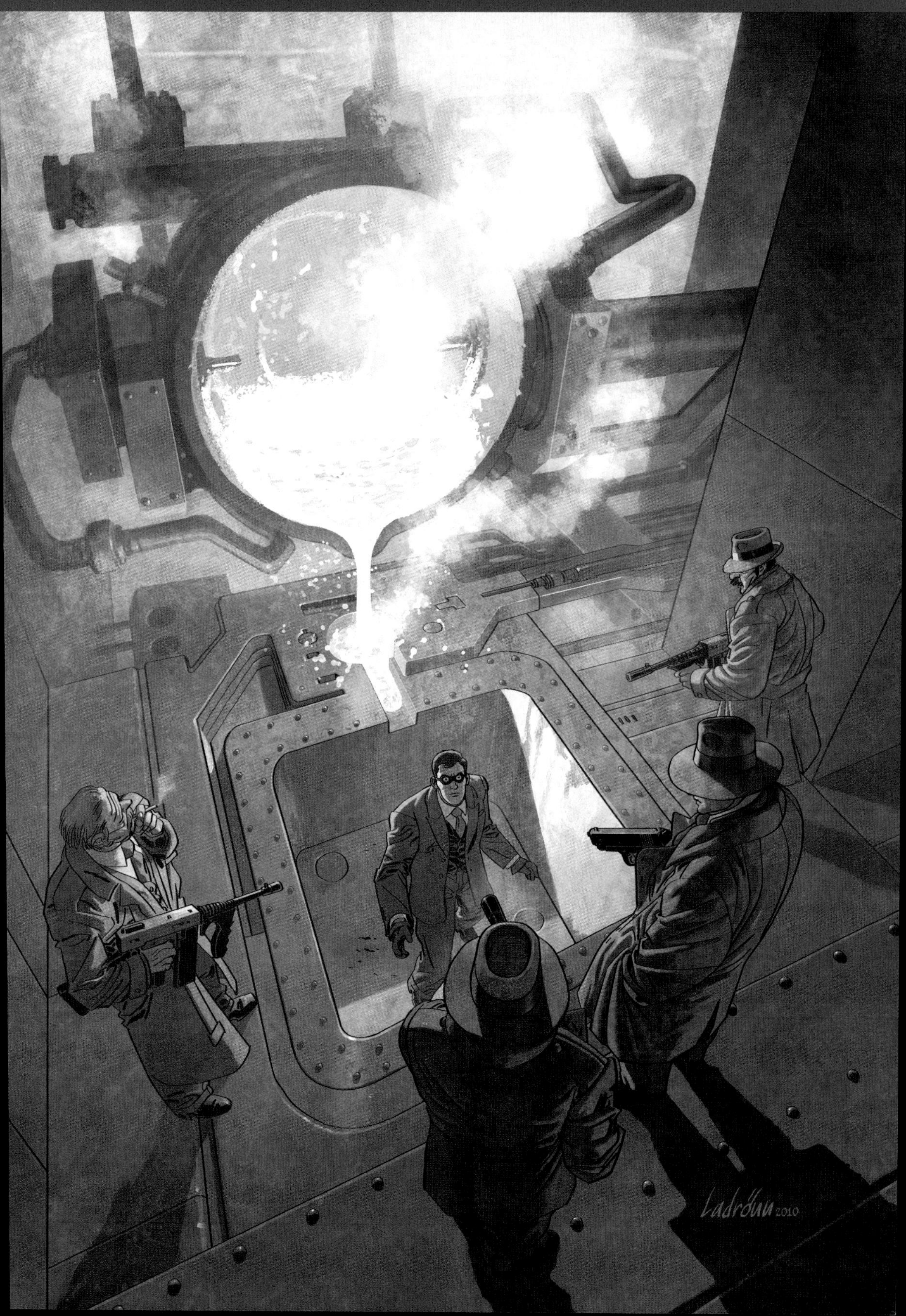
Ladrönn 2010

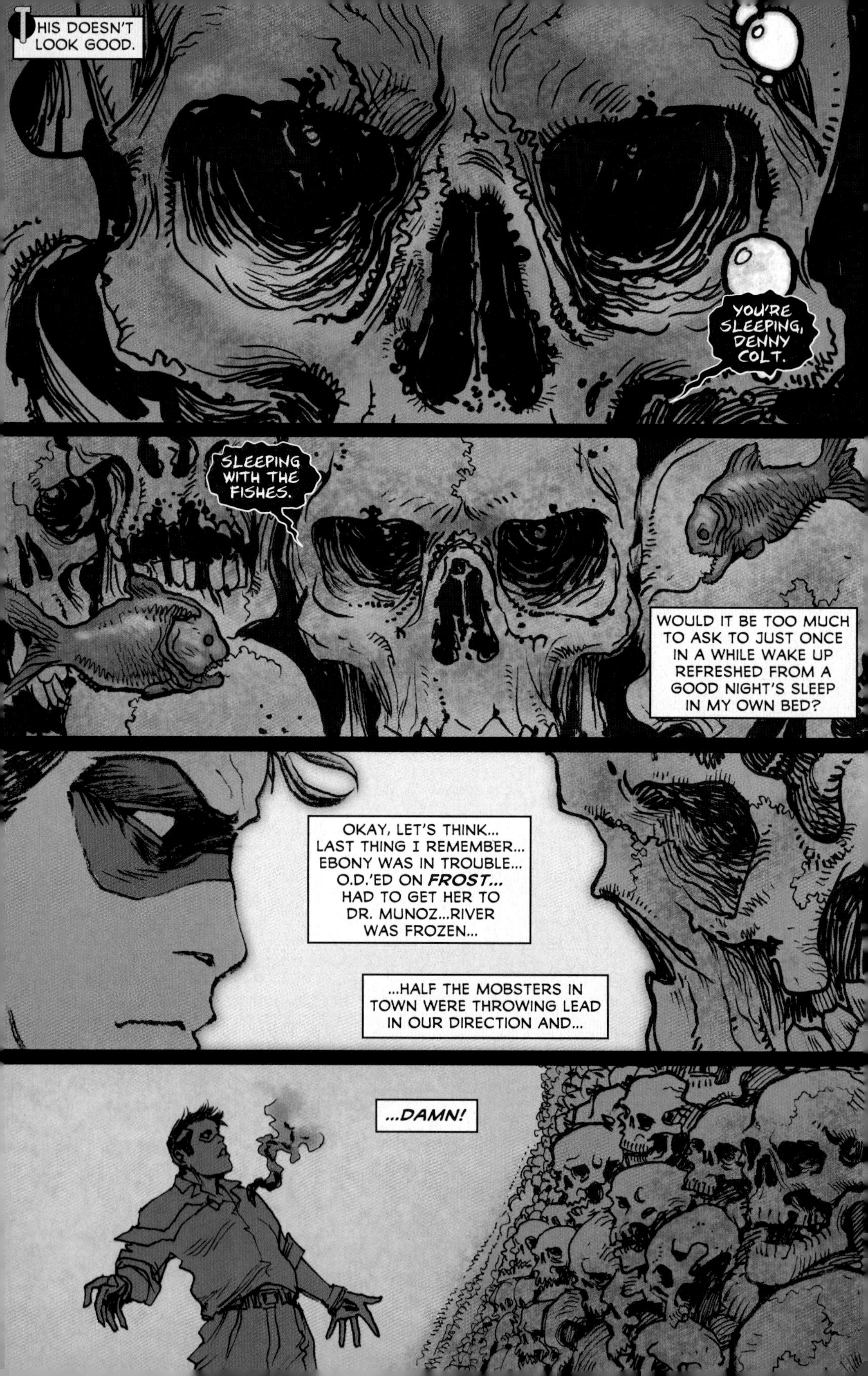
THIS DOESN'T LOOK GOOD.
YOU'RE SLEEPING, DENNY COLT.
SLEEPING WITH THE FISHES.
WOULD IT BE TOO MUCH TO ASK TO JUST ONCE IN A WHILE WAKE UP REFRESHED FROM A GOOD NIGHT'S SLEEP IN MY OWN BED?
OKAY, LET'S THINK... LAST THING I REMEMBER... EBONY WAS IN TROUBLE... O.D.'ED ON FROST... HAD TO GET HER TO DR. MUNOZ...RIVER WAS FROZEN...
...HALF THE MOBSTERS IN TOWN WERE THROWING LEAD IN OUR DIRECTION AND...
...DAMN!

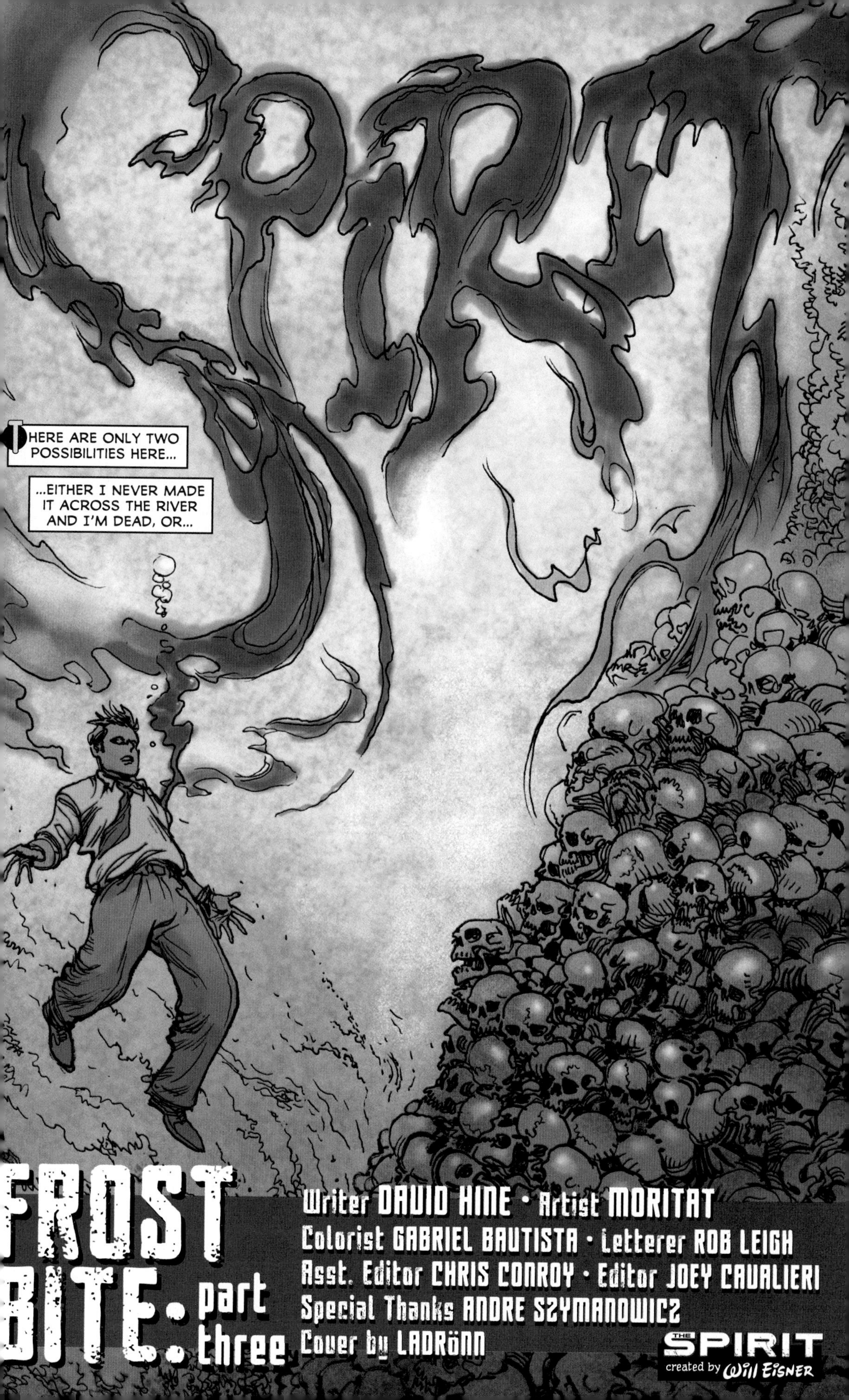
THE SPIRIT
THERE ARE ONLY TWO POSSIBILITIES HERE...
...EITHER I NEVER MADE IT ACROSS THE RIVER AND I'M DEAD, OR...
FROST BITE: part three
Writer DAVID HINE • Artist MORITAT
Colorist GABRIEL BAUTISTA • Letterer ROB LEIGH
Asst. Editor CHRIS CONROY • Editor JOEY CAVALIERI
Special Thanks ANDRE SZYMANOWICZ
Cover by LADRÖNN
THE SPIRIT created by Will Eisner

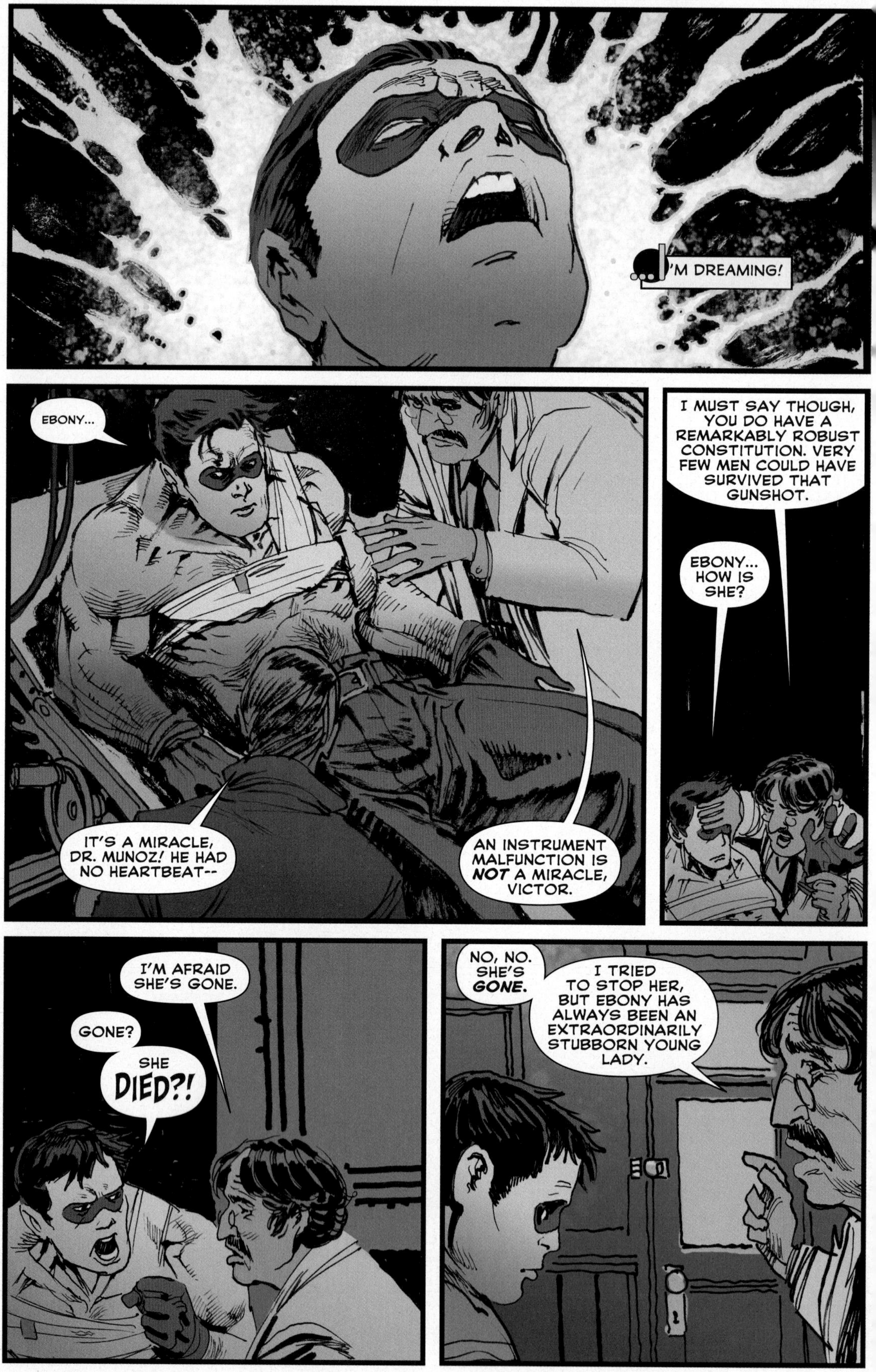
I'M DREAMING!
EBONY...
IT'S A MIRACLE, DR. MUNOZ! HE HAD NO HEARTBEAT--
AN INSTRUMENT MALFUNCTION IS NOT A MIRACLE, VICTOR.
I MUST SAY THOUGH, YOU DO HAVE A REMARKABLY ROBUST CONSTITUTION. VERY FEW MEN COULD HAVE SURVIVED THAT GUNSHOT.
EBONY... HOW IS SHE?
I'M AFRAID SHE'S GONE.
GONE?
SHE DIED?!
NO, NO. SHE'S GONE.
I TRIED TO STOP HER, BUT EBONY HAS ALWAYS BEEN AN EXTRAORDINARILY STUBBORN YOUNG LADY.

SHE RESPONDED WELL TO MY TREATMENT. THE LETHAL EFFECTS OF THE NARCOTIC HAVE BEEN BLOCKED, BUT THE *FROST IS* STILL IN HER SYSTEM.

SHE NEEDS *DAYS* OF BED REST.

WHERE DID SHE GO?!

TO FIND IMANI. DON'T YOU REMEMBER?

COMMISSIONER DOLAN CALLED.

KASS! HE HAS IMANI.

I HAVE TO GIVE MYSELF UP OR HE'LL KILL HER!

KASS IS WAITING FOR YOU IN THE OLD *FEIFFER AND FINE* IRON FOUNDRY.

EBONY WENT IN YOUR PLACE.

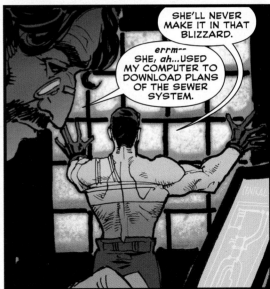

SHE'LL NEVER MAKE IT IN THAT BLIZZARD.

errm-- SHE, *ah...*USED MY COMPUTER TO DOWNLOAD PLANS OF THE SEWER SYSTEM.

AND SHE TOOK YOUR HAT AND COAT...

...AS A DISGUISE.

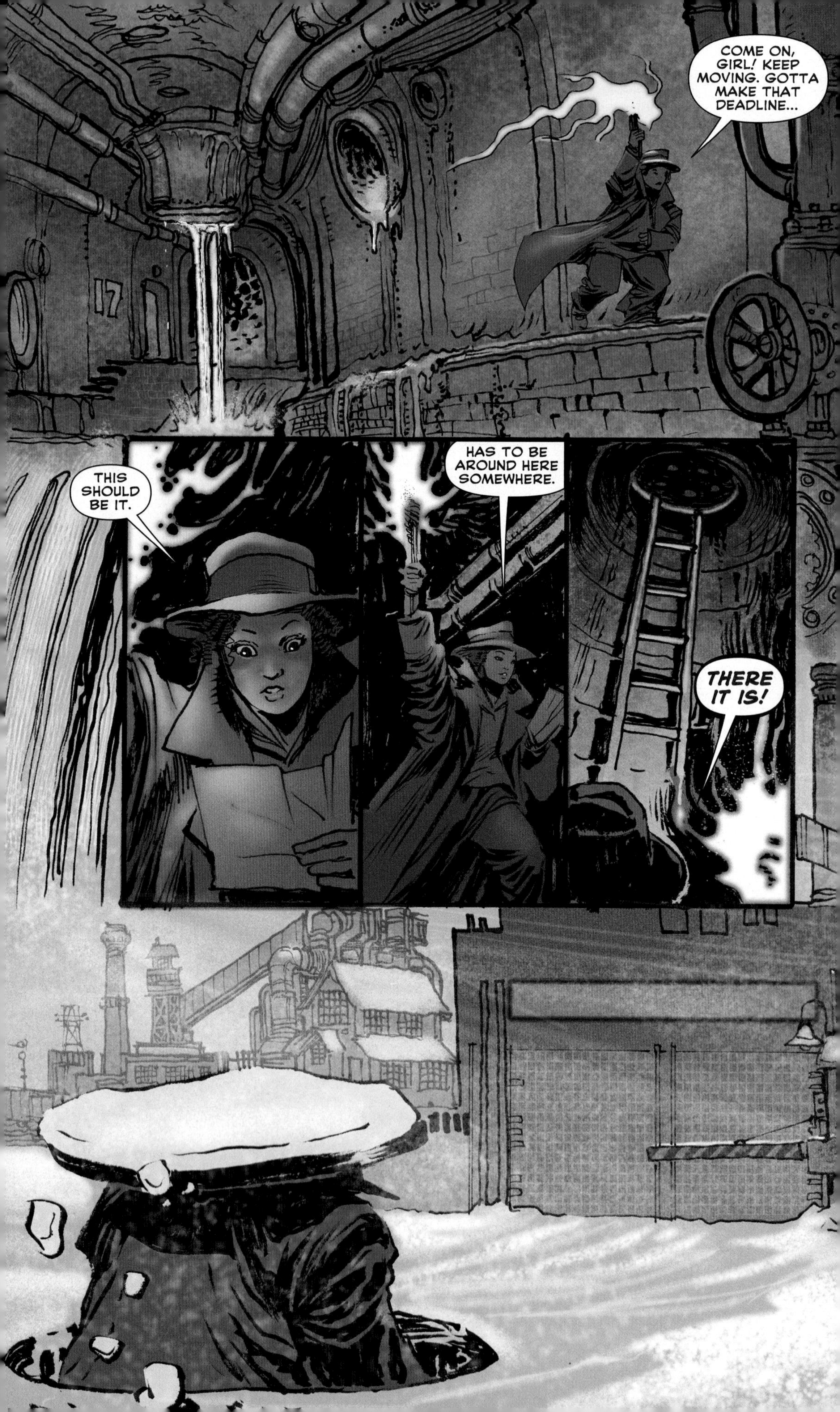
COME ON, GIRL! KEEP MOVING. GOTTA MAKE THAT DEADLINE...
THIS SHOULD BE IT.
HAS TO BE AROUND HERE SOMEWHERE.
THERE IT IS!
17

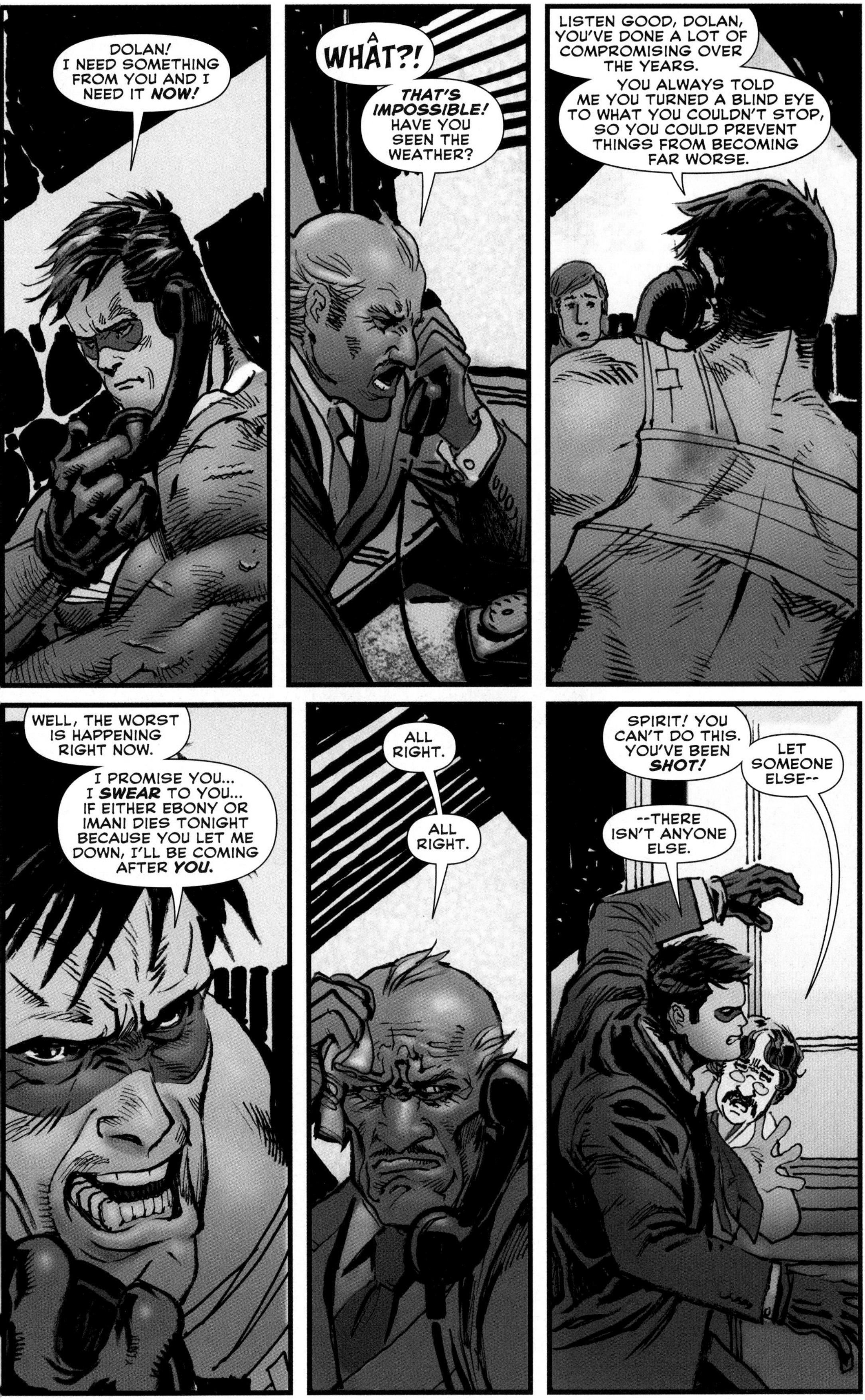
DOLAN! I NEED SOMETHING FROM YOU AND I NEED IT NOW!
A WHAT?!
THAT'S IMPOSSIBLE! HAVE YOU SEEN THE WEATHER?
LISTEN GOOD, DOLAN, YOU'VE DONE A LOT OF COMPROMISING OVER THE YEARS.
YOU ALWAYS TOLD ME YOU TURNED A BLIND EYE TO WHAT YOU COULDN'T STOP, SO YOU COULD PREVENT THINGS FROM BECOMING FAR WORSE.
WELL, THE WORST IS HAPPENING RIGHT NOW.
I PROMISE YOU... I SWEAR TO YOU... IF EITHER EBONY OR IMANI DIES TONIGHT BECAUSE YOU LET ME DOWN, I'LL BE COMING AFTER YOU.
ALL RIGHT.
ALL RIGHT.
SPIRIT! YOU CAN'T DO THIS. YOU'VE BEEN SHOT!
LET SOMEONE ELSE--
--THERE ISN'T ANYONE ELSE.

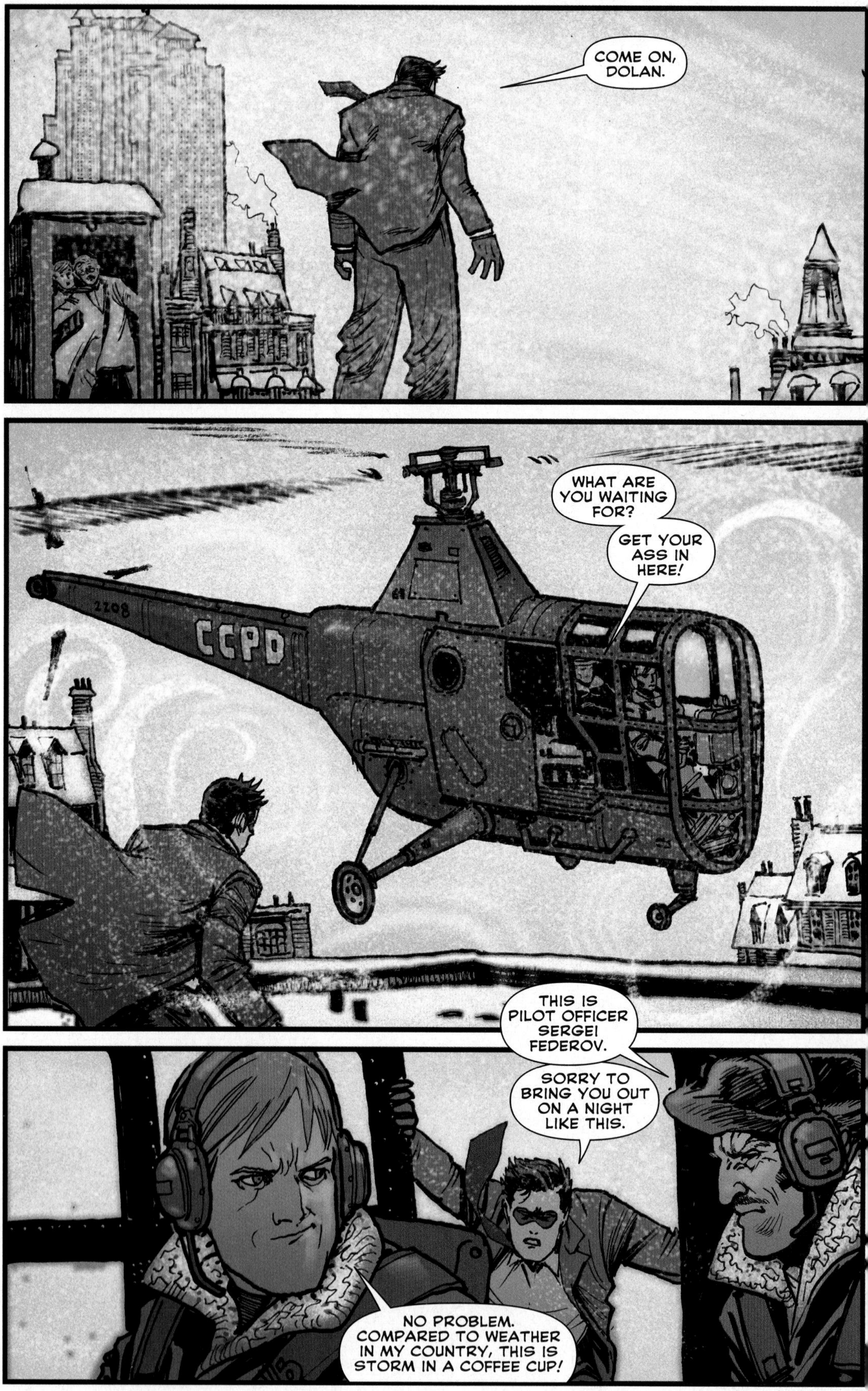

COME ON, DOLAN.
WHAT ARE YOU WAITING FOR?
GET YOUR ASS IN HERE!
CCPD
2208
THIS IS PILOT OFFICER SERGEI FEDEROV.
SORRY TO BRING YOU OUT ON A NIGHT LIKE THIS.
NO PROBLEM. COMPARED TO WEATHER IN MY COUNTRY, THIS IS STORM IN A COFFEE CUP!

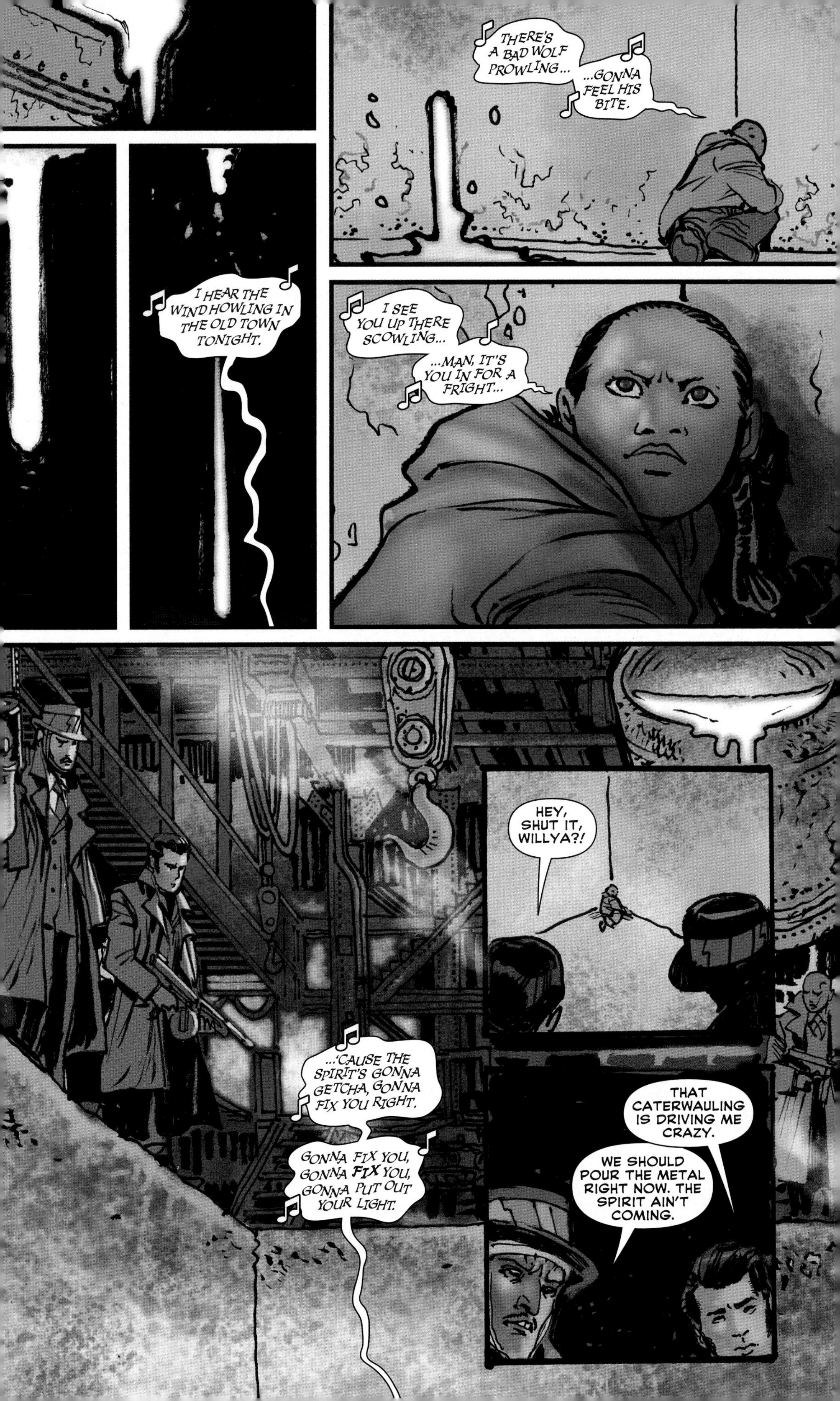

THERE'S A BAD WOLF PROWLING...
...GONNA FEEL HIS BITE.
I HEAR THE WIND HOWLING IN THE OLD TOWN TONIGHT.
I SEE YOU UP THERE SCOWLING...
...MAN, IT'S YOU IN FOR A FRIGHT...
HEY, SHUT IT, WILLYA?!
...'CAUSE THE SPIRIT'S GONNA GETCHA, GONNA FIX YOU RIGHT.
GONNA FIX YOU, GONNA FIX YOU, GONNA PUT OUT YOUR LIGHT.
THAT CATERWAULING IS DRIVING ME CRAZY.
WE SHOULD POUR THE METAL RIGHT NOW. THE SPIRIT AIN'T COMING.

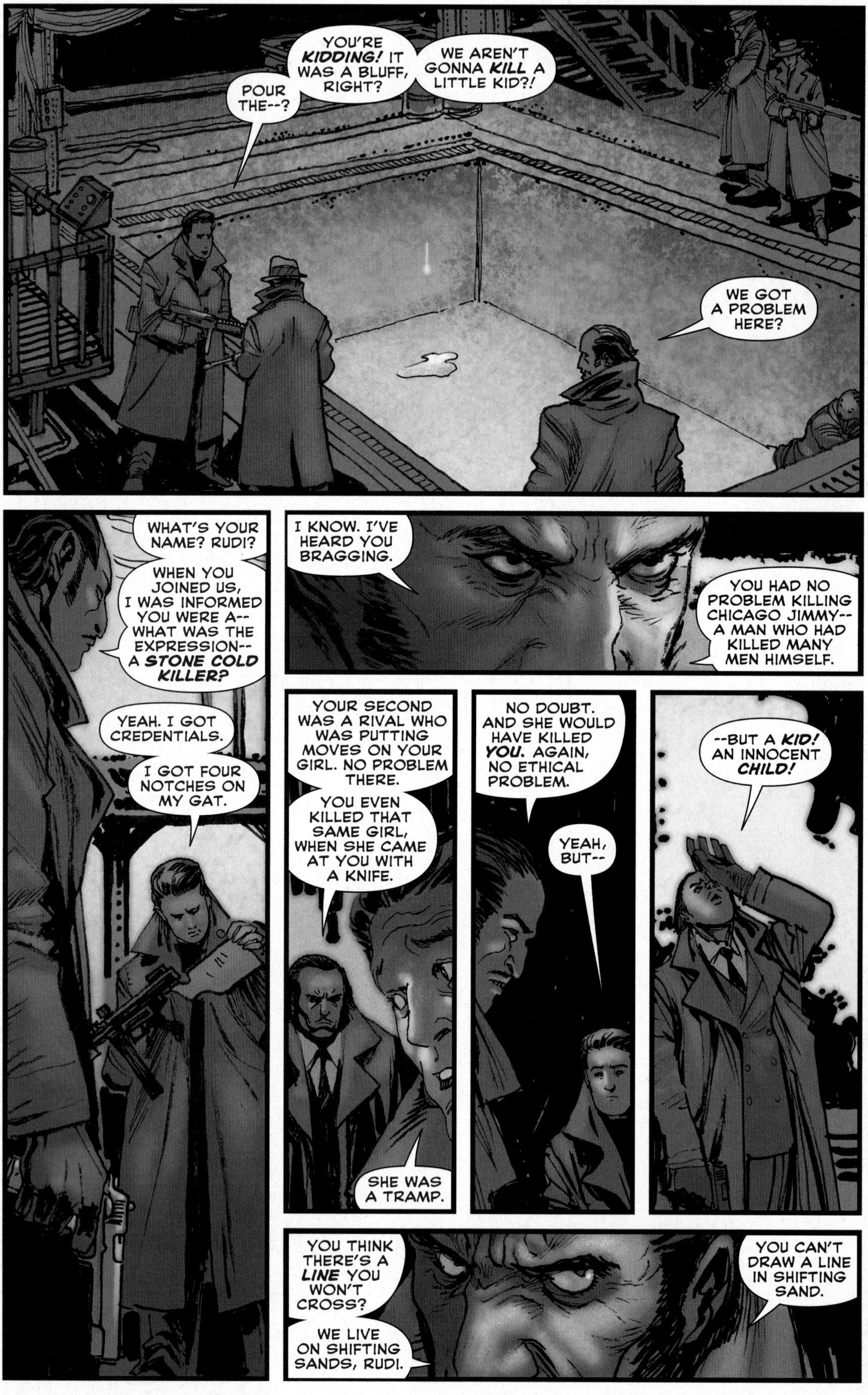
POUR THE--?
YOU'RE KIDDING! IT WAS A BLUFF, RIGHT?
WE AREN'T GONNA KILL A LITTLE KID?!
WE GOT A PROBLEM HERE?
WHAT'S YOUR NAME? RUDI?
WHEN YOU JOINED US, I WAS INFORMED YOU WERE A-- WHAT WAS THE EXPRESSION-- A STONE COLD KILLER?
YEAH. I GOT CREDENTIALS.
I GOT FOUR NOTCHES ON MY GAT.
I KNOW. I'VE HEARD YOU BRAGGING.
YOU HAD NO PROBLEM KILLING CHICAGO JIMMY-- A MAN WHO HAD KILLED MANY MEN HIMSELF.
YOUR SECOND WAS A RIVAL WHO WAS PUTTING MOVES ON YOUR GIRL. NO PROBLEM THERE.
YOU EVEN KILLED THAT SAME GIRL, WHEN SHE CAME AT YOU WITH A KNIFE.
SHE WAS A TRAMP.
NO DOUBT. AND SHE WOULD HAVE KILLED YOU. AGAIN, NO ETHICAL PROBLEM.
YEAH, BUT--
--BUT A KID! AN INNOCENT CHILD!
YOU THINK THERE'S A LINE YOU WON'T CROSS?
WE LIVE ON SHIFTING SANDS, RUDI.
YOU CAN'T DRAW A LINE IN SHIFTING SAND.

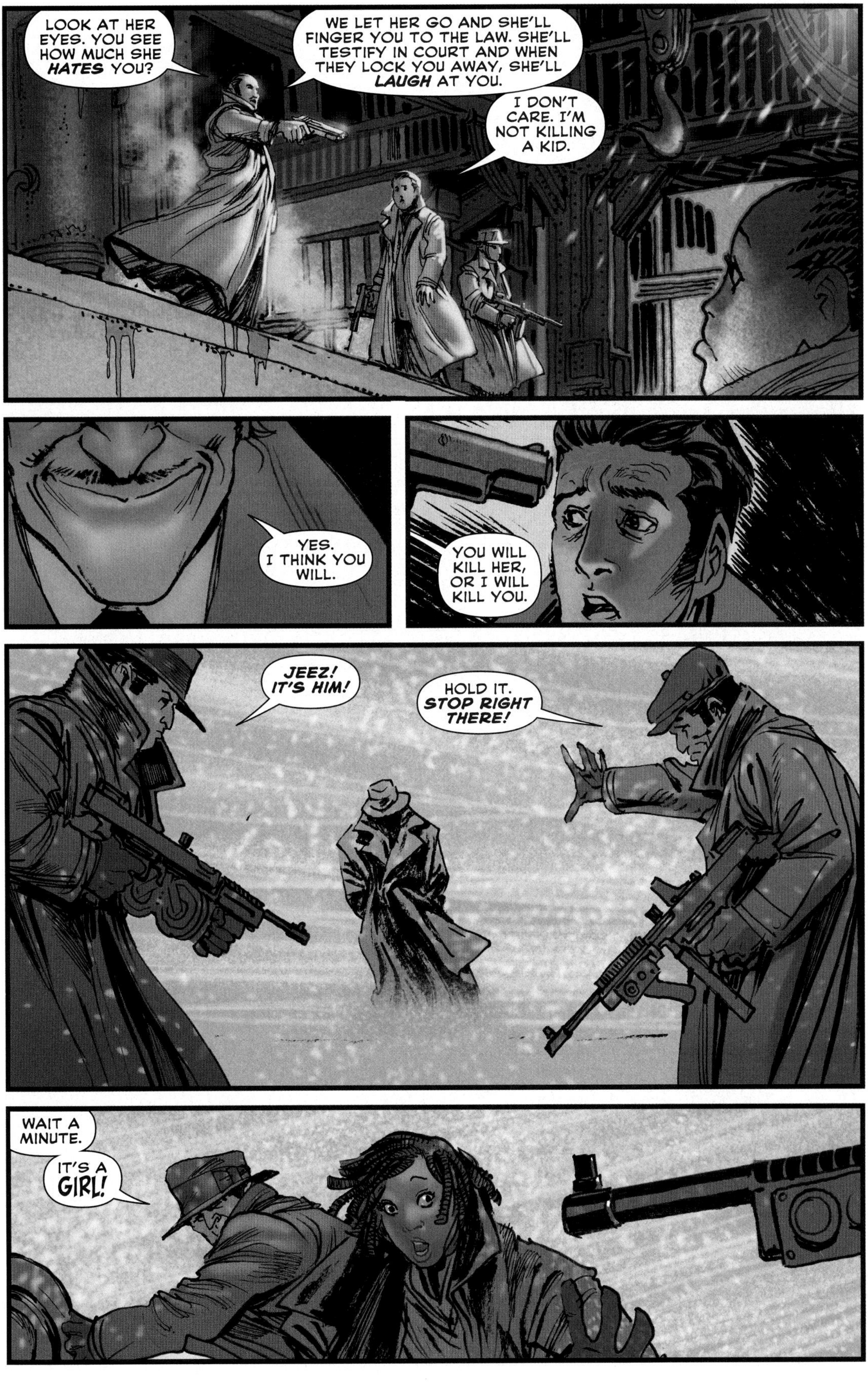
LOOK AT HER EYES. YOU SEE HOW MUCH SHE HATES YOU?
WE LET HER GO AND SHE'LL FINGER YOU TO THE LAW. SHE'LL TESTIFY IN COURT AND WHEN THEY LOCK YOU AWAY, SHE'LL LAUGH AT YOU.
I DON'T CARE. I'M NOT KILLING A KID.
YES. I THINK YOU WILL.
YOU WILL KILL HER, OR I WILL KILL YOU.
JEEZ! IT'S HIM!
HOLD IT. STOP RIGHT THERE!
WAIT A MINUTE.
IT'S A GIRL!

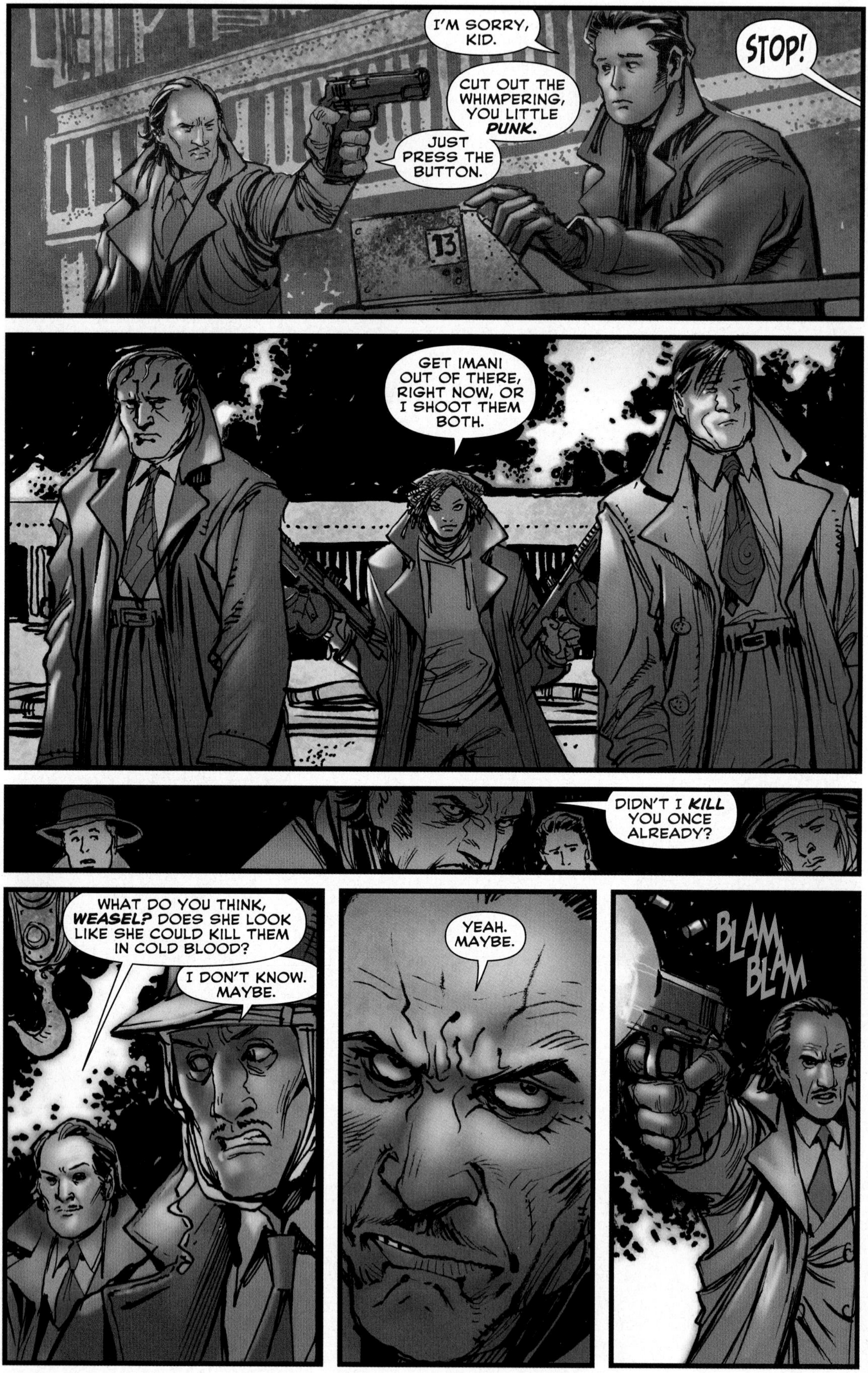

I'M SORRY, KID.
CUT OUT THE WHIMPERING, YOU LITTLE PUNK.
JUST PRESS THE BUTTON.
STOP!
13
GET IMANI OUT OF THERE, RIGHT NOW, OR I SHOOT THEM BOTH.
DIDN'T I KILL YOU ONCE ALREADY?
WHAT DO YOU THINK, WEASEL? DOES SHE LOOK LIKE SHE COULD KILL THEM IN COLD BLOOD?
I DON'T KNOW. MAYBE.
YEAH. MAYBE.
BLAM
BLAM

Tcch. NOW WE'LL NEVER KNOW.
OKAY. TAKE IT EASY, FELLERS.
THIS IS ME SURRENDERING.

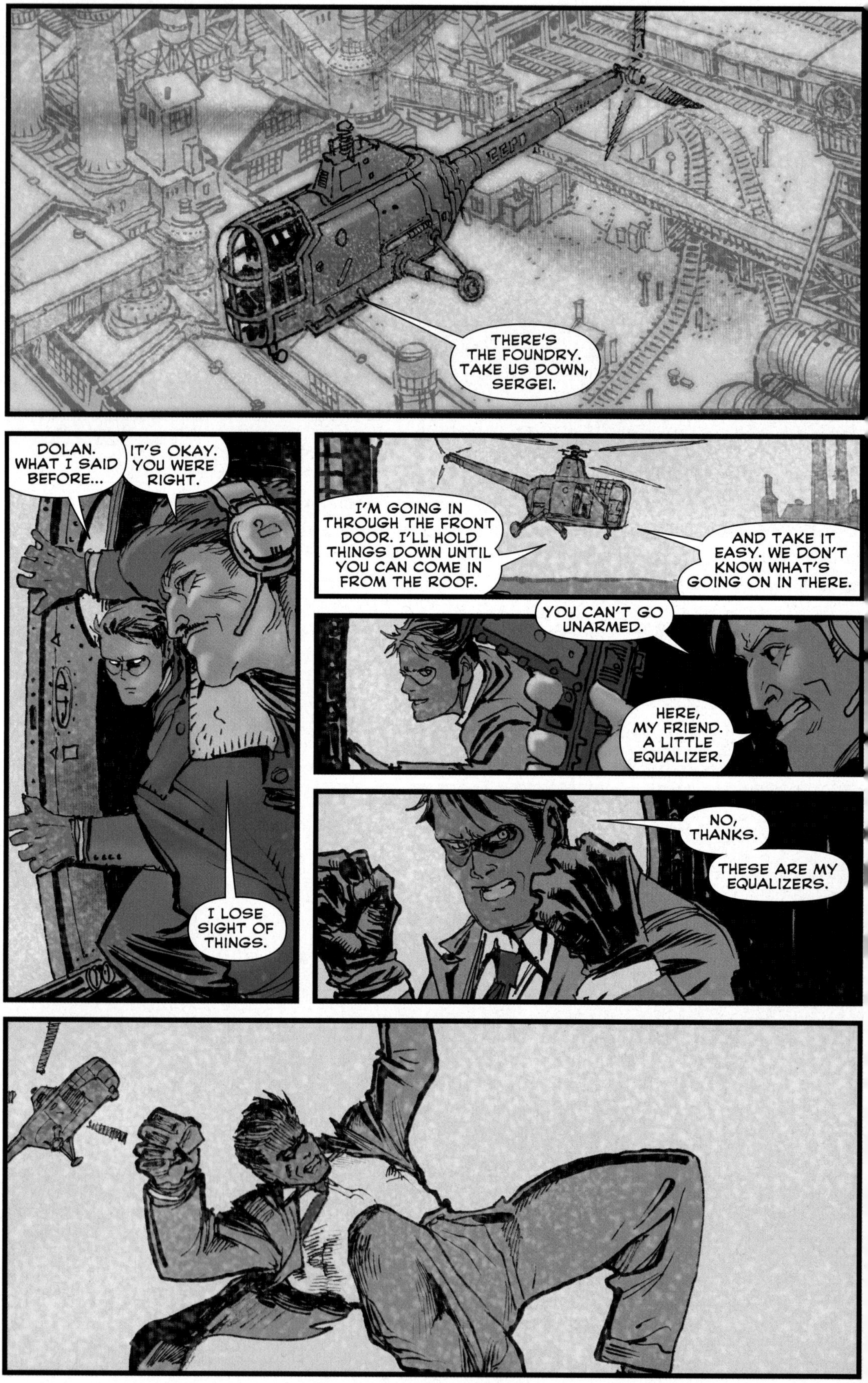
THERE'S THE FOUNDRY. TAKE US DOWN, SERGEI.
DOLAN. WHAT I SAID BEFORE...
IT'S OKAY. YOU WERE RIGHT.
I LOSE SIGHT OF THINGS.
I'M GOING IN THROUGH THE FRONT DOOR. I'LL HOLD THINGS DOWN UNTIL YOU CAN COME IN FROM THE ROOF.
AND TAKE IT EASY. WE DON'T KNOW WHAT'S GOING ON IN THERE.
YOU CAN'T GO UNARMED.
HERE, MY FRIEND. A LITTLE EQUALIZER.
NO, THANKS.
THESE ARE MY EQUALIZERS.

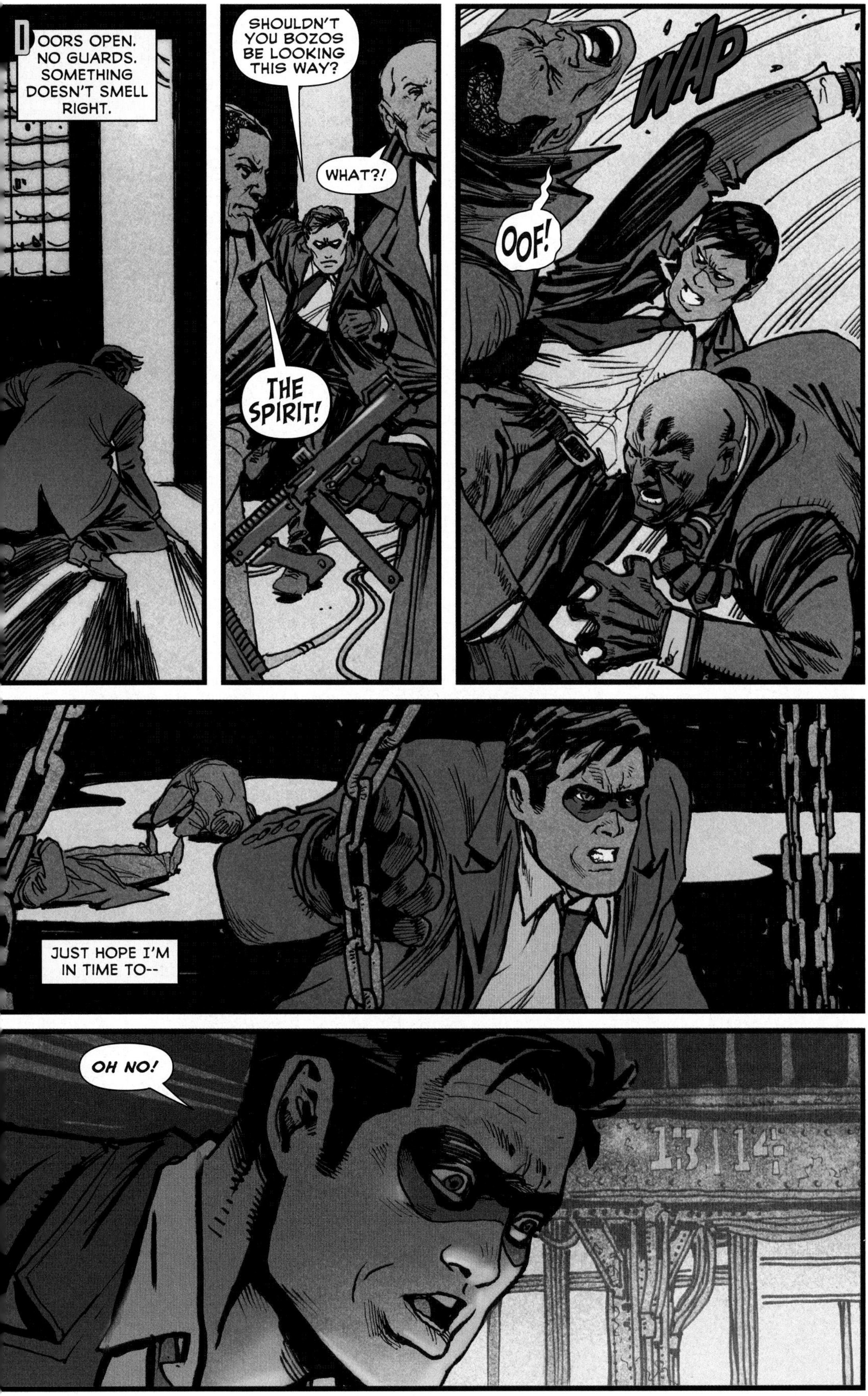

DOORS OPEN. NO GUARDS. SOMETHING DOESN'T SMELL RIGHT.
SHOULDN'T YOU BOZOS BE LOOKING THIS WAY?
WHAT?!
THE SPIRIT!
WAP
OOF!
JUST HOPE I'M IN TIME TO--
OH NO!
1314

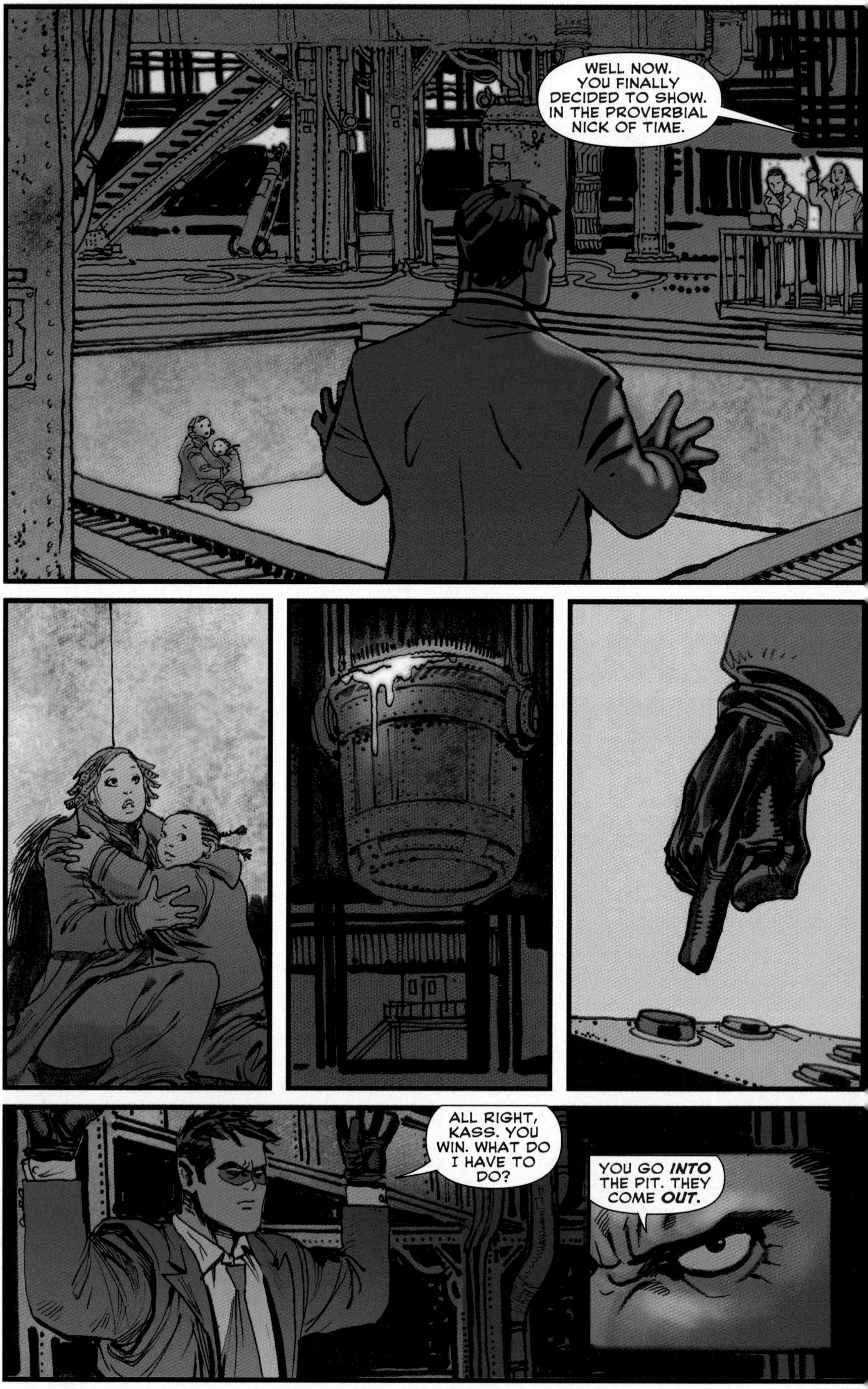
WELL NOW. YOU FINALLY DECIDED TO SHOW. IN THE PROVERBIAL NICK OF TIME.
ALL RIGHT, KASS. YOU WIN. WHAT DO I HAVE TO DO?
YOU GO *INTO* THE PIT. THEY COME *OUT*.

GET THEM OUT OF THERE FIRST.

YOU DON'T MAKE THE RULES.

YAAHH!

FUNNY. THEY TOLD ME THE SPIRIT WAS TOUGH. A REAL HARD MAN.

ALL THESE YEARS EVERYONE'S BEEN RUNNING SCARED OF YOU, AND TWO MINUTES AFTER YOU MEET *CARMINE KASS*, YOU'RE ROASTED MEAT.

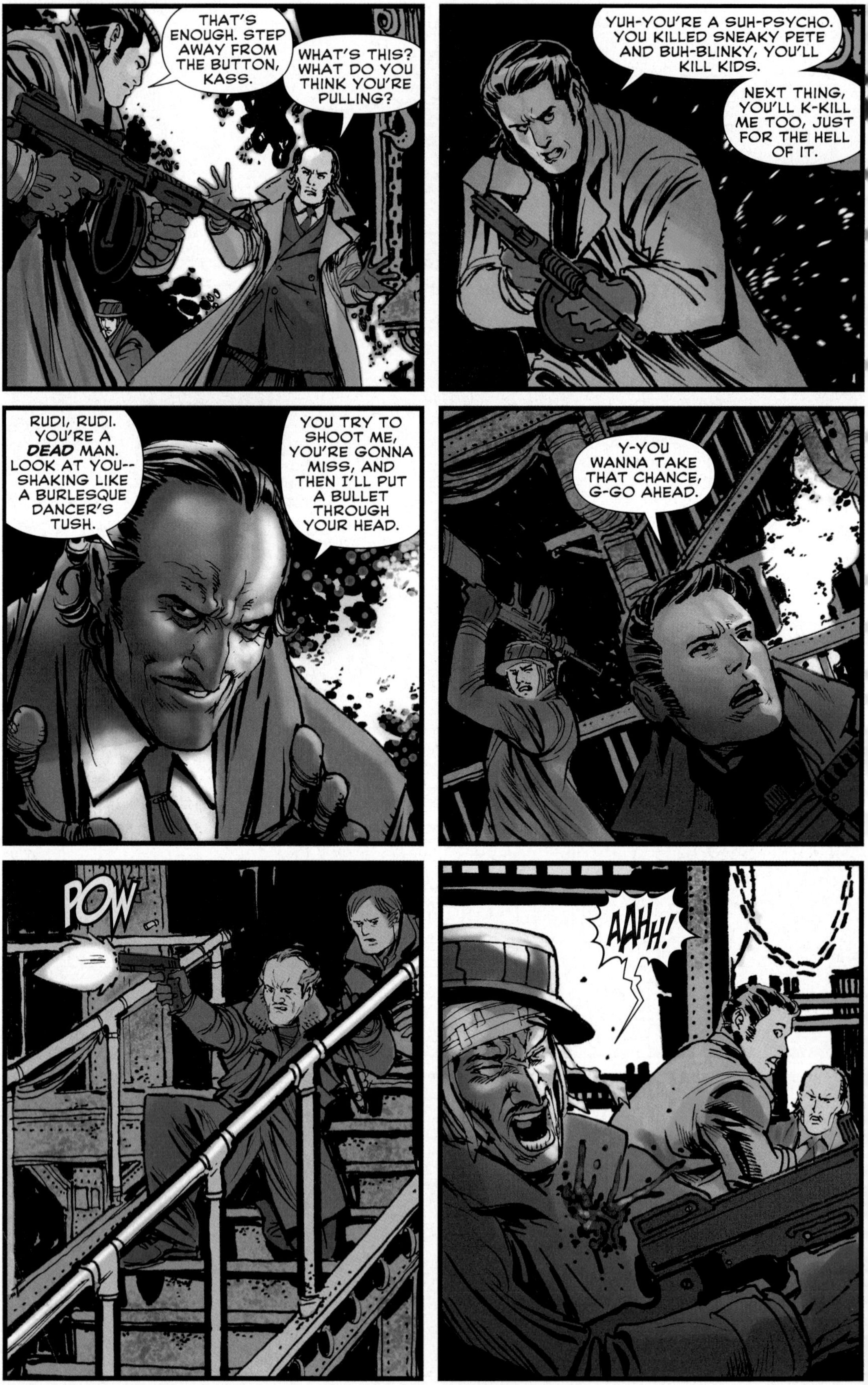
THAT'S ENOUGH. STEP AWAY FROM THE BUTTON, KASS.
WHAT'S THIS? WHAT DO YOU THINK YOU'RE PULLING?
YUH-YOU'RE A SUH-PSYCHO. YOU KILLED SNEAKY PETE AND BUH-BLINKY, YOU'LL KILL KIDS.
NEXT THING, YOU'LL K-KILL ME TOO, JUST FOR THE HELL OF IT.
RUDI, RUDI. YOU'RE A DEAD MAN. LOOK AT YOU--SHAKING LIKE A BURLESQUE DANCER'S TUSH.
YOU TRY TO SHOOT ME, YOU'RE GONNA MISS, AND THEN I'LL PUT A BULLET THROUGH YOUR HEAD.
Y-YOU WANNA TAKE THAT CHANCE, G-GO AHEAD.
POW
AAHH!

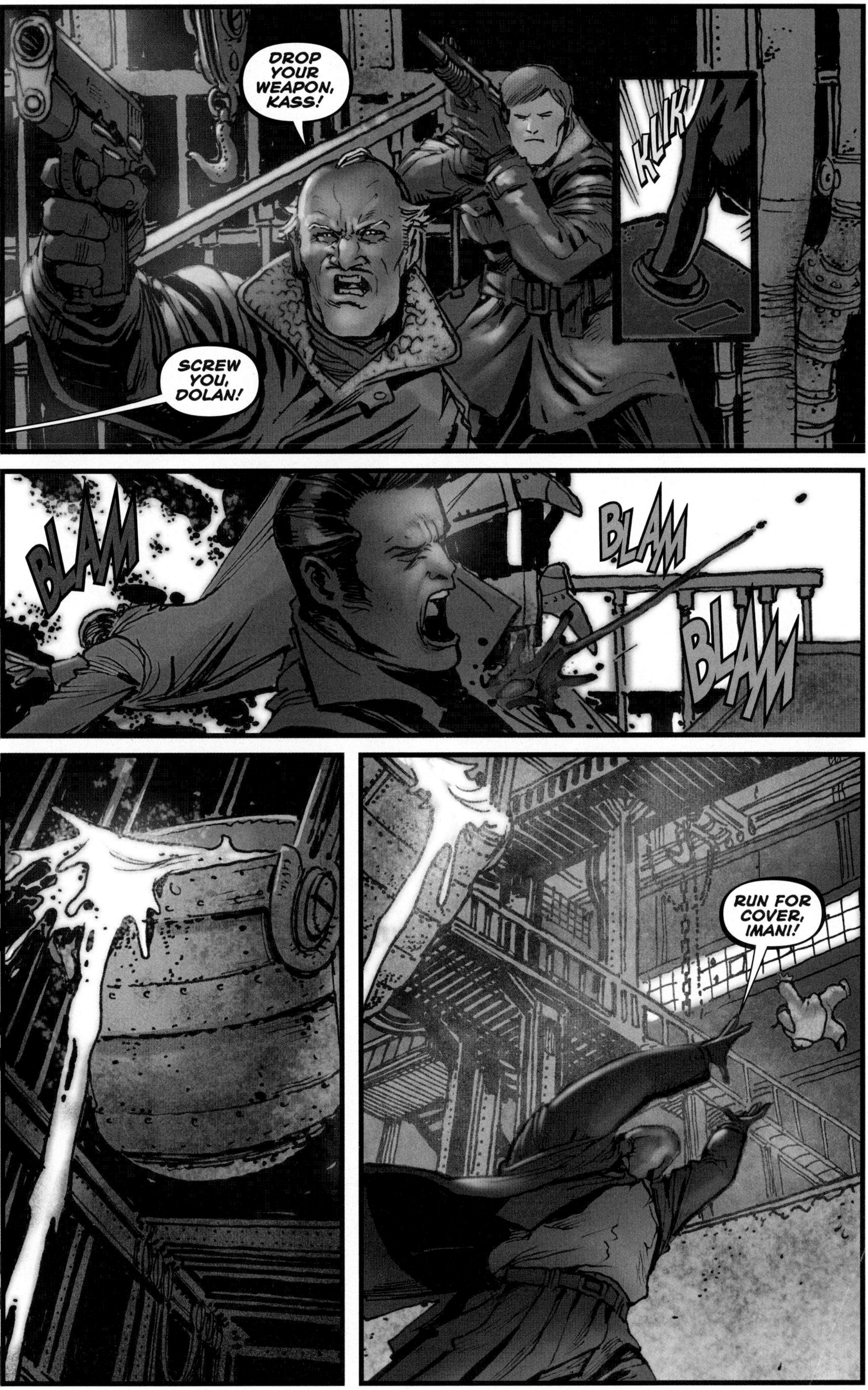
DROP YOUR WEAPON, KASS!
KLIK
SCREW YOU, DOLAN!
BLAM
BLAM
BLAM
RUN FOR COVER, IMANI!

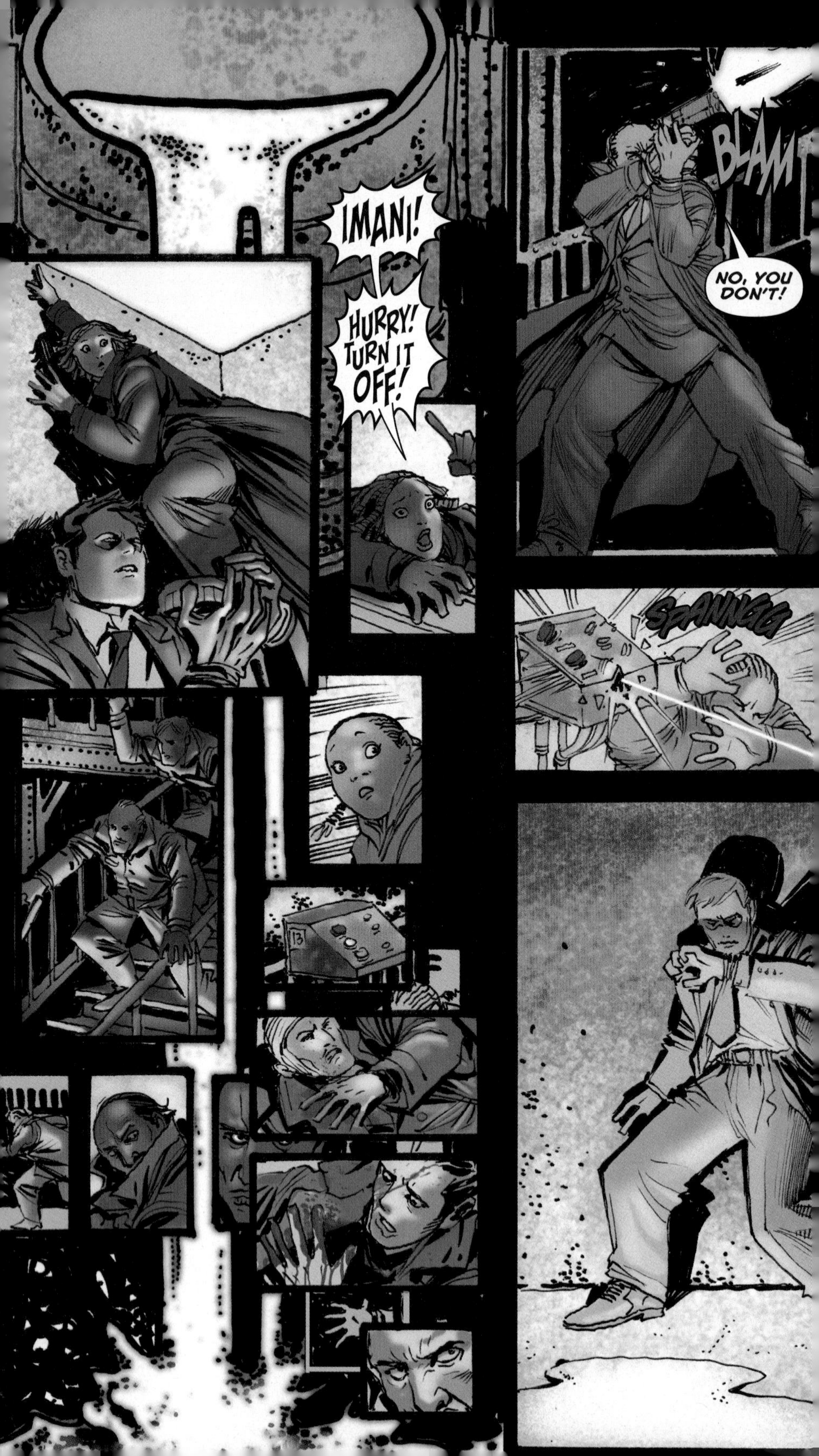
IMANI!
HURRY! TURN IT OFF!
BLAM
NO, YOU DON'T!
SPANNGG

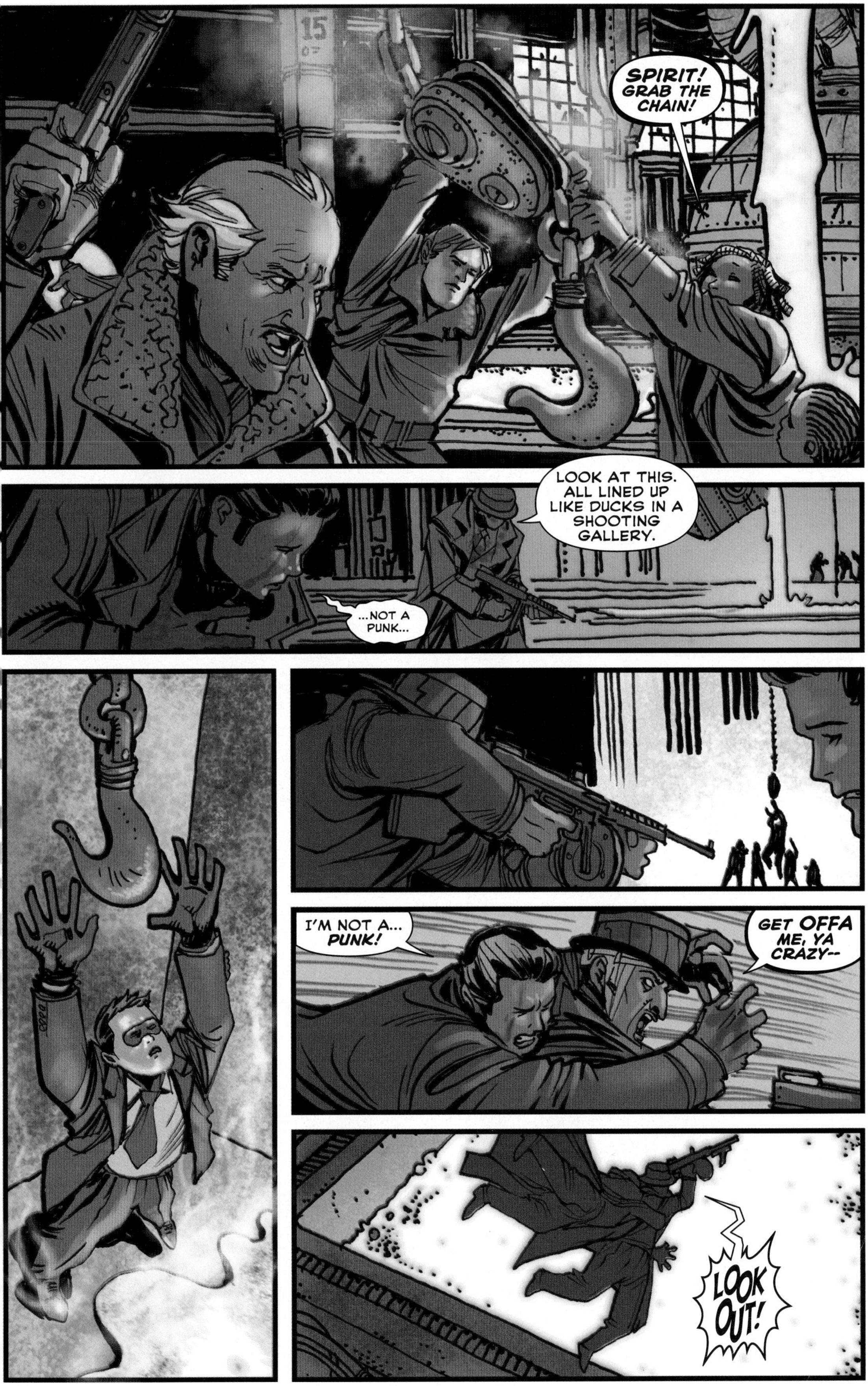
SPIRIT! GRAB THE CHAIN!
LOOK AT THIS. ALL LINED UP LIKE DUCKS IN A SHOOTING GALLERY.
...NOT A PUNK...
I'M NOT A... PUNK!
GET OFFA ME, YA CRAZY--
LOOK OUT!

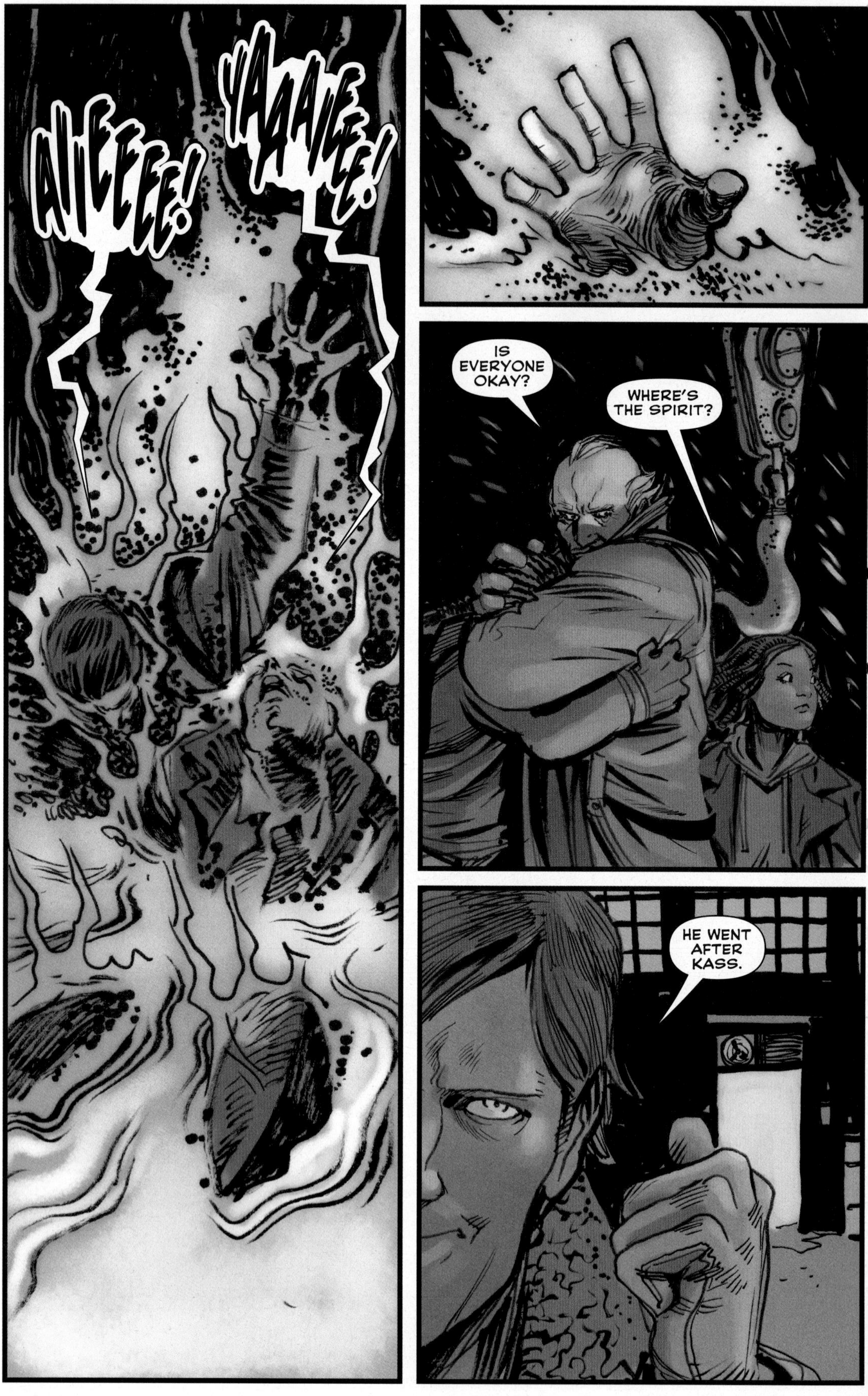

AIIEEEE!
YAAAIEE!
IS EVERYONE OKAY?
WHERE'S THE SPIRIT?
HE WENT AFTER KASS.

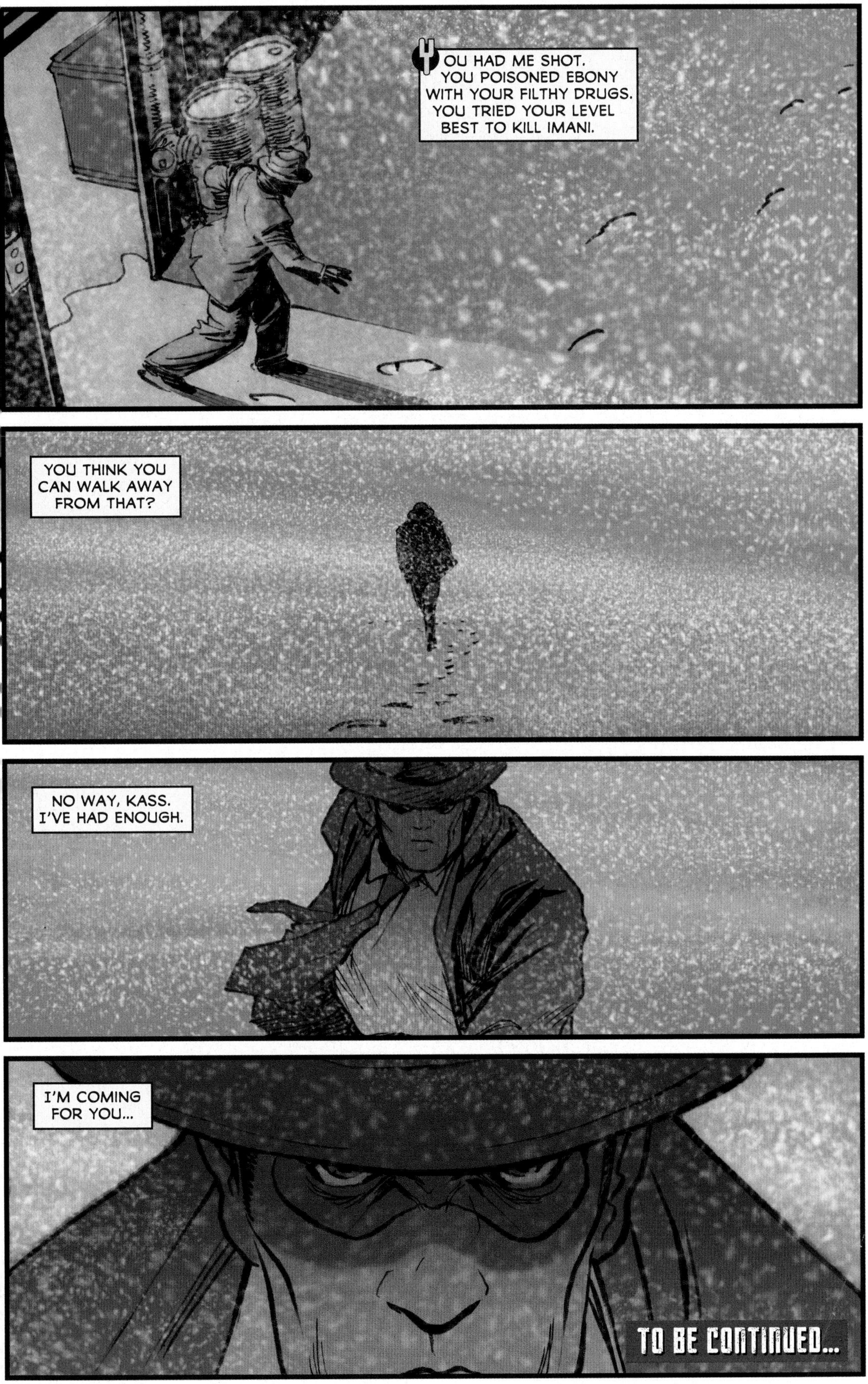
YOU HAD ME SHOT. YOU POISONED EBONY WITH YOUR FILTHY DRUGS. YOU TRIED YOUR LEVEL BEST TO KILL IMANI.
YOU THINK YOU CAN WALK AWAY FROM THAT?
NO WAY, KASS. I'VE HAD ENOUGH.
I'M COMING FOR YOU...
TO BE CONTINUED...

FROST BITE **PART FOUR**

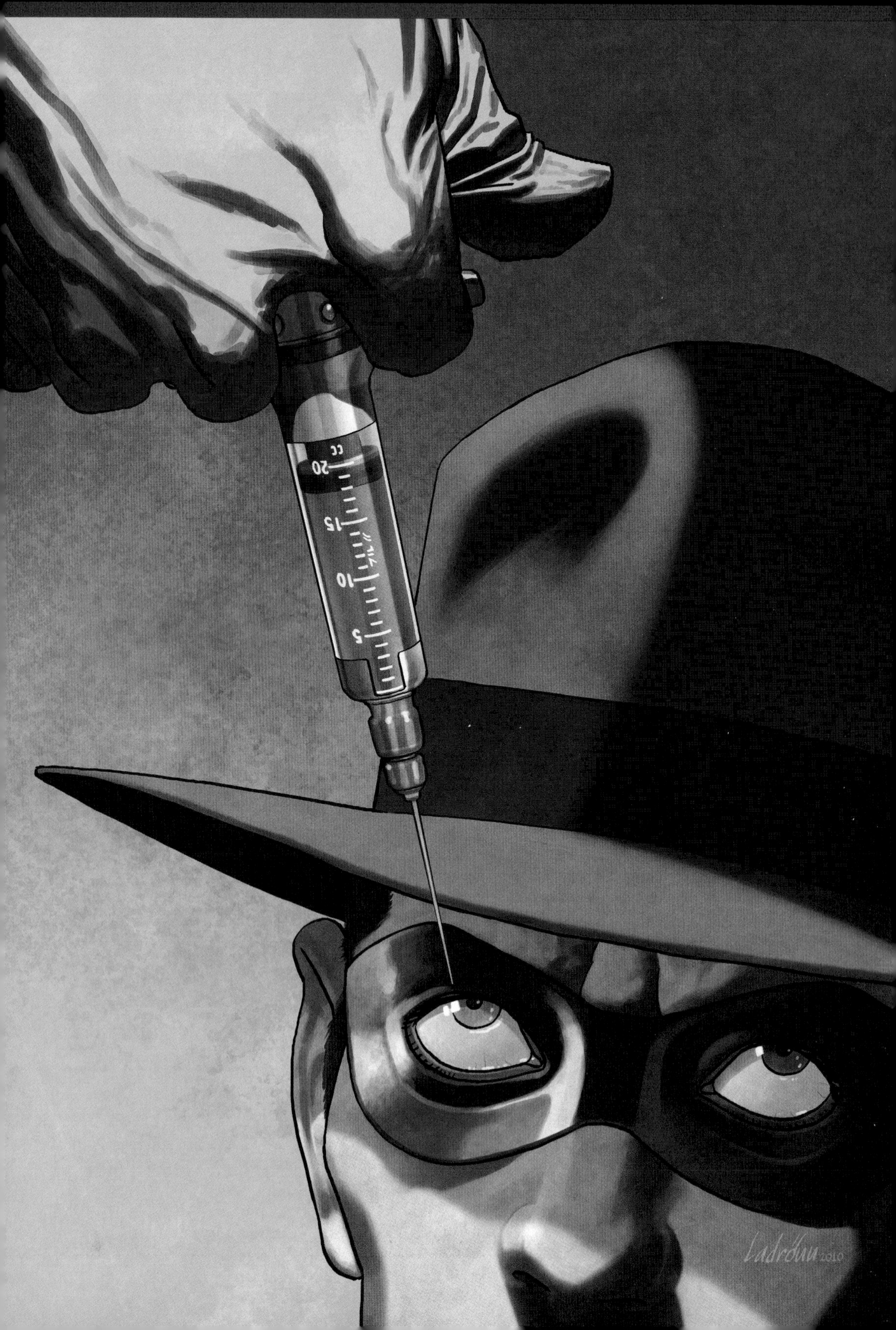

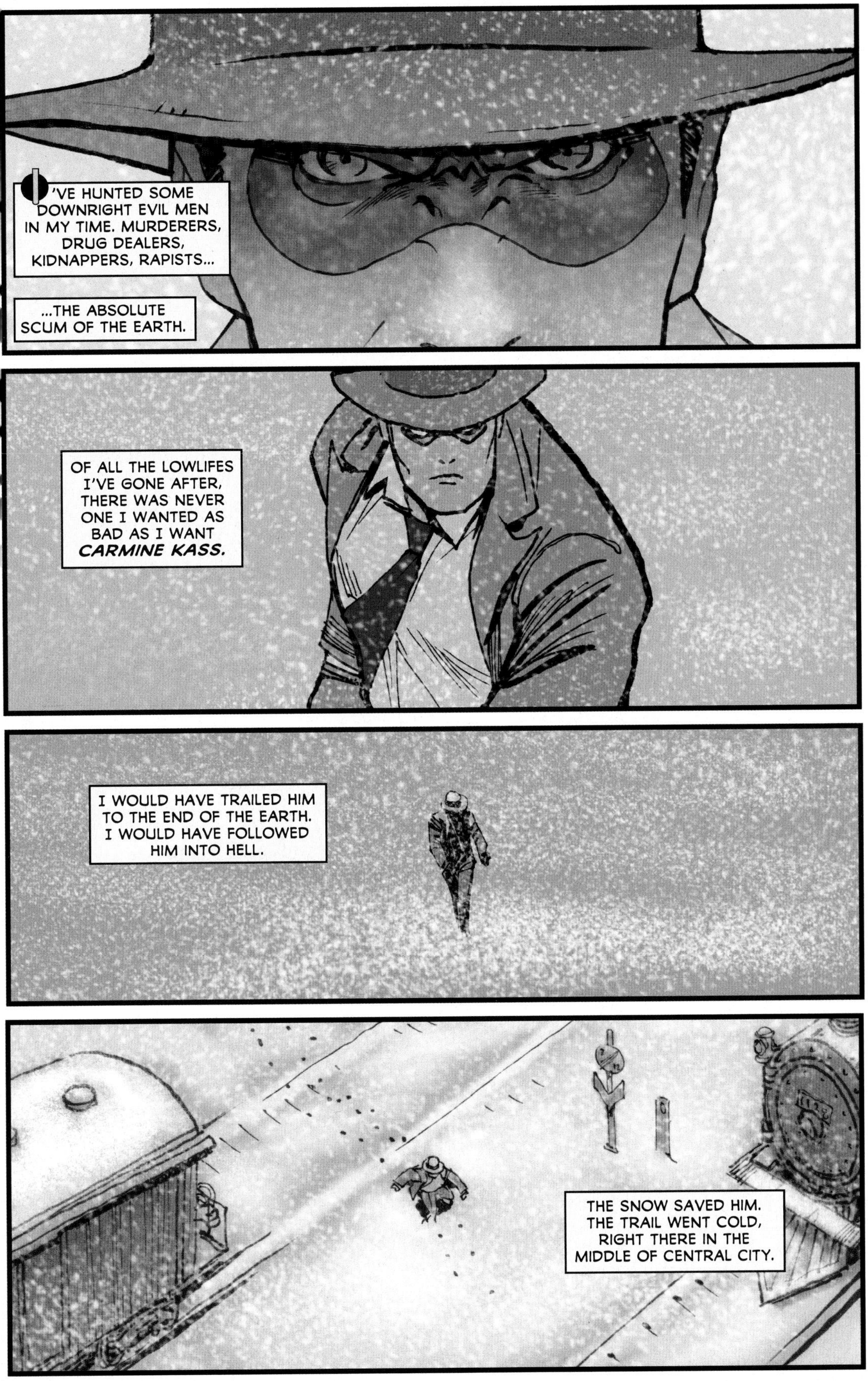
I'VE HUNTED SOME DOWNRIGHT EVIL MEN IN MY TIME. MURDERERS, DRUG DEALERS, KIDNAPPERS, RAPISTS...
...THE ABSOLUTE SCUM OF THE EARTH.
OF ALL THE LOWLIFES I'VE GONE AFTER, THERE WAS NEVER ONE I WANTED AS BAD AS I WANT *CARMINE KASS.*
I WOULD HAVE TRAILED HIM TO THE END OF THE EARTH. I WOULD HAVE FOLLOWED HIM INTO HELL.
THE SNOW SAVED HIM. THE TRAIL WENT COLD, RIGHT THERE IN THE MIDDLE OF CENTRAL CITY.

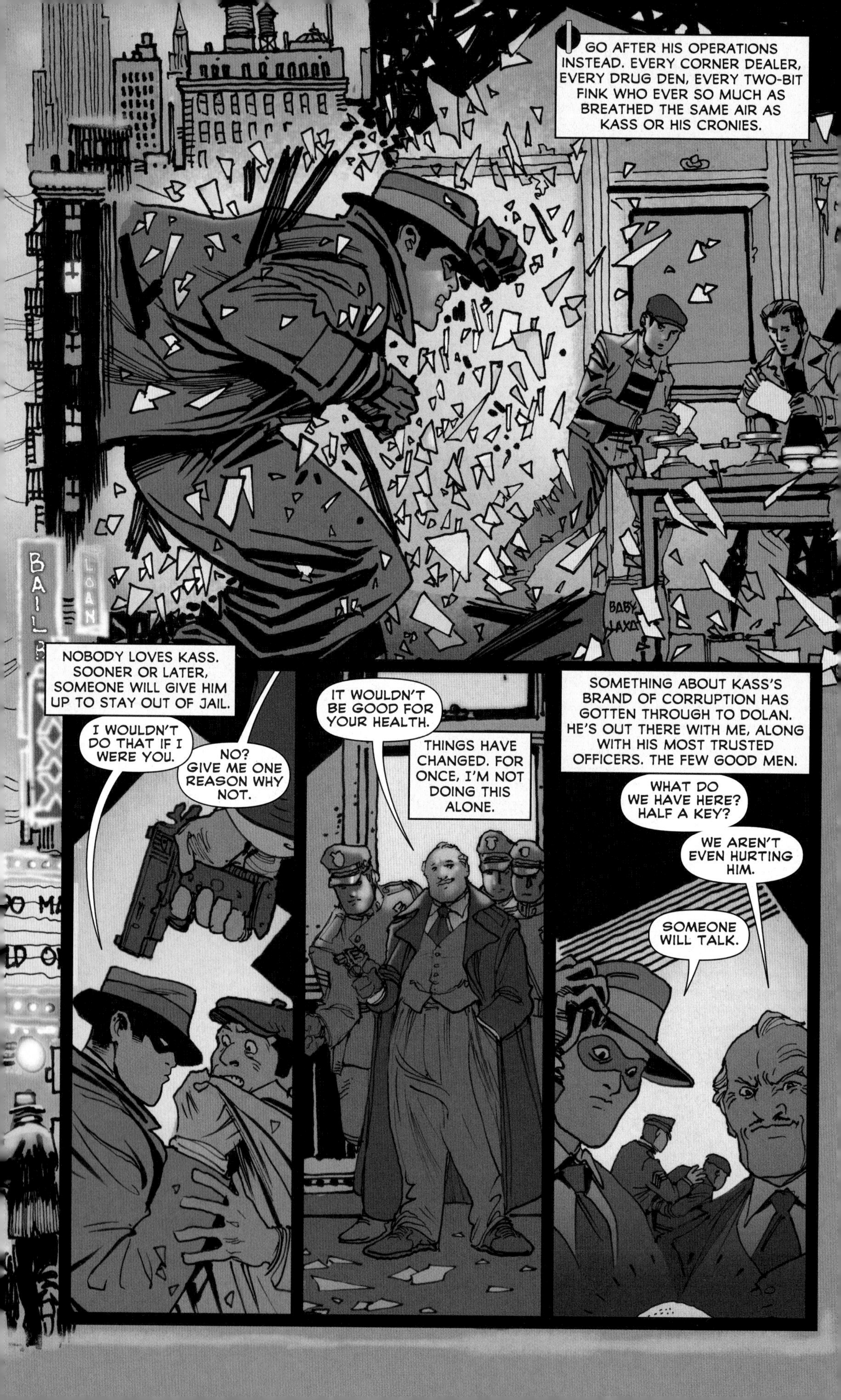
GO AFTER HIS OPERATIONS INSTEAD. EVERY CORNER DEALER, EVERY DRUG DEN, EVERY TWO-BIT FINK WHO EVER SO MUCH AS BREATHED THE SAME AIR AS KASS OR HIS CRONIES.
BAIL
LOAN
BABY LAXA
NOBODY LOVES KASS. SOONER OR LATER, SOMEONE WILL GIVE HIM UP TO STAY OUT OF JAIL.
I WOULDN'T DO THAT IF I WERE YOU.
NO? GIVE ME ONE REASON WHY NOT.
IT WOULDN'T BE GOOD FOR YOUR HEALTH.
THINGS HAVE CHANGED. FOR ONCE, I'M NOT DOING THIS ALONE.
SOMETHING ABOUT KASS'S BRAND OF CORRUPTION HAS GOTTEN THROUGH TO DOLAN. HE'S OUT THERE WITH ME, ALONG WITH HIS MOST TRUSTED OFFICERS. THE FEW GOOD MEN.
WHAT DO WE HAVE HERE? HALF A KEY?
WE AREN'T EVEN HURTING HIM.
SOMEONE WILL TALK.

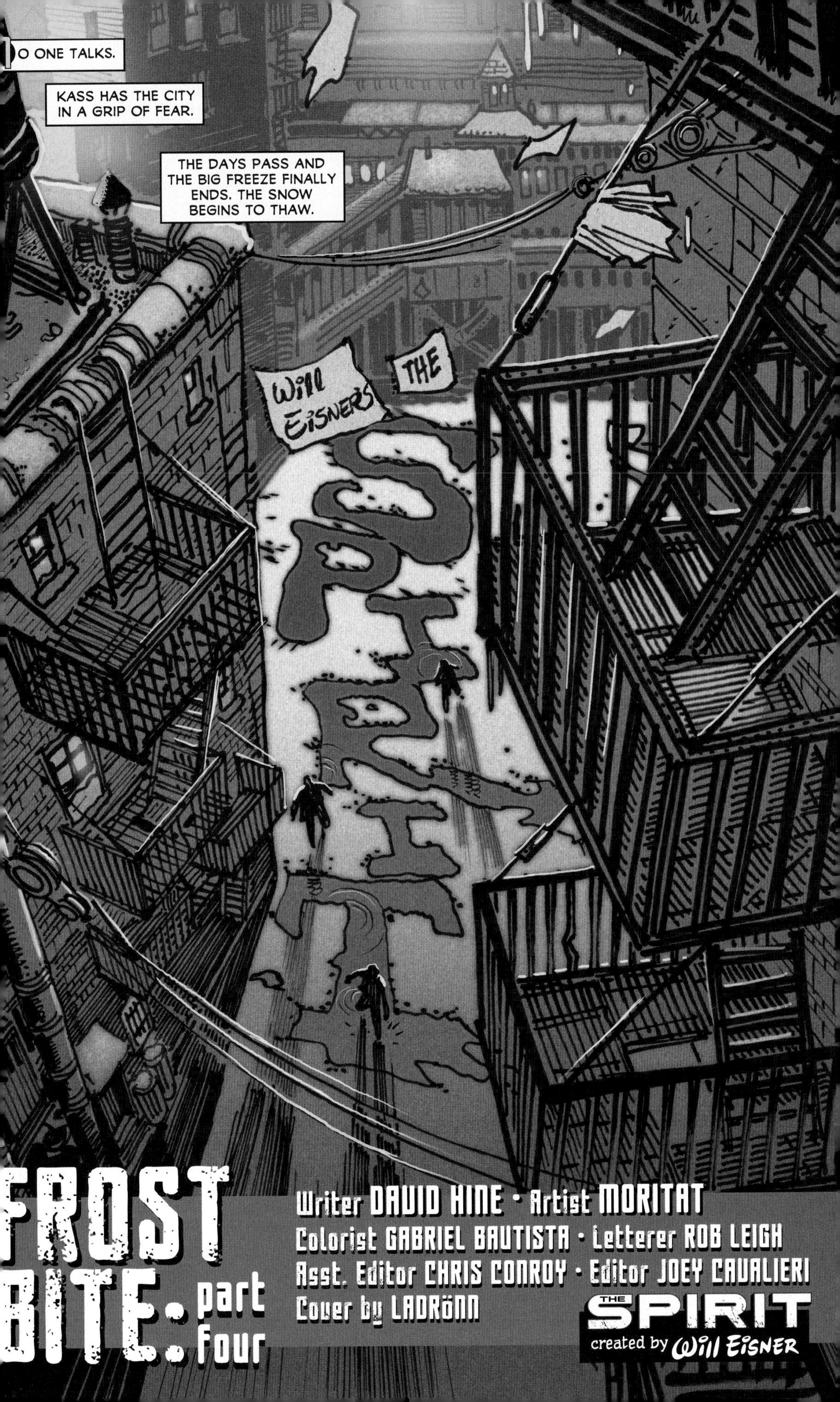
O ONE TALKS.
KASS HAS THE CITY IN A GRIP OF FEAR.
THE DAYS PASS AND THE BIG FREEZE FINALLY ENDS. THE SNOW BEGINS TO THAW.
WILL EISNER'S THE SPIRIT
FROST BITE: part four
Writer DAVID HINE • Artist MORITAT
Colorist GABRIEL BAUTISTA • Letterer ROB LEIGH
Asst. Editor CHRIS CONROY • Editor JOEY CAVALIERI
Cover by LADRÖNN
THE SPIRIT
created by WILL EISNER

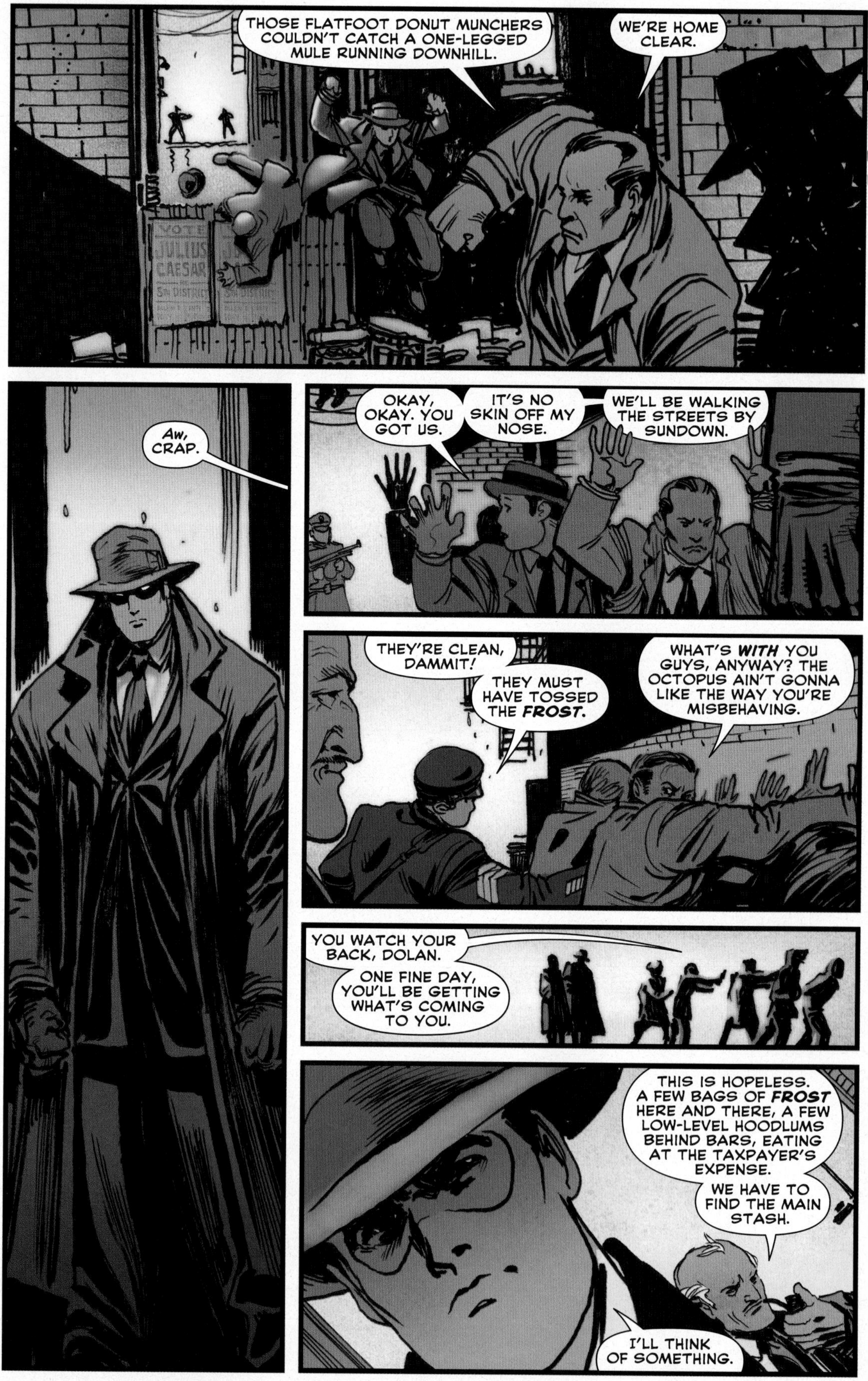

THOSE FLATFOOT DONUT MUNCHERS COULDN'T CATCH A ONE-LEGGED MULE RUNNING DOWNHILL.
WE'RE HOME CLEAR.
VOTE
JULIUS CAESAR
5th DISTRICT
Aw, CRAP.
OKAY, OKAY. YOU GOT US.
IT'S NO SKIN OFF MY NOSE.
WE'LL BE WALKING THE STREETS BY SUNDOWN.
THEY'RE CLEAN, DAMMIT!
THEY MUST HAVE TOSSED THE ***FROST***.
WHAT'S ***WITH*** YOU GUYS, ANYWAY? THE OCTOPUS AIN'T GONNA LIKE THE WAY YOU'RE MISBEHAVING.
YOU WATCH YOUR BACK, DOLAN.
ONE FINE DAY, YOU'LL BE GETTING WHAT'S COMING TO YOU.
THIS IS HOPELESS. A FEW BAGS OF ***FROST*** HERE AND THERE, A FEW LOW-LEVEL HOODLUMS BEHIND BARS, EATING AT THE TAXPAYER'S EXPENSE.
WE HAVE TO FIND THE MAIN STASH.
I'LL THINK OF SOMETHING.

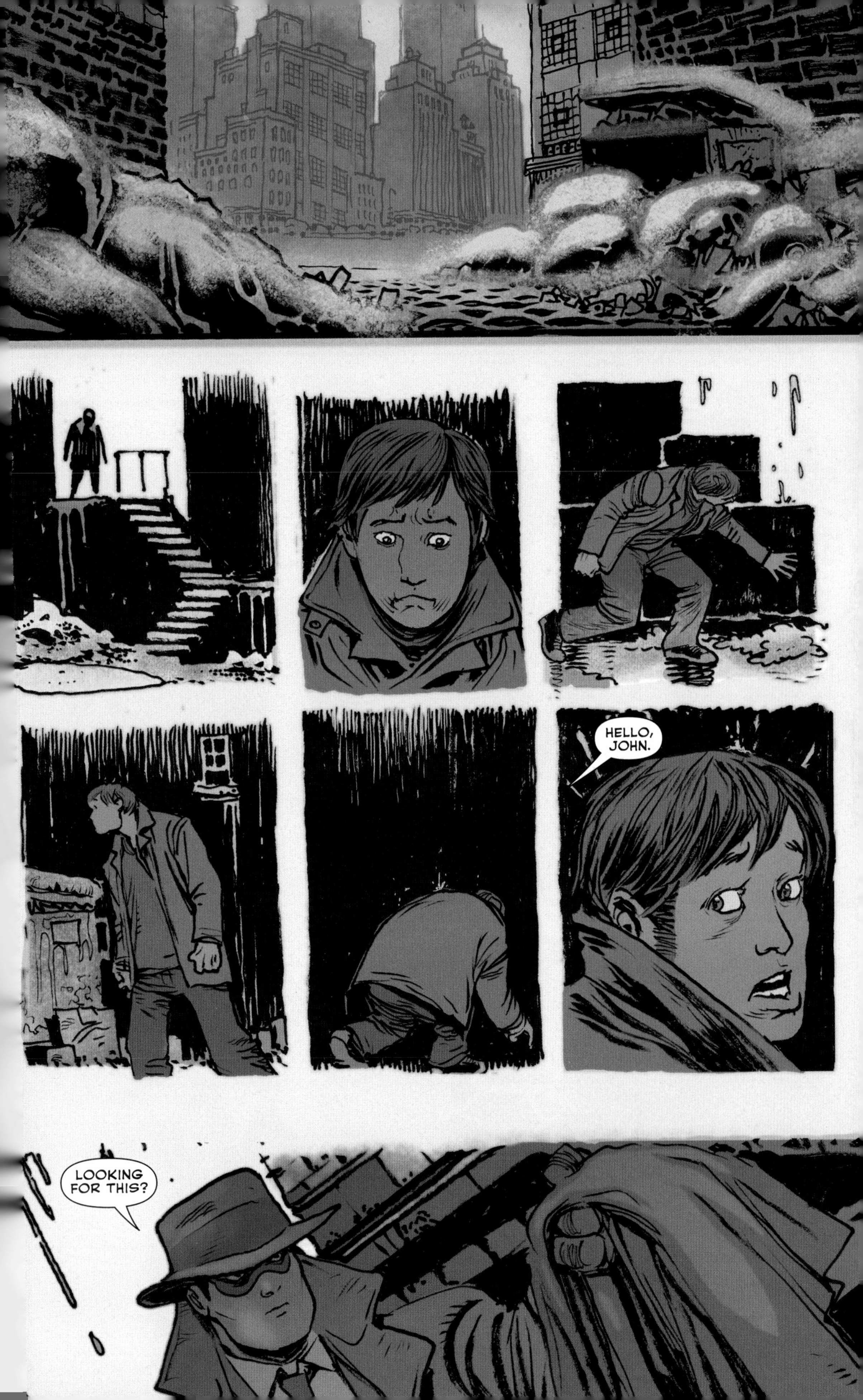
HELLO, JOHN.
LOOKING FOR THIS?

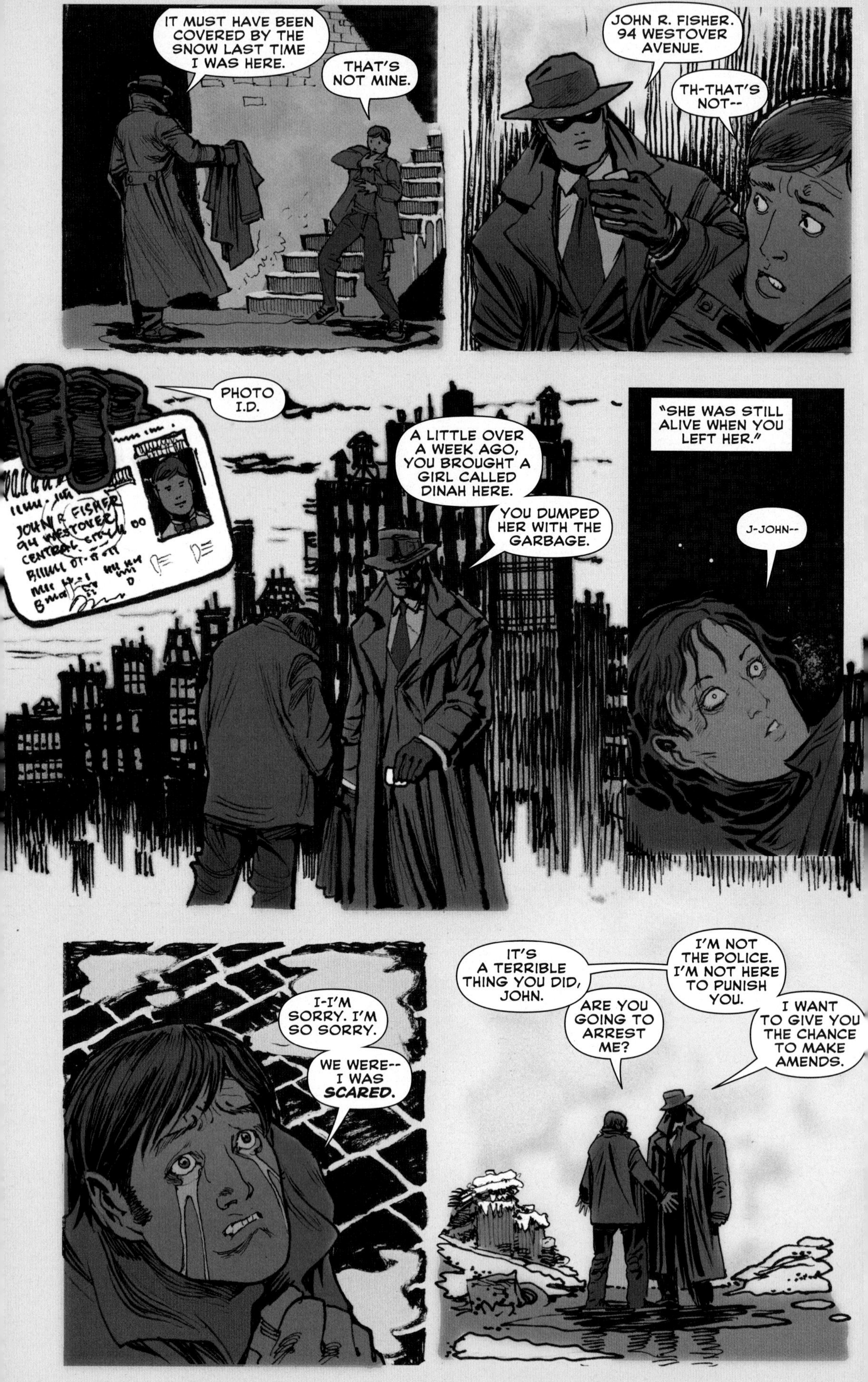

IT MUST HAVE BEEN COVERED BY THE SNOW LAST TIME I WAS HERE.
THAT'S NOT MINE.
JOHN R. FISHER. 94 WESTOVER AVENUE.
TH-THAT'S NOT--
PHOTO I.D.
JOHN R FISHER
94 WESTOVER
A LITTLE OVER A WEEK AGO, YOU BROUGHT A GIRL CALLED DINAH HERE.
YOU DUMPED HER WITH THE GARBAGE.
"SHE WAS STILL ALIVE WHEN YOU LEFT HER."
J-JOHN--
I-I'M SORRY. I'M SO SORRY.
WE WERE-- I WAS SCARED.
IT'S A TERRIBLE THING YOU DID, JOHN.
ARE YOU GOING TO ARREST ME?
I'M NOT THE POLICE. I'M NOT HERE TO PUNISH YOU.
I WANT TO GIVE YOU THE CHANCE TO MAKE AMENDS.

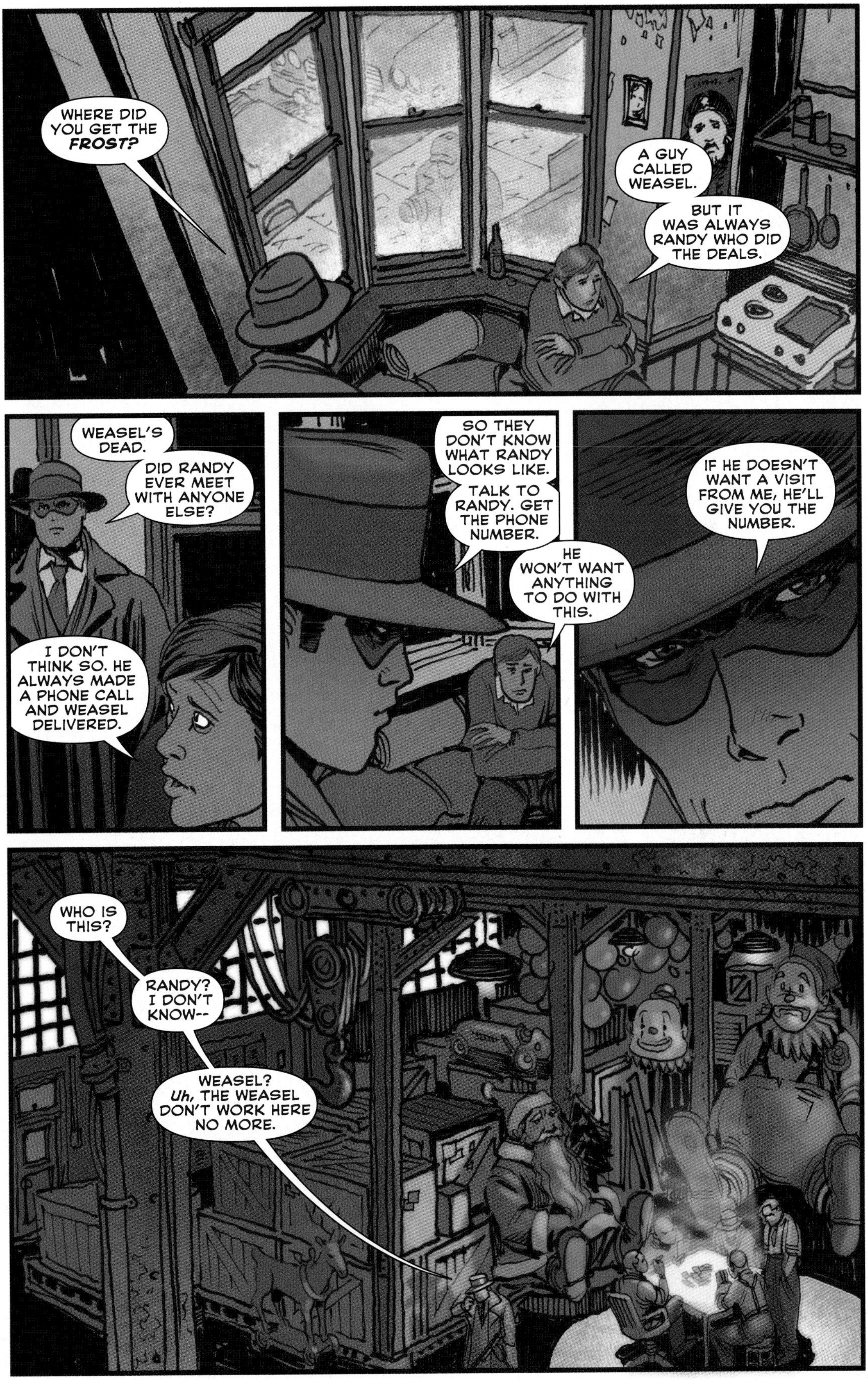
WHERE DID YOU GET THE *FROST?*
A GUY CALLED WEASEL.
BUT IT WAS ALWAYS RANDY WHO DID THE DEALS.
WEASEL'S DEAD.
DID RANDY EVER MEET WITH ANYONE ELSE?
I DON'T THINK SO. HE ALWAYS MADE A PHONE CALL AND WEASEL DELIVERED.
SO THEY DON'T KNOW WHAT RANDY LOOKS LIKE.
TALK TO RANDY. GET THE PHONE NUMBER.
HE WON'T WANT ANYTHING TO DO WITH THIS.
IF HE DOESN'T WANT A VISIT FROM ME, HE'LL GIVE YOU THE NUMBER.
WHO IS THIS?
RANDY? I DON'T KNOW--
WEASEL? *Uh,* THE WEASEL DON'T WORK HERE NO MORE.

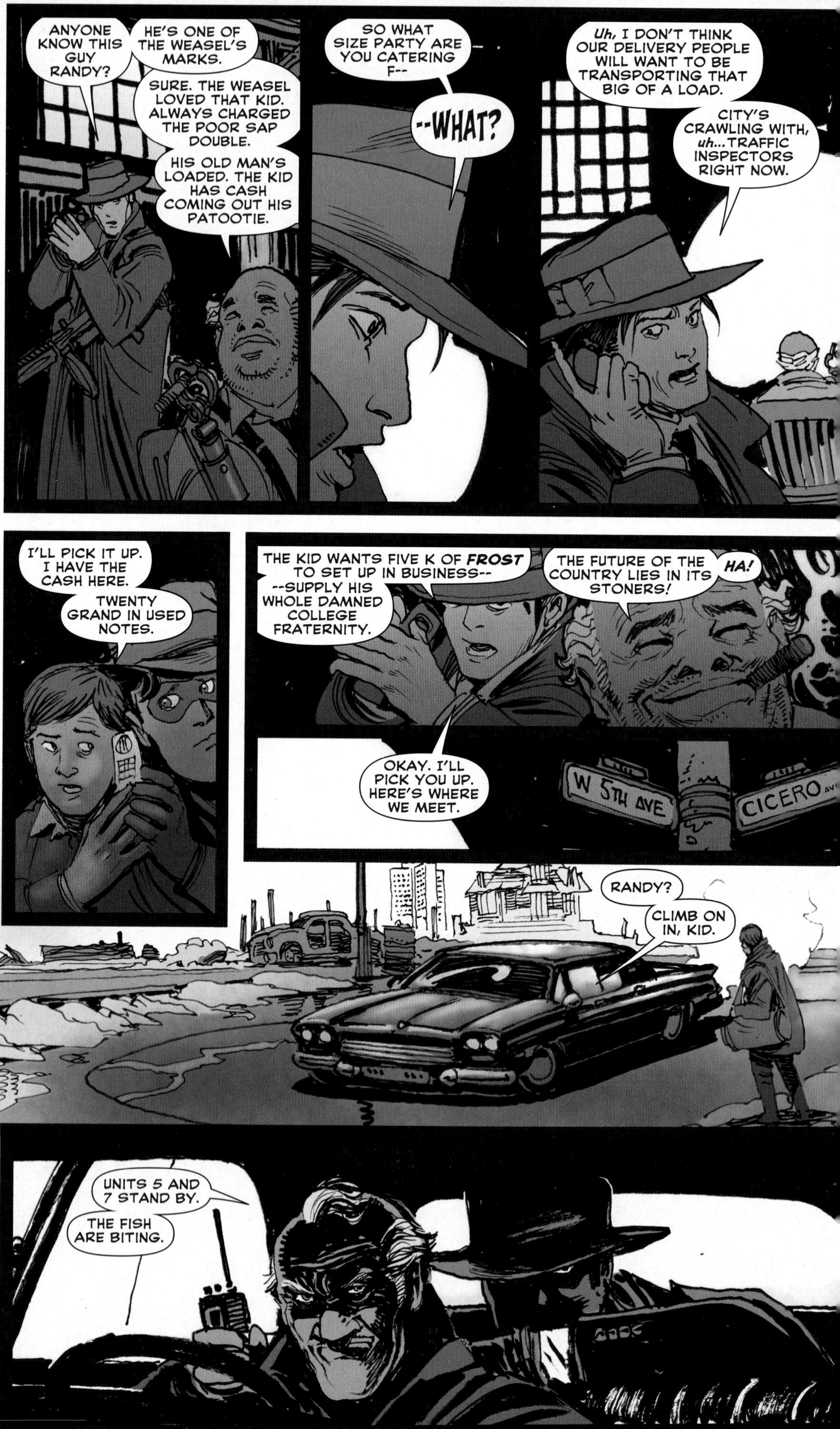
ANYONE KNOW THIS GUY RANDY?
HE'S ONE OF THE WEASEL'S MARKS.
SURE. THE WEASEL LOVED THAT KID. ALWAYS CHARGED THE POOR SAP DOUBLE.
HIS OLD MAN'S LOADED. THE KID HAS CASH COMING OUT HIS PATOOTIE.
SO WHAT SIZE PARTY ARE YOU CATERING F--
--WHAT?
Uh, I DON'T THINK OUR DELIVERY PEOPLE WILL WANT TO BE TRANSPORTING THAT BIG OF A LOAD.
CITY'S CRAWLING WITH, *uh*... TRAFFIC INSPECTORS RIGHT NOW.
I'LL PICK IT UP. I HAVE THE CASH HERE.
TWENTY GRAND IN USED NOTES.
THE KID WANTS FIVE K OF ***FROST*** TO SET UP IN BUSINESS--
--SUPPLY HIS WHOLE DAMNED COLLEGE FRATERNITY.
THE FUTURE OF THE COUNTRY LIES IN ITS STONERS!
HA!
OKAY. I'LL PICK YOU UP. HERE'S WHERE WE MEET.
W 5TH AVE
CICERO
RANDY?
CLIMB ON IN, KID.
UNITS 5 AND 7 STAND BY.
THE FISH ARE BITING.

FUN 'N' FROLIX
FUN 'N' FROLIX
WAIT HERE, KID. WE'LL GO GET THE PRODUCT.
THIS CASH WILL BUY YOU ENOUGH NOSE CANDY TO KEEP YOU AND YOUR BUDDIES HIGH ALL THE WAY THROUGH TO GRADUATION.
HEY, WHERE ARE YOU--?
YOU LITTLE RAT!
WHHEEEOOOOo-EEEEEOOOOO
WE'VE BEEN MADE! DAMNED KID BROUGHT THE COPS!

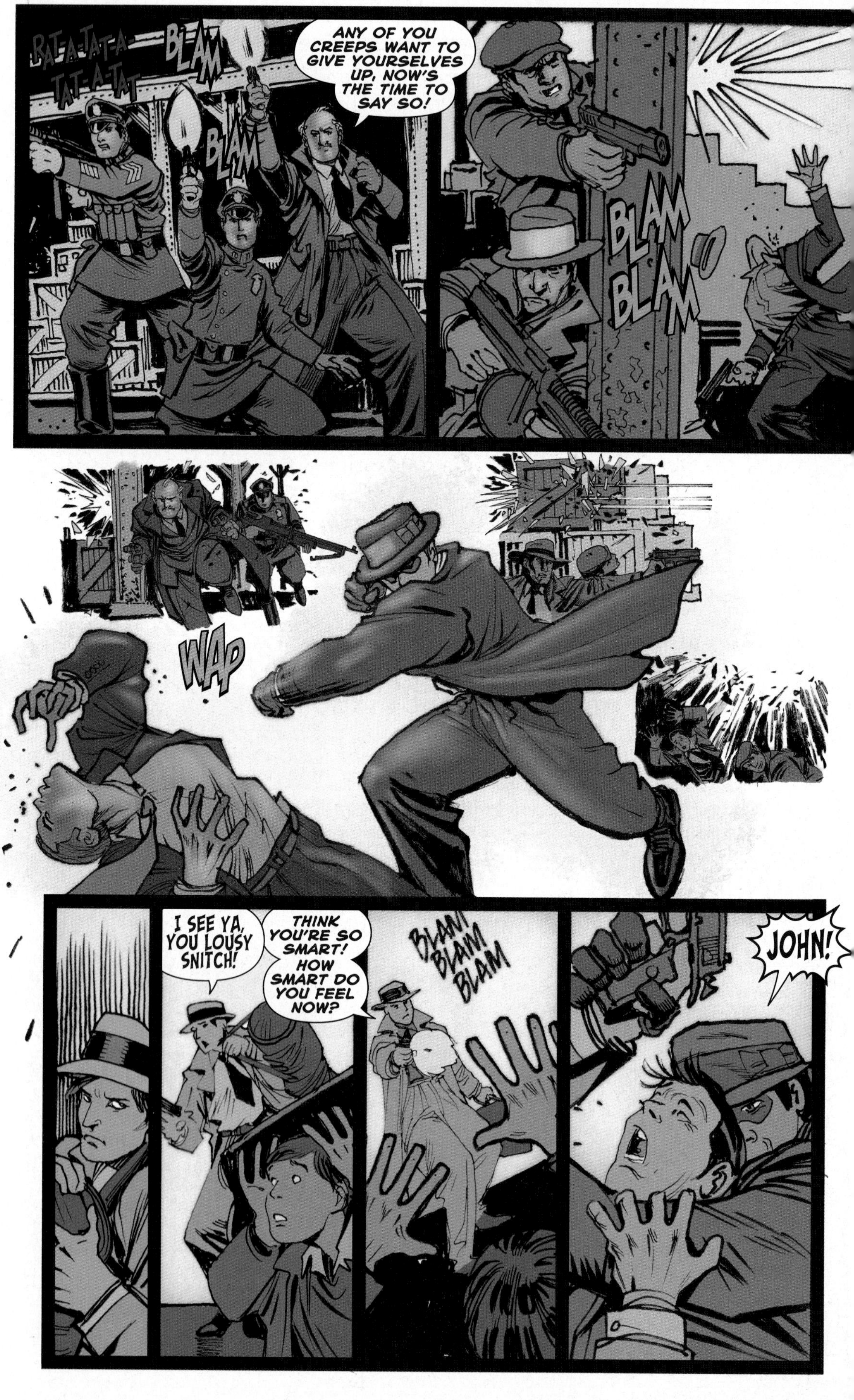
RAT-A-TAT-A-TAT-A-TAT
BLAM
ANY OF YOU CREEPS WANT TO GIVE YOURSELVES UP, NOW'S THE TIME TO SAY SO!
BLAM
BLAM BLAM
WAP
I SEE YA, YOU LOUSY SNITCH!
THINK YOU'RE SO SMART! HOW SMART DO YOU FEEL NOW?
BLAM BLAM BLAM
JOHN!

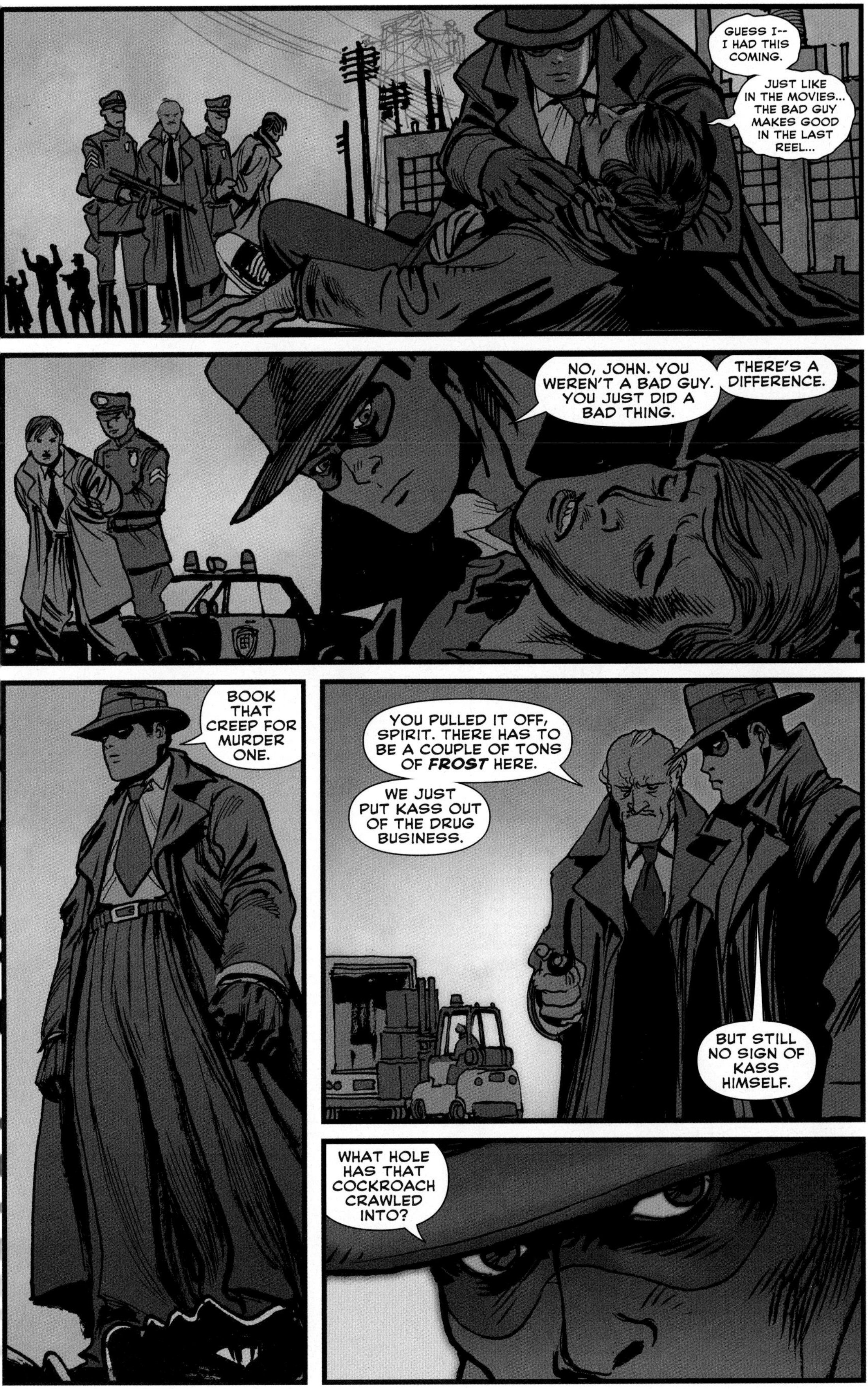
GUESS I-- I HAD THIS COMING.
JUST LIKE IN THE MOVIES... THE BAD GUY MAKES GOOD IN THE LAST REEL...
NO, JOHN. YOU WEREN'T A BAD GUY. YOU JUST DID A BAD THING.
THERE'S A DIFFERENCE.
BOOK THAT CREEP FOR MURDER ONE.
YOU PULLED IT OFF, SPIRIT. THERE HAS TO BE A COUPLE OF TONS OF FROST HERE.
WE JUST PUT KASS OUT OF THE DRUG BUSINESS.
BUT STILL NO SIGN OF KASS HIMSELF.
WHAT HOLE HAS THAT COCKROACH CRAWLED INTO?

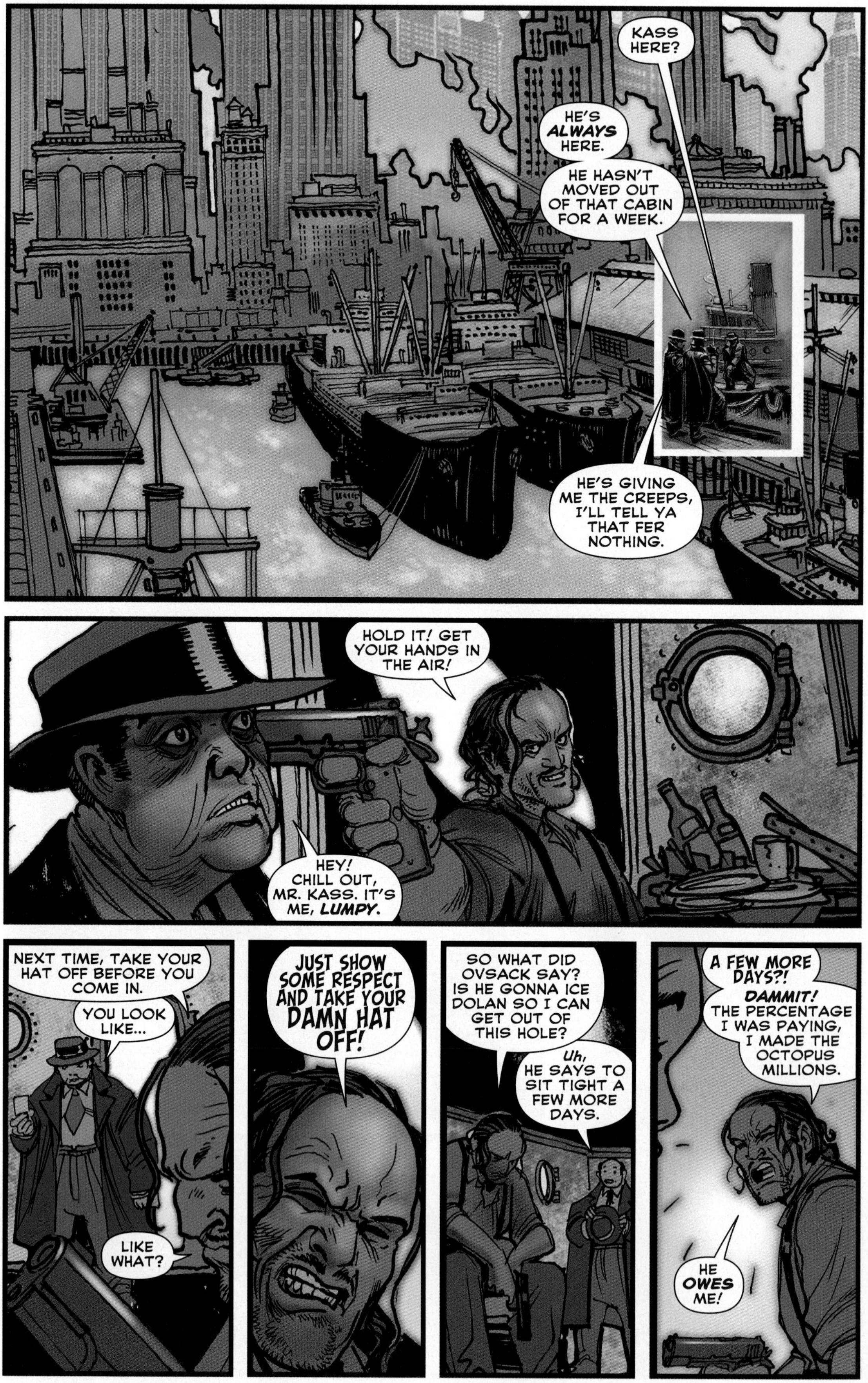
KASS HERE?
HE'S *ALWAYS* HERE.
HE HASN'T MOVED OUT OF THAT CABIN FOR A WEEK.
HE'S GIVING ME THE CREEPS, I'LL TELL YA THAT FER NOTHING.
HOLD IT! GET YOUR HANDS IN THE AIR!
HEY! CHILL OUT, MR. KASS. IT'S ME, *LUMPY*.
NEXT TIME, TAKE YOUR HAT OFF BEFORE YOU COME IN.
YOU LOOK LIKE...
LIKE WHAT?
JUST SHOW SOME RESPECT AND TAKE YOUR DAMN HAT OFF!
SO WHAT DID OVSACK SAY? IS HE GONNA ICE DOLAN SO I CAN GET OUT OF THIS HOLE?
Uh, HE SAYS TO SIT TIGHT A FEW MORE DAYS.
A FEW MORE DAYS?! *DAMMIT!* THE PERCENTAGE I WAS PAYING, I MADE THE OCTOPUS MILLIONS.
HE *OWES* ME!

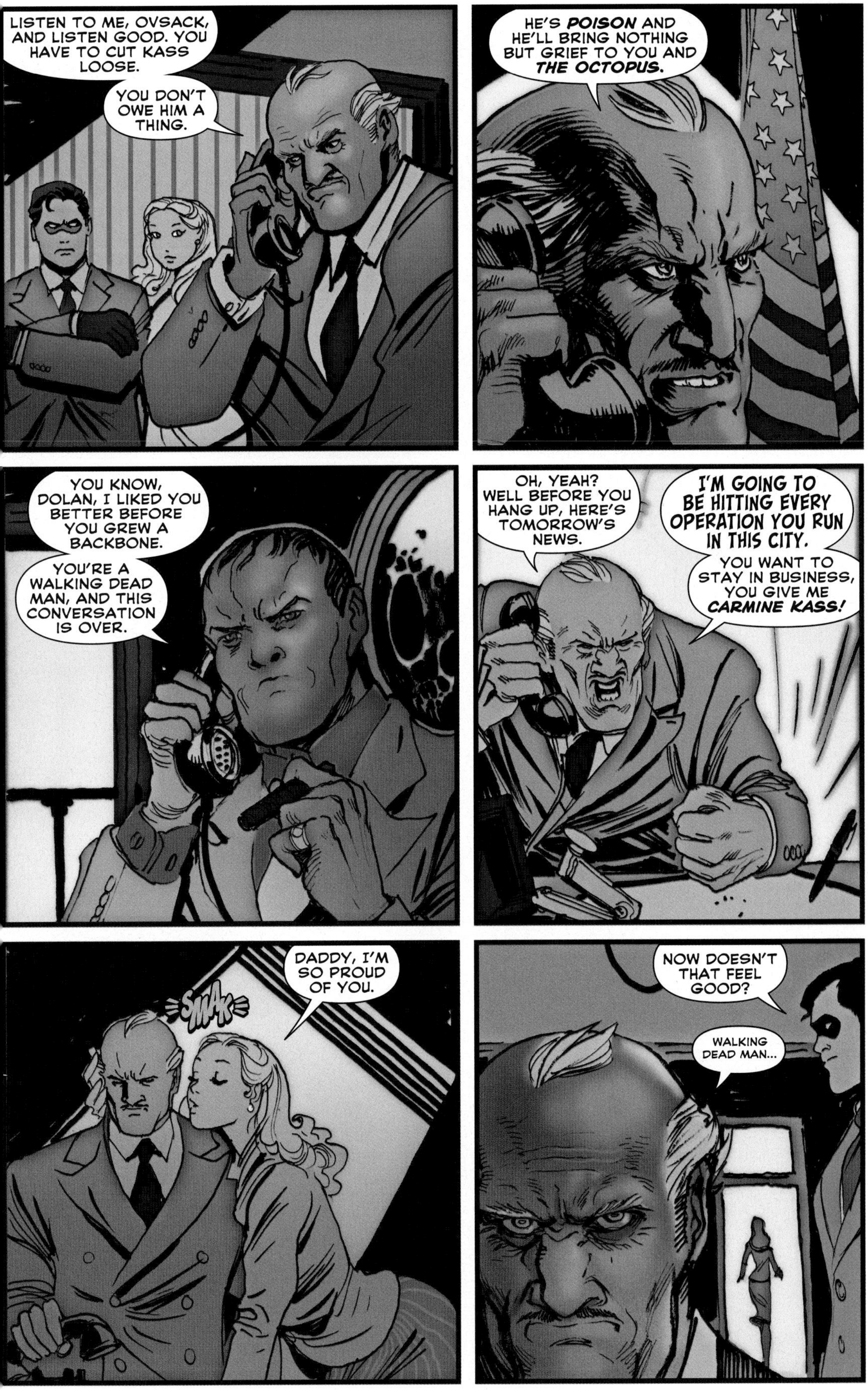
LISTEN TO ME, OVSACK, AND LISTEN GOOD. YOU HAVE TO CUT KASS LOOSE.
YOU DON'T OWE HIM A THING.
HE'S POISON AND HE'LL BRING NOTHING BUT GRIEF TO YOU AND THE OCTOPUS.
YOU KNOW, DOLAN, I LIKED YOU BETTER BEFORE YOU GREW A BACKBONE.
YOU'RE A WALKING DEAD MAN, AND THIS CONVERSATION IS OVER.
OH, YEAH? WELL BEFORE YOU HANG UP, HERE'S TOMORROW'S NEWS.
I'M GOING TO BE HITTING EVERY OPERATION YOU RUN IN THIS CITY.
YOU WANT TO STAY IN BUSINESS, YOU GIVE ME CARMINE KASS!
SMAK
DADDY, I'M SO PROUD OF YOU.
NOW DOESN'T THAT FEEL GOOD?
WALKING DEAD MAN...

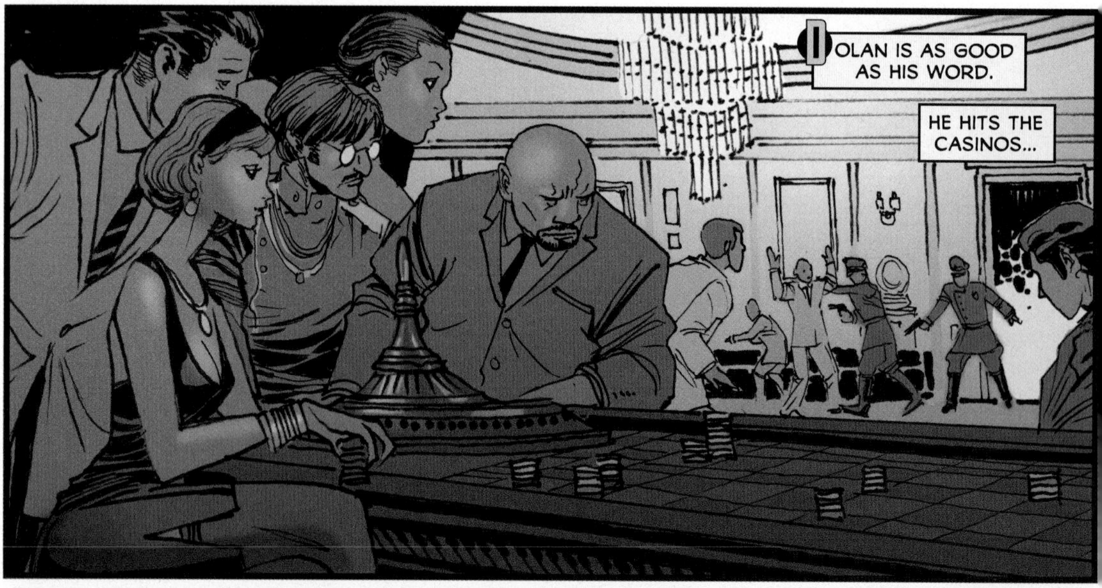
DOLAN IS AS GOOD AS HIS WORD.
HE HITS THE CASINOS...

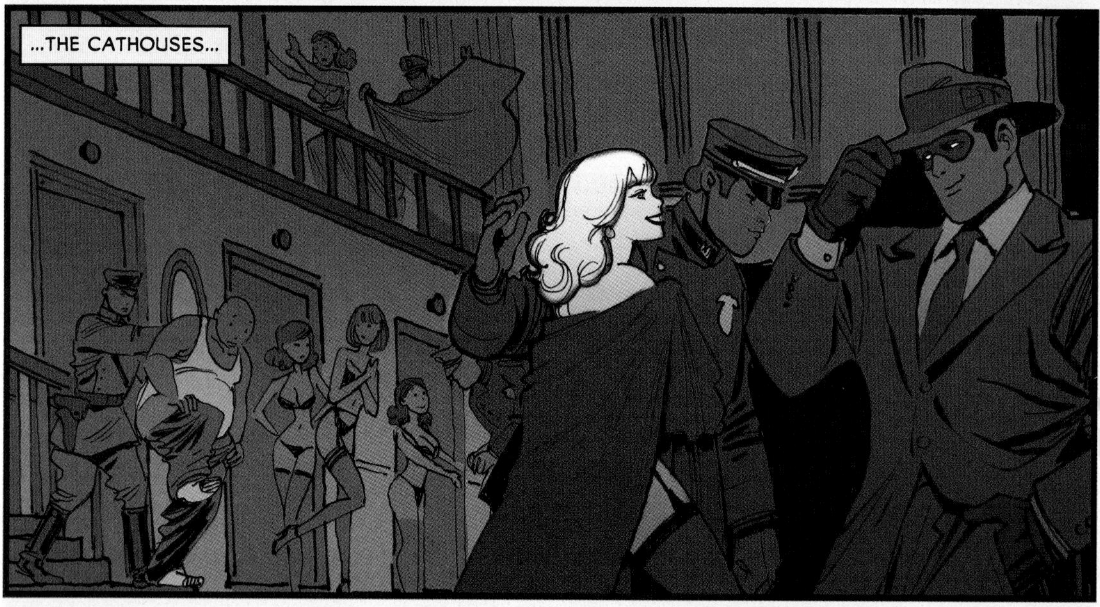
...THE CATHOUSES...

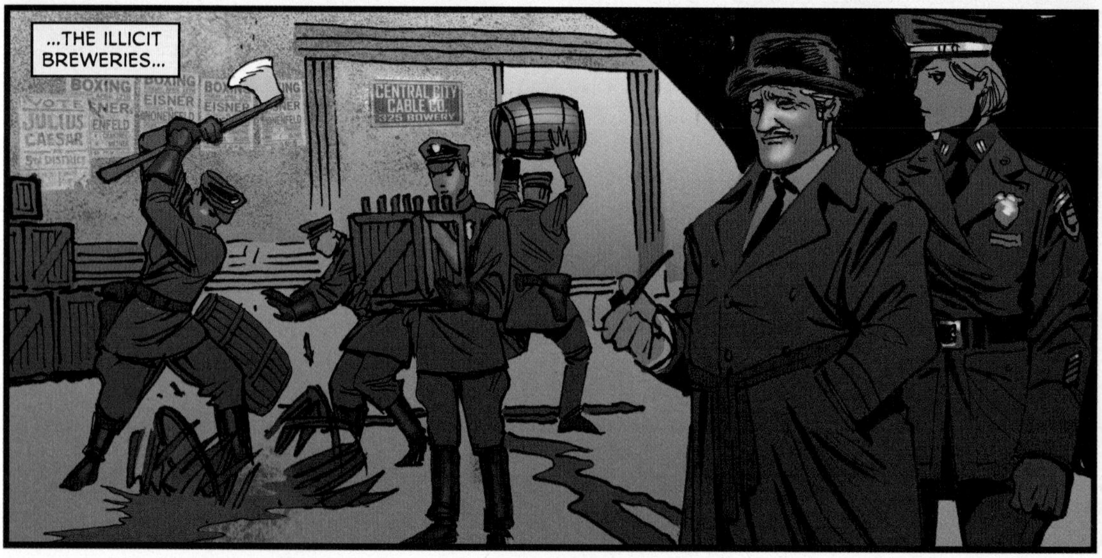
...THE ILLICIT BREWERIES...
CENTRAL CITY CABLE CO. 325 BOWERY

THIS HAS GOT TO STOP. WE'RE *HURTING!*

MY CLUBS ARE EMPTY. I GOT NO GIRLS, NO BOOZE...

WE GOTTA TAKE DOLAN DOWN.

DOLAN'S A POPULAR GUY. KILLING HIM IS TOO RISKY.

WE COULD ALWAYS DEAL WITH HIM BEFORE. HE'LL COME BACK IN LINE IF WE RUB OUT KASS.

WE SHOW WEAKNESS TO DOLAN NOW, WE LOSE RESPECT. EVERY TWO-BIT PUNK WITH A GUN WILL BE GOING UP AGAINST US.

RESPECT AND FEAR--TWO SIDES OF THE SAME COIN.

KASS NEEDS TO MEET *THE OCTOPUS.*

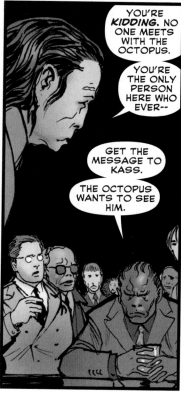

YOU'RE *KIDDING.* NO ONE MEETS WITH THE OCTOPUS.

YOU'RE THE ONLY PERSON HERE WHO EVER--

GET THE MESSAGE TO KASS.

THE OCTOPUS WANTS TO SEE HIM.

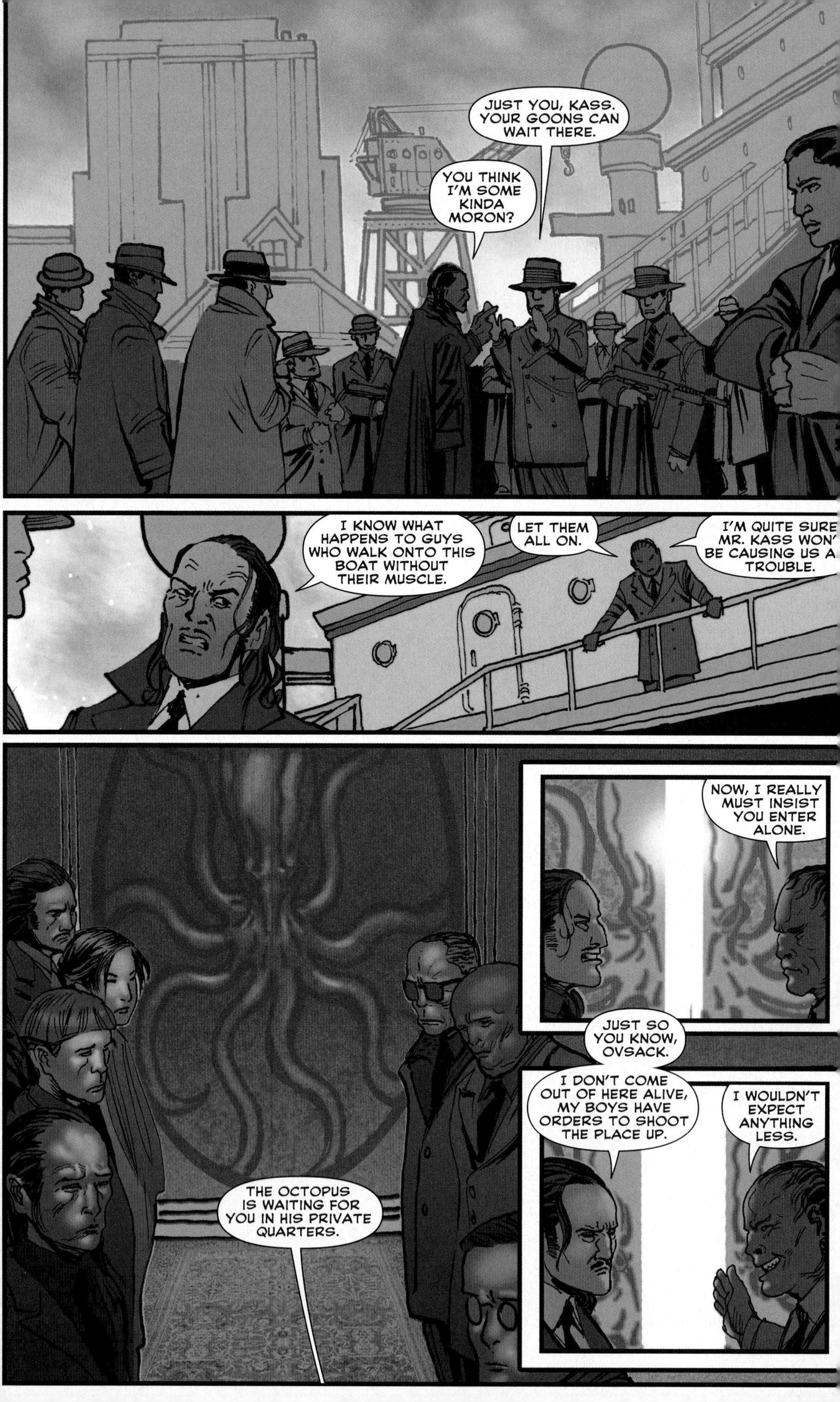
JUST YOU, KASS. YOUR GOONS CAN WAIT THERE.
YOU THINK I'M SOME KINDA MORON?
I KNOW WHAT HAPPENS TO GUYS WHO WALK ONTO THIS BOAT WITHOUT THEIR MUSCLE.
LET THEM ALL ON.
I'M QUITE SURE MR. KASS WON' BE CAUSING US A TROUBLE.
THE OCTOPUS IS WAITING FOR YOU IN HIS PRIVATE QUARTERS.
NOW, I REALLY MUST INSIST YOU ENTER ALONE.
JUST SO YOU KNOW, OVSACK.
I DON'T COME OUT OF HERE ALIVE, MY BOYS HAVE ORDERS TO SHOOT THE PLACE UP.
I WOULDN'T EXPECT ANYTHING LESS.

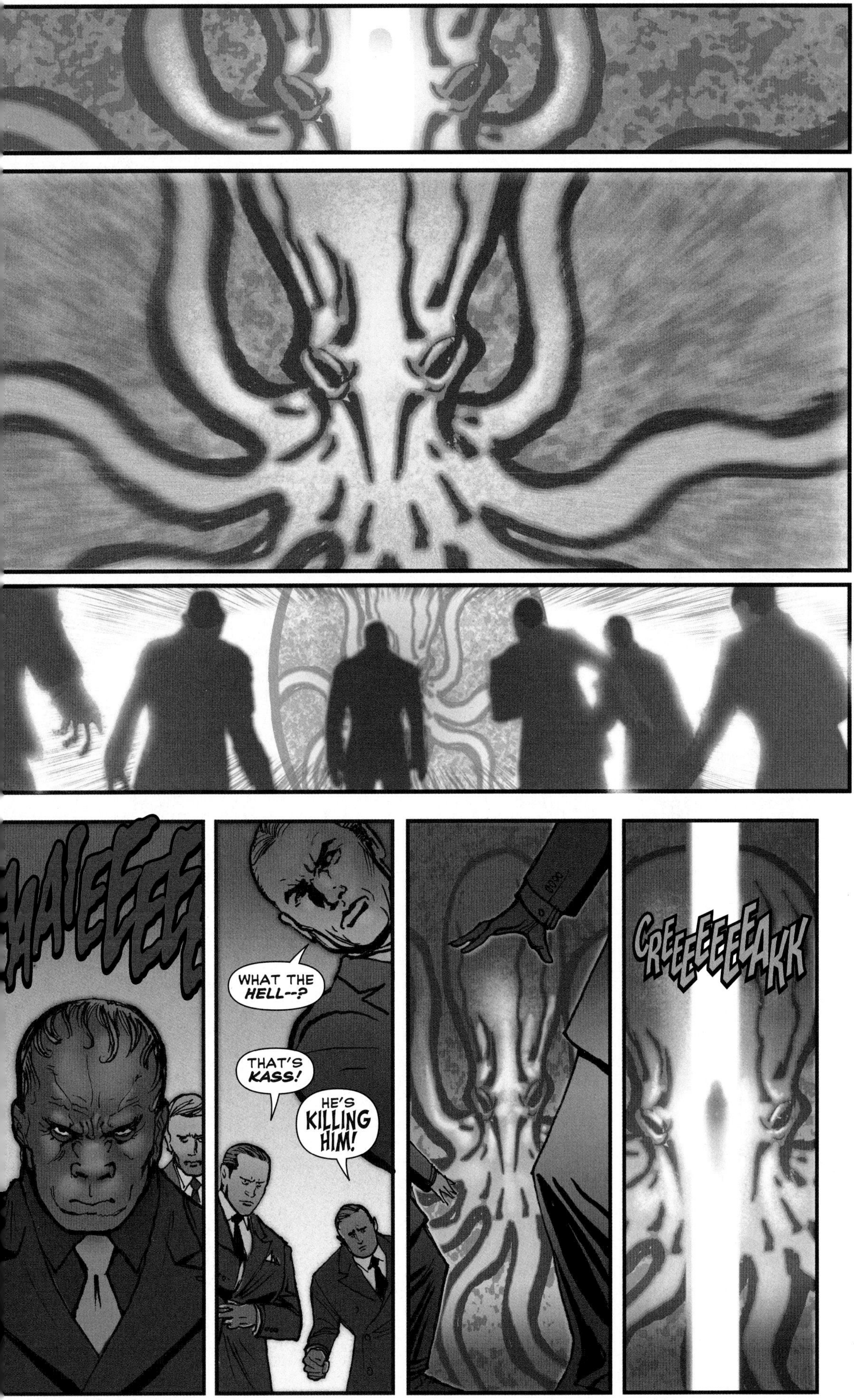
HAAIEEEEE
WHAT THE HELL--?
THAT'S KASS!
HE'S KILLING HIM!
CREEEEEEEAKK

heh-heh-heh-ock-kuk-

-ock-to-puss-heh-heh-heh

MY GOD!

THE OCTOPUS BLINDED HIM!

NO. KASS DID THIS TO HIMSELF.

LOOK!

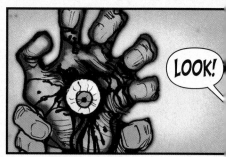

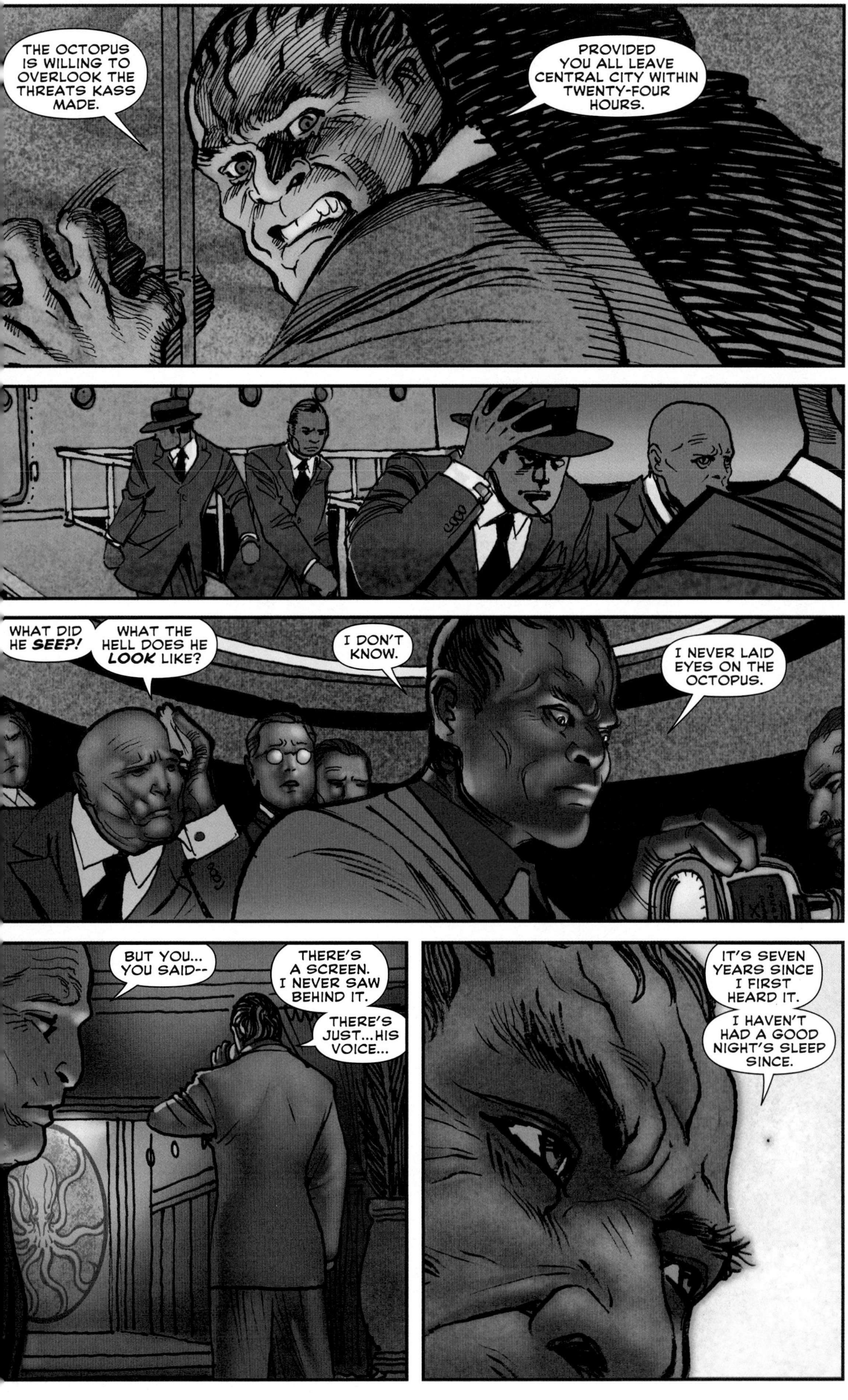
THE OCTOPUS IS WILLING TO OVERLOOK THE THREATS KASS MADE.
PROVIDED YOU ALL LEAVE CENTRAL CITY WITHIN TWENTY-FOUR HOURS.
WHAT DID HE *SEE?!*
WHAT THE HELL DOES HE *LOOK* LIKE?
I DON'T KNOW.
I NEVER LAID EYES ON THE OCTOPUS.
BUT YOU... YOU SAID--
THERE'S A SCREEN. I NEVER SAW BEHIND IT.
THERE'S JUST...HIS VOICE...
IT'S SEVEN YEARS SINCE I FIRST HEARD IT.
I HAVEN'T HAD A GOOD NIGHT'S SLEEP SINCE.

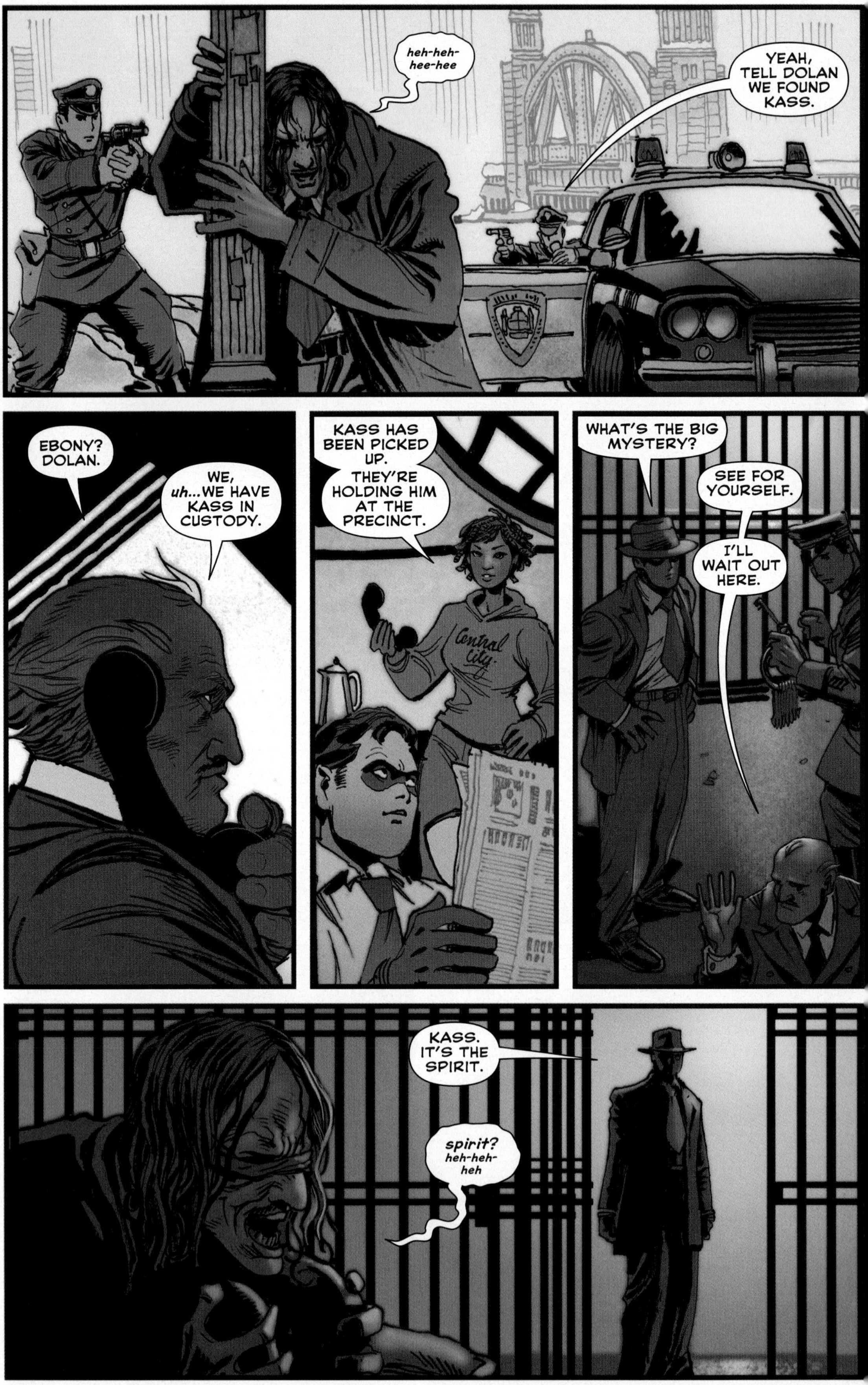
heh-heh-
hee-hee
YEAH, TELL DOLAN WE FOUND KASS.
EBONY? DOLAN.
WE, *uh*...WE HAVE KASS IN CUSTODY.
KASS HAS BEEN PICKED UP.
THEY'RE HOLDING HIM AT THE PRECINCT.
Central City
WHAT'S THE BIG MYSTERY?
SEE FOR YOURSELF.
I'LL WAIT OUT HERE.
KASS. IT'S THE SPIRIT.
spirit?
heh-heh-heh

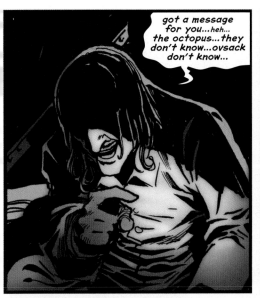

got a message for you...*heh*... the octopus...they don't know...ovsack don't know...

the octopus ain't a "he." she wants to hold you, spirit, wants to hold you in her... *heh-heh...*in her... arms...

THE OCTOPUS IS A **WOMAN?!**

...a woman?!... *ha-ha-ha-ha-ha*

YOU THINK HE'LL BE FIT TO STAND TRIAL?

LET HIM GO, DOLAN.

LET HIM GO.

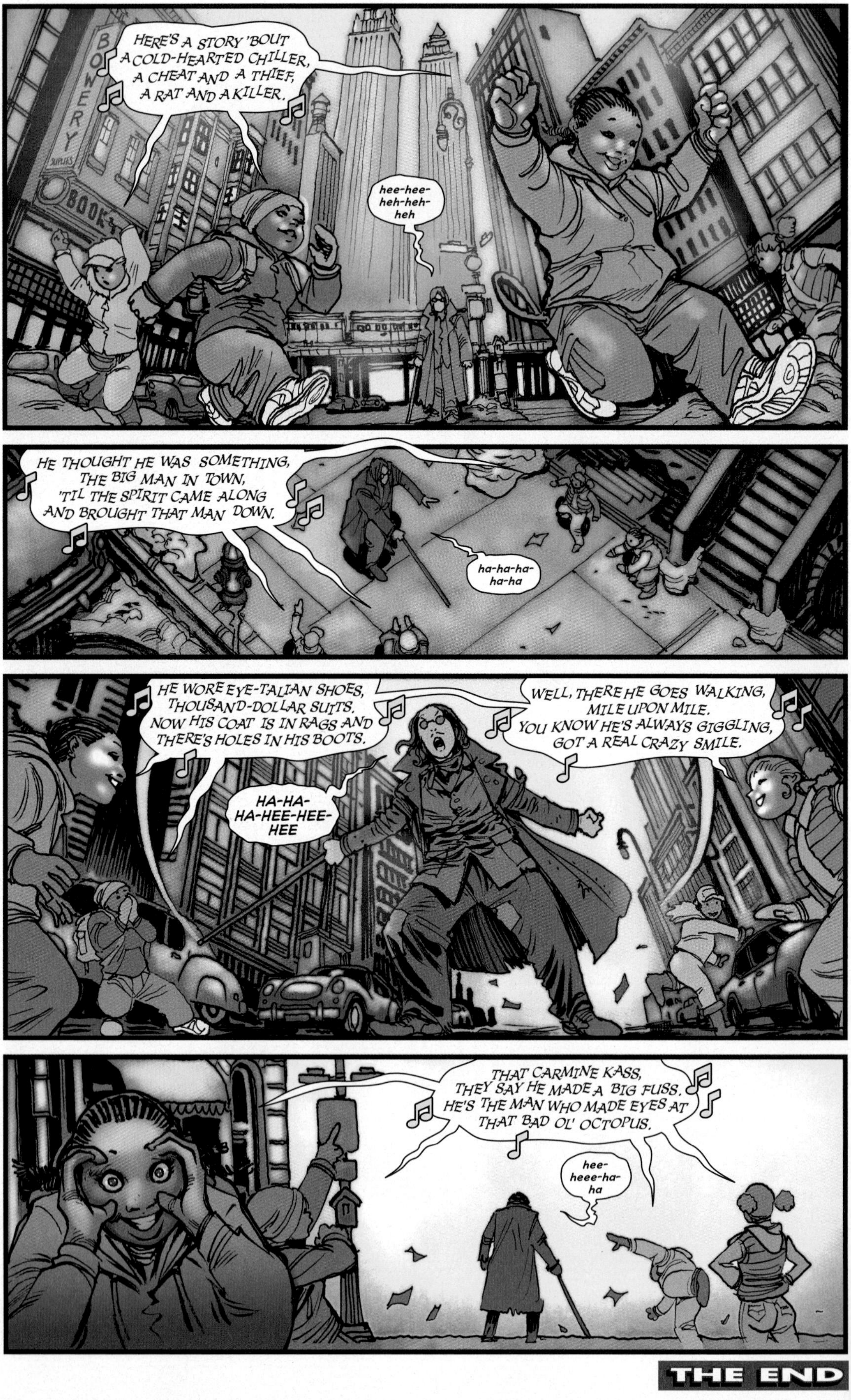
HERE'S A STORY 'BOUT A COLD-HEARTED CHILLER, A CHEAT AND A THIEF, A RAT AND A KILLER.
BOWERY
SUPPLIES
BOOKS
hee-hee-heh-heh-heh
HE THOUGHT HE WAS SOMETHING, THE BIG MAN IN TOWN, 'TIL THE SPIRIT CAME ALONG AND BROUGHT THAT MAN DOWN.
ha-ha-ha-ha-ha
HE WORE EYE-TALIAN SHOES, THOUSAND-DOLLAR SUITS. NOW HIS COAT IS IN RAGS AND THERE'S HOLES IN HIS BOOTS.
WELL, THERE HE GOES WALKING, MILE UPON MILE. YOU KNOW HE'S ALWAYS GIGGLING, GOT A REAL CRAZY SMILE.
HA-HA-HA-HEE-HEE-HEE
THAT CARMINE KASS, THEY SAY HE MADE A BIG FUSS. HE'S THE MAN WHO MADE EYES AT THAT BAD OL' OCTOPUS.
hee-heee-ha-ha
THE END

THE SPIRIT #1 VARIANT BY MARK SCHULTZ & JOHN KALISZ

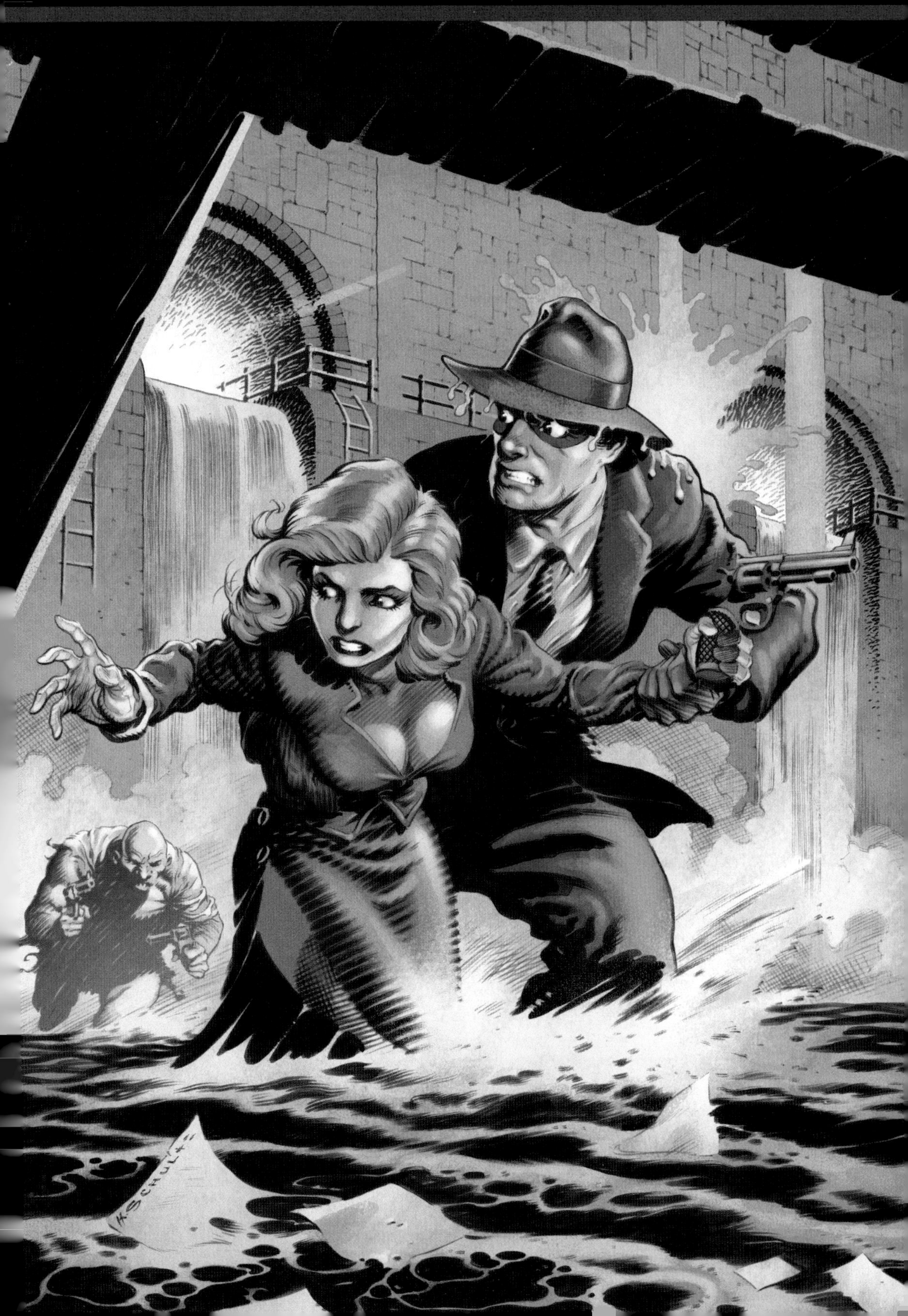

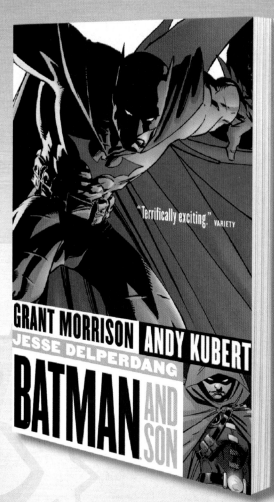
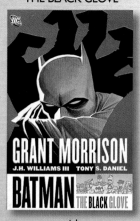